Habermas:
A Critical Reader

CRITICAL READERS

Blackwell's *Critical Readers* series presents a collection of linked perspectives on continental philosophers and social and cultural theorists. Edited and introduced by acknowledged experts and written by representatives of different schools and positions, the series embodies debate, dissent and a committed heterodoxy. From Foucault to Derrida, from Heidegger to Nietzsche, *Critical Readers* addresses figures whose work requires elucidation by a variety of perspectives. Volumes in the series include both primary and secondary bibliographies.

Althusser: *A Critical Reader*
Edited by Gregory Elliott

Bataille: *A Critical Reader*
Edited by Fred Botting and
Scott Wilson

Baudrillard: *A Critical Reader*
Edited by Douglas Kellner

Deleuze: *A Critical Reader*
Edited by Paul Patton

Derrida: *A Critical Reader*
Edited by David Wood

Frederick Douglass: *A Critical Reader*
Edited by Bill E. Lawson and Frank M.
Kirkland

Fanon: *A Critical Reader*
Edited by Lewis R. Gordon, T. Denean
Sharpley-Whiting and Renée T. White

Foucault: *A Critical Reader*
Edited by David Hoy

Habermas: *A Critical Reader*
Edited by Peter Dews

Heidegger: *A Critical Reader*
Edited by Hubert L. Dreyfus and
Harrison Hall

Kierkegaard: *A Critical Reader*
Edited by Jonathan Rée and Jane
Chamberlain

Nietzsche: *A Critical Reader*
Edited by Peter Sedgwick

Habermas:
A Critical Reader

Edited by
Peter Dews

BLACKWELL
Publishers

First published 1999
Reprinted 1999

Blackwell Publishers Ltd
108 Cowley Road
Oxford OX4 1JF
UK

Blackwell Publishers Inc.
350 Main Street
Malden, Massachusetts 02148
USA

British Library Cataloguing in Publication Data

A CIP catalogue record for this book is available from the British Library.

Library of Congress Cataloging-in-Publication Data

Habermas : a critical reader / edited by Peter Dews.
P. cm. — (Blackwell critical readers)
Includes bibliographical references and index.
ISBN 0–631–20134–3 (alk. paper). — ISBN 0–631–20135–1 (pbk : alk.paper)
1.   Habermas, Jürgen.   I. Dews, Peter.   II. Series.
B3258.H324H195   1999
193—dc21   99–17545
                                                            CIP

Typeset in 10 ½ on 12½ pt Bembo
By Best-set Typesetter Ltd, Hong Kong
Printed in Great Britain by MPG Books, Victoria Square, Bodmin, Cornwall

This book is printed on acid-free paper

For Jürgen Habermas,
at seventy

Contents

Notes on Contributors   ix
Preface   xii
Acknowledgements   xiv
Abbreviations   xvi
Introduction   1

Part I   Traditions

1   Does Hegel's Critique of Kant's Moral Theory Apply to Discourse Ethics?   29
Gordon Finlayson

2   Habermas, Marxism and Social Theory: The Case for Pluralism in Critical Social Science   53
James Bohman

3   Communicative Paradigms and the Question of Subjectivity: Habermas, Mead and Lacan   87
Peter Dews

4   Heidegger's Challenge and the Future of Critical Theory   118
Nikolas Kompridis

Part II Contexts

5   Between Radicalism and Resignation: Democratic
         Theory in Habermas's *Between Facts and Norms*   153
         William E. Scheuerman

6   Habermas, Feminism and the Question of Autonomy   178
         Maeve Cooke

7   Jürgen Habermas and the Antinomies of the Intellectual   211
         Max Pensky

Part III Contemporaries

8   Society and History: A Critique of Critical Theory   241
         Michael Theunissen

9   Openly Strategic Uses of Language: A Transcendental-
         Pragmatic Perspective (A second attempt to think with
         Habermas against Habermas)   272
         Karl-Otto Apel

10   What is Metaphysics – What is Modernity? Twelve
         Theses against Jürgen Habermas   291
         Dieter Henrich

11   The Social Dynamics of Disrespect: Situating Critical
         Theory Today   320
         Axel Honneth

         Select Bibliography   338

         Index   344

Contributors

Karl-Otto Apel is Emeritus Professor of Philosophy, University of Frankfurt. He has played a leading role in forging links between hermeneutics and analytical philosophy in post-war Germany, and was the pioneer, with Jürgen Habermas, of discourse ethics. His publications include *Transformation der Philosophie* (2 vols, 1973), *Diskurs und Verantwortung* (1988), and *Auseinandersetzungen* (1998). In English have appeared *Towards a Transformation of Philosophy* (1980), *Explanation and Understanding: A Transcendental-Pragmatic Perspective*, and *Selected Essays*, vol. 1: *Towards a Transcendental Semiotics* (1994), and Vol. 2: *Ethics and the Theory of Rationality* (1996).

James Bohman is Danforth Professor of Philosophy at Saint Louis University. He is author of *Public Deliberation: Pluralism, Complexity and Democracy* (1996) and *New Philosophy of Social Science: Problems of Indeterminacy* (1991). He has also edited *Deliberative Democracy* (with William Rehg, 1997) and *Perpetual Peace: Essays on Kant's Cosmopolitan Ideal* (with Matthias Lutz-Bachmann, 1997). He is currently writing a book on how moral and epistemic pluralism requires new interpretations of democratic ideals of equality, publicity and freedom.

Maeve Cooke is Senior Lecturer in the Department of German, University College Dublin. She is author of *Language and Reason: A Study of Habermas's Pragmatics* (1994), and editor of a reader on Habermas's writings on language and communication. She has published numerous articles on contemporary political and social theory, and is currently working on a book on the problem of evil.

Peter Dews is Professor of Philosophy and Head of the Philosophy Department, University of Essex. He is the author of *Logics of Disintegration: Post-Structuralist Thought and the Claims of Critical Theory* (1987) and *The Limits of Disenchantment: Essays on Contemporary European Philosophy* (1995). He has also edited *Autonomy and Solidarity: Interviews with Jürgen Habermas* (revised edn 1992) and (with Simon Critchley) *Deconstructive Subjectivities* (1996).

Gordon Finlayson is a Lecturer in Philosophy at the University of York, where he teaches Kant and Post-Kantian Philosophy, Ethics and Aesthetics. He is currently working on a philosophical monograph on 'The Idea of an Ethics of Discourse'.

Dieter Henrich is Emeritus Professor of Philosophy, University of Munich. He is well known for his path-breaking reconstructions of the thought of many of the key figures of German Idealism, including Kant, Fichte, Hegel and Hölderlin. His books include *Hegel im Kontext* (1967), *Identität und Objektivität* (1976), *Fluchtlinien* (1982), *Der Gang des Andenkens* (1987) and *Der Grund im Bewußtsein* (1992). His publications in English include *Aesthetic Judgement and the Moral Image of the World: Studies in Kant* (1993), *The Unity of Reason: Essays on Kant's Philosophy* (1994) and *The Course of Remembrance and other Essays on Hölderlin* (1997).

Axel Honneth is Professor of Philosophy, University of Frankfurt, and a leading contemporary representative of the Critical Theory tradition. He has published *Kritik der Macht: Reflexionsstufen einer kritischen Gesellschaftstheorie* (1985), *Die zerrissene Welt des Sozialen* (1990), *Kampf um Anerkennung* (1992) and *Desintegration: Bruchstücke einer soziologischen Gegenwartsdiagnose* (1994). In English have appeared *Critique of Power* (1991), *The Struggle for Recognition* (1995) and *The Fragmented World of the Social: Essays in Social and Political Philosophy* (1995).

Nikolas Kompridis is a Lecturer in the Philosophy Department at the University of Dundee. He is the author of *Crisis and Transformation: The Aesthetic Critique of Modernity from Hegel to Habermas* (forthcoming) and *In Times of Need: Heidegger, Habermas, and the Future of Critical Theory* (forthcoming).

Max Pensky is Associate Professor of Philosophy at the State University of New York at Binghamton. He is the author of *Melancholy Dialectics: Walter*

Benjamin and the Play of Mourning (1992), the editor of *The Actuality of Adorno* (1997), and has published articles on Critical Theory, post-structuralism and the contemporary German political public sphere.

William E. Scheuerman is Associate Professor of Political Theory, University of Pittsburgh. He is the author of *Between the Norm and the Exception: The Frankfurt School and the Rule of Law* (1994) and *Carl Schmitt: The End of Law* (1999).

Michael Theunissen is Emeritus Professor of Philosophy, Free University of Berlin. He has published many influential works on the thought of Hegel and Kierkegaard, on the theory of intersubjectivity and on social philosophy and philosophical theology. His publications include *Der Begriff Ernst bei Sören Kierkegaard* (1957), *Der Andere: Studien zur Sozialontologie der Gegenwart* (1965), *Sein und Schein: Die kritische Funktion der Hegelschen Logik* (1978) and *Negative Theologie der Zeit* (1991). *Der Andere* has been translated as *The Other: Studies in the Social Ontology of Husserl, Heidegger, Sartre and Buber* (1984).

Preface

In assembling this collection of essays I have sought to provide an image of Habermas's intellectual project which is not restricted to the latest stages of his theory, or to those aspects of his work which display the most obvious affinities with contemporary Anglo-American philosophy. I have tried to provide some insight into his context within the German – and, more broadly, the European – philosophical tradition, in terms both of his response to major predecessors, and of his relation to leading contemporaries. Despite his many fruitful borrowings, both substantive and methodological, from the thought of analytical philosophers, what is most remarkable about Habermas's work is the scope and synthetic power with which it carries forward the central preoccupations of the post-Kantian and post-Hegelian European tradition. To see his achievement in any other light is, I believe, to have only a limited and distorted picture of its significance.

After weighing considerations of space and utility, I have not included discussion of debates which Habermas has been involved in over the years which have already received wide coverage in the English-speaking world. These include the 'Positivist Dispute' of the early 1960s with Karl Popper and his German allies, the exchanges with Gadamer over the status of philosophical hermeneutics, and the wide-ranging arguments around Habermas's critique of post-structuralism, as presented in *The Philosophical Discourse of Modernity*, and his famous essay, 'Modernity – an incomplete project'.

I would like to thank the University of Essex for the granting of a year's sabbatical leave in 1995–6, during which most of the preliminary work for this anthology was done. I would also like to thank the Institut für die

Wissenschaften vom Menschen in Vienna for inviting me to spend a month as a Visiting Fellow in September 1997. The supportive and collegial atmosphere of the Institute made it an ideal place to carry out research, and to complete editorial and translation tasks. Finally, I would like to express my thanks to Chris Ellis for the many hours of work he put in correcting the disks and manuscripts.

With the exception of my essay, all the essays in Parts I and II of this volume are original contributions. Part III consists of seminal German articles on Habermas, and all but the last are newly translated. To reduce the number of notes, Habermas's major publications in German and English are referenced by means of abbreviations followed by a page number in the text. A list of abbreviations is provided.

Peter Dews
University of Essex
May 1999

Acknowledgements

Peter Dews, 'Communicative Paradigms and the Question of Subjectivity: Habermas, Mead and Lacan' (chapter 3), first appeared as 'The Paradigm Shift to Communication and the Question of Subjectivity: Reflections on Habermas, Mead and Lacan' in *Revue Internationale de Philosophie*, 194/4 (Dec., 1995) (special issue on Habermas), pp. 483–519. It is reprinted here by kind permission of the editors of the *Revue Internationale de Philosophie*.

Michael Theunissen, 'Society and History: A Critique of Critical Theory' (chapter 8) first appeared as 'Gesellschaft und Geschichte: Zur Kritik der Kritischen Theorie', in Theunissen, *Kritische Theorie der Gesellschaft* (Berlin and New York: Walter de Gruyter, 1969), pp. 1–40. It appears here by kind permission of the author and Walter de Gruyter and Co., and was translated by Gordon Finlayson and Peter Dews.

Karl-Otto Apel, 'Openly Strategic Uses of Language: A Transcendental-Pragmatic Perspective' (chapter 9) first appeared as 'Das Problem des offenen strategischen Sprachgebrauchs in transzendentalpragmatischer Sicht' in H. Burckhert (ed.), *Diskurs über Sprache* (Würzburg: Königshausen and Neumann, 1994), pp. 31–52. It was reprinted in Apel, *Auseinandersetzungen* (Frankfurt-am-Main: Suhrkamp Verlag, 1998), pp. 701–26. It appears here by kind permission of the author and Suhrkamp Verlag, and was translated by Peter Dews. © Suhrkamp Verlag, Frankfurt am Main, 1998.

Dieter Henrich, 'What is Metaphysics – What is Modernity? Twelve Theses against Jürgen Habermas' (chapter 10) was published as 'Was ist Metaphysik – was Moderne? Zwölf Thesen gegen Jürgen Habermas', in Henrich, *Konzepte* (Frankfurt-am-Main: Suhrkamp Verlag, 1987), pp. 11–43. It appears by kind permission of the author and Suhrkamp Verlag, and was translated by Peter Dews. © Suhrkamp Verlag, Frankfurt am Main, 1987.

Axel Honneth, 'The Social Dynamics of Disrespect: Situating Critical Theory Today' (chapter 11) first appeared as 'Die Soziale Dynamik von Mißachtung: Zur Ortsbestimmung einer kritischen Gesellschaftstheorie', in Christoph Görg (ed.), *Gesellschaft im Übergang: Perspektiven kritischer Soziologie* (Darmstadt: WBG, 1994), pp. 45–62. It first appeared in English in *Constellations*, 1/2 (1994), pp. 255–69, translated by John Farrell. It appears here by kind permission of the author and Blackwell Publishers Ltd. Translation © Blackwell Publishers Ltd.

Abbreviations of works by Habermas

AS   *Autonomy and Solidarity: Interviews with Jürgen Habermas*
BFN   *Between Facts and Norms*
CES   *Communication and the Evolution of Society*
EA   *Die Einbeziehung des Anderen*
ED   *Erläuterungen zur Diskursethik*
EI   *Erkenntnis und Interesse*
FG   *Faktitizität und Geltung*
JA   *Justification and Application*
KHI   *Knowledge and Human Interests*
KK   *Kultur und Kritik*
KPS   (followed by roman volume number) *Kleine Politische Schriften*
LC   *Legitimation Crisis*
LSS   *On the Logic of the Social Sciences*
MCCA *Moral Consciousness and Communicative Action*
MKH   *Moralbewußtsein und kommunikatives Handeln*
NC   *The New Conservatism*
ND   *Nachmetaphysisches Denken*
PDM   *The Philosophical Discourse of Modernity*
PDMo   *Der philosophische Diskurs der Moderne*
PF   *The Past as Future*
PhPP   *Philosophisch-politische Profile*
PPP   *Philosophical-Political Profiles*
PT   *Postmetaphysical Thinking*
STPS   *The Structural Transformation of the Public Sphere*

TCA1	*The Theory of Communicative Action*, vol. 1
TCA2	*The Theory of Communicative Action*, vol. 2
TK	*Texte und Kontexte*
TKH1	*Theorie des Kommunikativen Handelns*, vol. 1
TKH2	*Theorie des Kommunikativen Handelns*, vol. 2
TP	*Theory and Practice*
TuP	*Theorie und Praxis*
TWI	*Technik und Wissenschaft als 'Ideologie'*
WW	'Martin Heidegger: Work and *Weltanschauung*'
ZLS	*Zur Logik der Sozialwissenschaften*
ZRHM	*Zur Rekonstruktion des historischen Materialismus*

Introduction: Habermas and the desublimation of reason

I

Towards the end of his life, the greatest thinker of the early nineteenth century informed the audience gathered in his Berlin lecture theatre that 'the only thought which philosophy brings with it is the simple idea of *reason* – the idea that reason governs the world, and that world history is therefore a rational process'.[1] Even at the start of the 1830s, it required Hegel's compendious learning and unrivalled powers of synthesis to make this claim seem plausible. Now, after the political horrors and unspeakable moral disasters of the last two centuries, such a statement must surely be dismissed as expressing a naïve and irresponsible triumphalism. Most modern thinkers would regard Hegel's view as fit only for the kind of caustic mockery which Voltaire, in *Candide*, showered on Leibniz's claim that we live in the 'best of all possible worlds'. Or, as Max Horkheimer once put it, Hegel's claim must surely be seen as a 'purely private assertion, a personal peace treaty between the philosopher and an inhuman world'.[2]

Indeed, for many contemporary philosophers, the notion of reason which Hegel seems to employ here – reason as power abroad in the world, a kind of metaphysical puppeteer pulling the strings of history – would be almost unintelligible. Some present-day thinkers – the post-modernists, for example, or pragmatists in the mould of Richard Rorty – would reject the very notion of a reason which could be defined outside of any social and cultural context. For them, rationality runs no deeper than the conventions of a particular community; it is a crystallization of specific shared assumptions. If such philosophers think about history at all, they are likely to regard it as the domain of contingency and accident, a chaotic and often dismal narrative. For others, the concept of reason does refer to a general human capacity – our ability to choose the most appropriate or effective means to achieve a desired goal. But if we take the further step of describing this capacity as triumphing in history (or at least in the history of the West), then the result is not a tale which gives much cause for celebration. Max Weber was merely the first of many who have understood the 'rationalization' of modern society to mean the ever more constricting enclosure of our lives within an iron cage of technology, bureaucracy and dehumanizing calculation. Finally, there are authors such as John Rawls and Hilary Putnam who believe that reason is not simply a matter of matching means to ends. Political structures, moral responses, ways of living together, can also be described as more or less reasonable. Such a notion of reason does have affinities with the conception of reason found in thinkers such as Kant and Hegel. But Rawls and Putnam would entirely repudiate the Hegelian notion that history, viewed from a philosophical perspective, can be seen as the working out of a destiny inscribed in reason itself.

Against the backdrop of this general scepticism about the role of reason in history, the uniqueness of Habermas's philosophical project emerges clearly. For, throughout his career, Habermas has tried, in different ways, to pull off what looks like an impossible balancing act. On the one hand, he has sought to be thoroughly 'post-metaphysical', to renounce philosophy's venerable, but no longer plausible, claim to provide an interpretation of the world as a whole. Yet, on the other hand, he has struggled to hold on to the notion of an inner relation between reason and history, or what he terms the 'Vernunftbezug der Geschichte' – a relation which might give us grounds for hope.[3] In a suitably humbled and modified form, Habermas suggests, we can retain a central element of Hegel's grandiose claim. There are two principal motives for trying to do so. First, we should not allow the concept of reason to be commandeered by those who equate rationalization with uniformity and regimentation. To do so is to imply that opposition to the oppressive advance of reason can come only from the domain of the non-rational. Powerful and moving as it may sometimes be to unleash the forces of the body, sensuality, mysticism and derangement against the cold calculation of the modern world, such efforts are always likely to be dismissed as the expression of a hopeless, evanescent romanticism, which can provide no basis for alternative social arrangements. The situation looks different, however, if it can be shown that the equation of rationalization with increased technical control tells only half the story. But this brings us to the second, connected point. It is not enough to show that reason, *in principle*, has another side, one linked with the promise of self-determination, of democracy and community, rather than with domination. Unless there is historical evidence that this other side of reason has made itself felt, has had some real effect in the world, then there would be nothing to build on, no practical basis for change. Such a recovery of the traces of reason in history need not, and cannot, take the form of Hegel's triumphalism, of course. But it could show, for example, that the 'democratic' aspect of reason has – for the most part – been crippled or even suppressed by its calculating, technical aspect. It could equally acknowledge that there is no *guarantee* that reason, in either form, will eventually overcome the forces of chaos and destruction. But without any historical support whatsoever, the philosophical proof that reason has a 'communicative' as well as an 'instrumental' aspect, to use Habermas's terminology, would remain no more than an empty invocation. Indeed, in Habermas's view, there are no purely philosophical proofs which can dispense entirely with empirical support.

Habermas often makes his point that we cannot give up on the connection between reason and history by asserting that, philosophically, 'we remain contemporaries of the Young Hegelians' (PDM 53). The allusion may at first seem obscure, but once it is understood, many features of Habermas's basic stance become clearer. The Young Hegelians were the radical followers of Hegel who, during the 1830s and 1840s, found themselves in a strangely ambivalent relationship to their master. On the one hand, they were convinced that Hegel had 'completed' the history of Western philosophy – he had shown that all one-sided metaphysical positions, such as idealism or materialism, monism or pluralism, cannot help being eventually undermined by what they are forced to leave out of account. He proposed a dialectically unfolding system which situated and incorporated the *partial* truth of each of these views. But at the same time Hegel left behind one final contradiction: the gulf between his claim that the dialectical process, which unites thought and history, culminates in the fundamental triumph of reason, and the obvious continuing irrationality of the social world. The Young Hegelians drew the conclusion that Hegel was in one sense right about the relation between reason and history – there was indeed a historically accumulated rational *potential* which his thought had made visible. But this potential still needed to be *realized*. Reason alone was impotent. It had to be retrieved from the abstruse, abstract world of metaphysical concepts, and made concrete in the lives of finite, embodied beings. In other words, the inner relation of reason and history had to be preserved, without transfiguring history into the already completed *expression* of reason, as Hegel tended to do.

Habermas sometimes terms this task of bringing reason down to earth the 'desublimation of reason', and the historical and intellectual moment when it emerged, has obviously always fascinated him. For example, his 1954 doctoral dissertation on one of the great philosophers of the Idealist generation, F. W. J. Schelling, begins with a lengthy discussion of the Hegelian aftermath, which runs to over seventy pages.[4] Clearly, what excited the young Habermas's interest was the range of ways in which thinkers after Hegel, from Bruno Bauer, Max Stirner and Ludwig Feuerbach to Marx and Kierkegaard, sought to acknowledge the openness of human freedom and the irreducible contingency of history, without lapsing back into the one-sided metaphysical postures whose untenability Hegel's system had definitively exposed. Habermas portrays Schelling's internal disruption of Idealism, his insistence that the conceptual realm has a 'ground' which cannot be rationally comprehended, as paving the way for these more radical anti-metaphysical protests.

II

The early 1950s, when Habermas gained his doctorate, was also the period when he first came into contact with the thought of the Frankfurt School, especially via Adorno and Horkheimer's *Dialectic of Enlightenment*. He has recalled that he found the book a revelation. It is from this point that we can date the first major phase of his work, which was dominated by the critical appropriation of the thought of Marx and the Marxist tradition, and its application to the analysis of contemporary society. But despite this reorientation towards 'Western Marxism', Habermas continued to pursue the central concerns of his dissertation in a different guise: he was still seeking a philosophical interpretation of 'reason in history' which would not pre-empt the contingencies of the real historical process. Accordingly, he criticized all those who regarded Marxism as an objective, 'scientific' theory of history. He argued that Marxism is a hypothesis – based on the evidence of history – concerning ourselves, human beings, as the potential *makers* of history. This meant that Marxism was a theory with a distinctive cognitive status, for which Habermas coined the rather cumbersome phrase 'empirically falsifiable philosophy of history with practical intent' (cf. TuP 271–9). Marxism was neither an explanatory theory in the usual scientific sense, nor pure philosophical speculation, but rather something in between. To describe this anomalous, rather awkward location, Habermas employs the term 'Kritik'.

In this context, 'critique' refers to a type of theory first developed by Marx, who had himself learned from Kant and Hegel. Critique seeks not to *disprove* other theories, but to establish the *limits* of their validity, by showing that they unknowingly reflect a social reality which is itself distorted, an 'alienated' and impoverished version of what it could become. Of course, the reality of alienation, of the suppression of unrealized potentials, is not something which can simply be pointed out like an empirical fact. Accordingly, unlike traditional metaphysics, the truth of critique is dependent on confirmation through the *realization* of the possibility which it projects into the future, a possibility which provides it with its yardstick for assessing the present. However, such confirmation is not comparable to theory testing in the experimental sciences either, since it is not detached observation, but a *practical* readiness to realize the projected possibility, which first generates the vantage-point of critique. Neatly summarizing the views of the founder of this type of theory, Habermas writes that 'Marx declares . . . the readiness to make to be the precondition of the ability to know' (TuP 433).

But what exactly is the potential whose realization critique anticipates? What could human beings make, which currently makes them? In an extended review and assessment of the philosophical discussions around Marxism in the twentieth century, written in 1957, Habermas interprets this potential in terms of the traditional Marxist categories of 'alienated labour', or 'alienation' more generally – and we can understand this as referring to all forms of human activity which are apparently determined by external forces, rather than by the agents themselves. By the time of his major essay on 'Marxism as critique', however, which was first published in 1963, Habermas refers more generally to the 'makeability of history'. He argues that the possibility of human beings controlling their own historical destiny has not always existed, but rather has itself emerged historically, through the network of global interconnections which capitalism – as Marx predicted – has put in place. Hence there is no basis for projecting a permanent underlying 'subject of history, which would allow us to grasp history philosophically as a metaphysical whole':

A specifically materialist philosophy of history would have to derive its presuppositions exclusively from the epochal context in which it has itself historically emerged. In its critical self-consciousness it would have to incorporate the fact that the categories of the unity of the world and the makeability of history have been made true by history itself in one of its phases. (TuP 279)

This insistence on deriving as much as possible from the actual historical context, rather than from philosophical presuppositions, points towards the second aspect of Habermas's account of Marxism as critique. From a sceptical standpoint, the content of the *practical* projection of an emancipated society which makes possible the *theoretical* standpoint of critique could be dismissed as a utopian fantasy. To counter this objection, Habermas insists that the assumption of a potentiality for social transformation has to be backed up by historical and sociological enquiry and analysis. To the further objection that the results of such investigations, despite their empirical aspect, will in fact simply mirror the original philosophical projection, Habermas replies by insisting on the gap between objectifying science and philosophy: 'The data of a scientifically objectified reality are to be interpreted with reference to the conceptualized goal of society; but in such a way that the concept which is to be practically realised, the *vérité à faire*, can be unequivocally falsified. The theory regards itself as empirically refutable. In this way it is precisely the hiatus between philosophy and science which guarantees the continuum of rationality.'[5] In other words, Habermas's conception of Marxism as critique is directed against both those who claim Marxism to be a science and those who assume that Marxism, being based on a philosophical projection of an idealized human future, can dispense with empirical support altogether.

By working out this rather elaborate division of labour between philosophy and empirical social science, Habermas clearly wanted to avoid accusations of intellectual – and political – irresponsibility. He sought to establish as many checks and contraints as possible, so as to fend off the suggestion that Marxism is no more than an irresponsibly utopian social fantasy. As an 'empirically controllable philosophy of history', Marxism is dependent on two kinds of 'verification': through empirical social enquiry and through the possibility of its practical realization. And this means, Habermas argues, that Marxism must not try to be a successor to 'first philosophy' (Aristotle's and Descartes's term for metaphysics), with its function of providing ultimate grounds for knowledge. Critique, as the successor to philosophy, cannot claim to ground itself. It is exposed to the revisability of empirical knowledge – and the contingency of the future.

Unfortunately, this argument raises a serious problem. For if critique cannot ground its own projected ideal of a conscious 'making' of history, why should this specific practical goal be accepted as binding, or be regarded as more valid than any other? This is a question which has haunted the Critical Theory tradition ever since its beginnings, and in the work of founders of the Frankfurt School, such as Max Horkheimer, it never received more than an allusive or promissory answer. In the 'Postscript' to 'Traditional and Critical Theory', for example, Horkheimer describes Critical Theory as following 'quite consciously, in the formation of its categories and in all phases of its progress, the interest in the rational organization of human activity, an interest which it is also its task to clarify and legitimate'.[6] But this is an ambivalent formulation. For if Critical Theory *legitimates* the interest in rational organization, it seems to claim the traditional self-sufficiency of philosophy, which Horkheimer opposes. On the other hand, if it merely follows this interest, why should one such interest be privileged over any other? Is it really sufficient simply to assert, as Horkheimer does, that 'the goal of a rational society, which admittedly seems to exist today only as fantasy, is really innate in every human being'?[7]

III

In *Knowledge and Human Interests* (1971, German original 1968), his most important treatise on epistemology, Habermas attempts to provide a systematic solution to this problem. It is one which already marks a shift away from his early reliance on the philosophy of history, even in an 'empirically controlled' form. Habermas's strategy in this book is to show that the basic conceptual structures of human knowledge are determined by interests which are deeply anchored in the social existence of human beings as such. He argues that since different interests shape qualitatively distinct ways of knowing, cognitive claims can be assessed along dimensions other than that of truth and falsehood. Knowledge can *also* be appraised with reference to the *appropriateness* of the relationship between the interest which guides it and the objects with which it is concerned. More specifically, Habermas argues that the 'empirical-analytical sciences' – classically, the natural sciences – are guided by an interest in the technical control of their objects, while the hermeneutic sciences (for example, various branches of the humanities) are guided by an interest in 'the preservation and expansion of the intersubjectivity of possible action-orienting mutual understanding' (KHI 310). From such a standpoint, knowledge which enables us to predict and control human behaviour may be possible. But we should not lose sight of the fact that such knowledge suppresses the role of its 'object' as a potential partner in dialogue, accessible to the qualitatively different kind of knowledge embodied in 'understanding' (*Verstehen*).

At first glance, it might seem that Habermas is reducing knowledge to the status of a 'tool' in the service of interests, so that the 'utility' of knowledge becomes more important than its 'truth'. But in fact, he is careful to avoid this implication, and indeed criticizes Nietzsche for carrying out precisely such a reduction.[8] Knowledge is not just an implement, because 'these basic orientations do not aim at the gratification of immediately empirical needs but at the solution of system problems in general' (KHI 196). In other words, our basic cognitive orientations to the world arise from our interest in successful, productive 'work' and interpersonal understanding achieved through 'interaction'; these two achievements are essential to the very continuation of socal life. But since social life always already embodies technical knowledge and forms of mutual understanding, the cognitive interests do not explain the *nature* of knowledge and understanding as such. They account only for the contrasts in concept formation and method between different ways of knowing.

So the cognitive interests must not be seen as biological or psychological constraints or limitations of knowledge. Indeed, to view them in this way would be to look at ourselves 'objectivistically', as if from the outside, and so presuppose one of the very cognitive interests we are seeking to illuminate. In other words, only a being capable of examining its own process of knowing reflectively, 'from within', can grasp the cognitive interests as what Habermas calls 'quasi-transcendental' conditions of possibility of knowing. The phrase 'quasi-transcendental' is meant to point to the fact that these conditions are contingently grounded in the life of the human species, yet have a priori status for us: they do not *constrain* knowledge, but make it possible. The implication of Habermas's argument, however, is not just that only a being able to reflect on its own ways of knowing could have *access* to its cognitive interests, but also that only such a being could *have* cognitive interests. An animal whose perception of the world was shaped by its needs and drives (and this is the way Nietzsche tends to describe human beings) might be *adapted* to its environment, but it would not have *cognitive* interests, since no claim to objectivity could be made for what it perceived. In view of this, Habermas writes, in *Knowledge and Human Interests*, that 'the category of cognitive interest is authenticated only by the interest innate in reason. The technical and practical cognitive interests can be comprehended *as* knowledge-constitutive interests only in connection with the emancipatory cognitive interest of rational reflection' (KHI 198).

So Habermas's strategy is first to demonstrate that our knowledge is guided by interests. This he achieves through an *internal* analysis of causal-explanatory and hermeneutic ('interpretative') knowledge, in which he shows how those who pursue these forms of knowledge are tacitly oriented by practical interests in their ways of assessing truth claims. He then argues that only a self-reflective being can have such interests, and suggests that such self-reflection must itself be the expression of an interest – namely, an emancipatory interest. Self-reflection, we might say, is 'emancipatory' for two reasons. It enables us to acknowledge forms of access to the world as definitive *for* us, without their being definitive *of* us. And it puts us in a position to *use* explanation and understanding in order to free ourselves – at least partially – from entrapment in the causal nexus of nature and from patterns of social life permeated by relations of power. At last, it seems, a solid basis for critique has been found (needed, we recall, because critique cannot ground itself). But of course, in line with his intuitions about the dependence of philosophical truth on empirical substantiation, Habermas must be able to point to an *existing* form of knowledge which expresses such an emancipatory interest.

In *Knowledge and Human Interests* psychoanalysis takes on this role. Psychoanalytic theory, Habermas argues, is distinguished by its distinctive interweaving of interpretative and causal forms of explanation, an intertwining which makes it distinct from both purely 'hermeneutic' and purely 'causal-explanatory' forms of knowledge. In psychoanalytic therapy, unconscious causal connections running between past and present are identified in the speech and behaviour of the patient; but the aim of the therapy is precisely to dissolve the rigidity of these connections by helping the patient to grasp the personal *meaning* of the traumatic experience which under lies them. Thus, psychoanalysis, self-reflection and emancipation coincide in the achievement of what Habermas calls 'Mündigkeit'. (*Mündigkeit* means 'maturity' in a quasi-legal sense, but is often translated as 'autonomy and responsibility'.) Given this distinctive cognitive structure, Habermas suggests, psychoanalysis can be taken as the model for a critical social science guided by the emancipatory interest. Such a science seeks to unmask 'ideologically frozen relations of dependence', the power structures distorting communication and interaction, at the level of society as a whole (KHI 310).

However, the notion of an emancipatory interest is much more contentious than its two counterparts. Psychoanalysis offers Habermas the chance of a 'transcendental deduction' of the emancipatory interest – he can try to show that such an interest is its necessary 'condition of possibility'. But this is a 'weak' deduction, because psychoanalysis presupposes such an interest *only* if one already accepts something like Habermas's account of its cognitive structure. In short, the notion of emancipation cannot be defined independently of what our supposed *interest* in emancipation aims at, whereas the criteria of technical achievement and of successful mutual understanding need make no reference to corresponding interests. Approaching the problem from another angle, we can see that liberation from needlessly oppressive power structures is not a process which is *essential* for the continuation of social life as such. Hierarchical, violent and restrictive societies can endure for centuries, whereas a degree of control over nature and a minimum level of intersubjective agreement are indeed necessary for social life. Not surprisingly, therefore, Habermas has recourse to a notion of primordial insight, in order to explain the status of the emancipatory interest. In a celebrated passage from his Frankfurt inaugural lecture of 1965, he claimed:

The human interest in autonomy and responsibility is not merely a fancy, for it can be apprehended a priori. What raises us out of nature is the only thing whose nature we can know: *language*. Through its structure, autonomy and responsibility are posited for us. Our first sentence expresses unequivocally the intention of universal and unconstrained consensus. (KHI 314)

Clearly, Habermas has already moved a good way from his earlier philosophy of history. But he still insists in the inaugural lecture that philosophical insight reaches fruition only when *applied* to history:

The ontological illusion of pure theory . . . promotes the fiction that Socratic dialogue is possible everywhere and at any time. From the beginning philosophy has presumed that the autonomy and responsibility posited with the structure of language are not only anticipated but real. It is pure theory, wanting to derive everything from itself, that succumbs to unacknowledged external conditions and becomes ideological. Only when philosophy discovers in the dialectical course of history the traces of violence that deform repeated attempts at dialogue and recurrently close off the path to unconstrained communication does it further the process whose suspension it otherwise legitimates. (KHI 315)

However, the conception of reflection at work in this passage falls prey to a fatal ambiguity, as Habermas's long-standing friend and colleague Karl-Otto Apel was quick to point out. On the one hand, self-reflection involves the exploration of the universal conditions of forms of knowledge and practice in general – for example, the identification of the cognitive interests. On the other hand, it can also take the form of a breaking down of the specific constraints and barriers to self-knowledge which have marred an individual life history (as in psychoanalysis), or possibly a collective history (as in the critique of ideology). In Apel's view, a clear distinction between these two forms of self-reflection is *politically* essential. For reflection on the nature of general human competences claims an unqualified, universal status which it would be dangerous for reflection on *particular* collective histories to claim. Apel writes: 'Theoretical reflection and material-practical engagement are not identical, despite the identity of reason with the interest in reason. They separate again, on the highest level of philosophical reflection, as diametrically opposed moments within the emancipatory interest in knowledge.'[9] The problem which Habermas generates by fusing these two notions of reflection can be discerned in the quotation given above. For, on the one hand, Habermas seeks to undermine the 'illusion of pure theory' by arguing that truth can only be *anticipated* – truth is dependent upon an unconstrained communication which is yet to be realized. On the other hand, any presumed 'unity of knowledge and interest [which] proves itself in a dialectic that takes the historical traces of suppressed dialogue and reconstructs what has been suppressed' (KHI 315) would have to be *already* in possession of the criteria of undistorted communication. What this suggests is that Habermas cannot entirely eliminate the 'self-grounding' dimension of philosophy – even his version of critique relies on an appeal to timeless insight which, from the standpoint of the original project of a desublimation of reason, looks suspiciously 'idealist'.

Nevertheless, in the 1971 'Postscript' to *Knowledge and Human Interests* and in other writings of the same period, Habermas fully accepted the force of Apel's criticism. He began to distingush between two forms of 'self-reflection', dividing critique into two distinct activities. One of these he still termed 'critique' (*Kritik*), the other 'reconstruction' (*Nachkonstruktion*). The principal differences between these two activities, Habermas now suggests, are as follows: (1) *Critique* is directed at objects whose 'pseudo-objectivity' is to be revealed, whereas reconstruction deals with processes which are already acknowledged as the activity of subjects; (2) *Critique* deals with the deformations of particular identities, whereas reconstructions are concerned with anonymous systems of rules; (3) *Critique* makes conscious something unconscious, altering what determines a *false* consciousness with practical results, whereas reconstructions retrieve a correct but implicit know-how, and have no immediate practical effects (Postscript to KHI 378). As this final point makes clear, reconstruction reinstates a form of knowledge detached from interest, and so signals a fundamental shift in Habermas's conception of the tasks of philosophy. All the same, he did not immediately abandon the notion of philosophy as *Kritik*. Indeed, it continued to play the key role in his two main metaphilosophical essays of the early 1970s.

In his 1971 essay 'Wozu noch Philosophie?' (Does philosophy still have a purpose?) (PPP 1–19), Habermas stresses four features which distinguish philosophy-as-critique from the tradition of metaphysics: (1) philosophy abandons its claim to provide ultimate foundations for knowledge; (2) philosophy understands itself as a dimension of social praxis, inverting the traditional relation between theory and practice; (3) philosophy criticizes the claims of metaphysical and religious world-views to interpret the meaning of the world as a whole, releasing their contents for a future-oriented project of emancipation; (4) philosophy becomes aware of its own socially restricted basis and elitist self-understanding. Similar claims are made in the 1975 essay 'Die Rolle der Philosophie im Marxismus' (The role of philosophy in Marxism). Here Habermas particularly stresses the fact that philosophy cannot retreat – as phenomenologists and existentialists assume – into a sanctum of privileged insight, distinct from the domain of science, whose positivistic self-understanding it leaves untouched. The noblest function of philosophy,

Habermas suggests, is to break down, through a process of reflection, reifications and objectifications of all kinds (ZRHM 49–59).

In 'Does philosophy still have a purpose?', however, Habermas makes the important additional claim that philosophy is currently undergoing a major transformation. This shift of register, he suggests, is comparable only to the Hegelian aftermath, which – as we have seen – he regards as a crucial historical and intellectual turning-point. The shift consists in the fact that philosophy is ceasing to be an expression of personal wisdom. It no longer articulates the stance towards the world of particular, often charismatic individuals. Philosophy is becoming a form of 'research' (*Forschung*) – in other words, a co-operative quest for truth comparable to that of other specialized sciences. Admittedly, even after Hegel, philosophy – especially in Germany – often retained the stamp of a personal rhetoric, a distinctive individual style – one need think only of Kierkegaard, Marx, Nietzsche or Heidegger. But Habermas suggests that the continuing salience of the style of the 'great thinker' – if not of great philosophy – must be understood in terms of the aberrant development and belated normalization of Germany as a modern, constitutional state.

Habermas's description of this new transformation of philosophy is not without ambivalence. After all, he refers explicitly in the essay to Adorno's argument that Germany's retarded development made deeper insights – as well as deeper aberrations – possible. Furthermore, as a historical generalization, Habermas's prognosis seems questionable, to say the least. Just think of what was happening across the Rhine in the early 1970s, where a style of thought emphatically defined by the personal gesture, in the shape of the work of Foucault, Derrida, Lacan, Deleuze and others, was on the point of achieving world-wide resonance. In view of this, Habermas's prediction is perhaps best understood as part of a new strategy for continuing the project of the 'desublimation of reason', a response to difficulties with the notion of critique which he was still thinking through. As we observed, the concept of 'self-reflection' ultimately implied a stance too close to 'first philosophy', a fusing of the particular and the universal. But perhaps a gentle insistence that philosophy can preserve its influence only by abandoning claims to privileged insight, and approximating to the intellectual style and fallibilistic awareness of the sciences, will humble in a more reliable way the excessive ambition of thinkers to interpret the world as a whole.

The problem here, of course, is that the emphasis on philosophy as *Forschung*, and the claim that philosophy must conform to the same standards of assessment as the empirical sciences, leaves an important dimension of philosophy out of account – namely, its role in offering insight into human existence and in seeking to understand our place as self-conscious beings in a perplexing universe. The problems raised by this elision are made clear by Habermas's own use of a quote from Adorno to open 'Does philosophy still have a purpose?' In the passage which he cites, Adorno insists that philosophy must forbid itself the thought of the Absolute precisely in order not to betray it, and must hold on to the 'emphatic concept of truth'. This contradiction, Habermas suggests, has been 'the element of any philosophy that is to be taken seriously, ever since the death of Hegel' (PPP 1). But, in fact, his own account of the normalization of philosophy as 'research' implies that the emphatic claim to truth (the claim to offer a glimpse of the truth of the whole) must be given up entirely in favour of corrigible results. With it − of course − would have to be abandoned the claim of philosophy to offer any general orientation towards the world, including towards the significance of the knowledge claims of the individual sciences.

IV

The solution which Habermas eventually adopts to this problem, his strategy for retaining at least a trace of the emphatic concept of truth, involves distinguishing two basic tasks of philosophy. In the first, philosophy acts as a 'stand-in' (*Platzhalter*) for scientific theories making strong universalist claims. Combatting a myopic empiricism, it paves the way for ambitious research programmes in the social and human sciences, and collaborates in theoretical initiatives which attempt to 'reconstruct' the universal bases of human competences in such areas as cognitive and moral development, argumentation and linguistic communication. In this 'stand-in' role philosophy cannot make purely a priori claims to knowledge or insight. It must work hand in hand with forms of empirical research, simultaneously shaping their orientation and being confirmed − or possibly disconfirmed − by them:

Starting primarily from the intuitive knowledge of competent subjects − competent in terms of judgement, action and language − and secondarily from systematic knowledge handed down by culture, the reconstructive sciences explain the presumably universal bases of rational experience and judgement, as well as action and linguistic communication. Marked down in price, the venerable transcendental and dialectical modes of justification may still come in handy. All they can be fairly expected to furnish, however, is reconstructive hypotheses for use in empirical settings. (MCCA 15−16)

Habermas is aware, however, that this cannot be the whole story. Indeed, he concedes that there is an element of truth in the conservative philosopher

Robert Spaemann's warning that 'every philosophy makes a practical and theoretical claim to totality and . . . not to make such a twofold claim is to be
doing something which does not qualify as philosophy' (MCCA 16). The
problem is how to accommodate this dimension of philosophy without reviving the emphatic concept of truth which, according to Habermas, Adorno
both invokes *and* revokes, in the endless self-cancelling movement of his
'negative dialectics'.

Habermas's solution is to preserve the notion of the whole, but at the
same time restrict its application to the totality of a lifeworld or a culture.
He insists that philosophy cannot attain an external vantage-point from which
it can survey, assess and pass judgement on an entire culture, let alone the
world as a whole. But, in its role as 'interpreter', it is able to explore a culture
hermeneutically from within, diagnosing rigidities and internal conflicts
against the background of an implicit global sense of the culture. A particularly urgent task here is posed by the modern separating out of different
cultural value spheres – science, law and post-traditional morality, and
autonomous art. For in each of these spheres a different aspect of rationality
predominates: cognitive, normative and aesthetic, respectively. For Habermas,
this achievement of modernity, while progressive in one sense, calls for a
mediation *between* the value spheres, one which can correct their one-
sidedness without undermining the primacy of the aspect of reason which
defines each of them. It also calls for a mediation between the cultural value
spheres and the domain of everyday life – the domain where cognitive, normative and aesthetic orientations are still inextricably fused. Philosophy,
Habermas suggests, is particularly suited to play these mediating roles because
of its multilingual capacity (*Mehrsprachigkeit*) and its simultaneous intuitive
closeness and subversive, reflective distance from everyday discourse. 'Everyday life', Habermas concludes, 'is a more promising medium for regaining
the lost unity of reason than are today's expert cultures or yesteryear's classical philosophy of reason' (MCCA 18).

The contrast between 'stand-in' and 'interpreter' roles has continued to
define Habermas's conception of philosophy right up to the present day. Yet
it is unsatisfactory in several respects. For one thing, a paradox seems to result
from this division of labour. On the one hand, Habermas attributes the cognitive progress of modernity to the differentiation of the three value spheres
of 'truth', 'rightness' and 'authenticity'. For example, it was only when problems of knowledge could be filtered out from the symbolic and ethical contexts in which they were formerly embedded, and addressed through specific
institutionalized forms of enquiry, that the take-off of modern natural science
became possible. Similarly, modern moral universalism implies the existence
of a sphere within which questions of justice can be treated by legal and

other experts who are skilled in isolating normative issues. At the same time Habermas stresses that – within the lifeworld – the three dimensions of validity continue to be intrinsically interwoven (to describe an act as 'courageous', or someone's taste as 'insipid', for example, is to make a claim which is both cognitive *and* evaluative). Yet, if this is the case, we are faced with the question of which 'ontology' (which conception of what is ultimately 'out there') should be taken as more fundamental. As the younger Critical Theorist Martin Seel has put the issue, does the lifeworld exhibit an *illusory integration* of dimensions of rationality, which is exposed as such by their modern institutional separation? Or is it, rather, the integration of the lifeworld which reveals the *illusory separation* of rationality dimensions characteristic of specialized cultures of expertise?[10]

This problem can also be put another way. Habermas's conception suggests that the knowledge of the natural sciences – to take this example – is *universal* in its scope, but can be produced only through a process of cognitive abstraction. Scientists have, first of all, to be communicating persons embedded in the lifeworld in order to produce scientific knowledge. But they also have to screen out most of what they know about themselves and others in order to take up an 'objectivating' attitude. Objective knowledge thus remains epistemically *secondary* in relation to our encompassing, implicit awareness of the lifeworld. On the other hand, the lifeworld, which appears as existentially more *fundamental* because of its fusion of validity claims, will always be exposed as particular and *relative* in terms of the content which its common sense articulates.

Habermas, in his reply to Seel, appears not to appreciate the force of this objection. He states that each specialized form of argumentation can indeed, under the pressure of problems encountered, be abandoned in favour of another form. He also admits that judgement, a sense of appropriateness which cannot be formalized, will play an important role in deciding if and how this takes place. In this way, Habermas acknowledges a coherence and interdependence of the forms of argumentation, but at the same time he asserts that 'every discourse stands, so to speak, directly before God'.[11] He goes on to suggest that this is not surprising, since 'communicative action encounters in the different types of argumentation only its own reflected forms'. But this reply overlooks the fact that types of argumentation also have *ontological* implications. For example, specialized discussion within the scientific rationality complex presupposes the existence of a world of normatively neutral facts, while discourse in the legal–moral sphere presupposes the existence of a normative dimension which is logically independent of any specific states of affairs. This splitting apart of ontological domains is incompatible with the fusion of considerations of truth, rightness and aesthetic appeal which characterizes the everyday world which we all inhabit. So the question arises: which conception of the world is more fundamental? Are the fusions of fact and value typical of the lifeworld projections on to an essentially value-neutral reality or not?

In itself, this may appear to be a relatively minor problem. But it takes on greater significance as soon we try locate philosophy on one or other side of the divide between the lifeworld and the specialized value spheres. In its role as 'stand-in', philosophy is located unambiguously within the compart-mentalized system of scientific research. But, despite the claims of 'Does philosophy still have a purpose?', Habermas knows that philosophy cannot be reduced to *Forschung*. It would betray its age-old inheritance if it were to view itself merely as one specialized form of knowledge amongst others, and lost its connection with common sense and everyday life. But if philosophy, as interpreter, has to swim in the waters of the lifeworld (albeit against the current), what cognitive standards must it satisfy? Surely it cannot be expected to meet criteria which are themselves *abstracted* from the lifeworld whose integrity philosophy seeks to explore and defend?

Habermas himself appears to sense this problem when he remarks that 'this mediating task [of interpretation] is not devoid of a certain paradox, because in the expert cultures knowledge is always treated under individual aspects of validity, whereas in everyday practice *all* functions of language and aspects of validity encroach on each other, constitute a syndrome'.[12] Although he does not say so directly, the task of mediation appears 'paradoxical' because the philosophical language which translates specialized validity claims back into the terms of the lifeworld must itself *fuse* the various dimensions of valid-ity, and in this case will not be susceptible to any straightforward assessment of its 'cognitive' truth. Habermas, perhaps unwillingly, highlights this elusive status of philosophical discourse when he states: 'Like [common sense], philosophy moves within the vicinity of the lifeworld; its relation to the totality of the receding horizon of everyday knowledge is similar to that of common sense. And yet through the subversive force of reflection and of illu-minating, critical and dissecting analysis, philosophy is completely opposed to common sense' (PT 38). As this description makes clear, reflexivity as such need not dissolve the interfusion of validity dimensions. Art, for example, is another form of reflexive exploration of experience; but in the aesthetic domain, too, all the dimensions of validity remain intertwined. Knowledge of the world and moral insight are intrinsic features of the work of art.

Yet, despite his awareness of the difficulties, Habermas has continued to assert, in some of his recent writings, that contemporary philosophy must satisfy the specialized criteria of scientific truth: 'Today, philosophy could establish its own distinct criteria of validity – in the name of genealogy, of recollection (*Andenken*), of elucidating *Existenz*, of philosophical faith, of deconstruction, etc. – only at the price of *falling short* of a level of differentiation and justification that has already been reached, i.e. at the price of surrendering its own plausibility (*Glaubwürdigkeit*)' (PT 17). But can the types of philosophical activity listed here really be regarded as primarily concerned with *evading* assessment of their truth? Would it not be more accurate to say that they seek to perform the *interpretative* task which Habermas himself goes on to describe as 'an illuminating furtherance of lifeworld processes of achieving self-understanding, processes that are related to totality'? This task, Habermas claims, is vital, because 'the lifeworld must be defended against extreme alienation at the hands of the objectivating, the moralizing, *and* the aestheticizing interventions of expert cultures' (PT 17–18). This dismissal of the currently predominant styles of philosophy becomes even more surprising when we recall that Habermas himself has stressed the 'multilingual' virtues of philosophy (TK 41) in its role of mediator between the laboratory, the court room, the museum and the lifeworld. For what can these multiple languages be, if not precisely the phenomenological, hermeneutic, genealogical and deconstructive currents of twentieth-century thought? What other discourses are available which weave between validity dimensions, reflecting upon the textures of the lifeworld as a whole, and thus simultaneously confirming and disrupting them? To suggest that such discourses are not 'plausible' (*glaubwürdig*) seems, at best, a clumsy accusation. For whoever thought that they aspire to provide 'knowledge' in the modern scientific sense?

V

Enough has been said by now to confirm that Habermas's division between the 'stand-in' and 'interpreter' roles of philosophy is fraught with difficulties. But this does not mean that there is any simple alternative solution to the problem of philosophizing after Hegel. While many trends in twentieth-century philosophy achieve their sensitivity to the particular at the cost of any comprehensive vision, others strive for a universality which is reductive or homogenizing. The virtue of Habermas's dual metaphilosophy is that it tries to do justice to both impulses, while insisting that we must abandon the illusion that they can be conflated. Arguably, the problems which his approach generates are no graver than those of any of the other – usually more one-sided – conceptions of philosophy currently available. Accordingly,

rather than posing the question of absolute success, it may be more pertinent to ask: how far is Habermas's mature conception of philosophy adequate to his own original project of the desublimation of reason?

We have seen that Habermas's account of reason is marked by an insistent naturalizing and historicizing drive. In *Knowledge and Human Interests*, for
example, Habermas sought to ground reason in interests ultimately connected
with the survival of the species, although the result of his attempt was
ambiguous, since the very notion of a cognitive interest seemed to presuppose a spontaneous capacity for self-reflection that is difficult to naturalize.
In later writings, he moves from a minimal philosophical anthropology to a
'universal' or 'formal' pragmatics of language, arguing that 'Reason is by its
very nature incarnated in contexts of communicative action and in structures
of the lifeworld' (PDM 322). Once reason is viewed in this way, Habermas
contends, the old metaphysical idea of reason as an ideal power originating
beyond the transient, finite world, or entirely pervading it, can at last be laid
to rest:

> The concept of reason that is identified in the presuppositions of action oriented
> toward mutual understanding frees us from the dilemma of having to choose between
> Kant and Hegel. Communicative reason is neither incorporeal, like the spontaneity
> of a subjectivity that is world-constituting, yet itself without a world, nor does it twist
> history into a circular teleology for the sake of the absolute self-mediation of a his-
> toricized spirit. (PT 142)

But however much he stresses the embodiedness and embeddedness of communicative reason, Habermas cannot abolish the tension between the ideal
and the real entirely. As he writes:

> The transcendental gap between the intelligible and the empirical worlds no longer
> has to be overcome through the philosophy of nature and the philosophy of history.
> It has instead been reduced to a tension transferred into the lifeworld of the com-
> municative actors themselves, a tension between the unconditional character of
> context-bursting, transcendent validity-claims on the one hand and, on the other
> hand, the factual character of the context-dependent 'yes' and 'no' positions that create
> social facts *in situ*. (PT 142)

Thus, even communicative reason cannot be *entirely* naturalized; there is 'a
moment of *unconditionality* . . . built into *factual* processes of mutual understanding (PDM 322). Reason, in other words, still transcends the given; it
orients us towards an ideal point of resolution which always lies beyond
the present, although Habermas is now more reluctant to describe this point
even in terms of an ideal speech situation.[13] Indeed, in some of his recent

writings, Habermas employs the phrase 'transcendence from within' to describe the way in which 'the validity claimed for propositions and norms . . . "*blots out*" *space and time*', even though such claims are always raised within specific contexts of communication and action (PDM 323). Of course, unless one goes entirely naturalistic, a move which Habermas vigorously combats in the case of thinkers like Richard Rorty, or returns to some kind of Hegelian synthesis, in which reason and the historical process ultimately fuse, such a transcendent dimension of reason is inevitable. But if this is so, what can still be meant by the 'desublimation' of reason?

As Habermas's lifelong reference to the Young Hegelians makes clear, in order for reason to be 'desublimated', it is not enough for it to be theorized as a *potential* of social and communicative practice. It has to be actually progressively embodied in the activities and institutions of society. In other words, reason remains an impotent ideal unless, as Habermas often says, it is 'met half-way' by modern forms of life which are receptive to, and can foster, its democratic and universalizing impulses. Habermas connects this thought explicitly with Marx's notion of the 'realization of philosophy'. In the contemporary world, he argues, such a realization 'can . . . be understood in the following way: what has, following the disintegration of metaphysical and religious worldviews, been divided up on the level of cultural systems under various aspects of validity, can now be put together – and also put right – only in the experiential context of lifeworld practices' (PT 51).

But here a final peculiarity of Habermas's view emerges. Reason is dependent for its realization on the lifeworld, which is woven from the deep implicit assumptions which imbue the culture and practices of a society. But Habermas is remarkably reluctant to allow philosophy, even in its guise as interpreter, any role in shaping a culture which would be more receptive to the claims of reason. Indeed, there is a basic unresolved tension in his more recent work between the tendentially *universal* character of philosophy's claims and the attempt to confine philosophy-as-interpreter within the particularism of traditions. This tension appears, for example, in the account of 'evaluative' discourse in *The Theory of Communicative Action*, which Habermas explicates primarily in terms of aesthetic critique.

Habermas suggests that the claim raised by evaluative discourse is the relative one of the 'appropriateness of adequacy of value standards' (TCA1 39). Above all, he suggests,

the type of validity-claim attached to cultural values does not transcend the local boundaries in the same way as truth and rightness claims. Cultural values do not count as universal . . . Values can be made plausible only in the context of a particular form of life. Thus the critique of value standards presupposes a shared pre-understanding among participants in the argument, a pre-understanding that is not at their disposal but constitutes and at the same time circumscribes the domain of the thematized validity claims. (TCA1 42)

As an account of 'aesthetic critique', this description already seems tendentious, since aesthetic critique undoubtedly strives for universality, even whilst conceding that this is far harder to achieve than in the case of straightforward cognitive claims. Furthermore, in cases where the aesthetic standards at the basis of the discussion are themselves made problematic by the fact of disagreement, the philosophical issue of the *appropriateness* of these standards, assessed in the light of what is essential to a work of art *as such*, will inevitably be raised. Aesthetic critique and therapeutic critique, in many of their modes, and *a fortiori* philosophy, cannot help but address the question of the relation between our culturally embedded standards and values and the ultimate or true nature of the relevant phenomena (uncomfortably essentialist though this may sound).

   This avoidance of ultimate questions leads to similar difficulties in the case of Habermas's austere account of the scope of moral philosophy. Programmatically, Habermas suggests that interpretative philosophy must hold open a channel of communication between the specialized sphere of normative rationality and the lifeworld. But when it comes to the crunch, he simply states that 'a postmetaphysical philosophy is too belated to perform the one task, the awakening of moral sensibility, and is overtaxed by the other, overcoming moral cynicism' (JA 75). In Habermas's view, 'The inarticulate, socially integrating experiences of considerateness, solidarity and fairness shape our intuitions and provide us with better instruction about morality than arguments ever could' (JA 76). Indeed, he insists that 'Philosophy is overtaxed by . . . "the existential question concerning the meaning of being moral". For moral despair demands an answer to the fundamental ethical question of the meaning of life as such, of personal and collective identity. But the ethical-existential process of reaching an individual self-understanding and the ethical-political clarification of a collective understanding are the concern of those involved, not of philosophy' (JA 75). This exclusion of philosophy from the domain of 'ethical' debate (discussion of the nature of the good society and the good life) seems artificial. For surely, any such debate which arises from deep differences of opinion and intuition will eventually be driven towards an exploration of conceptual issues, an exploration which can properly be called philosophical. In other words, philosophy − as an attempt to transcend the lifeworld − arises from *within* the lifeworld. It does not have to be imported into it.

Of course, it is always tempting to be sceptical about the possibility of transcending our cultural and linguistic confines, in the manner currently exemplified by Richard Rorty, who bluntly claims that 'we have no prelinguistic consciousness to which language needs to be adequate, no deep sense of how things are which it is the duty of philosophers to spell out in language'.[14] However, such a position overlooks the fact that the linguistically disclosed lifeworld is not simply *a* world, but also *the* world: there is no neutral space in which it could be situated as one relatively self-enclosed world amongst others, since to envisage such a space would presuppose precisely the kind of metaphysical objectivism which the notion of the lifeworld aims to overcome. The assumptions and values which structure the lifeworld are not projections on to the blank screen of a value-neutral reality, but rather perspectival ways of experiencing the world as such. Implicitly Habermas recognizes this, since he is highly critical of Rorty's celebration of the final victory of metaphors of self-creation over metaphors of discovery, insisting that frames of world disclosure shift in response to the resistance of what they disclose. Yet, by describing the task of interpretation as a rendering explicit of the intuitions of a particular lifeworld, Habermas fails to acknowledge that philosophical thought cannot help but weave back and forth in the field of tension between a culturally sedimented interpretation of the world and the experience of the world *tout court*. Suggestions that one can be neatly disentangled from the other are no more plausible than those totalizing, 'post-modern' unmaskings of truth and reason as effects of power which Habermas rightly resists.

In one sense, of course, Habermas's reluctance to claim superior wisdom or to prescribe to the lifeworld can be seen as the reflection of a sound intuition: the desublimation of reason cannot be exclusively – or even primarily – a theoretical or philosophical task. It requires cultural and ethical sensitivity and political imagination, much more than a definitive account of the nature of things – and indeed is incompatible with the very notion of such an account. But at the same time, the refusal to allow philosophy to strive beyond the boundaries of tradition, to say something general about our human place in the world, risks depriving us of a source of illumination and insight. For in the long run there is no point in trying to impose a 'cognitive' strait-jacket on philosophy, or insisting that 'world-disclosing arguments that induce us to see things in a radically different light are not essentially philosophical arguments' (JA 79). While rejecting the elitist posture of the philosopher as seer, a posture whose political dangers Habermas rightly underlines, we have to recognize that philosophy does not just speak many languages – it also reveals many kinds of truths. As long as we remain aware that philosophical truth is oblique, that it is not to be equated with the knowledge produced by the sciences, there seems no reason to refuse philosophy a role as a *discloser* of possibilities. Indeed, such a refusal would run counter to one of Habermas's deepest aims: to illuminate the suppressed traces of communicative reason in the history which has shaped us, and thereby show that our own modern identity confronts us with the demand for a less destructively irrational world.

★   ★   ★

I began by suggesting that the Young Hegelian critique of Hegel has remained a defining philosophical moment for Habermas throughout his career. The notion that philosophy after Hegel must retrieve the rational content of the metaphysical tradition, but in a desublimated form, has been a constant of his thought. It seems clear, for example, that when Habermas deciphers the world as a whole which metaphysics sought to grasp as the *projected* totality of a specific lifeworld, he is ultimately inspired by the dialectic of externalization and recuperation which is the basis of Feuerbach's critique of theology. But, of course, the process of 'reappropriating' supposedly objectified or over-rationalized philosophical contents did not end with the Young Hegelians; indeed, it has been a constant feature of the European tradition ever since. One need only think of the development of phenomenology, where Husserl's own return to experience and the 'things themselves' is repeatedly unmasked by later thinkers as insufficiently radical, for imposing its own rigid, preconceived grid on our experience of the world; or the response of the Wittgenstein of the *Philosophical Investigations* to earlier analytical theories of meaning, including his own. One of the ironies here is that, very often, a theoretical tradition which begins with the aim of effecting a radical desublimation of reason ends up being criticized by its successors for producing new hypostatizations. The Greek social philosopher Cornelius Castoriadis, for example, directed against Marx and the Marxist tradition the very charges of reification and objectification which the young Marx had himself directed against Hegel (and it is worth recalling that the young Hegel wrote passages which sound almost like Feuerbach).[15]

Given the seeming ineluctability of this process, it is scarcely surprising that something similar has occurred in the case of Habermas himself. Among the current critiques of Habermas inspired by a general sympathy for his project, the prevalent tendency is to identify those features of his theory which seem to constrain or exclude the very dimensions of experience from which the critical impulse might emerge in the first place. The need for a retrieval of occluded pre-theoretical sources is argued for by some critics in relation to moral and ethical experience, by others in relation to forms of communication and recognition, and by yet others in relation to the body and the emotions and to the domain of the aesthetic in general. The second, correlative feature of this line of critique is, of course, a sense that overarching theoretical constructs and overly formal procedures of justification have constricting, even repressive, aspects which their internal logic renders them unable to acknowledge or even to envision.

In their different ways, the essays in Part I of this collection develop criticisms of Habermas along these lines. Gordon Finlayson (ch. 1) argues that the Kantianism of Habermas's moral theory screens out access to important wellsprings of ethical experience and social commitment which feed into the dynamic of universalization. The importance of these wellsprings was highlighted by Hegel in his critique of Kant. James Bohman (ch. 2) argues that Habermas still has a residual commitment to a comprehensive, unifying framework for a critical theory of society which inhibits the pluralistic bent and critical potential of his thought. I argue, in my contribution (ch. 3), that Habermas's account of linguistic intersubjectivity tends to exclude dimensions of the self which cannot be fitted readily into an intersubjective frame. And finally, Nikolas Kompridis (ch. 4) suggests that Habermas's stress on the primacy of the dimension of validity in language underplays the revelatory (as opposed to representational) function of language and other practices – that process of world disclosure which was at the heart of Heidegger's concerns. In probing these different aspects of Habermas's theory, the essays in this section are also intended to provide a perspective on his relation to some of the major philosophical traditions on which he draws.

The contributions in Part II bear on more directly political, social and cultural dimensions of Habermas's work. Nevertheless, similar worries concerning the hypostatizing tendencies of his theory are in evidence here. This is most evident in Maeve Cooke's essay (ch. 6), which assesses the strengths and weaknesses of Habermas's notion of autonomy from a feminist perspective. While defending the view that feminists need some ideal of autonomy and that Habermas's account is a promising one, she also argues that the value of moral autonomy depends on an ethical context, and that the role of ethical autonomy – and the form of validity it presupposes – is not adequately acknowledged in Habermas's work. William Scheuerman (ch. 5), examining Habermas's major contribution to the philosophy of law and political theory, *Between Facts and Norms*, suggests that he is too ready to endorse a disillusioned 'realist' account of decision making within the modern state, one which is in theoretical and political tension with his own radical democratic impulses. And finally, Max Pensky (ch. 7) assesses the history of Habermas's engagement in the day-to-day political controversies of the Federal Republic of Germany. Pensky points out that Habermas's adamant opposition to any resurgence of German national feeling, his conviction that this continues to be the key political issue, sometimes leads him to assume a priori that his opponents' stance is strategic, in a way which violates his own conception of the intrinsic norms of debate.

The essays in Part III are intended to illuminate Habermas's work from an angle which is rather unusual in the English-speaking world. I have already traced the development of Habermas's conception of the philosopher's task, from his doctoral dissertation up to the formulation of his now well-established distinction between the reconstructive and hermeneutic roles of philosophy. This division of labour currently defines Habermas's conception of Critical Theory and its relation to practice. But, of course, as well as being the leading international figure in Critical Theory, Habermas is also one of a number of powerfully original thinkers, politically on the Left and committed to the defence of modernity, who have set their stamp on German philosophy in the latter part of the twentieth century. Contemporaries such as Karl-Otto Apel, a fellow student from his Bonn days with whom Habermas has maintained a lifelong friendship and collaboration, the innovative interpreter of German Idealism Dieter Henrich, and the religiously oriented theorist of communicative freedom Michael Theunissen, have each propounded their own conception of philosophy's contemporary role. This has led to a series of fascinating debates in which Habermas has been engaged in recent years, concerning fundamental issues of philosophical method and orientation. The essays translated here can offer only a glimpse of the alternative perspectives of Habermas's peers, but I hope they will help to establish a sense of the specifically German intellectual context in which Habermas's own project has been elaborated. To round out this picture, I have concluded the book with an essay by Axel Honneth, widely regarded as the leading representative of the Critical Theory tradition amongst the younger generation of German philosophers. Honneth proposes a return to the notion of Critical Theory as the articulation of a pre-theoretical interest in emancipation, classically formulated by Max Horkheimer. He argues that Habermas's formal theory of communication tends to screen out the concrete relations of recognition it presupposes, and has thereby lost sensitivity to the distortions and breakdowns of intersubjective acknowledgement which give rise to movements for social change. In response, Honneth attempts to renew Critical Theory's socially *diagnostic* role, by providing a framework for deciphering the critique of social power structures and inequalities which is *already* morally coded in the emotions and reactions of the despised and socially excluded. In so doing, he makes his own contribution to the continuing project of the desublimation of reason, which, for all its Habermasian inspiration, today sometimes finds itself in conflict with the imposing architectonic of Habermas's own mature thought.

Notes

A few paragraphs of this introduction are a revised version of material that first appeared in Peter Dews, 'Law, solidarity and the tasks of philosophy', *Theoria*, 88 (Dec. 1997), pp. 107–27 (repr. in René von Schomberg and Kenneth Baynes, eds, *Democracy and Discourse: Essays on Habermas' Between Facts and Norms* (Albany, NY: SUNY Press, forthcoming).

1   G. W. F. Hegel, *Lectures on the Philosophy of World History. Introduction: Reason in History*, tr. H. B. Nisbet (Cambridge: Cambridge University Press, 1975), p. 27.

2   Max Horkheimer, 'Traditional and Critical Theory', in *Critical Theory: Selected Essays*, tr. M. O'Connell (New York: Herder and Herder, 1972), p. 204.

3   Habermas employs the phrase 'Vernunftbezug der Geschichte' in PDMo 392n.

4   Jürgen Habermas, 'Das Absolute und die Geschichte: Von der Zwiespältigkeit in Schellings Denken' (doctoral dissertation, University of Bonn, 1954), pp. 15–86.

5   'Literaturbericht zur philosophischen Diskussion um Marx und den Marxismus (1957)', in TuP 443. The phrase '*vérité à faire*' is taken from Merleau-Ponty, an important influence on the early Habermas's understanding of the philosophical status of Marxism.

6   Max Horkheimer, 'Postscript' in *Critical Theory*, p. 245 (translation altered).

7   Ibid., p. 251.

8   See 'Zu Nietzsches Erkenntnistheorie (ein Nachwort)', in KK 239–63.

9   Karl-Otto Apel, 'Wissenschaft als Emanzipation? – Eine kritische Würdigung der Wissenschaftskonzeption der "Kritischen Theorie"', in *Transformation der Philosophie*, vol. 2 (Frankfurt am Main: Suhrkamp, 1976), p. 153.

10 See Martin Seel, 'Die Zwei Bedeutungen "kommunikativer" Rationalität: Bemerkungen zu Habermas' Kritik der pluralen Vernunft', in *Kommunikatives Handeln*, ed. Axel Honneth and Hans Joas (Frankfurt am Main: Suhrkamp, 1986), p. 55.

11 '. . . denn jeder Diskurs ist sozusagen unmittelbar zu Gott': 'Entgegnung', in *Kommunikatives Handeln*, p. 343. The allusion is to Ranke's famous description of historical epochs.

12 'Exkurs: Transzendenz von innen, Transzendenz ins Diesseits', in TK 38.

13 See Jürgen Habermas, 'Rortys pragmatische Wende', *Deutsche Zeitschrift für Philosophy*, 5 (1996), p. 732.

14 Richard Rorty, *Contingency, Irony and Solidarity* (Cambridge: Cambridge University Press, 1989), p. 21.

15 See Cornelius Castoriadis, *The Imaginary Institution of Society*, tr. Kathleen Blamey (Cambridge: Polity Press, 1987), ch. 1.

Part I
Traditions

1

Does Hegel's critique of Kant's moral theory apply to discourse ethics?

Gordon Finlayson

The universal in the *sense of the universality of reason*, is **also** universal in the sense . . . that it presents itself *for* consciousness in the mode of thinghood and sensuous being, without thereby losing its nature and having regressed into inert existence. . . . What is universally valid (*gültig*) is **also** universally operative (*geltend*); what *ought* to be in fact **also** *is* and what **only** *ought* to be without being has no truth.[1]

Several years ago Jürgen Habermas wrote a short answer to the question: 'Does Hegel's critique of Kant apply to discourse ethics?' The gist of his short answer is, 'no'. In so far as Hegel's criticisms of the formalism and abstract universalism of the moral law failed to apply to Kant's moral theory in the first place, they also fail to apply to discourse ethics. In so far as Hegel's criticisms of the rigorism of the moral law and of Kant's conception of autonomy do hit the mark, discourse ethics successfully draws their sting by reconceiving Kant's moral standpoint along the following lines. (1) Where Kant wrongly undertakes to establish the moral law as a 'fact of reason', discourse ethics derives the moral standpoint from two premises: one formal, a rationally reconstructed logic of argumentation, and one material, concerning the cognitive competence of participants in discourse. (2) Where Kant insists that we must be able to think of ourselves both as intelligible characters, inhabiting a noumenal world, and as empirical characters, inhabiting the world of appearances, discourse ethics allows that in the contexts of action and moral discourse we have just one character, with needs and interests that are empirically based, though not fixed and immune from criticism. (3) Where Kant mistakenly argues that moral autonomy requires that human beings abstract away from their needs and interests and will maxims of action in virtue of their universal form alone, discourse ethics understands moral autonomy to consist in the free adoption of a standpoint from which conflicts of interest can be regulated impartially, by giving special weight to the satisfaction of universalizable interests. (4) Where Kant misconceives the Categorical Imperative as an objective test of universalizability that is applied by individual wills in isolation, discourse ethics reconceives the moral universalism as an ideal of intersubjective agreement of participants in discourse. On this, which he takes to be the defining difference between the two approaches, Habermas is wont to cite Thomas McCarthy's summary:

Rather than ascribing as valid to all others any maxim that I can will to be a universal law, I must submit my maxim to all others for the purposes of discursively testing its claim to universality. The emphasis shifts from what each can will without contradiction to be a general law, to what all can will in agreement to be a universal norm. (MCCA 67)

Against Habermas, I shall argue that some of Hegel's objections to Kant do apply to discourse ethics. For Habermas's interpretation obscures the ways in which Hegel's criticism applies to Kant's ethics, and thus ignores the ways in which Hegel's objections apply *mutatis mutandis* to discourse ethics. True, discourse ethics is immune from Hegel's objection to Kant's thesis that *pure* reason can be practical, in so far as this thesis rests on the idea of a pure rational will, a noumenal causal influence on the empirical world. But Hegel's wider arguments against the formalism and abstract universalism of Kant's conception of the will demonstrate that Kant has no convincing account of how content is given to the Categorical Imperative, construed as a formal principle of universalization, and these arguments can be turned against Habermas's principle U and the notion of a 'universalizable interest'. This is my thesis in section IV. In the three preliminary sections I (I) introduce the relevant principles and presuppositions of discourse ethics; (II) report Habermas's reasons for denying that Hegel's criticisms of Kant's ethics apply to discourse ethics; (III) offer an interpretation of Hegel's objections to Kant which differs from Habermas's.

I Presuppositions and Principles of Discourse Ethics

Habermas's notion of 'discourse' is not just a synonym for speech; it is based on the by no means uncontroversial theory of language and meaning contained in his *Theory of Communicative Action*. Habermas's theory begins from the assumption that 'The process of reaching agreement inhabits human speech as its telos' (TCA1 287). According to Habermas there are always two dimensions to reaching agreement: the propositional content of an utterance, which picks out what we reach agreement about, and the 'performative' use of an utterance, which picks out the way in which one subject reaches agreement with another. Habermas analyses this performative dimension of speech as follows: it is a feature of every speech act that it necessarily, albeit implicitly, raises three different claims to validity: with respect to the truth of the proposition, the rightness of the utterance and the truthfulness of the speaker.[2] Habermas contends that the interpreter of an utterance is always in principle free to take up a 'yes' or 'no' stance to the validity claims raised by that utterance, and thus to accept or reject it. When a validity claim is challenged with respect to its truth or its rightness, participants enter into a 'context of discourse'. Practical and theoretical discourse are reflective modes of communication in which the speaker will attempt to justify the disputed validity claim by adducing reasons for its normative rightness or truth, respectively. Habermas maintains that meaningful utterances must satisfy certain reciprocal conditions of acceptability. That is, in order to understand the meaning of any utterance, I must be able to bring to mind and accept the reasons which would 'redeem' its validity claim in discourse. Without getting embroiled in the details of the theory, the important point is that, according to Habermas, the conditions of acceptability of validity claims to truth and those of validity claims to normative rightness are more or less isonomic. In other words, truth claims can be justified in theoretical discourse in much the same way that normative claims can be justified in practical discourse.

For Habermas it is the perceived analogy between the validity domains of truth and normative rightness that underlies the meta-ethical cognitivism of discourse ethics.[3] This means that Habermas is not a cognitivist in the usual sense. He does not think that normative statements are capable of being true or false in the same way that descriptive statements are. But they are alike in so far as they can be right or wrong and stand in need of justification; 'for normative statements a claim to validity is only analogous to a truth claim' (MCCA 76, 68, 56). Everything depends on how deep the analogy goes. If the analogy is one of surface structure, limited to the claim that we treat moral judgements as if they were truth-apt, then not just Kant, but error theorists like J. L. Mackie and even quasi-realists like Simon Blackburn (despite his protestations to the contrary) turn out to be 'cognitivists'.[4] But this is not the issue here. The issue is that discourse ethics embraces 'cognitivism', but not at the price of crude moral realism.[5]

So 'discourse' is the attempt in speech to reach a reasoned consensus over disputed validity claims, on the basis of mutually acceptable reasons (TCA1 42). A reasoned consensus is a consensus that would be reached by participants under ideal conditions – that is, if they argued long enough and well enough and were constrained by nothing external to the discourse situation, only by the unforced force of the better argument. '*Practical* discourse' refers to the process of moral argumentation, the attempt in speech to reach a rationally motivated consensus over a disputed validity claim to normative rightness. More broadly, it picks out the phenomenon of moral argumentation as the way in which rational, mature, social agents regulate conflicts of interest, by means other than those of deception and force – namely, by attempting to repair a damaged intersubjective consensus.[6] When such disputes are resolved successfully, then a new consensus is reached that settles back into contexts of action and allows the participants confidently to base their actions on justified and mutually acceptable norms of behaviour.

What makes discourse theory attractive to the ethicist is that the notion of discourse already harbours a stock of normative rules and commitments that can serve as a premiss of a normative moral theory which is not already morally weighted. Habermas claims that, by rationally reconstructing the pragmatic conditions of discourse, it is possible to isolate a set of ideal conditions that every competent speaker who is oriented towards reaching a reasoned consensus must suppose to be satisfied. These rules of discourse formalize the intuitive know-how of participants in discourse. Analysis of these rules shows that, amongst other things, argumentation in principle excludes no one, renders no assertion immune from question and criticism, and prohibits the use of all coercion except the unforced force of the better argument. These rules have the status of idealizing presuppositions that are necessarily invoked by all participants in discourse (MCCA 87–94; JA 50, 55–6).[7] The thought here is familiar from Kant and elsewhere: namely, that if you will the end, you will the means to this end. As soon as you are engaged in discourse or argumentation, you implicitly accept both the ideal aim of discourse – to reach a rationally motivated consensus – and the means of achieving this aim – the rules of discourse. It is important to note that the aim of discourse and its necessary presuppositions are ideal, although of course real dialogue situations are limited in time and depend on the participants' finite capacity for reasoning, and thus can only approximate these ideals. Still, participants in real discourses must, if only implicitly, take themselves to be aiming at the consensus that would be reached by participants under ideal conditions. If their actual conduct falls short of this aim and they flout the rules of discourse (for example, if they exclude some participant, refuse to listen to their interlocutors, or threaten them with force), then, in so far as they are oriented towards reaching reasoned consensus, they are committing a 'performative contradiction', by violating the very rules they implicitly enjoin.

For present purposes we need only bear in mind the main idea: that there is a normative core to the conception of discourse. 'The ideas of justice and solidarity are already *implicit* in the idealising presuppositions of communicative action, above all in the reciprocal recognition of persons capable of orienting their actions to validity claims' (JA 50). One consequence of this is that Habermas's modest conception of normative moral theory is partly premissed, as he readily concedes, on the 'outrageously strong' empirical claim that a 'universal core of moral intuition' is germane to all forms of life in which action is co-ordinated by communication (AS 201).

Taken alone, even this strong generalization cannot ground a normative moral theory, for fundamental moral principles do not follow directly from the presuppositions of argumentation. If they did, he suggests, it might be clear why these moral principles were binding within practical discourse, but it would remain wholly obscure why they should be binding on actions outside the discourse situation. So Habermas adduces a richer, second premiss about the level of cognitive competence that is possessed by participants in discourse. Participants in discourses must know intuitively 'what it means to discuss hypothetically whether norms of action should be adopted' (MCCA 92, 198).

What this second premiss amounts to is a moot point. Certainly it entails that participants can adduce universalizable reasons in order to justify norms.[8] But Habermas wants to claim that cognitive competence involves knowledge that universally acceptable reasons must also be impartial – that is, agent-neutral.[9] So cognitive competence presupposes the ability to go beyond the contingency of one's own perspective, beyond one's own needs, values and interests, and to empathize with the needs, values and interests of others.

Habermas argues that, from these two premisses, the principle of universalization U can be derived by 'material implication'. More recently, Habermas has weakened his position, now maintaining that U is 'no more than a suggestion won through abduction' – the best guess given the evidence! (EA 60).[10] Since this is not my main concern here, I will assume that U can be derived as Habermas claims. U is a moral principle that links rationally motivated consensus (concerning the validity of norms) with agreement about the existence of universal interests that would be satisfied by them. U states that a norm is valid 'if and only if all affected can *freely* accept the consequences and the side effects the *general* observance of a controversial norm can be anticipated to have for the satisfaction of the everyone's interests.' (MCCA 65). A more recent reformulation of the principle, which emphasizes that moral norms be acceptable from all perspectives, is that 'a norm is valid if the foreseeable consequences and side effects of its general observance for the interests and value-orientations of *each individual* could be freely accepted *jointly* by *all* concerned.' (EA 354).

The idea captured by U is quite straightforward. U projects the ideal of a discourse in which everyone affected by the implementation of a norm would have equal say in its adoption. Moreover, each participant can consent to a norm only if he or she has an interest in – that is, only if he or she has reason to want – the circumstances which would ensue from the general implementation of the norm. What constitutes a universalizable interest is something I shall discuss in section IV. But we should note that everyone assents to norms on the basis of interests: namely, those interests that they share with everyone affected by the implementation of the norm.

Note that Habermas's position is different from Kant's conception of practical reason. Participants in discourse do not assent to moral norms on the basis of unalloyed insight independent of all interest. It is not the case that everyone blindly and freely volunteers to be bound only by all norms that satisfy everyone's interest, which would introduce a large dose of decisionism into the spontaneity of reaching reasoned consensus. Nor, obviously, is it the case that participants agree for moral reasons to be bound by those norms that look like they are in everyone's interest. In that case discourse ethics would presuppose the moral standpoint, not explain it. U links the free acceptance of the consequences of a norm in each case with the satisfaction of not just of one's own, but of everyone else's interests. In discourse, reasons are tested from all perspectives, and those that rest on interests that are particular to some participants are 'ultimately discarded as not being susceptible to consensus' (MCCA 103). U thus posits a kind of ideal end-point of moral enquiry, in which agreement would settle on only those norms that were equally in the interests of all. It represents the standpoint of impartial judgement from which everyone's interests would be weighed.[11]

The kind of impartiality aimed at by discourse ethics, unlike that of Kant or Rawls, does not require participants to abstract away from their own interests; nor is it gained by taking up a neutral, third-person perspective on one's own interests, as recommended by Adam Smith, in his *Theory of the Moral Sentiments.*[12] In these cases the attainment of impartiality gives rise to the problem of dissociation between the self that considers its interests and needs and the self that has those needs.[13] Habermas claims that the intersubjective ideal of impartiality embodied in principle U is immune from what has come to be known as the 'communitarian' criticism of the disinterested moral self. For in discourse ethics impartiality results from a process in which every participant in discourse empathetically attempts to occupy the standpoint of all others affected by a norm and imaginatively to identify with their needs and interests. The idea is not to adopt the external perspective of a spectator on, and thus to dissociate oneself from, one's own interests, but, through the empathetic occupation of the standpoint of all others, to associate oneself with theirs.[14] Impartiality is gained through the mutual adoption, adjustment and integration of multilateral perspectives. This process of 'ideal role taking' which lies at the heart of practical discourse is more than just an epistemic check on whether or not one can universalize from the existence of an interest in one's own case to its existence in all other cases; it opens up one's view of one's own needs and interests to the critical interpretation of others: 'Only under this social-cognitive presupposition can each person give equal weight to the interests of the others when it comes to judging whether a general practice could be accepted by each member on good grounds, *in the same way that I have accepted it*.'[15]

II Habermas on Hegel's Kant Critique

I am going to look at two of Hegel's objections to Kant that Habermas claims do not apply to discourse ethics. These are the objections to the formalism and the abstract universalism of Kant's moral theory. According to Habermas, the objection to formalism runs: 'Since the moral principle of the Categorical Imperative requires that the moral agent abstract from the concrete content of duties and maxims, its application necessarily leads to tautological judgments' (MCCA 195). The objection to abstract universalism runs: 'Since the Categorical Imperative enjoins separating the universal from the particular, a judgment considered valid in terms of that principle, necessarily remains external to individual cases and insensitive to the particular context of a problem' (ibid.).

Habermas rejects Hegel's attempted knock-down objection that the formalism of the moral law implies emptiness, by pointing out that, on Kant's theory and his own, the moral principle is both formal and not empty. The procedure captured by U is 'not formal in the sense that it abstracts from content. Quite the contrary . . . practical discourse depends on contingent content being fed into it from outside' (MCCA 103). It is thus not true that a formal moral principle can have no purchase on the 'substantive problems of everyday life'; it bears directly on all those problems that concern norms embodying 'universalizable' interests (MCCA 204).

What is notable here is that Habermas largely accepts Kant's conception of the will as a tester of maxims in the *Groundwork of the Metaphysics of Morals* and the *Critique of Practical Reason*. Indeed, he invites comparison between the way in which content is fed into the formal testing procedures represented by U and the formula of the universal law respectively (MCCA 204). U relates to norms as the Categorical Imperative does to maxims. For Kant, maxims embody interests: so, for Habermas, do norms. Kant was the first thinker systematically to link interests with the faculty of reason. In the second *Critique*, he writes that 'the concept of a maxim rests on that of an interest': 'From the concept of an incentive [*Triebfeder*, literally "mainspring"] arises that of an interest, which is never attributed to a being except when that being possesses Reason, and an incentive of the will means an incentive insofar as it is represented by Reason.'[16] For Habermas, as we have seen, interests imply reasons for participants freely and jointly to assent to norms in practical discourse.

In response to the second charge of abstract universalism, Habermas argues that although both Kant's theory and his own involve abstractions, it is not true that 'a moral point of view based on the universalizability of norms necessarily leads to the neglect . . . of existing . . . interests' (MCCA 204). The abstractions made by a moral theory that concentrates on the question of justification are unavoidable. However, this necessary decontextualization is counterbalanced by a capacity for nuanced, appropriate and context-sensitive judgement, whereby justified moral norms are applied to particular cases.

III Hegel's Criticisms of Kant's Moral Theory

The objection to formalism that Habermas rejects occurs in Hegel's 1802 essay on *Natural Law*, and again in the *Phenomenology of Spirit*. Hegel claims that the Categorical Imperative is a merely logical test of universalizability which any maxim can be made to pass: 'The criterion of law which Reason possesses within itself, fits every case equally well, and is thus in fact no criterion at all.'[17]

However, Habermas is right: this attempted knock-down argument does not stand up. At least, some maxims can be made to fail the test, in particular those which contain what Kant calls a 'contradiction in conception' – for example, the maxim 'I shall make deceiving promises when convenient'.[18] But if some maxims fail the test of universalizability, then Kant can at least show that the negation of those failed maxims expresses a strict duty: 'Do not break promises when convenient.' In which case it is not true that *any* maxim can be made to pass the test, and hence not true that the Categorical Imperative is empty.

Hegel has a second, more careful objection to the Categorical Imperative, which is that valid moral principles emerge successfully from the test of universalizability only because Kant presupposes the existence of substantive moral values against which the results of the test of universalizability can be weighed. He adduces Kant's example of a man wondering whether he should keep hold of an unrecorded deposit that has been entrusted to his care. Kant declares that, in answering the question of whether or not the maxim 'I shall keep a deposit entrusted to me whenever the opportunity presents itelf' can be universalized: 'I become immediately aware that such a principle would destroy itself if made into a law, for it would entail that there would be no deposits.'[19] Hegel's response is that there is no contradiction here. It is just as self-consistent to will a world in which no such deposits are made, because property does not exist, as it is to will a world in which deposits are made and property exists. 'Property, simply as such, does not contradict itself . . . non-property, the non-ownership of things, or a common ownership of goods is just as little self-contradictory.'[20]

The contradiction arises, argues Hegel, only because Kant presupposes that the moral world ought to be a property-owning world, where deposits can be made and where depositees can be trusted. The maxim can be made self-consistent, but it conflicts with existing values, beliefs and institutions. But the Categorical Imperative was supposed to provide a critical test through which we could reflectively endorse those of our moral intuitions which were contained in justifiable maxims. The resultant justified maxims, the permissions or prohibitions that survive the test, are supposed to be valid a priori, regardless of context. It is not part of that theory that the survivors may be rejected if they conflict with our untested intuitions. That would compromise the autonomy of the moral law, by making it depend upon the 'heteronomous' content of our untested beliefs, desires and practices.

So Hegel's argument, such as it is, is hindered rather than helped by this example. Kant's deposit example does contain a contradiction in conception. This contradiction may only come to light because of the meaning of the concept of 'deposit', which is interwoven with a set of background assumptions about property rights and relations of trust. None the less, a contradiction in conception arises because, when I attempt to universalize my appropriation of the deposit, I have at the same time to will the existence of a world in which relations of trust obtain between the givers and receivers of deposits, and the existence of a world in which everyone would appropriate deposits if they could, and in which, therefore, such relations of trust would not obtain.[21]

But although Hegel did not choose a convincing example to support his argument, he still has a point. The problem is not that any principle which is formal is empty, but that, so long as the principle is just a test of the universalizable form of the maxim, the results of the application of the test will be insufficiently determinate. The charge that formalism implies emptiness was the bogus one that any maxim could be made to pass the test; the charge that formalism implies 'indeterminacy' is that too many maxims pass the test, so that it alone is not sufficient to determine their moral worth. The objection needs to be fleshed out with an example of one of many possible 'rogue' maxims – that is, maxims which produce counter-intuitive, not to say absurd, results when subjected to the test of universalization. 'Always open doors for other people.' This is a plausible example of a maxim. It is at least as plausible as any of the examples that Kant himself discusses. Yet, given the fact that two people cannot open the same door for each other, the maxim clearly fails the test of universalizability. It would, however, be absurd to conclude that it was therefore morally impermissible always to open doors for other people, or that one had a strict duty not to do so.

One response to the problem of 'rogue' maxims has been to introduce a scope restriction on what can count as a candidate maxim, thereby ensuring that only 'morally relevant' maxims are available for testing by the moral will. This is the response that is usually offered in Kant's defence. Onora O'Neill draws a distinction between 'underlying intentions' – for example, to be hospitable to one's guests – and 'ancillary intentions' – for example, to offer them a cup of tea. She reserves the term 'maxim' for the former. In the same spirit, Ottfried Höffe draws a distinction between maxims, which are general (subjective) principles of the will and capture the 'fundamental normative pattern' of actions, and rules, or precepts of action, which reflect more or less arbitrary decisions about how to order one's life, such as to rise early in the morning.[22] I suspect that any scope restrictions on candidate maxims that are sufficiently determinate to rule out examples like 'Always open doors for other people' as trivial or irrelevant must ultimately refer to the content, not just the form, of the maxim. But the moral will is supposed to abstract from considerations of content. So this defence of Kant is vulnerable to the objection that, under the guise of redescribing the function of maxims in shaping a life, it smuggles in normative considerations to determine candidature, considerations which are supposed to result from the reflective testing of maxims, not to be fed into it in the premises.

In spite of its unpromising formulation in his early works, Hegel does have here the lineaments of a good argument against the indeterminacy of Kant's moral standpoint. It is this argument that Hegel, in the *Elements of the Philosophy of Right*, directs against its proper target, not the Categorical Imperative itself, but Kant's wider conception of the will as a tester of maxims. His claim is that the 'indeterminacy' of the moral standpoint results from the attempt to settle the question of the validity of moral laws formally – that is, prior to and independent of their relation to a possible content. Note that Hegel here does not attack a crude caricature of Kant's moral theory, as the early Hegel and Schiller were wont to do. Maxims are not the content on to which moral form is stamped. Maxims are not identical with the 'materials' of moral psychology, however these materials – sensations, feelings, emotions, needs, wants, interests – may rate on the scale of refinement and complexity. Rather, maxims are first-order principles of the will that contain and form this material and serve as candidate moral norms, available for uptake into the moral will. The Categorical Imperative is a second-order principle of the will that reflectively selects maxims on the basis of their universalizability, and, more importantly, rejects those that are not universalizable. It is this quite sophisticated picture of the will as a tester of maxims against which the later Hegel directs his fire.

It would be wrong, however, to suggest that the later Hegel rejects Kant's conception of the will in all respects. On the contrary, to a great extent he shares Kant's moral psychology.[23] Hegel agrees with Kant that the moral will is autonomous.[24] He agrees that the autonomous will is one which gives itself a law or adopts a maxim.[25] He agrees that the law which the will gives to itself or the maxim it adopts is universal, not one which merely ministers to particular inclinations.[26] He even agrees that the law or maxim be adopted in virtue of its universality – that is, that the moral agent performs 'duty for its own sake'.[27] Yet he claims that Kant reduces the moral standpoint to an 'empty formalism' when he insists that the maxim be adopted *only* for the sake of its universal form, not *also* for the sake of any desires or interests the maxim may advance.

However essential it may be to emphasise the pure and unconditional self-determination of the will as the root of duty – for knowledge of the will first gained a firm foundation and point of departure in the philosophy of Kant, through the thought of its infinite autonomy – to cling on to a merely moral point of view without making the transition to the concept of ethics reduces this gain to an *empty formalism*. . . . **From this standpoint, no immanent doctrine of duties is possible.** One may indeed bring in material from outside and thereby arrive at particular duties, but it is impossible to make the transition to the determination of particular duties from the above determination of duty as *absence of contradiction*, as *formal correspondence with itself*, which is no different from the specification of *abstract indeterminacy*; **and even if such a particular content for action is taken into consideration, there is no criterion within that principle for deciding whether or not this content is a duty.** . . . A contradiction must be a contradiction with something, that is, with a content which is already fundamentally present as an established principle. Only to a principle does an action stand in a relation of agreement or contradiction. **But if a**

duty is to be willed merely as a duty and not because of its content, it is a *formal identity* **which necessarily excludes every content and determination.**[28]

Hegel's argument is that Kant fails to show how the moral will can give itself contentful moral principles whilst remaining truly self-determining and free. His initial reproach, that Kant can give no 'immanent doctrine of duties', cuts deeper than the familiar charge that Kantian morality is deficient in substantial, determinately action-guiding duties. Such an argument could easily be deflected by pointing out that in the *Groundwork* and the second *Critique*, Kant's principal aim is *to justify the moral law*, not to provide a doctrine of determinate duties; this is a task he undertakes later in the second part of the *Metaphysics of Morals* (the 'Doctrine of Virtue').[29] Hegel's deeper point is that, because Kant conceives of the autonomy of the moral will as an a priori determination of itself – that is, a determination that abstracts from the ends it adopts – he introduces a hiatus between the moral will, with its principle of maxim selection, the Categorical Imperative, and the empirical will, the bearer of the candidate maxims.

The hiatus can be brought into view by considering the reflective structure of the will that Hegel attributes to Kant. I morally will (on the basis of the Categorical Imperative) that I empirically will (adopt the maxim) not to make deceiving promises. The categorical 'ought' comes from the moral will. But it is addressed to the human, empirical will that is both rational and sensible and which has interests. According to Hegel, Kant claims that there is a partial identity between the moral will and the empirical will, since the former is wholly rational and the latter both rational and sensible. Hegel insists, by contrast, that there is only a formal identity, that Kant's moral will is characterized by 'formal correspondence with itself' and 'abstract indeterminacy'.[30] For the moral will incorporates maxims on the basis of their universal form alone. Thus the moral will remains, ultimately, discontinuous with the 'content' or the interest that is contained in the maxim. But having a content, an interest, is what distinguishes the empirical from the moral will. So the moral will must be discontinuous with the empirical will. They remain, ultimately, different agencies. The content of the maxim itself exerts no constraints on the adoption of the maxim, only on the form of the content. What this means more concretely is that my desire to keep my promises and my wanting not to let the person to whom I promise down are not morally relevant considerations to the adoption of my maxim not to make deceiving promises. In so far as these desires form part of the content of the maxim, this content remains a moment of heteronomy within the will or, as Hegel writes elsewhere, 'the last undigested lump in the stomach'.[31] Hegel concludes that this discontinuity obscures the relation of the a priori principle to its possible content: 'there is no criterion within that principle for deciding whether this content is a duty.'

Let me now review my reconsideration of Hegel's Kant critique. (1) Hegel's most plausible objection to the Categorical Imperative is that it captures too many maxims. The results of the testing process are thus not sufficiently determinate to capture our moral intuitions successfully. (2) Hegel challenges Kant to show how, in his view, the moral will can acquire a determinate content, if a maxim must be adopted in virtue of its universalizable form alone, not also in virtue of the interest it contains. This way of putting the point makes Hegel's criticism of 'abstract universalism' concerning the rigid separation of universal and particular into an aspect of the criticism of formalism. But this is not a difficulty. Rather, Habermas's suggestion that Kant's separation of universals and particulars forms a separate problem, one that arises only in the application of valid moral norms to particular situations, is misleading. In Hegel's eyes, Kant's insuperable problem is to show how there can be valid, contentful moral norms. Of course there *are* such norms, and he presupposes that there are. But he fails to show how this is possible. If my interpretation is right, Hegel's answer to this question would involve giving a plausible account of how a universalizable maxim can be adopted in virtue of its form *and* in virtue of its content. And to show that, Hegel would have to give some account of how particular interests acquire universal form. This is one of the tasks, arguably the most important one, that Hegel assigns to the philosophy of objective spirit.

IV A Critique of the Formalism of Discourse Ethics

Do Hegel's criticisms of Kant apply *mutatis mutandis* to discourse ethics, and if so how? We can begin to answer this question by asking whether the results of the test of universalizability in principle U would capture enough of our moral intuitions. We know that U rules out any norm the general observance of which would not be likely to satisfy 'everyone's interests'; that is, U rules out all norms that do not embody, to use Habermas's term, a 'generalizable' or 'universalizable interest'. But what counts as 'in everyone's interest'? Or, to put it differently, what are the conditions of the universalizability of interests? Looking closely, there is a worrying ambiguity in Habermas's formulation and subsequent explanations of U. A norm is not valid unless 'all affected can *freely* accept the consequences and the side effects its *general* observance can be anticipated to have for the satisfaction of everyone's interests' (MCCA 65). The ambiguity is captured by a different translation of the principle later in the English translation of the same work: 'For a norm to be valid, the consequences and side effects of its general observance for the satisfaction of *each person's particular interests* must be acceptable to all' (MCCA 197). The text should read 'for the interests of each individual', not 'for each person's particular interests'. Habermas's formulation of U should not specify that the interests, the hypothetical satisfaction of which constitutes the validity of a norm, be particular; for, elsewhere, Habermas defines a 'particular' interest as one which fails the test of universalizability.[32] But even in the original, U is open to such an interpretation.[33] U could mean that validity is conferred on a norm only if everyone has *an* interest in its general observance, but not necessarily the same interest. Such interests could be particular, not common to all, which would imply that different people could assent to a norm for different reasons. I shall call this the 'unofficial interpretation'. Alternatively, U might mean that validity is conferred on a norm only if everyone has *one and the same interest* in its general observance, which would imply that a rationally motivated consensus about a norm can be reached only if everyone can freely accept it for *one and the same reason*. I shall call this the 'official version'.

It is by no means implausible to claim that a valid norm must satisfy *an interest* of everyone affected by its general observance, though not necessarily the same one. But, given what Habermas argues elsewhere, he must rule out the unofficial version of U and, with it, the possibility that participants in discourse can assent to norms for different reasons, on the basis of different interests. Take the example of an isolated, self-sufficient farming co-operative consisting of vegetarians, who also happen to be atheists, and religious believers, who happen not to be vegetarian, all agreeing that it is wrong to eat pork. The norm that one ought not to eat pork commands universal assent, in spite of the fact that the reasons for the norm are not themselves universally recognized as valid, but, rather, are relative to some other context – vegetarianism and religion, respectively. Indeed, assent is universal in spite of the fact that, since this context is not generally shared, neither group can be persuaded by the reasons advanced by the other. Yet, on the unofficial interpretation of U, the norm would be valid, since it would pass the test of universalization.

The unofficial version validates norms on the basis of a contingent overlap of particular interests, on condition that all participants in discourse can judge that everyone affected by the norm has some interest in its general observance. However, U is supposed to function as a criterion that would enable participants in discourse to distinguish sharply between a rationally motivated consensus that can withstand reflective scrutiny and a merely *de facto* consensus or compromise resting on a contingent overlap of two particular interests. It lies at the heart of Habermas's disagreement with Rawls that consensus in practical discourse meet this cognitive condition.[34] 'Whereas parties brokering a compromise can assent to the result each for different reasons, participants in argumentation aim to secure a rationally motivated consensus, if at all, then on the basis of the same reasons'. (EA 108).

On the unofficial interpretation, U cannot fulfil this requirement. It can distinguish only between *de facto* universal consensus and *de facto* dissent. Worse still, if U permits the validity of norms to rest on a merely contingent overlap of interests, rather than on the universal acceptability of good reasons, a mainstay of discourse meta-ethics – the analogy between normative rightness and truth – breaks down. Newtonian and Einsteinian physicists might agree that light consists of particles rather than waves, but they would do so for very different reasons. It would not count as a 'rationally motivated' consensus only on the basis of good reasons. In other words, justifying reasons, as well as the conclusions they warrant, must converge if we are to speak of convergence proper. To the extent that normative rightness is analogous with truth, the same must hold of a rationally motivated consensus about norms.

What about the official version, according to which a norm is valid only if participants can assent to it for the same reasons – that is, on the basis of the same interest?[35] There is more than one way of 'sharing' or 'having the same' interest. A couple can be said to share an interest in their child's education, a bit like they share a flat. The same interest provides them both with a common aim, just as the shared flat provides them with a common living space. By contrast, human beings can be said to share an interest in avoiding pain. Here the 'same' interest provides each with a different aim, you with avoiding your pain, me with avoiding mine, and so on, aims which we hold and pursue independently. As a consequence of these two ways of individuating interests, there are two different ways in which everyone can have the same interest. Interests can be universalizable collectively or distributively.

To begin with the latter, the interest in avoiding pain is distributively universalizable in avoiding pain if and only if everyone has an interest in avoiding their own pain. As I said earlier, to have an interest is to have a reason to want. Now, distributively universalizable interests are agent-relative reasons to want. Following McNaughton and Rawling, we can say that a reason is agent-relative 'if its full articulation would involve ineliminable pronominal back-reference to the agent: agent-neutral otherwise'.[36] By contrast, the interest is collectively universalizable if and only if everyone has an interest in everyone's avoiding their pain. Collectively universalizable interests, then, imply reasons which do not contain an ineliminable pronominal back reference to the agent, and are thus agent-neutral.

The question is, does discourse conforming to U provide a test of distributive or collective universalizability? Habermas is not as clear as he might be on this issue. I think he is committed to the view that discourse conforming to U permits consensus only on the basis of collectively universalizable interests. I think this for two reasons. First, Habermas equates the moral standpoint with the standpoint of impartial judgement, and impartiality usually implies both universalizability and agent neutrality. And he thinks that all *impartial* reasons to assent to norms can be universally shared on the basis of universalizable interests. 'True impartiality pertains only to that standpoint from which one can universalize precisely those norms that can count on universal assent because they perceptibly embody an interest common to all affected' (MCCA 65, 198).[37] Secondly, and decisively, there is Habermas's repeated insistence that moral reasons must be agent-neutral, not agent-relative. He has recently argued that moral justification is possible only on the basis of rational reasons (*Vernunftgründe*): 'But in contradistinction to the empirical varieties of contractualism, these reasons are no longer understood as agent-relative motives, with the result that the epistemic core of the validity of ought-claims (*Sollgeltung*) remains in tact' (EA 15). In much the same spirit he writes: 'Normative reasons are – unlike mere declarations of intent or simple imperatives – not agent-relative reasons for one's own . . . instrumental behavior, but – as in the case of assertions – agent-neutral reasons, though not reasons for states of affairs, but for the fulfillment of normative expectations'.[38]

Habermas's point seems to be that not only must the content of moral norms be agent-neutral, so must the reasons that justify those norms. Note that the claim is not that agent-neutral principles are justifiable only by agent-neutral reasons, which is certainly untrue. (A community of rational egoists can agree to a system of morality which contains some agent-neutral principles.) Habermas's claim is, rather, that moral principles cannot be justified by agent-relative reasons, which implies that agent-neutral principles that are justified only by agent-relative reasons are not yet moral principles. The further step to moral normativity requires agent-neutral justification on the basis of collectively universalizable interests.

It is counterintuitive for the moral authority of a public conception of justice to rest on reasons that are not public. Everything valid must also be publicly justifiable. Valid utterances deserve to be universally recognized on the basis of the same reasons. . . . Such a practice of justification [i.e. moral discourse not compromise] aims at a publicly and collectively achieved consensus. (EA 108)

If we take the liberty of changing the vocabulary from 'public' to 'agent-neutral', and add in his claim that collectively, but not distributively, universalizable interests imply agent-neutral reasons, we get an unambiguous statement of his position.

The trouble is that, whereas the unofficial version of U is too weak, the official version is now too strong. At least, it is too strong to pass itself off as a plausible reconstruction of everyday moral intuitions. It is true that morality is more than a matter of enlightened agent-relative interest, which itself is much more than just a matter of 'enlightened self-interest', for agent-relative rules – for example, grandchildren ought to respect their grandparents – do not have to be selfish. And it is possible to argue, as Habermas does, that ultimately the content of all genuinely 'moral' norms is agent-neutral. Whereas tradition tells us to show respect to our *own* grandparents, morality demands that we show equal respect to other people's grandparents, so the underlying moral norm here might be something like. 'Respect old people'. But none of this implies either that moral norms are not sufficiently justified by agent-relative reasons, which is doubtful, or that agent-relative reasons can play no part in the justification of moral norms, which is false.

Why is Habermas led to these implausible conclusions? He sometimes suggests that the analogy between the validity domains of truth and normative rightness, between epistemic and moral reasons, requires that U permit consensus only on the basis of agent-neutral reasons. It is true that good epistemic reasons tend not to contain ineliminable references to believers; they tend to be both universalizable and, as it were, thinker-neutral, but this is not always the case. My reason for believing that I wrote this chapter is that GF wrote this chapter and I am GF. Here we have a belief that is fully justified by a 'thinker-relative' reason. Be that as it may. It seems reasonable to think that the norm 'Harm no one' can be morally justified by reference to everyone's interest in avoiding harm to him or herself, and unreasonable to deny that this distributively universalizable interest can enter into the moral justification of such a norm. Hence, if U were to permit agent-relative justification of moral norms, there would be no threat to the analogy between epistemic and moral reasons presupposed by discourse meta-ethics.

To find out just what is and what is not entailed by the analogy between epistemic and moral reasons is a long and difficult task which I cannot undertake here. Suffice it to say that, if I am right and Habermas's argument is that the official version of U is a necessary condition of the justifiability of moral norms, then the official version is too strong. For, as many commentators have remarked, the number of justifiable moral norms that could meet such a stringent condition, would be too few. Habermas apparently does not see this as a problem. True, there are not many norms that can be justified in practical discourse, but there are some. And the number of collectively universalizable interests is anyway a historical and empirical question (JA 91).[39]

But this undoubtedly *ought* to be a problem for a modest conception of moral theory that claims merely to clarify and explicate our intuitions about morality. Discourse ethics supposedly sets out to explain our moral intuitions, not challenge them or radically to revise them (MCCA 44; JA 40). Yet, the official version of U poses such a stringent test of universalizability that it leaves few survivors. Consequently, it fails to capture the moral intuitions that discourse ethics supposedly sets out to clarify.[40] Albrecht Wellmer goes so far as to claim that U makes 'a fully justified moral judgement' into an impossibility (ED 155). But his objection is overdrawn. In fact, U does not claim to specify the necessary conditions under which practical reasoners can reach action-guiding moral judgements, but only the conditions under which alone moral norms are valid. Besides, this objection fails in the same way as Hegel's initial formulation of the objection to the empty formalism of the Categorical Imperative fails. Habermas has only to adduce one example of a justified moral norm, and the objection is refuted. My way of running the objection is not disposed of so easily; nor is it rebuffed by Habermas's distinction between justification and application (ED 156–8).

Thomas McCarthy and Maeve Cooke point to a ramification of the objection from intuition: the redundancy of the moral standpoint. Because U leaves so few survivors, moral discourse can at most regulate only a negligible proportion of our moral lives.[41] But that is tantamount to conceding that moral discourses are more or less useless for the purpose of regulating moral conflicts. In which case it is methodologically inappropriate for moral discourse to occupy centre stage in his theory of practical reason, let alone provide the normative foundation for critical social theory.

If I am right here, then, discourse ethics is beset by a dilemma of its own making. The unofficial version of U is too weak, and the official version too strong, to do any real work in determining contentful moral norms. The question is: what do these objections to Habermas's too demanding conception of the justifiability of moral norms have to do with Hegel's objection to the 'abstract indeterminacy' of Kant's Categorical Imperative and of Kant's formal conception of the will? Sure, Habermas's difficulties stem from the way in which discourse ethics tries to respond to the problem of the relation between the moral and the empirical will, the problem of the way in which content is introduced into the procedure of moral discourse. Habermas addresses this problem by making universalizability not just a rational requirement on willing that can be met by each individual, but a constraint exerted by the content of what can be collectively willed – universalizable interests. Thus Habermas demonstrates Hegel's point that a duty is willed 'not merely as a duty', but also 'because of its content'.[42] However, while Kant's difficulties arose from the fact that the Categorical Imperative justified too many maxims, requiring the introduction of *ad hoc* scope restrictions, principle U justifies too few. At most, then, Kant and Habermas are vulnerable to similar criticisms directed towards the same problematic relation between form and content.

In the process of addressing Hegel's criticism of the empty formalism of Kant's Categorical Imperative, however, Habermas falls foul of Hegel's criticism of abstract universalism, the rigid separation of universal and particular. There is a slight difference. For in Hegel's eyes Kant is guilty of separating universal form from particular content, whereas the procedural principle U separates universalizable content from particular (that is, non-universalizable) content. The result, however, is equally incapacitating. We have seen that Habermas tries to corral the two logically independent distinctions between universalizable and non-universalizable interests, and agent-neutral and agent-relative reasons, into line, and to make this line serve as the 'razor-sharp' distinction between values and norms, as the boundary of the moral standpoint. In this way the official version of U creates a blind spot with regard to the complex dialectic in which agent-relative concerns feed into and support the agent-neutral content of norms which we more readily recognize as 'moral'.

One obvious solution here would be to weaken the official version of U to allow either distributively or collectively universalizable interests to provide the criterion for moral validity. Another possibility would be to adopt the unofficial version. Either way, this would entail redrawing the distinction between norms and values and blurring the boundary between *Moralität* and *Sittlichkeit* that discourse ethics erects. Interestingly, such a move would push Habermas away from a neo-Kantian position in which norms/justice/morality and values/the good life/ethical life are located in separate, supposedly complementary spheres, towards a more inclusive Hegelian conception of ethical life – that is, towards a more complex dialectical account of the good as 'the unity of the concept of the will and the particular will'.[43]

This would not violate discourse meta-ethics, which, as we have seen, offers no compelling epistemological support for Habermas's very strong official version of U. Indeed, Habermas is well aware that he needs to close the hiatus between norms and values, justice and the good, morality and ethical life; a hiatus which opens up, if I am right, as a result of his analysis, rather than of historical and social forces. This hiatus comes clearly and crucially into view when discourse ethics now attempts to answer the question: in virtue of what are universalizable interests especially worthy of recognition from the moral standpoint? Hitherto, Habermas has been content to give an epistemological answer: in virtue of the demanding conception of validity proper to both moral and theoretical discourse. But his moral epistemology is unsound. Hence, either Habermas must answer that communicative subjects already have a moral interest in recognizing universalizable interests as specially reason-giving from the moral standpoint, which is circular; or discourse ethics is forced to say, as Habermas concedes, 'something relevant about substance as well . . . about the hidden link between justice and the common good' (MCCA 202). That is, discourse ethics must offer some account of why it is good to be moral. Yet it cannot do this, because, on Habermas's understanding, ethical values ultimately consist in particular interests and merely contingent, subjective preferences, and can say nothing about this connection that is not merely descriptive, value-laden and culturally parochial. Habermas is right that the link between morality and the good remains hidden, but it is his own taxonomy that is the source of the obscurity.

In fact, Habermas's unfulfilled demand that the interrelation between morality and ethics, justice and the common good, be made clear is nothing less than a Hegelian insight, a call to uncover a suppressed dialectical relation between a Kantian dichotomy of particular and universalizable interests. Unlike the moral theories of Kant and Habermas, Hegel's philosophy of objective spirit, which culminates in the moment of 'ethical life', emphasizes the continuity between the moral content – the interests embodied in the candidate maxims – and the moral form – the principle of the will. Roughly speaking, it does this in the form of a narrative, in which rational human subjects reflectively revise, refine and realign the particular desires, interests and ends they pursue in concert with others within the framework of their social and political practices and institutions. The point is that, in this framework, the reflective pursuit of particular interests can advance and sustain more universal interests in such a way that formal considerations of fairness, reciprocity and universality come to acquire enduring recognition. This summary is no doubt too brief and too vague to be convincing. I have not undertaken to defend it here. But, if I have shown how, *pace* Habermas, Hegel's criticism of Kant's moral theory applies to discourse ethics, I will have gone some way to demonstrating the enduring relevance of Hegel's ethical insight to the criticism of the moral standpoint, an insight that is captured most pregnantly in the passage from the *Phenomenology of Spirit* which I chose as the epigraph to this chapter.

Notes

Thanks to Christian Piller, Jason Gaiger and Peter Dews for comments on earlier drafts, to Tom Baldwin, John Skorupski and the members of the Political Theory Workshop at the University of York.

1 Hegel, G. W. F. *Hegel Werke*, vol. 3, ed. E. Moldenauer and R. Michel (Frankfurt am Main: Suhrkamp Taschenbuch Wissenschaft, 1986), p. 192; *Phenomenology of Spirit*, tr. A. V. Miller (Oxford: Oxford University Press, 1977), p. 151; Hegel's emphasis in italics, mine in bold.

2 'Necessarily' is meant transcendentally, referring to the conditions of the possibility of reaching a reasoned consensus. Originally Habermas outlines four validity claims, the fourth being that of intelligibility, but he soon pares it down to three (CES 2). These three validity claims correspond to the three types of illocutionary act which Habermas's suggested taxonomy of speech acts allows: constatives, regulatives and expressives (TCA1 322). These in turn relate to the three value spheres which structure the lifeworld: the scientific-technical, the legal-moral and the aesthetic-expressive. I shall focus for the most part on the validity claims to truth and rightness.

3 According to Habermas's theory of meaning, the two sets of predicates true/false and right/wrong are specifications of a single dimension of validity.

4 Interestingly, Habermas's concession that moral utterances, though like truth, do not refer in the same way as assertoric utterances, or refer to a different ontological order (the 'subjective world' or 'social reality' as opposed to the 'objective external world'), pushes him away from a genuinely anti-realist explanation of truth, into the camp of Mackie, Williams and Blackburn, who are scientific realists about assertoric statements but not about moral ones. Crispin Wright, for instance, denies the narrow 'correspondence' model of truth in virtue of which the disanalogy with moral utterances arises. For Wright, 'truth' just is the way in which a sentence is suitably embedded within the syntactic discipline of a language. See J. L. Mackie, *Ethics: Inventing Right and Wrong* (London: Penguin, 1977); Simon Blackburn, *Spreading the Word* (Oxford: Oxford University Press, 1984), ch. 6: 'Evaluations, projections and quasi-realism'; Crispin Wright, 'Truth in ethics', *Ratio*, NS 8 (1995), pp. 213–26.

5 'I defend a cognitivist position . . . namely that there is a universal core of moral intuition . . . In the last analysis, they stem from the conditions of symmetry and reciprocal recognition which are unavoidable presuppositions of communicative action. . . . Any attempt . . . to defend a cognitivist-universalist ethical theory involves the public assertion that in your own society and in others all practical and political questions have a moral core which is susceptible to argument' (AS 201).

6 Since Habermas now makes an analytic distinction between morality and ethics, he uses the term 'moral discourse' for what he previously called 'practical discourse', and the latter ranges over moral, ethical and pragmatic discourse. Concomitantly he now recognizes that he ought to call discourse ethics 'the discourse theory of morality' (JA 2).

7 For an elaboration of the premises in the derivation of the principle of universalization see W. Rehg, 'Discourse and the moral point of view: deriving a dialogical principle of universalisation', *Inquiry*, 34 (1991), pp. 27–48.

8   Roughly speaking, there is good reason for one person to believe *p*, if and only if, in face of all the relevant evidence, there is good reason for any rational person faced with the same evidence to believe *p*. Similarly, there is good reason for one agent to do *f* in situation *S*, if and only if there is good reason for any rational agent to do *f* in situation *S*. See J. Skorupski, 'Reasons and reason', in *Ethics and Practical Reason*, ed. G. Cullity and B. Gaut (Oxford: Oxford University Press, 1997), pp. 352–3.

9   This is dubious, because it does not follow from the claim that all good reasons are universalizable that all good reasons are agent-neutral. For it is not true that only agent-neutral reasons are universalizable; some agent-relative reasons are universalizable too. On agent relativity and universalizability see the excellent discussion of D. McNaughton and P. Rawling, 'Value and agent-relative reasons', *Utilitas*, 7 (1995), pp. 31–47.

10 Habermas does not provide the derivation; rather, he states that such a derivation is possible. Some of the difficulties posed by the derivation of U are unearthed by W. Rehg, 'Discourse and the moral point of view'. In particular, the second premiss brings culturally specific and value-laden assumptions into play, assumptions about the moral relevance of interests and needs. But this threatens to blur the strict distinction which Habermas wishes to draw between values and norms, between moral questions of justice and ethical questions of the good. See below.

11 'True impartiality pertains only to that standpoint from which one can generalize precisely those norms that can count on universal assent because they perceptibly embody an interest common to all affected' (MCCA 65, 198; JA 12–13). Elsewhere Habermas claims that the principles of discourse ethics explicate the moral standpoint – that is, 'the point of view from which norms of action can be impartially grounded' – and that moral discourses aim at 'the impartial evaluation of action conflicts' (BFN 97).

12 'We must view them (his interests and my interests) neither with our own eyes nor with his, but from the place and with the eyes of a third person who has no particular connexion with either and who judges with impartiality between us': Adam Smith, *Theory of the Moral Sentiments*, III. 3.3, cited from David Wiggins, 'Universality, impartiality, truth', in *Needs, Values, Truth: Essays in the Philosophy of Value* (Oxford: Blackwell, 1987), p. 74.

13 Bernard Williams, *Ethics and the Limits of Philosophy* (London: Fontana, 1985).

14 See Jürgen Habermas, 'Individuation through socialization: on George Herbert Mead's Theory of Subjectivity', in PT 149–204.

15 Jürgen Habermas, 'Justice and solidarity: on the discussion concerning "stage 6"', *Philosophical Forum*, 21 (1989–90), p. 39, my emphasis.

16 Immanuel Kant, *Gesammelte Schriften*, Akademie-Ausgabe, 29 vols, Berlin: Prussian Academy of Sciences, 1902–), vol. 5, p. 80.

17 G. W. F. Hegel, *Werke*, vol. 3, p. 319; *Phenomenology of Spirit*, p. 259.

18 Immanuel Kant, *Gesammelte Schriften*, vol. 4, p. 424.

19 Ibid., vol. 5, p. 27.

20 Hegel, *Werke*, vol. 3, p. 317; *Phenomenology of Spirit*, p. 258; see also *Werke*, vol. 2, p. 460.

21 See C. Korsgaard, 'Kant's formula of the universal law', *Pacific Philosophical Quarterly*, 66 (1965), p. 31; see also A. W. Wood, *Hegel's Ethical Thought* (Cambridge: Cambridge University Press, 1990), p. 157.

22 Onora O'Neill, 'Kant after virtue', in *Constructions of Reason* (Cambridge: Cambridge University Press, 1989), pp. 145–65; Ottfried Höffe, *Immanuel Kant*, tr. Marshall Farrier (Albany, NY: SUNY Press, 1994), pp. 149–51; Henry E. Allison, *Kant's Theory of Freedom* (Cambridge: Cambridge University Press, 1990), pp. 85–94.

23 On this see H. Lottenbach and S. Tenenbaum, 'Hegel's critique of Kant in the philosophy of Right', *Kant-Studien* (1995), pp. 219–21.

24 G. W. F. Hegel, *Philosophy of Right*, §133. The moral will here refers to what Kant terms 'Wille' as opposed to 'Willkür'. See John R. Silber, 'The ethical significance of Kant's religion', in Immanuel Kant, *Religion within the Limits of Reason Alone* (New York: Harper and Row, 1960), pp. xciv–cvi, and Allison, *Kant's Theory of Freedom*, pp. 129–36.

25 Hegel, *Philosophy of Right*, §135.

26 Ibid., §137R.

27 Ibid., §133.

28 Ibid., §135R; Hegel's emphasis in italics, mine in bold.

29 The task Kant sets himself in these works is that of justifying the moral law. Sally Sedgwick makes this point comprehensively in 'On the relation of Pure Reason to content: a reply to Hegel's critique of formalism in Kant's ethics', *Philosophy and Phenomenological Research*, 49/1 (1988).

30 Hegel, *Philosophy of Right*, §135R.

31 Hegel, *Vorlesungen über die Geschichte der Philosophie III, Werke*, vol. 20, p. 369.

32 'Particular interests are those that prove on the basis of discursive testing not to be susceptible of generalization and thus to require compromise' ('Reply to my critics', in *Habermas: Critical Debates*, ed. D. Held and J. Thompson (London: Macmillan, 1982), pp. 258).

33 The translator is not wholly at fault here, since his rendering, although inaccurate, is permitted by an ambiguity in the formulation of U in the German: 'daß die Folgen und Nebenwirkungen, die sich jeweils aus ihrer *allgemeinen* Befolgung **für die Befriedigung der Interessen eines *jeden* Einzelnen** . . . ergeben, von allen Betroffenen akzeptiert . . . werden können' (MCCA 65, my emphasis in bold).

34 See Habermas (EA 113–15); *idem*, 'Reconciliation through the public use of Reason', *Journal of Philosophy*, 92 (1995), pp. 109–31; and Thomas McCarthy, 'Kantian constructivism and reconstructivism: Rawls and Habermas in dialogue', *Ethics*, 105 (1994), pp. 44–63.

35 Felmon John Davis thinks that discourse meta-ethics requires the official version: 'parties must have the same reason (to the same degree) to agree.' See his 'Discourse ethics and ethical realism: a realist realignment of discourse ethics',

European Journal of Philosophy, 2/2 (1994), pp. 125–43. He fails to note that, since having the same reason means having the same interest, what counts as the same reason will depend on the way in which interests are individuated.

36 See McNaughton and Rawling: 'Value and agent-relative reasons', p. 33. Habermas follows Thomas Nagel, who claims that 'if it is a reason for anyone to do or want something that it would be in *his* interest, then that is a relative reason': *View from Nowhere* (Oxford: Oxford University Press, 1986), p. 153.

37 Habermas claims that the ideal role undertaken in moral discourse results in the occupation of an 'impartial standpoint which overcomes the subjectivity of the individual participant's perspective' (JA 12–13).

38 Jürgen Habermas, 'Sprecht-theoretische Erlänfeningen zum Begriff der KommuniKativen Rationalität', in *Zeitschrift für Philosophie Forshung*, 50 (1996), p. 76.

39 Initially, in response to Steven Luke's objection that U was too strong, Habermas denied that there is a paucity of universalizable interests and justifiable norms ('Reply to my critics', p. 257). Nowadays he denies only that this is a consequence of his analysis of the moral standpoint.

40 Steven Lukes also invoked an objection usually levelled at Rawls's contractualism. Either the contracting parties are real, in which case there may well be no norm or principle they can agree upon, or they are ideally rational agents, in which case their ideally rational consensus will not bind real agents. The moral standpoint is not explained, but already presupposed, in the combined premisses of the existence of ideally rational agents and the conditions of agreement. However, as Habermas points out, this objection just ignores the status of U as an idealizing presupposition, which participants cannot but invoke, in so far as they are oriented to reaching agreement in practical discourse ('Reply to my critics, pp. 141–2).

41 Thomas McCarthy, *Ideals and Illusions* (Cambridge, Mass.: MIT Press, 1991), p. 198; and Maeve Cooke, 'Habermas and consensus', *European Journal of Philosophy*, 1/3 (1993), pp. 257–8.

42 Hegel, *Philosophy of Right*, §135R.

43 Ibid., §129.

2

Habermas, Marxism and social theory: the case for pluralism in critical social science

James Bohman

I The Idea of a Critical Social Science

Although myriad in its forms, 'Critical Theory', or, more generally, critical social science, shares a distinctive purpose and overall structure. Critical theorists aim at constructing social theories that link explanation and criticism, and thus have both normative and explanatory features. Furthermore, such theories must also be 'practical'. 'Practical' here does not mean useful; nor does it mean that they are connected to practice generally, but to a particular purpose. As Horkheimer put it, such theories seek 'to liberate human beings from the circumstances that enslave them'.[1] Such a combination of theoretical features and emancipatory purposes serves to narrow the field of useful candidate theories and frameworks and to eliminate, for example, neo-classical economics, systems theory or structural-functionalist sociology. However, it still leaves a variety of plausible candidates at various levels, from causal to interpretive approaches, as well as ones with Marxist and radical democratic political goals or feminist or post-colonial orientations. But, historically, one theory has claimed a pre-eminent status as the uniquely adequate critical social theory: historical materialism. This theory finds few defenders today.

Critical Theory is now less unified than ever before, and is marked by ever more eclectic approaches to social theory, none more so than the social

theory of Jürgen Habermas. In this essay, I want to discuss the implications
of Habermas's clear rejection of such claims to uniqueness and his equally
clear acceptance of both theoretical and methodological pluralism in critical
social science. Indeed, although it is obvious that few Critical Theorists today
still hold the strong claim that some particular theory alone can fulfil the
aims of criticism, full realization of the political and practical implications of
the rejection of this claim to uniqueness for emancipatory theories is not as
evident. In particular, I want to explore whether there is any need at all for
a single, comprehensive social theory as the basis for social criticism, especially since there is also little evidence that there is a single moral and political goal upon which all emancipatory criticism somehow converges.

Habermas was perhaps among the first contemporary philosophers of
social science and social theorists to realize the full implications of irreducible
methodological and theoretical pluralism in the social sciences, incorporating
diverse theoretical and empirical sources in his attempt to revitalize critical
social theory. None the less, there is a tension in Habermas's ongoing project
of a 'reconstruction' of critical social theory: the tension between retaining
the Marxian project of elaborating a comprehensive social theory as the basis
for criticism, on the one hand, and accepting the Weberian insight into irreducible methodological pluralism in the social sciences, on the other hand.
In the end, Habermas's methodological pluralism requires that he also adopt
a theoretical pluralism, and thus abandon the search for some convergent,
general Critical Theory. I want to show why such a thoroughgoing pluralism has always been part of the enterprise of the 'Critical Theory' of the
Frankfurt School, and how it strengthens, rather than weakens, the social-
scientific side of its critical endeavours. It is also more consistent with Habermas's attempt to provide a post-positivist philosophy of social science, where
positivism is defined as the 'lack of reflection' on the conditions of possibility of the theoretical enterprise itself (KHI 67). Nowhere is this lack of
reflection more evident than in the positivist thesis of the methodological
unity of the sciences, and the search for a comprehensive theory makes little
sense if such unity is neither conceivable nor desirable.

The search for a comprehensive Critical Theory has not only derived from
a conception of scientific method; it also has a practical motivation. As Marx
argues in the 'Preface' to *The German Ideology*, the explanatory and scientific
status of historical materialism as a rigorous, non-idealistic historical social
theory was not only supposed to show the superiority of theoretically
grounded criticism over 'moralizing' or 'critical criticism'; it was supposed to
be uniquely tailored to the purpose of emancipation under contemporary
circumstances.[2] That is because Marx thought that only a particular sort of
politics, embodied in a particular social movement with a particular collec-

tive actor, could bring about the sort of change necessary: the transformation not of ideas, but of large-scale, powerfully entrenched social structures. The appropriateness of historical materialism was hence primarily *practical* for Marx, and its superiority was even more fundamentally defined in terms of specific political goals. Even given these same goals, the theory itself has long been in need of revision, and the only way to achieve this is to incorporate the best theories and results of contemporary social science, as Marx himself did when he first constructed it. Such a revision is truly a 'reconstruction' in Habermas's sense: 'taking a theory apart and putting it back together again in order to more fully attain the goal it has set for itself' (CES 95). However, once pulled apart, historical materialism, like Humpty-Dumpty, does not go back together again. After throwing out most of its central assumptions, contemporary social science can put only a few pieces back together at a time. This is indeed what Habermas does in his writings on social theory: he does not provide a comprehensive social theory, but rather an innovative, pluralistic approach that integrates existing theoretical and methodological perspectives wherever empirically possible for the sake of criticizing diverse features of modern societies.

The difficulties of reconstructing a comprehensive social theory occur at two distinct levels. First, the best contemporary social science does not suggest that such a reconstruction, even if successful, would yield a single theoretical framework that is consistent with all the goals of critical social science. Second, it is no longer plausible to believe, as Marx did in his historical period, that theoretically grounded criticism suggests a single goal of human emancipation, as, for example, the liberation of the labouring subject in socialism. I want to argue that both these results ought to be embraced by critical social science. We should abandon not only Marx's particular theory, but the very project of reconstructing an analogue to historical materialism as a comprehensive framework for critical social science: contemporary Critical Theory must be theoretically, methodologically and practically pluralistic. This means that we must surrender the goal that Marx saw as defining the superiority of historical materialism: a unique fit between critical explanation and political practice. Whereas empirical theories are indeterminate to the extent that they do not yield *unique* predictions, Critical Theories are indeterminate when they do not establish a unique relation to a set of emancipatory political goals.[3] None the less, adequate Critical Theories have *some* relation to such a political practice; it follows, then, that adequate Critical Theories may be indeterminate. If there are many dimensions and axes of emancipation, then they *must* be indeterminate.

The unique fit between historical-materialist theory and emancipatory practice was meant to solve the obvious problem of conflicts between different political purposes and programmes that lay claim to human emanci-pation: the best theoretical framework cuts the Gordian knot of conflicting values and norms of justice. Against Marx, Weber argued that criticism is theory-laden and theory-dependent, and that this circularity limits what social science can do. As in the case of the hermeneutic circle, once we reject uniqueness, it is easier to accept that this 'critical circle' is not a vicious, but a reflexive aspect of the pluralism of the social sciences. Like the theory-laden character of observation in the natural sciences, it has broad ramifications, particularly for the nature of social-scientific knowledge itself. Indeed, one of the main issues here is epistemological, concerning the nature and limits of theoretical knowledge in the social sciences. Critical science, therefore, cannot be so pluralistic as to incorporate all theories and perspectives without becoming empty. Still, its scope must be rather wide, determined for the most part on case-by-case, empirical grounds. Pluralism also best fits the practical character of the critical enterprise, in which theories must be useful in clari-fying the 'struggles of the age'.

The critical social theory of the Frankfurt School has always had a ten-dency towards pluralism. However, such a pluralistic critical social science goes well beyond Horkheimer's call for an 'interdisciplinary materialism'. It no longer makes sense to think of historical materialism as a philosophical framework for the presentation of the 'results' of other theories. Extending the many good arguments against empiricism in the philosophy of science to this context shows that Horkheimer's proposal is incoherent, given the difficulties of separating theory and evidence pointed out by post-empiricist philosophers of science. Nor is there any reason to think that the best and most critically useful results of recent social science are compatible with the premisses of historical materialism. As Marx's theoretical programme shows, critical social science in its past forms has typically been oriented primarily to macro-sociological theories. But there is no reason to think that criticism is confined to such theories alone, or even best done in this way: just as there can be explanations that do not refer to theories, such as narratives; so, too, interpretations can at times be critical without being informed by explicit theoretical commitments.

Even given such pluralism, there are still important differences between criticisms that are informed by theories and those that are not: interpretive critics are limited to the internal perspective of participants in the prac-tices they criticize, with all the normative and epistemic limitations that might be the price of increased persuasiveness and rhetorical effectiveness. The critical social theorist, too, can adopt the interpretive stance in order to clarify, as Marx put it, 'the struggles and aspirations of the age'. When informed by social theory, the effective critic is perhaps able to articulate those aspirations and struggles in a new language, perhaps creating a new, more self-reflexive audience of historical agents in the process. In order to do so, the critic requires self-reflexive and practical social theories, each emerging from, and appropriate to, particular historical circumstances. Habermas thinks that such theories should be diverse in approach and subject-matter, yet at the same time be united within a comprehensive theoretical and practical framework that explains the problems and prospects of modern societies. This dual approach leaves Habermas with an unresolved tension: between method-ological pluralism and theoretical integration in the social sciences.

II Methodological Pluralism Versus Theoretical Integration: The Tension in Habermas's Philosophy of Social Science

Already in *Knowledge and Human Interests*, Habermas had recognized the inherent pluralism of the social sciences. He identifies three distinct, irre-ducible 'knowledge-constitutive interests', each with its own distinct presup-positions, modes of enquiry and epistemic goals.[4] Habermas also ties each to 'social media' of work, language and power, as distinct means for structuring social relationships and creating modes of social organization. The technical cognitive interest aims at control, and is connected with nomological sci-ences; the practical interest of the hermeneutic-historical sciences aims at increasing mutual understanding and unimpeded communication; and finally, the emancipatory interest of critically oriented science aims at liberating human beings from relations of force, unconscious constraints and depen-dence on hypostatized powers. While the first two interests can be developed through the 'self-reflection of the existing sciences', the third, emancipatory interest has a unique status – at least in so far as it does not correspond to a single, well-developed form of enquiry. While Habermas thinks that there are exemplars of such activity in psychoanalysis and the critique of ideology, there is no determinate or well-accepted form of enquiry that corresponds to 'critical reflective knowledge'. This gap has to do not only with the 'sci-entistic misunderstandings' of Marxism, but also with the comprehensive character of the interest in emancipation: such forms of knowledge can be developed in a broad account of the self-formative process of the human species as a whole. Thus, this interest aims at self-reflection, where self-reflection 'articulates itself substantially in the concept of a self-formative process' (TP 22–3).[5]

Regardless of what we think of this analysis of cognitive interests as an epistemology of the social sciences, it is striking that the emancipatory inter-est has a particular status that already encompasses the two-sidedness of

Habermas's conception of critical social theory. On the one hand, he recognizes a variety of epistemic goals or interests in social science and the role of critical self-reflection in achieving them; on the other hand, he argues that critical self-reflection and, with it, critical social theory have a special comprehensive status in unifying all forms of social enquiry in the enquiry into 'the self-formation of all humanity'.

The justification of this two-sided, pluralistic, yet comprehensive approach is worked out more specifically in Habermas's writings on the philosophy of social science, and is the common thread that connects *On the Logic of the Social Sciences* (1967) to *The Theory of Communicative Action* (1981). The problem of pluralism is not new in the philosophy of social science. As Habermas argues in *On the Logic of the Social Sciences*, Max Weber was among the first to recognize that the social sciences combine various cognitive operations: explanation and interpretation, historical comparison and trans-historical theoretical terms. This mixed status leads social scientists to combine seemingly contradictory and heterogeneous methods, aims and theories into more or less coherent wholes. Just as in the analysis of forms of enquiry tied to distinct knowledge-constitutive interests, Habermas accepts that various theories and methods each have 'a relative legitimacy'. Indeed, he goes so far as to argue that it is 'the apparatus of general theories' typical in the natural sciences, not their causal or functional forms of enquiry, that cannot be applied to society. Failing such general theories, the most fruitful approach to social-scientific knowledge is to bring all the various methods and theories into relation with each other. 'Whereas the natural and the cultural or hermeneutic sciences are capable of living in mutually indifferent, albeit more hostile than peaceful coexistence, the social sciences must bear the tension of divergent approaches under one roof' (LSS 3).

Habermas's affirmation of pluralism in the social sciences has two sides. Even while accepting pluralism, the social sciences cannot be satisfied with mere pluralism or indifference; they must also seek the relationships between the various fundamental approaches and modes of empirical research and explanation. It is establishing the connections among these various forms of research that is the hallmark of Critical Theory. To the extent that it is self-reflexive about the social-scientific enterprise itself and the need to hold different approaches in tension, Critical Theory reveals how the social sciences as a whole can properly handle theoretical and methodological pluralism.

Later, in *The Theory of Communicative Action*, Habermas casts critical social theory in a similar pluralistic, yet unifying way. In discussing various accounts of societal modernization, Habermas argues that the main existing theories have their own 'particular legitimacy' as developed lines of empirical research, and that Critical Theory takes on the task of critically unifying the various theories and their heterogeneous methods and presuppositions. 'Critical Theory does not relate to established lines of research as a competitor; starting from its concept of the rise of modern societies, it attempts to explain the specific limitations and relative rights of those approaches' (TCA2 375). Here Habermas adds a particular theoretical task that is not present in his previous recognition of methodological pluralism in the social sciences. Other theoretical approaches can be positively incorporated into Critical Theory (the continuation of the Frankfurt School's project) by recognizing the relative rights of all competing approaches. Thus, Critical Theory does not seek to eliminate any possibly fruitful line of empirical research on theoretical grounds. However, recognizing the rights of diverse approaches implies also recognizing their limitations, and there must be some more comprehensive standpoint from which the Critical Theorist may do so: it is the comprehensive standpoint of an overall account of the process of modernization that incorporates what is right about each other approach while criticizing its weaknesses and limitations. From the point of view of the problematic of reflection with which Habermas began in *Knowledge and Human Interests*, Habermas sees Critical Theory as performing a self-reflective *Aufhebung* of other empirically valid approaches, eliminating none and locating them all in a more comprehensive framework. Taken on their own, each such approach is an inadequate, one-sided explanation of those phenomena that it seeks to explain from a particular methodological perspective and set of theoretical assumptions.

This Hegelian response to the fact of pluralism in the social sciences contrasts sharply with the Kantian answer favoured by Habermas in other philosophical domains, particularly in normative theory. Whereas a Hegelian response tries to incorporate the partial truths of various theories into an encompassing, unifying theory, the Kantian approach leaves the plurality of theories in place. Instead of unifying them into a super-theory, reflection on the nature and limits of social-scientific methods and theories establishes the proper domains and limits of each theory and approach. The Kantian answer is given sharpest formulation by Weber, in his philosophy of social science: Weber recognized the hybrid nature of social science, but saw different methods and theories as truly heterogeneous in their presuppositions. According to this contrasting approach, 'the relative rights and specific limitations' of each theory and method are recognized by assigning them to their own particular (hence limited) empirical domain. Rather than establishing these judgements of scope and domain through a more comprehensive theory that encompasses all others and thereby shows their limitations, the Kantian approach proceeds case by case, seeing the way in which these theories run up against their limits in trying to extend beyond the core phenomena of their domain of validity.[6] Such an approach need not deny the possibility of fruitful large-scale theories, whose success is established by the weight of empirical evidence and by their capacity to integrate various domains of explanation. Indeed, the mixed status of the social sciences as combining explanation and interpretation indicates that elaborating such combinations and connections (rather than producing some grand theory such as historical materialism) is the proper goal of social theory.

The problem with the idea of a comprehensive theory is that it presupposes some standpoint 'above the battle' of conflicting explanations and methods. As opposed to the Hegelian solution of encompassing such conflicts in a comprehensive theory, Kant's dialectic points out the contradictions that theoretical reason falls into once it tries to validate knowledge from some non-empirical, metaphysical standpoint. By analogy, Kant supplies good arguments that suggest how comprehensive social theories fall back into making dubious metaphysical claims, as endless debates between materialists and idealists in the social sciences have shown. Once we see that such an attempt to unify the social sciences theoretically exceeds the available evidence, we can see why the reconstruction of historical materialism is not the central theoretical task of critical social science. We might still be able to talk about the ways in which the social sciences are rational enterprises and the extent to which they (like all the sciences) are dependent on procedures of justification in a free and open community of enquirers. In his Kantian mode, Habermas has argued for such a 'procedural unity of reason' (TCA1 249), based on the presuppositions of the discursive form of communication in which any claim would be justified. This unity, however, is only formal; the procedures and forms of justification employed in practical and theoretical discourses are quite different and form distinct domains. Habermas even concedes that the question of the unity of reason and enquiry 'awaits an adequate resolution this side of Hegelian logic'.[7] This admission suggests the need to embrace a more radical pluralism than Habermas has suggested in his more Hegelian approach to empirically oriented critical social theories.

An examination of Habermas's own way of actually doing critical social science with empirical content and practical orientation provides the best case for such a more consistent, Kantian-style pluralism in the social sciences. If we look at Habermas's practice, not his philosophical interpretation of it, we get a quite different picture than is suggested by the official Hegelian argument for a comprehensive theory. When Habermas is critically appropriating various theories, he is in the first instance concerned to make distinctions between various perspectives, domains and purposes in the social sciences. These distinctions are then sometimes overcome in the particular unified theories that Habermas proposes; but these theories, in turn, do not amount to some comprehensive social theory that the first generation of the Frankfurt School always called for but never developed.[8] However, Habermas is correct about his method in a central respect: when he is able to unify various approaches and theories into a more comprehensive approach (typically involving explanations at both the micro-level of social action and the macro-level of structures and systems), the result is a powerful theoretical tool for social criticism of the present form of complex, modern societies. I develop the two most successful examples of this type below: the first is Habermas's early treatment of the theory of ideology; the second is the account of social complexity and the colonization of the lifeworld formulated in his more recent writings. However, such a unification of various approaches and domains within one theory could be made an even more successful exemplar of a critical social theory through the clearer recognition of the role of both methodological and theoretical pluralism in achieving its goals.

Besides the Hegelian problems of unity and diversity, yet another sort of tension pervades Habermas's social theory: namely, the tensions between the terms of the various neo-Kantian dualisms with which Habermas describes his theory: between nomic and interpretive sciences, communicative and strategic actions, system and lifeworld, ideal and actual conditions, instrumental and communicative forms of rationality, and so on. At times Habermas seems to suggest that these distinctions cut the social world, the 'symbolically prestructured domain' that is the object of the human sciences, at its structural joints (TCA1 109). In this vein, Habermas argues that such dualisms represent 'real' distinctions, rather than analytically useful tools for describing different aspects of certain social phenomena; he has made this argument, for example, in defending the 'real distinction' between communicative and strategic action.[9] If the theory of communicative action is to fulfil the Hegelian goal of unifying the various domains of social science, then the theory that is the basis for these distinctions must illuminate the structural features of the object domain of the social sciences as a whole, the pre-structured social world. Similarly, Habermas sharply distinguishes two ways in which modern societies are integrated: social and system integration. Social integration occurs via communication against the unproblematic background of the 'lifeworld', the taken-for-granted certainties and pre-reflective assumptions of culture and social institutions. By contrast, system integration occurs 'behind the backs' of agents, and does not depend on their beliefs or intentions. However, in both these cases, Habermas turns distinctions into dichotomies, and fails on his own terms: he fails to provide a systematic and comprehensive account of the actual empirical phenomena, in which such 'pure types' of action, speech or social process are rather rare, if they exist at all. Most importantly, 'pure' cases are not the ones that interest a Critical Theory of action or speech. It is certainly also the case that the systems of the market and bureaucracy depend on the social, integrative effective of law; they are, as Habermas admits, 'anchored' in, not separated from, the lifeworld.

If we ignore Habermas's methodological understanding of these distinctions and look instead at the particularly successful cases of critical social science in Habermas's work, we get a different picture. The critical uses of his theories succeed not by employing idealizations, but by developing hybrid mixtures that cut across distinctions, fusing together different theories and ontological domains. In these cases, Habermas successfully employs a multidimensional approach to social theory, and constructs complex, critical explanations of complex, hybrid phenomena. But these hybrid theories are not constructed according to any general method; nor do they converge upon a reconstructed historical materialism. Indeed, Habermas is sometimes misled in his development of such Critical Theories by his Hegelian and sometimes overly synthetic approach, which weakens the empirical robustness of his own theoretical proposals at various levels. This self-understanding misplaces the efforts of the Critical Theorist into constructing a general theory of modern societies, rather than employing multiple theories with robust empirical interconnections, which replace the effort at more general theoretical unification. Instead of such a pluralistic approach, Habermas has consistently sought a comprehensive social theory to unify and ground his social criticism, beginning with 'a philosophy of history with practical intent', a 'reconstruction of historical materialism', and, finally, a 'two-level' theory of social integration and societal rationalization. In what follows, I show that Habermas succeeds when he constructs mixed theories in a much more limited, Kantian way, primarily by making fruitful connections between various theories and methods for the practical task of social criticism.

III Action, Meaning and Critical Social Science: Habermas's Methodological Pluralism in the Theory of Ideology

Habermas's criticisms of Marxist social theory have, from the start, implied that pluralism is necessary for any critically useful theory. In *Theory and Practice*, he not only criticized the excesses of a politics based on the 'correct' theory; he also pointed out that Marxist objectivism gives the critic no epistemic foothold in the social world from which to communicate his criticism. This lack of a common social location, coupled with the supposed epistemic superiority of the theorist over participants in social practices, leads to a strategic relation to the addressee of criticism (TP 37–40). Even while seeking a reconstruction, Habermas criticizes the theory of historical materialism for its reliance on the conception of history as 'unilinear, necessary, uninterrupted and progressive development of a macro-subject' (CES 138). This criticism gives a new role to moral consciousness and normative structures as the 'pace-makers' of social evolution.[10] Most of all, Marxism fails on its own terms as a critical social theory, primarily because of 'lack of clarity about its norma-tive foundations' (CES 96). The attempt to supply such foundations could be read as an attempt to supply an independent normative standard, through a foundational moral theory along the lines of discourse ethics. But even if a moral theory is needed to explore the structure of moral justification, such an independent, foundational theory would tell us very little about how to reconstruct a practically useful critical social theory. In responding to such deficits, Habermas takes a very different direction, laboriously reconstructing the presuppositions of various types and levels of critical social science, from the micro-interpretive level to the macro-level of social integration of complex societies.

These criticisms make sense only if one of the main tasks of critical social theory is to integrate the insights of theories of social action into its frame-work. In adapting Hegel's framework for the analysis of action from the Jena writings, Habermas distinguishes early on those social processes based on labour from those based on language (TP 142–69). Each of these different social processes has its own distinct normative structure. The point of a criti-cal explanation, according to Habermas, is to work out the implications of such normative structures and to show the different ways in which these norms are violated through the influence of other social media (as previously explained) upon them, such as the way domination distorts linguistic com-munication. For example, Habermas shows that understanding linguistic expressions normally follows the route of ordinary hermeneutic understand-ing, particularly as conceived by Gadamer as ongoing dialogue (LSS 149). However, such dialogue can be distorted by social relations of power and mechanisms that are not accessible to ordinary understanding. In this case, understanding requires an entirely different sort of self-reflection, which can be achieved only in the distanced attitude and third-person perspective of the social theorist. None the less, this approach to self-reflection on the effects of power on language and dialogue requires granting a particular conception of interpretive agency, the epistemic perspective of which gives the enquirer sole access to the meanings of actions and practices. Such a conception of agency and meaning is precisely absent from perhaps the most exemplary of Critical Theories, the critique of ideology.

From the time of his early pronouncement of the need for 'ruthless criticism of everything existing', Marx's writing represents a sustained attempt to find the methods and basis for such an adequate critical endeavour.[11] Marx's historical social theory provides a basis for his more thorough, searching criticism of capitalism than the mere 'critical criticism' offered by the Left Hegelians. This explanatory social theory, however, does not exhaust the critical resources of many of Marx's writings. *Capital*, for example, is a multigenre work of social criticism, using a variety of interpretive and explanatory techniques: Marx develops, among other things, a theory of the developmental tendencies of capitalism towards recurrent and cyclical crises, a theoretical account of working time in the theory of the value of commodities, and detailed and novelistically crafted documentary accounts of the life conditions of workers in the nineteenth century. *Capital* also employs techniques of ideology critique, particularly in its analysis of the 'fetishism of commodities'; Marx wants to explain why it is that members of capitalist societies falsely endow certain things (commodities) with subjective and social powers (of producing value on their own).

A theory of ideology is a Critical Theory about the formation of social beliefs and about the relation of meaning and domination. For Marxists with monistic, Eleatic tendencies, it works by presenting a simple contrast between the 'true' beliefs of historical-materialist social science and the 'false' beliefs of unscientific participants: a contrast between the way of knowing and the way of seeming. In light of the theory of forces and relations of production, the historical materialist can explain the false beliefs of actors both causally and functionally; the economic structure of society, or base, causes the superstructure, the prevalent set of beliefs that agents have, particularly those of law, morality and theology. The beliefs that become widely shared in a society are the ones that fulfil the function of promoting and maintaining the social relations of production – that is, the relations of domination between classes. As Elster and others have pointed out, Marx usually only sketches these relationships between actors' beliefs and their positions in the social structure, so that the Marxian theory of ideology offers no account of the process by which such beliefs are formed 'behind our backs'. Marx's descriptions of these formation processes remains strictly on the macro-level, and must therefore be supplemented by a variety of contemporary approaches to social action.[12]

What makes this a Critical Theory of belief formation? The critical features of such an explanation of beliefs can be seen by contrasting Marx's theory of ideology with Mannheim's 'neutral' theory.[13] Like Marx, Mannheim constructed his explanation in terms of large-scale relationships between the content of beliefs and their social context and origins, claiming that 'ideas are always bound up with the existing life-situation of the thinker'.[14] Unlike Marx's, Mannheim's account claims to be neutral and non-evaluative. Mannheim bases this neutrality on the reflexivity of his theory: once all thoughts relate to some 'life-situation', then the critic has no place *hors de combat* to stand and pass judgements. By contrast, Marx's theory does not see the situated, historical character of thought as a limit on social criticism. While he accepts the reflexive character of his theory, he attempts to turn its theoretical paradox of being situated in a historical epoch into a fruitful circle for practical knowledge that would empower agents to overcome their cognitive limits. Marx's critical, non-paradoxical reflexivity is possible only if the theory of ideology accepts extra burdens and standards of proof for its explanations and for how its social and cultural status also enables it to be critical. It must not only fit the empirical evidence, but it must also be able to account for its own social and historical conditions of possibility, as well as for its potential emancipatory effects and consequences. These reflexive conditions have too often been assumed in dogmatic social criticism and objectivistic understandings of social theory.

Marx's theory of ideology not only offers an account of the processes which relate large-scale social structures and historical trends to agents' beliefs, but also analyses conditions of greater social transparency under which beliefs can be changed and a more truthful interpretation of social practice generated. Its weaknesses are the limitations of Marx's theory of action, which permits only the contrast between agents' self-interpretations and the rigorous descriptions of the materialist social theory; such explanations have, as Elster put it, no 'micro-foundations' in a the theory of action or cognition.[15] In order to overcome this deficit, Habermas takes a quite different strategy from Elster, who develops his own theory of rational action. Habermas shifts the focus of the theory of ideology from belief formation to the public use of shared meanings. More specifically, he shifts the discussion in a methodologically pluralist direction. Instead of developing an alternative theory out of the weaknesses of Marx's approach, the critique of ideology can be developed internally by demonstrating the limitations of the approach which is most at home in the domain of meaning, understanding and communication: the hermeneutic sciences. With their emphasis on intersubjective and symbolically transmitted meanings and traditions, these sciences help Habermas rethink the status of the social sciences from the point of view of the critic as a participant historically situated in a form of life.

Habermas makes common cause with hermeneutics against their shared enemies. Epistemic arguments for the necessity of interpretive access to the social world provide the proper corrective to positivist models of social science and objectivist conceptions of critique. Once social science recognizes the force of this argument, the critic can no longer be a detached spectator, but rather 'a reflective participant' (LSS 153). But whereas hermeneutics considers participants' reflective knowledge to be limited in principle to the horizon of their given culture or tradition, Habermas argues that such reflection breaks down the limitations of unconscious, implicit presuppositions, the dependence of any given symbolic framework on non-normative conditions of power and domination. Once 'hermeneutic experience encounters this dependency of the symbolic framework on actual conditions it changes into the critique of ideology' (LSS 174). The hermeneutic approach runs up against its own limitations to the extent that it cannot explain such constraints upon meaning and understanding; they are not the object of interpretation, but can be understood only in 'an objective framework that is constituted by language, labor and domination' (LSS 173). As applied to meaning and communication, 'depth hermeneutics' combines both explanation and understanding, reasons and causes, in arriving at an explanation of 'the incomprehensibility of distorted communication'. The model for such an approach is psychoanalysis, which can then be extended to other areas of communication distorted by domination and power. When actually applied to cases of ideological constraint on interpretation, the 'objective framework of social action' does little explanatory work. Rather, the critic employs the hybrid form of 'explanatory understanding' necessary in cases of hermeneutic failure such as distorted communication, and thereby mixes interpretive and causal approaches to the explanation of incomprehensible expressions in situations marked by domination and asymmetries of power.

More recently, Habermas has attempted to develop an account of this comprehensive framework of social action and his own specific conception of interpretive agency, which is closely linked to a multi-dimensional conception of rationality. Both these undertakings are part of an overall theory of communicative action, which conceives of the intelligibility of social actions in terms of agents' capacity to reason. According to this theory, interpretation is reflective participation; the situated character of the interpreter requires that 'all understanding is evaluation' (TCA1 107, 111). But a closer examination of the details of the theories that make up the account of rationality shows that they are fundamentally pluralistic. The theory of communicative action and its accompanying multi-dimensional theory of rationality depend on sharp conceptual distinctions between ideal-typical acts: strategic and instrumental action, on the one hand, and communicative action, on the other, each with ideal-typical subcategories. Conceived in this way, the theory can simply incorporate whole other theories of action, as, for example, a game-theoretical account of strategic interaction. Here, too, as in the case of the limits of hermeneutic experience, the role of the comprehensive theories of social action or of rationality is not really to stand on their own, but to provide a corrective. They provide the basis for criticisms of other one-sided theories, showing their limitations and proper scope. At the same time, the theories of action and rationality both compensate for the weaknesses of contextual interpretation, showing that it depends on a more complete act of evaluation. Thus, the theory of communicative action is a comprehensive theory of a peculiar sort, at best a placeholder for a theory which depends on working out all the relations between the various types of action and their presuppositions. Coupled with the fact that developing the theory requires idealizations which prescind from the empirical complexity of actual cases, the theory of action *per se* has very little empirical content or application of its own.[16] For that reason, it is not itself an explanatory Critical Theory, but rather presents an example of how to construct a critical social theory, the theory of ideology, that is informed by diverse social-scientific theories and approaches, from which it borrows its empirical content.

The force of this interpretation of Habermas's theory of communicative action can best be seen in the fate of the theory of ideology within it. Ideology is here understood as manifested in a particular relationship between strategic and communicative action. It is indeed 'latent strategic action', and ideology critique has now become a form of 'therapeutic discourse' rather than of explanation (TCA1 21). None the less, the theory suggests only a general approach to understanding 'meaning in the service of power',[17] not a full theory of ideology or a specific way to exercise such critique. For all the sophistication of Habermas's newer theory of action, the basic model of critical social science remains the same: critical self-reflection emerging at the limits of interpretive approaches to the social sciences is established by specific empirical connections between various domains of explanation, such as between strategic and communicative action, between an account of the norms of communication and their violation in pathological forms of communication, and in the effects of different forms of rationality upon each other. In this way, this type of comprehensive framework does very little actual work, since all the empirical and critical analysis is done by the particular theories and approaches that it ties together. Indeed, this result suggests that the critique of ideology can be practised by any combination of first- and third-person perspectives which brings together any number of empirically useful theories and methodologies. There are many different ways to achieve the goal common to the many Critical Theories of ideology: increasing self-reflection on the conditions of use and the norms governing linguistic interaction and discursive practices.

IV Macro-sociology and Critical Theory: System and Lifeworld as an Example of Habermas's Theoretical Pluralism

In light of the critical indeterminacy and essential pluralism most apparent in theories of action, Critical Theorists have long argued that only large-scale, agent-independent, macro-level theories could integrate the results of the social sciences. Why do Marxists favour such a conception of social theory? Part of the answer is the particular sort of practical goals that they had and the types of social structure that they wished to change: market economies. Here, too, the problem is that implicit positivist and empiricist assumptions about scientific theories are taken over unreflectively by Critical Theorists. Marx himself seems to have thought that science progressed by constructing large-scale, organizing theories in which particular observations are organized and explained.[18] For example, the theory of evolution in biology can organize a large range of phenomena, from the fossil record to adaptation strategies of individual animals. However plausible this goal may be, no precise analogues to this sort of theory are available in the social sciences. Large-scale social phenomena can have relatively independent explanations at various levels. This can be shown by examining the most important macro-level explanation in historical materialism: its theory of the crisis of capitalist societies. Such historical-materialist explanations fail to the extent that they lack practical means of verification. Many versions of interpretive social science are non-critical for an opposite, though related, reason. In this section, I want to argue that the necessary interrelationships between macro-sociological explanation and critical interpretation also give us reason to abandon the project of reconstructing historical materialism or any particular comprehensive critical social theory, even Habermas's weaker version of a Critical Theory of modernity.

Because of the character of its concepts and activities, social criticism is difficult to achieve at both extremes: in macro-sociological and in micro-interpretive social scientific analyses, which together range from the most practical and embedded, in the case of interpretation, to the most theoretical and abstract, in the case of macro-sociology. The features relevant to criticism in each case are in direct contrast: as Clifford Geertz has put it, interpretive concepts are 'experience-near', while those of macro-sociology are 'experience-distant'; the latter offer the 'thin' descriptions of general theories, while the former's descriptions are 'thick', rich in the textures of lived experience. Thin descriptions do not depend so directly on the meanings and cultural significance of actors' own interpretations; they apply to general and multiple contexts, and are thus less local and context-bound. Geertz shows that anthropologists necessarily use both types of concepts. 'An experience-near concept is, roughly, one that someone – a patient, a subject, in our case an informant – might himself naturally and effortlessly use to define what he and his fellows see, feel, think, imagine and so on. . . . An experience-distant concept is one that specialists of one sort or another – an analyst, an experimenter, an ethnographer, even a priest or an ideologist – employ to forward their scientific, philosophical and practical aims.'[19]

As the second sentence in the above quotation indicates, Geertz in no way restricts ethnography itself to experience-near concepts; rather, the point for an ethnographer is to find adequate connections between the two, as part of what it is to understand others' categories in our terms. The interpretive task is to understand other people's experience-near concepts 'well enough to place them in illuminating connection with experience-distant concepts theorists have fashioned to capture the general features of social life'.[20] Like interpretation, criticism also must aim at such illuminating connections between explanations and the social experiences of different groups within a society, mixing experience-distant concepts with experience-near descriptions in their explanatory theories. Restricting social science to either of the extremes of this conceptual continuum makes for inadequate, uncritical explanation. The goal of critical social science is to connect experience-near and -distant descriptions, and any explanation that does this adequately I shall call 'complete', in the sense that it is multi-dimensional in the way required by methodological pluralism.

As opposed to such multi-dimensional, but well-integrated explanations, both interpretive and macro-level social science can easily lose their critical force, as they become too experience-near or too experience-distant. On the one hand, structural, functional and systemic explanations can simply be too independent of lived experience to be connected back to agents' beliefs and attitudes. In this case, social science adopts so entirely an external, third-person point of view that it has no foothold from which to change internal, first-person beliefs or goals. On the other hand, interpretations can be so immersed in the texture of ongoing social life as to fail to provide any critical distance from it. In this case, the categories of social science are insufficiently distinct from those of the subjects studied to provide anything like critical illumination or insight. Quite apart from these difficulties, both forms of non-critical social science fail even as explanations and interpretations, and do not possess any reflective character in their theoretical or practical knowledge. Such failures occur even when theories claim to be reflective, as in the case of unconvincing attempts at demystification. However, exemplars of critical interpretive and macro-level social science are available, and they exhibit how critics can use the resources of both experience-near and experience-distant concepts to co-ordinate internal and external perspectives, all the while becoming neither too engaged and embedded nor too detached and distant. While Habermas has criticized hermeneutics as too embedded, he has also criticized systems theory as too detached to have any critical potential (TCA2 280). While hermeneutics approaches the social world entirely from the agents' point of view, systems theory uses only a third-person perspective, conceiving of societies as made up of interdependent parts integrated into wholes by anonymous and non-intentional mechanisms such as markets.

Suitably modified, even the most holistic, macro-level explanation can acquire a critical potential. That structural and functional concepts can be put to critical use is most evident in perhaps the greatest work of critical social science: Marx's *Capital*. In it, Marx gives a holistic account of the structure and functioning of capitalism as a system of production and commodity exchange, developing a simple abstract model of the complex relationships that make up the conditions for its continued existence. The critical pay-off of such an analysis lies not in providing technical knowledge of how this complex system can be maintained or made more efficient, but in practical, diagnostic knowledge of its recurrent structural tendencies. Marx's ultimate aim at the macro-level is to provide a theory of capitalism's crisis tendencies, which emerge as the result of economic actors and classes pursuing their goals and interests within a set of institutional structures and constraints. Since these crises are 'systemic', hence tied to the very identity of capitalism as a system of commodity production, any measures taken to correct them, such as technical innovation, government intervention or the concentration of capital, only deepen and widen the difficulties. Thus, the system integration of production, in which many actors relate to each other through the unintended consequences of their actions, breaks down as the market mechanisms of co-ordination are no longer able to contain its driving force – namely, the process of accumulation.[21] In this case, a more complete, macro-level analysis of crisis serves to explain the inherent conflict of a collectively irrational social institution. The goal of a complete macro-sociological crisis theory seems to be the one piece of historical materialism that is worth taking apart and putting back together again, even if the particular crisis-producing conditions and mechanisms that Marx himself described no longer hold.

Throughout his writings, Marx challenges non-critical explanations of the structure and functioning of capitalism, from 'invisible hand' explanations of the benefits of the market to views of capitalism as automatically self-equilibriating. His critical claims are supported by arguments that show the superiority of his explanations in accounting for all the evidence and piercing the veil of appearances to reveal the reality of the way capitalism functions. Marx credits many of the explanations of classical political economy with going beyond the mere appearances and crude illusions of everyday life: 'Nevertheless even the best spokespersons of classical economy remain more or less in the grasp of the world of illusion which this criticism has dissolved . . . and then they all fall into inconsistencies, half-truths and unsolved contradictions.'[22] Thus, critical self-reflection is necessary to make such explanations more adequate. The documentary evidence of the lived crisis of the working class serves an epistemological and a theoretical function: it serves as empirical evidence that the classical model is wrong and that Marx's own diagnosis that capitalism is in crisis is correct.

None the less, perhaps the greatest weakness of Marx's explanation is its failure to achieve a thorough co-ordination of the various perspectives contained in his analysis of these crises. The documentary chapters of *Capital* serve a primarily theoretical function, and Marx does not adequately reflect upon whether they supply practical verification as well; he simply takes the objective facts of the overwhelming suffering of workers to be sufficient motivation for transformative collective action.[23] Under current conditions of a global economy, practical verification of a critical analysis of capitalism is more difficult to come by, as the conditions giving rise to potential lived and systemic crises have changed as well. To meet these changing requirements of a Critical Theory of the macro- and micro-effects of economic processes, Habermas generalizes the idea of system integration and system crises so as to indicate multiple locations for the occurrence of lived crises and their indicators, conflict and struggle. The cumulative effect of the emergence of markets and bureaucracies is that their power to co-ordinate action depends less and less on the norms of social life contained in institutions such as those in a democracy, so that they become cut off from the lifeworld contexts and the linguistic medium in which processes of reaching understanding are always embedded. Even as systems become 'detached' from the lifeworld and operate according to the internal imperatives of money and power, they are still subject to crisis and contestation, now including tendencies towards anomie, the fragmentation of life, the failure of the state to solve certain recurrent problems, breakdowns in socialization and much more. Like Marx, Habermas contrasts his critical explanation to non-critical ones employing similar concepts, and argues for the empirical superiority of his own theory. As opposed to non-critical forms of holism that analyse social order as a seamless whole, Habermas's theory depicts systemic order as causing crises in other areas of social life and as being open to challenge by collective actors – that is, by social movements organized around the unresolved problems and consequences of systemic interventions in everyday life and sometimes of systemic breakdowns, such as the destruction of the natural environment and the failure of the state to manage economic growth and the unequal distribution of wealth and opportunities. A wide variety of social theories is needed to explain these complex, interrelated processes.

If one examines the wide spectrum of social theories that Habermas employs in *The Theory of Communicative Action*, what they all have in common is not just the substantive concern with explaining the emerging order of modern, complex societies. They also share the general methodological assumption that only holistic social theory can produce the most appropriate explanations of these phenomena. Parsons, Marx, Weber and Mead all share with Durkheim the view that any attempt to explain everything at the level of individuals or constituent parts reduces society and social organization to 'only artificial and more or less arbitrary combinations'.[24] Accordingly, all these theorists construct 'macro-sociological explanations', explanations that do not refer merely to the actors' intentions or to their face-to-face interaction, but to higher-level generalizations about the interrelationships between parts and levels of the social totality. In this way, Weber's explanations show relationships between the institutions of the state and the economy, or between the emergence of Protestantism and the development of capitalism. Similarly, Habermas explains various pathologies of modern social life in terms of the relationships between different types of social order, between 'system' and 'lifeworld'. Many critics have pointed out the inadequacies and reifications involved in some formulations of this macro-sociological explanation of modernity, usually with reference to the consequences of Habermas's 'unfortunate' use of systems theory to work out his thesis that systems 'colonize' the lifeworld. But the appropriation of systems theory serves the purpose of raising Marx's questions about the consequences of dialectically interrelated processes of social order and breakdown in large, complex, market societies.

My interest here is not the particular macro-social theory that Habermas uses, but the type of explanation he constructs. I want to argue that he does provide something like a defensible 'explanation sketch', to use Hempel's term, that is an adequate, critical and theoretically pluralistic explanation: an explanation that establishes a macro–micro linkage via institutions. Indeed, the problem with the debate about Habermas's use of the system–lifeworld distinction is that it has focused not on the *explanation* that he offers, but rather, only on *conceptual* problems with the theories that he uses. I will argue that the explanation fits the main criterion of adequacy for macro-to-micro explanation: it is at least potentially *complete* if it can show the relationships between these various levels of analysis. Once we abandon endless metaphysical and conceptual debates about individualism versus collectivism, we see that the only real empirical issue at stake is the adequacy of the explanation to the many different factors operating in the social phenomenon at hand. The problem with many holistic explanations is not so much their implausible ontology or conceptual flaws, as their empirical incompleteness.

This approach to Habermas's macro-sociology is aided by a new consensus regarding reductionism and holism that is emerging in the social sciences. The proper theoretical and methodological question is not how to reduce one level to the other, but how they are linked and interconnected: theoretical debates are no longer about reduction, but about 'linkage'.[25] For the empirical purpose of constructing better explanations, it is increasingly clear that the distinction between micro- and macro-levels is at best an analytic one, marking the ends of a continuum of theoretical concepts that figure in an adequate explanation, rather than a dichotomy between distinct levels of a social ontology. Taken in this way, the macro–micro linkage becomes an *empirical* question.

As methodological pluralism already implies, there can be different types of macro–micro linkage and different theories that explain them. Durkheim's notion of the 'pre-contractual basis of the contract' was supposed to explain how patterns of interaction can persist and how a society can integrate itself through recurrent social practices. Social theorists have called this aspect of social order 'social integration', the cultural structure in which the coordination of action takes place. Speaking a language is one such structure: in formulating my beliefs and intentions in a language, I accomplish my purposes by generally reproducing its grammatical structures and rules, which form a social order that is not the product of any single individual's intentional actions. For Habermas, the lifeworld concerns the shared, taken-for-granted presuppositions of social action that enable actors to interpret each others' actions and to participate in common institutions. Among its many uses, Habermas employs the concept to discuss the Weberian idea of rationalization as a process by which a cultural domain ceases to be merely taken for granted and becomes the subject for explicit, formalized knowledge in institutions like law and science.

As opposed to the concept of syst ily useful for describing those aspec might be called their 'cultural struct that (1) persist and are inherited fron understanding and are not necessaril strain beliefs and actions without dete of macro-level explanation related to In contrast to explanations of the cu theories have developed explanation ships typical of modern, complex societies: the systemic order of functional interdependence between parts of a whole that are not directly dependent on the shared beliefs and norms of actors. As formulated prior to Habermas, such explanations have been non-critical, placing modern social order beyond actors' intentions. This results from their use of exclusively experience-distant concepts and the observer perspective of the detached theorist.

This contrast between 'system' and 'social' integration, as sociologists have called it since Lockwood's ground-breaking discussion,[26] can be developed along a number of dimensions. First, the two forms, or processes, of integration can be distinguished according to 'the degree of interdependence of action', along a continuum from cultural constraint as the weakest to system dependence as the strongest form. Lifeworld constraints can best be seen in pre-reflective conditions of co-ordination in practices. Greater degrees of interdependence require a far greater predictability of outcomes and consequences than is permitted in simple cultural integration. Indeed, it is the existence of such stronger constraints like those of the market as a system of interdependent actions that makes economics a more determinate science on the macro-level; some degree of predictability is a condition of market order. Second, greater interdependence also follows from another characteristic of systemic order: complexity. Complex webs of interrelated actions allow spatially and temporally distant actors to affect each other, often without their knowledge. Third, system and structure can be distinguished only as contrasting analytic levels, which can then be connected empirically in a variety of ways. As Giddens puts it, 'Patterns of social relationships only exist insofar as the latter are organized as systems, reproduced over the course of time.'[27] The converse is also true: systems exist only if they are organized in social institutions. In the case of modern markets, states and corporate organizations, their breadth, complexity and scale all require this level of macro-analysis, although all of them have interconnected macro- and micro-cultural levels of order as well. As the contrast of 'corporate cultures' in Japan and the United States shows, there is no one-to-one relationship between these forms of order.

Even if connected to culture and action, it is precisely the complexity of systems that gives rise to a fourth, most highly problematic feature: their relative autonomy from any particular set of cultural norms or beliefs. Indeed, this feature is often offered as an explanation of interdependence and scale. This notion of independence also admits of degrees, with the most extreme version of it found in Habermas's description of systems as 'blocks of norm-free sociality' (TCA2 258). On this view, some aspects of social order, specifically material reproduction, may become (relatively) 'uncoupled' from the normative or cultural order. The primary examples of such phenomena are markets and bureaucracies, both of which also begin to have reifying effects upon the cultural order out of which they have emerged. A second, more moderate and pluralist position merely contrasts and interrelates two different processes of integration and two different forms of description of the same social order. In developing his thesis of the 'colonization of the lifeworld', Habermas employs both types of descriptions, and the problems of modern order emerge only in seeing their interrelationships.

At first glance, Habermas's colonization thesis seems to be an exclusively macro-structural explanation, explaining one macro-pattern (cultural frag-mentation and the disruption of socialization) by another (the spread of bureaucracies and markets). Indeed, Habermas borrows the exclusively 'macro' concepts of Parsons' and Luhmann's systems theories, neither of which uses all the elements of the scheme of explanation that I outlined above. Does this borrowing from a one-sided theory make for explanatory deficits, or for a basically sound, but 'overly reifying vocabulary'[28] in describing the integra-tion of social systems? A closer examination of the explanations employed in the colonization thesis shows that Habermas does make the requisite empiri-cal linkages between the various levels of good macro-to-micro explanations: his explanations refer to the macro-level of social systems, to institutions typical of them, and to the micro-level of action and belief formation. Prop-erly reconstructed, Habermas's explanation of the colonization of the cultural lifeworld by the advance of social systems such as markets provides a good example of an adequate macro–micro link for the purposes of showing the dysfunctions of the social system and its undesirable unintended effects.

In explaining how systems 'invade' and 'colonize' the lifeworld, Habermas must show how each level is both autonomous and interconnected. In one of his more successful 'reconstructions of historical materialism', Habermas reinterprets Marx's base–superstructure distinction to establish the causal role of mechanisms operative on both sides of this distinction. Put simply, Haber-mas's appeals to institutions and the social processes that go on within them are necessary to explain how macro-to-micro relationships are established. Systems relate to institutions as superstructure to base: systems must be 'anchored' in the lifeworld through institutions (TCA2 259). The organiza-tion of the economy through market mechanisms requires that the systemi-cally organized sphere of material production be 'anchored' in new cultural institutions such as civil law and bureaucratic offices. This interdependence makes 'increases in [system] complexity dependent on the structural differ-entiation of the lifeworld'.[29] Furthermore, it is only through their anchoring institutions (and not some mysterious 'internal logic') that systems spread, as when social relations become increasingly governed by law or mediated through money. In other words, it is the increasing capacity of institutions of law and exchange to define the character of social relationships (and not the intrinsic properties of the systems themselves) which has the dysfunctional structural effects and the bad, unintended consequences. Further analysis of the continued role of micro-level social order shows the implausibility of a stronger interpretation of the colonization of the lifeworld. For example, rational choice theory shows that rational agents in a bureaucracy do not seek the maximum information regarding all aspects of the process they are regulating; they 'satisfice', rather than maximize, by getting just enough information, as needed, and thereby economize on the costs of further search. Furthermore, ethnomethodology shows that social order in the organizations that anchor systems is constantly renegotiated.[30] These less frightening analyses of such processes have practical consequences: they show that such large-scale institutional order is still vulnerable to collective action and to the refusal of agents to co-operate in large collective enterprises that have only the appearance of being tightly integrated. Indeed, incomplete and one-sided macro-level explanations also lose their critical power to initiate self-reflection. But their failure to refer to human agency is due to the inadequate social theories on which they are based, not to putative facts about the ungovernability of complex societies and their institutions. Macro-sociological theories and explanations must therefore integrate various levels and types of analysis 'under one roof' if sociology is to fulfil one of its main goals: that it be a practical science.[31]

If Habermas's theory were truer to his own aim of methodological and theoretical pluralism, he would see that the overly strong versions of system integration that he borrows from Luhmann and Weber are inadequate as empirical descriptions of what actually goes on in the settings of formal institutions. In the case of macro-sociological explanation, a more self-conscious methodological pluralism would emphasize the corrective role of theoretical pluralism at the macro-level. Once again, the false picture that the largest level of social order is the most comprehensive basis for social theory weakens the critical appropriation of other social theories. In a reply to critics of his 'unhappy marriage' of hermeneutics and functionalism, Habermas admits that his analysis is not pluralist enough: it does not show that each type of description is 'relevant to an analysis of social phenomena at both levels', and thus that it is misleading for him to separate them so sharply at the analytic level that they appear to apply only to specific sorts of actions or social domains.[32] This position is consistent with the sort of pluralism that I have been recommending here for macro-sociological explanation, and entails abandoning the need for comprehensive theory at the macro-sociological level. Critical Theory requires multi-dimensional explanations that integrate the results of many different theoretical perspectives. While never fully comprehensive, explanations that consider and criticize social phenomena from the available methodological and theoretical perspectives are as complete as social-scientific explanations can be.

A more pluralistic conception of complex social order such as this still faces greater difficulties in practical verification than Marx's less mediated, more objectivistic and comprehensive theory. It is now no longer possible to count on the obvious effects of system malfunctioning to supply motivating reasons for transformative action. For this reason, Habermas has attempted to rethink the problem of emancipatory change on the model of social learning, rather than as the proper resolution of a crisis. As Habermas puts it, 'If a socialist organization of society were the adequate response to crisis-ridden developments in capitalist society, then it would have to be explained in terms of a process of democratization; that is, the penetration of universalistic structures into action domains previously reserved to the private autonomous setting of ends' (CES 124).[33] A critical social theory can still diagnose present obstacles to such a transformation (privatism, for example, or the depoliticization of the public sphere) and uncover locations (systemic breakdowns, invasions) where challenges to the current systemic structures can occur. If social change requires competent agents capable of social learning, then the social scientist is but one participant in this democratic, self-reflective process. The key to critical social science in this context is to make such self-reflexivity non-paradoxical. As the history of the Frankfurt School, particularly the later work of Adorno, shows, it is very difficult to avoid the temptation to political scepticism and helplessness that follows from the paradoxes of self-reflexivity in macro-level theories of societal integration 'behind our backs'. Post-modernism shows that such paradoxical reflexivity is an equally seductive stance in the interpretive domain as well. Multi-dimensional explanations, rather than comprehensive theories, provide the basis for reflexivity consistent with pluralism. Such pluralism best fulfils the corrective role that Habermas ascribes to macro-sociological theory: it gets us beyond the potentially ideological limits of one-sided theories.

V The Dilemma of Critical Theory: Crisis or Dissolution?

Critical social theory is a reflexive theory with intellectual and moral interests. Habermas has provided a general interpretive and explanatory framework for a theory of human emancipation. More than any other theorist, he has furthered this endeavour. His actual theoretical framework does not

> Even though Habermas argued he is not pluralist enough – he's provided a basis for reflexivity – Giddens

require a single comprehensive theory such as historical materialism. Such a theory serves only the methodological purpose of correcting for the one-sidedness of existing theories and approaches while integrating them into adequate critical and practical explanations. Historical materialism has long been tied to the project of a politically and scientifically determinate Critical Theory; abandoning this goal and accepting the weaker criterion of adequacy also entails that we accept a different picture of the practical character of social-scientific knowledge consistent with the irreducibility of heterogeneous methods and theories in the social sciences. A plurality of adequate theories and methods is not only required for good explanations with normative content; it is also more appropriate to the role that critics play in democratic political change. Habermas's methodological and political writings have pushed critical social science in this direction, as has his critical appropriation of diverse social theories from Durkheim and Mead to Parsons and Luhmann. This critical purpose of his social theory, I have argued, is best served by a more consistent methodological and theoretical pluralism. The problems remaining in Habermas's framework for a sociological criticism of modern society, whether in the theory of ideology or in his conception of social complexity, emerge when he violates his own insights into the irreducible pluralism of the social sciences.

However, accepting the fact of methodological and theoretical pluralism also raises new epistemological and political problems for critical social science. These problems could be corrected by a thoroughgoing pragmatism with respect to two central features of the epistemology of critical social science that Habermas has already identified: both its social contexts of enquiry and the 'practical verification' of its consequences. Such pragmatism might also solve the problem of the choice between often contradictory theories and methods that Habermas's pluralism leaves unresolved if his attempts at a comprehensive theory fail.

Besides analysing the 'emancipatory interest' as the specific purpose of certain forms of social enquiry, Habermas's view that critical social science has a distinctive relationship between theory and practice pushes his theory in the direction of pragmatism.[34] Merely to identify a number of different methods and a number of different theories connected with a variety of different purposes and interests leaves the social scientist with a rather hopeless epistemological dilemma. *Either* the choice among theories, methods and interests seems utterly arbitrary, *or* the Critical Theorist has some special epistemic claim to survey the domain and make the proper choice for the right reason. While the former, more sceptical horn of the dilemma is one endorsed by 'new pragmatists' like Richard Rorty (who sees all knowledge as relative to particular purposes) and by Weber in the more decisionist moments in his methodological writings, the latter makes strong objectivist claims for social science generally, and for the epistemic superiority of the Critical Theorist in particular, that Habermas and others have been at pains to reject.[35] Is there any way out of the epistemic dilemma of pluralism? The way out, it seems to me, has already been indicated by pragmatism's emphasis on the social context of enquiry and the practical character of social knowledge.

The problems of pluralism cannot be easily avoided simply by shifting the debate to practical criteria. Not only are there many distinct practical interests or purposes, but the social sciences may be practical in many different senses. To the extent that we can identify the epistemological basis of the social sciences in forms of practical knowledge, the dilemma of pluralism becomes more tractable as a problem: identifying the type of knowledge required by the specific social context of enquiry. The analysis of interests takes us some of the way. Technical knowledge does not represent only a particular interest, say the interest in controlling outcomes; in the case of the social sciences, it also presupposes a particular practical relation between the social scientists and the subjects of their enquiry. In order to control certain social outcomes or processes, a particular context of enquiry must be created: the regulative control of institutions over certain kinds of practices or processes. Critical social enquiry presupposes and attempts to create a different social context of enquiry: it addresses the subjects of enquiry as equal reflective participants, as knowledgeable social agents. In this way, the asymmetries of the context of technical control are suspended; this means that critical social enquiry must be judged by a different set of practical consequences, by appeal to increasing the 'reflective knowledge' that agents already possess to a greater or lesser degree. As themselves agents in the social world, social scientists participate in the creation of the sort of contexts in which their theories are verified.

The goal of critical enquiry is not to control social processes or even to influence the sorts of decisions that agents might make in any determinate sort of way. Instead, its goal is 'to initiate processes of self-reflection' (TP 38). Thus, critical social science can measure its success against the standard of attaining such a practical goal. In certain cases, the goal may be attained simply by addressing agents as members of a functioning public sphere characterized by free and open communication among equal citizens; hence, the success of critical social enquiry may be measured by its practical consequences for members of the public sphere. Such a standard offers the same measure of success for the contributions of all reflective participants in the public sphere, particularly those who are concerned about its public character or the quality of public opinion formed within it.[36] But it may not always be the case that a well-functioning public sphere exists; and even if one exists, it may be difficult to initiate reflection on various social themes or self-reflection on aspects of the public sphere. Such cases are the subject-matter of most critical theories, such as the theory of ideology, which seem to introduce certain asymmetric features into critical social knowledge, leaving the critic once again in a position of epistemic superiority. This problem, too, is less intractable from a pragmatic point of view: no such claims are required, since the critic's theory does not provide the practical warrant of critique.

In its context of enquiry, critical social science treats social actors as knowledgeable social agents to whom its claims are publicly addressed. Such claims are successful not in so far as they bring agents to particular true insights, but rather in so far as they initiate processes of self-reflection, the outcome of which agents determine for themselves. Social-scientific knowledge brings agents to see their circumstances differently, indeed to a point where they can see that change of some sort or another is practically necessary. In this way, critics do not employ reflexive theories in an 'objectivating fashion', as Habermas argues. Rather, their form of enquiry seeks to bring about those social conditions in which their insights and proposals could be validated or falsified by agents themselves. The fact that agents do not now accept some proffered interpretation of their practices does not refute such a criticism; the practical conception of verification allows that agents could be mistaken about the character of their practices. Just as technical knowledge seeks to create the social conditions necessary to validate its predictions, so too, critical enquiry seeks to create the appropriate social conditions under which agents themselves may verify or falsify the criticism offered. Agents in this new social context can retrospectively judge their past knowledge as reflectively inadequate; but apart from undertaking this process of practical verification, there is no way of knowing the truth or falsity of a criticism as a 'fact of the matter'. Rather, a criticism is verified if it proves acceptable to those to whom it is addressed under the appropriate reflective conditions in a public process of judgement and validation.

Pragmatism adds a further dimension to such a view of practical verification: the relationship between democracy and science, especially as developed by Dewey, suggests that such a process must be social and institutionally organized. In this regard, pragmatism emphasizes an 'intelligent' form of democracy that is broadly experimental in seeking and testing open, flexible and informed policies. Even this weak analogy to science points to the underemphasized role of knowledge in democracy, a role that seems lacking when we think of democracy solely in terms of moral fairness. Dewey argues that the most desirable and applicable epistemic features of science are primarily the consequence of its division of labour, since it is the division of labour which makes scientific intelligence co-operatively and 'socially organized'. As it is structured now, democratic practice ignores the existence of occupational groups, whose combined efforts produce results that no other group or individual could attain. While the division of labour requires experts and specialists, it does not demand that knowledge be located in a group or class of experts; ideally, every citizen participates as an expert in making his or her irreplaceable contribution to the whole. Thus, a democratic social organization of knowledge is essentially co-operative, in that it is decentralized among all participants in the democratic process. This is especially important for improving deliberation on issues of sufficient complexity: in such cases, there could be no particular group which possesses all the knowledge necessary to accomplish a particular large goal. Such an emphasis on the social organization and distribution of knowledge helps us to understand the role of the critical social scientist differently: as one among many reflective participants engaging in an ongoing process of deliberation and self-reflection. The critic's role can be to restart stalled processes of co-operation, diagnosing cases of restrictions and blockages and enlisting the co-operation of others to overcome them. Socially distributed knowledge is not represented anywhere specific, but in the group as a whole. This mutual dependence makes it impossible for any subgroup of individuals to possess knowledge in such a way as to control the social process, since only the full collective knowledge and co-operation of the group can achieve social control and effective social policies.

In such an ongoing and socially organized process, the critic's role is practical in a variety of ways. The regulation of means and ends has more to do with determining what is acceptable to those participating in this large collective and co-operative enterprise than with approximating some ideal state of full causal knowledge of society. The epistemic features of democracy make it the location not only for social criticism, but also for critical social enquiry. In it, we engage in a self-reflective practice that seeks constantly to create and re-create the conditions for the practical verification of judgements and interpretations. When understood as solely dependent upon the superiority of theoretical knowledge, the critic has no foothold in the social world and no way to choose among the many competing approaches and methods. But such a conception is based on the wrong model of verification for critical social enquiry. On the pragmatic account that I have been defending, we can see why it is that critical enquiry aims at creating the conditions for its own practical verification, with the proviso that agents may not in the end find these insights acceptable, and thus may not change their beliefs or practices.

Conclusion: Democracy as the Location for Critical Practice

My argument depends on a contrast between two interpretations of critical social science: one is theoretical and dependent on the heritage of German Idealism, whereas the other is practical and pluralistic in the spirit of pragmatism. The main epistemic weakness of the first interpretation is that it depends on the overly ambitious goal of a comprehensive social theory which can unify all the diverse methods and practical purposes of social enquiry. In the absence of such a theory, the choice between various approaches or methods seems fundamentally arbitrary. The practical alternative offers a solution to this problem by taking critical social theory in a pragmatic direction. In this respect, I have argued that a pragmatic reinterpretation of the verification of critical enquiry solves seemingly intractable epistemic problems for the social theorist. But it is also true that Critical Theory can help us to understand pragmatism better, avoiding pragmatism's often rather naive faith in the progressive power of scientific knowledge, on the one hand, and the relativistic pluralism of recent 'new' pragmatism, on the other. Critical Theory and pragmatism are therefore mutually informative, especially when united around an epistemic interpretation of democratic practices of socially organized judgement. Habermas calls such formal and informal practices 'deliberative politics', and it is in this context that a pluralistic critical social science has a social location. Pragmatism's emphasis on the social organization of knowledge provides a model of how this form of politics might work: democracy depends on a co-operative form of social enquiry involving all citizens. Co-operative enquiry allows for the division of critical labour, where the overall legitimacy of institutions and policies can be tested by a variety of participants from different perspectives and with different social knowledge. Properly organized and defined, such social-scientific knowledge is a resource that may be socially diffused and shared and used by everyone. Under these conditions, already entrenched asymmetries of information and power can be transformed by the practical consequences of organized critical social enquiry.

Notes

1   Max Horkheimer, 'Traditional and Critical Theory', in *Critical Theory* (New York: Seabury Press, 1982), p. 244.
2   The 'German ideology' that Marx refers to consists of variants of the thesis that criticizing 'false conceptions' will change 'existing realities'. As he put it: 'Let us

teach human beings, says one, to exchange these imaginations for thoughts that correspond to the essence of man; says the second, to take up a critical attitude toward them; says a third to knock them out of their heads — and existing reality will collapse.' He compares these views of criticism to attempting to keep human beings from drowning by keeping the idea of gravity out of their heads. See Karl Marx and Friedrich Engels, *The German Ideology* (New York: International Publishers, 1970), p. 38.

3   I am here following Jon Elster's distinction between the inadequacy and the indeterminacy of social-scientific theories: empirical theories are inadequate when they fail to yield *any* predictions; they are indeterminate when they fail to yield *unique* predictions. Critical theories are inadequate if they do not bear *any* relationship to emancipatory political practice (however that may be defined by the theory); they are indeterminate if they do not bear a *unique* relationship to political practice, and thus to a specific political goal. I am arguing that critical theories ought to be adequate, but not determinate. See Jon Elster, *Solomonic Judgements* (Cambridge: Cambridge University Press, 1989), p. 1. For a longer discussion of these conceptions of indeterminacy and adequacy, see the 'Introduction' to my *New Philosophy of Social Science* (Cambridge, Mass.: MIT/Polity Press, 1991).

4   Introducing the concept of interests not only overcomes a positivist conception of the social sciences; it also ties 'the achievement of the transcendental subject to the natural history of the human species' (KHI 312). This sort of epistemological argument puts Habermas closer to current naturalized epistemologies than does his neo-Kantian dualism of the natural and the human sciences as ontological domains accessible to distinct epistemic operations of causal explanation and interpretation.

5   For an excellent discussion of the weaknesses of such a philosophy of history with practical intent as a comprehensive framework for criticism, see Thomas McCarthy, *The Critical Theory of Jürgen Habermas* (Cambridge, Mass.: MIT Press and Polity, 1978), pp. 94ff.

6   This is my approach to the problem of pluralism in explanation and interpretation throughout my *New Philosophy of Social Science*.

7   Habermas, 'Questions and counter-questions', in *Habermas and Modernity*, ed. Richard Bernstein (Oxford: Blackwell, 1986), p. 216.

8   On the failure of the Frankfurt School to develop a comprehensive 'dialectical' social theory and the way in which Benjamin's notion of constellations gradually replaced it, see Rolf Wiggershaus, *The Frankfurt School* (Cambridge, Mass.: MIT Press, 1994), pp. 177–91.

9   As Habermas puts it, 'I do not want to use the terms "strategic" and "communicative" only to designate two analytic aspects under which the same action can be described' (TCA1 286). However, as I shall show later, Habermas does think that the contrasting descriptions of the theory of communicative action and systems theory can be seen in precisely this way.

10   For this modification of historical materialism, see Habermas, 'Historical materialism and the development of normative structures' (CES 95–129); the devel-

opment of normative structures is 'the pacemaker of social evolution, for new principles of social organization mean new forms of social integration; and the latter, in turn, first make it possible to implement the available productive forces or to generate new ones, as well as making possible a heightening of social complexity' (CES 120).

11 See Seyla Benhabib, *Critique, Norm and Utopia: A Study of the Foundations of Critical Theory* (New York: Columbia University Press, 1986), esp. chs 1–4, for a good discussion of the different phases and models of Marx's project. She distinguishes at least three forms of criticism in Marx: immanent or internal critique borrowed from Hegel, disillusioning critique in the theory of ideology, and the defetishizing methods of the theory of commodities.

12 For an account of how rational choice theory can describe mechanisms for the formation of ideology, see Jon Elster, *Sour Grapes* (Cambridge: Cambridge University Press, 1983). The problem with such explanations is that, because they appeal to micro-level, psychological processes, they cannot specify why it is that such ideological beliefs become widely shared. For an account of how the theory of communicative action can formulate a theory of different mechanisms related to restrictions in communication, see my *New Philosophy of Social Science*, pp. 211–17.

13 See Paul Ricoeur, *Lectures on Ideology and Utopia* (New York: Columbia University Press, 1986), for a good comparative treatment of Mannheim and Marx.

14 Karl Mannheim, *Ideology and Utopia* (New York: Harvest Books, 1936), p. 59.

15 For this criticism of the theory of ideology, see Jon Elster, *Making Sense of Marx* (Cambridge: Cambridge University Press, 1985), ch. 8.

16 On this problem, see my 'Empirical weaknesses and theoretical strengths: formal pragmatics and the social sciences', *Pragmatics and Cognition*, 3/2 (1995), pp. 293–312.

17 For the fruitfulness of such a definition relative to its competitors, see John Thompson, *Studies in the Theory of Ideology* (Stanford, Calif.: Stanford University Press, 1984).

18 Such analogies are to be found in the preface to the 1st edn of *Capital* (New York: International Publishers, 1967), pp. 7–9.

19 Clifford Geertz, *Local Knowledge* (New York: Basic Books, 1983), p. 57.

20 Ibid., p. 58.

21 The analysis of these crisis mechanisms culminates in ch. 25 of vol. 1 of *Capital*, in which Marx develops the spiralling effects of accumulation crises, aggravated by actors' attempts to correct them.

22 Marx, *Capital*, vol. 3, p. 830.

23 Sometimes Marx also seems committed to the false view that crises are 'inevitable' by some teleological necessity, although he clearly recognizes that an exploitative social system can last for centuries if agents do not change it through self-conscious, collective effort, as was the case in many empires.

24 Émile Durkheim, *Rules of Sociological Method* (New York: Free Press, 1938), p. 18.

25   See the essays in *The Micro–Macro Link*, ed. J. Alexander et al. (Berkeley: University of California Press, 1987), especially the introductory essay by Alexander and Giesen, 'From reduction to linkage'.

26   David Lockwood, 'Social integration and system integration', in *Explorations in Social Change*, ed. G. K. Zollschan and W. Hirsch (Boston: Brown and Littlefield, 1964); for a good discussion of the relation between Lockwood's distinction and Marxian social theory, see Alex Callinicos, *Making History* (Ithaca, NY: Cornell University Press, 1988), ch. 2.

27   See Anthony Giddens, *Central Problems of Social Theory* (Berkeley: University of California Press, 1979), pp. 61–2.

28   See Habermas's reply to such criticisms, in his 'A reply' in Axel Honneth and Hans Joas, eds, *Communicative Action* (Cambridge: Polity Press, 1991), pp. 250–1.

29   Ibid., p. 258.

30   For a reconstruction of such explanations, see my 'The completeness of macro-sociological explanations', *Protosoziologie*, 5/3 (1993), pp. 80–9.

31   A fuller discussion of the issue of agency in complete macro-sociological explanations, and of other issues of the macro–micro link not developed here, can be found in my *New Philosophy of Social Science*, ch. 4.

32   See Habermas, 'A reply', p. 253.

33   Habermas has recently modified this position, and argued that the conditions of social complexity undermine the democratic self-organization of society. See also BFN, chs 7 and 8. For a criticism of this argument, showing that it is based on a false view of complexity, see my *Public Deliberation: Pluralism, Complexity and Democracy* (Cambridge, Mass.: MIT Press, 1996), ch. 4. For an argument directed explicitly against the notion of complexity in *Between Facts and Norms*, see my 'Complexity, pluralism and the constitutional state: on Habermas's *Faktizität und Geltung*', *Law and Society Review*, 28/4 (1994), pp. 801–34. Habermas's 'two-level' social theory of modern social complexity leads him to develop a 'two-track' conception of democracy appropriate to such societies, with the formal and law-making institutions of the constitutional state as one track and the informal public sphere as the other. For a more general account of the relation of democracy and complexity, see my 'Modernization and impediments to democracy: the problems of hypercomplexity and hyperrationality', *Theoria*, 86 (1995), pp. 1–20.

34   Horkheimer and the first-generation Critical Theorists refuse to recognize the similarity between their epistemological views of social science and pragmatism. They invariably criticize the latter for reducing truth to usefulness. However, the similarities are more striking than such difference produced by rather hasty judgements. For example, Horkheimer's criticism of Cartesian conceptions of knowledge as articulating the epistemology of 'traditional theory' is remarkably similar to Dewey's criticism of the epistemic criterion of certainty and the spectator theory of knowledge.

35   This view of the social sciences is defended by Rorty in 'Inquiry as recontextualization', in *The Interpretive Turn*, ed. D. Hiley et al. (Ithaca, NY: Cornell Uni-

versity Press, 1991), where he argues that we ought to 'switch our attentions from the "demands of the object" to the purpose a particular inquiry is supposed to serve' (p. 79). Similarly, Weber argues that the complex set of factors that make up any social phenomenon should be selected according to what is 'decisive for our interest', not in terms of all 'objective possibilities'. See Max Weber, *The Methodology of the Social Sciences* (New York: Free Press, 1949), pp. 180ff.

36 See Bohman, *Public Deliberation*, ch. 1.

3

Communicative paradigms and the question of subjectivity: Habermas, Mead and Lacan

Peter Dews

I

The central contention of Jürgen Habermas's book *The Philosophical Discourse of Modernity* is that the emancipatory intention of the radical critique of reason which derives from Nietzsche, and which has recently enjoyed a new florescence in the form of post-structuralism, can only be salvaged through a change of philosophical 'paradigm'. The self-defeating dynamic of this critique will remain insuperable until the move is made from a standpoint which still remains – albeit by negation – within the force field of the 'philosophy of consciousness' to a standpoint which affirms the primacy of communication. According to Habermas, 'freedom, as the principle of modernity, cannot really be grasped by means of the basic concepts of the philosophy of the subject' (PDM 292). This is because, 'in all attempts to grasp self-determination and self-realization, that is, freedom in the moral and aesthetic senses, with the tools of the philosophy of consciousness, one immediately runs up against an ironic inversion of what is actually intended. Repression of the self is the converse side of an autonomy that is forced into subject–object relationships; the loss – and the narcissistic fear of loss – of self is the converse of an expressivity brought under these concepts' (PDM 292). In his reconstruction of the history of philosophy since Hegel, Habermas suggests that, from Marx onwards, opportunities to make such a paradigm shift were repeatedly missed. Contemporary philosophy therefore needs to return to the 'alternative that Hegel left in the lurch back in Jena – to a concept of communicative reason which places the dialectic of enlightenment in a different light' (PDM 74).

It is curious that in much of the discussion aroused by *The Philosophical Discourse of Modernity* – in the English-speaking world, at least – the essential force of Habermas's criticism has not been recognized, or its thrust has been avoided. Habermas is habitually – and inaccurately – accused of aspiring to the impossible ideal of a transparent, non-metaphorical philosophical discourse,[1] of having failed to grasp the subtlety or the authentic critical potential of the writings of Derrida and Foucault,[2] or of seeking to *impose* a repressive normative framework on communication.[3] When the issue of a paradigm shift *is* raised, the response is often either to deny that such shift has taken place at all, or to point out that concepts of intersubjectivity still make reference to human *subjects*, as if this were an indictment, while refusing to confront Habermas's warning of the dangers of an '*undialectical* rejection of subjectivity'.[4] In such contexts, it is rarely observed that, in later phases of their work, both Foucault and Derrida have made tangible concessions to the essential rightness of Habermas's criticism; that in much of Derrida's more recent work, and in some of the last statements Foucault made before he died, there is an unmistakable shift towards a concern with issues of intersubjectivity – perhaps even towards an intersubjective paradigm.

One could instance, for example, the approach which Derrida takes in his essay 'The politics of friendship'. Here he no longer argues that metaphysical enquiry is disrupted by the movement of an abstract 'general text', but rather that such enquiry is always embedded within a relation between speakers which establishes its conditions of possibility: 'The very possibility of the question, in the form of "what is . . . ?", seems always to have supposed this friendship prior to friendships, this *anterior* affirmation of being together in the collocution. Such an affirmation can no longer be simply integrated, above all it cannot be *presented* as a being-present (substance, subject, essence, or existence) within the space of an ontology, precisely because it opens this space.'[5] Derrida can now be seen as acknowledging – at least implicitly – that this 'collocution' cannot be understood in terms of pure *différance*, if such *différance* is viewed as logically prior to any element of shared identity. For he admits that even the most radical exercise in deconstruction must rely on, and take its departure from, a grounding moment of agreement, regardless of how many aspects of this agreement are questioned subsequently. Without an underlying core of semantic stability, it would be impossible for 'dissemination' even to begin. Thus, in the 'Afterword' to *Limited Inc.*, Derrida refers to the 'minimal consensus' which is necessary for access to 'structures that are "relatively stable" (and hence destabilizable!), and from which even the most venturesome questions and interpretations have to start'.[6]

Both in this most recent phase of Derrida's work, and in the last statements made by Foucault, one can sense the emergence of a new sensibility. During the 1970s, Foucault had reduced the status of truth to that of a product of systems of power, arguing that '"Truth" is linked in a circular relation with systems of power which produce and sustain it, and to effects of power which it induces, and which extend it'; or, even more bluntly – and without the inhibiting inverted commas – that 'Truth is a thing of this world: it is produced only by multiple forms of constraint'.[7] This is a position which Habermas justly criticizes in *The Philosophical Discourse of Modernity*. In 1984, however, shortly before he died, Foucault began to discuss a new ethics of dialogue required by the co-operative search for truth:

In the serious play of questions and answers, in the work of reciprocal elucidation, the rights of each person are in some sense immanent in the discussion. They depend only on the dialogue situation. The person asking the questions is merely exercising the right that has been given him: to remain unconvinced, to perceive a contradiction, to require more information, to emphasize different postulates, to point out faulty reasoning, etc. As for the person answering the questions, he too exercises a right that does not go beyond the discussion itself; by the logic of his own discourse he is tied to what he has said earlier, and by the acceptance of dialogue he is tied to the questioning of the other.[8]

There is no suggestion here on Foucault's part that such 'rights', that such a 'logic of discourse', and the truth which they bring forth, are merely the masquerade of more fundamental forces and constraints, any more than Derrida now seeks to reduce what he terms 'minimal friendship' to an 'effect' of an all-embracing 'general text'.

In the case of both these thinkers, it appears, a realization has occurred – the realization that structures of intersubjectivity cannot be automatically assumed to embody, in another form, the repressive features of consciousness-centred philosophical models. There seems to be a new recognition that the concept of intersubjectivity can represent the possibility of a *breakthrough*, a disruption of some of the constraining, 'logocentric' features of the subject-object framework. In fact, in this respect both Derrida and Foucault have merely made explicit insights which had been touched upon, but then passed over, in their previous work. As early as his 'Introduction' to Husserl's essay on 'The origin of geometry', for example, Derrida had already hinted at the difficulties which the primacy of intersubjectivity would pose for the project of a transcendental phenomenology. And, as Habermas points out in *The*

Philosophical Discourse of Modernity, Derrida, in *Speech and Phenomena*, explicitly highlights the difficulties which the indicative dimension of communication poses for Husserl's monological account of meaning and expression, before he veers off into his discussion of a supposedly more originary 'staging' of transcendental consciousness.[9] Similar hints can also be found in Foucault, whose analyses of power are haunted by the sense of a disrupted communicative reciprocity, which is nevertheless only ever evoked in the most fleeting and elusive manner. In *Discipline and Punish*, for example, Foucault protests that the prisoner within the panoptic system 'is seen, but he does not see; he is the object of information, never a subject in communication'.[10]

II

There is thus good evidence for the fundamental correctness of Habermas's critique of post-structuralism and for his claim that a communicative concept of reason breaks down the boundaries of what are fashionably – but not unjustifiably – attacked as the repressive structures of Western rationality. In Habermas's view, the 'paradigm of mutual understanding' (*Verständigungspara-digma*) does not need to invoke a disruptive, extramundane alterity which is heterogeneous to reason in order to validate its critical standpoint, since it 'conceives of intersubjective understanding as the telos inscribed into communication in ordinary language, and of the logocentrism of Western thought, heightened by the philosophy of consciousness, as a systematic *foreshortening* and *distortion* of a potential always already operative in the communicative practice of everyday life, but only selectively exploited' (PDM 311)

In what follows, however, I aim to raise some questions about the way in which Habermas constructs the opposition between the philosophy of consciousness, on the one hand, and the theory of communicative action, on the other. Difficulties arise from the fact that, just as there is a multiplicity of positions within the general paradigm of the philosophy of consciousness, so there is a variety of positions within the paradigm of intersubjectivity, not all of which favour the conclusions which Habermas wishes to reach. Furthermore, as we shall discover, it is not always easy to keep the two paradigms opposed to each other in the straightforward manner which Habermas seems to intend.

Habermas's fundamental conviction is that the move to the paradigm of mutual understanding will *defuse* the self-destructive totalization of the critique of reason, by showing the possibility of a 'more far reaching and *comprehensive* reason' (PDM 302). The crucial difficulty with the critique of modernity deriving from Nietzsche is that it is based on an '*exclusion model* of reason'. According to this model, the 'other' of reason can only be understood as 'the vital forces of a split-off and repressed subjective nature, it is the sorts of phenomena rediscovered by Romanticism – dreams, fantasies, madness, orgiastic excitement, ecstasy – it is the aesthetic, body-centred experiences of a decentred subjectivity that function as the placeholders for the other of reason' (PDM 306). The problem here is that '[t]he spatial metaphor of inclusive and exclusive reason reveals that the supposedly radical critique of reason remains tied to the presuppositions of the philosophy of the subject from which it wanted to free itself. . . . Hence inside and outside are linked with domination and subjugation; and the overcoming of reason-as-powerholder is linked with breaking open the prison gates and vouchsafing release into an indeterminate freedom' (PDM 309).

Against this exclusion model, Habermas opposes what he terms a '*diremption model* of reason [which] distinguishes solidary social practice as the locus of a historically situated reason in which the threads of outer nature, inner nature, and society converge' (PDM 306). As we have just seen, it is arguable that some elements of the diremption model – which Habermas traces back to the early Hegel – are once more coming to the fore in some 'post-post-structuralist' philosophizing. However, the reference to this model immediately poses a crucial philosophical problem. For although the young Hegel asserts the reconciling power of intersubjectivity – which irrupts in the form of the 'causality of fate' – the ground of this power is accessible to human awareness only through privileged experiences, such as those of love and religious communion. Hegel is initially dependent on an appeal to an idealized model of ancient ethical totalities, whose cohesion and homogeneity would be incompatible with the differentiation of modern society. By contrast, as Habermas argues, when Hegel seeks – in his mature work – to articulate the structure of this reconciling power theoretically, he develops a concept of *comprehensive reason* which is no longer intersubjectively structured, but is grounded in the meta-subjectivity of *Geist*. The consequence of this is that 'the question of the genuine self-understanding of modernity expires in the ironic laughter of reason. For reason has now taken over the place of fate and knows that every event of essential significance has already been decided' (PDM 42).

Thus the success of Habermas's argument basically depends on the possibility of evading this Hegelian dilemma. Habermas must make good his claim that 'the theory of communicative action can reconstruct Hegel's concept of the ethical context of life (independently of the premises of the philosophy of consciousness)' (PDM 316). It is this claim which we shall be examining more closely. What will be at issue is Habermas's implicit assumption that, with the vanishing of pre-modern forms of *Sittlichkeit*, there is no longer the possibility of a philosophical position which accepts the existence of a reconciling, intersubjective power of reason, but denies that this power is *theoretically* retrievable. If such a position were conceivable, however, then a third possibility would have to be reckoned with, obviating the stark choice offered us by Habermas. The options would no longer simply be between, on the one hand, a hypostatized 'other' *heterogeneous* to reason, which reduces reason to a thin veneer masking more elemental forces, and, on the other hand, reason as the advance towards the *telos* of agreement inhabiting communication. There would emerge a different conception of what might be termed 'reason *as* and *in* the other', a reconciling power which nevertheless transcends the conceptual grasp of finite human subjects.

It is the possibility of this third standpoint, and its implications for Habermas's argument, which I will first explore through a discussion of the thought of the French psychoanalyst Jacques Lacan. At first sight, this may appear an unlikely point of comparison. But, as I hope to show, Lacan's conception of the structure of linguistic intersubjectivity bears remarkable similarities to that of Habermas, while diverging – in an illuminating way – at certain philosophically crucial points.

III

Lacan hardly figures in *The Philosophical Discourse of Modernity*, and, when he does, it is as a critic – perhaps even a genealogist – of a 'reason grounded in the principle of subjectivity', in the tradition running from Nietzsche to Bataille and Foucault (PDM 55, 97). The omission of any substantive discussion of Lacan can hardly be considered a flaw in a work already so wideranging. But the classification of Lacan within the post-Nietzschean tradition is symptomatic of a certain simplification of fronts. For although Lacan is indeed a powerful critic of subjective reason, his standpoint is arguably far closer to that of Habermas than to the French contemporaries with whom he is habitually associated.[11] Like Habermas, Lacan – who attended Kojève's lectures on the *Phenomenology of Spirit* in Paris during the 1930s – learned fundamental lessons concerning the intersubjective structuring of human identity from Hegel. These lessons remained indelible, even when, during the 1950s, structuralist influences began to enter his work.

In this context, much could be said about the striking convergences between the interpretations of Freud offered by Habermas and Lacan. Both agree that Freudian psychoanalysis should not be interpreted as an explanatory account of the dynamics of quasi-biological drives, but rather as providing a means of deciphering the distortions of symbolic structures. For Habermas the unconscious must not be viewed naturalistically, as a reservoir of purely pre-social impulses, but rather as a 'sphere which has become second nature through self-objectification' (KHI 271). The unconscious cannot be made available to objectifying theory, since it can be grasped only privatively, through its effects, the gaps and distortions of everyday language, and thus from an essentially *normative* standpoint: 'Starting with the experiences of the physician's communication with his patient, Freud derived the concept of the unconscious from a specific form of disturbance of communication in ordinary language' (KHI 238). Accordingly, the process of analysis can be viewed as the communicative transformation of a subjectivity which has become alienated from itself, whose own process of self-formation has become opaque and inaccessible: 'Analysis has immediate therapeutic results because the critical overcoming of blocks to consciousness and the penetration of false objectivations initiates the appropriation of a lost portion of life history' (KHI 233).

Lacan similarly argues for a 'disentanglement' of 'the technique of deciphering the unconscious and the theory of instincts', and defines the unconscious as 'that part of my history which is marked by a blank or occupied by a falsehood: it is the censored chapter'.[12] As in Habermas, the process of analysis is understood not as the making conscious of quasi-natural drives, but as the recovery and reconstruction by the analysand of a distorted and partially obliterated autobiography, in which what has been repressed is not so much the events themselves, as their *meaning* for the individual. In accordance with this conception, the aim of analysis is 'the restitution of the wholeness of the subject', which takes the form of a 'restoration of the past'.[13] This restoration can be achieved only through speech, through the communicative relation with the analyst, since it is only in this medium that the desire of the analysand can make itself recognized: 'It is through the intersubjectivity of the "we" which it assumes that the value of a language as speech is measured.'[14]

Thus Lacan's initial reformulation of psychoanalytic theory is not only linguistic and hermeneutic in orientation; it also lays much stress on the primacy of the intersubjective relation. In the first *Seminar* Lacan states emphatically: 'we must begin from a radical intersubjectivity, from the total acceptance of the subject by the other subject. . . . It is only retrospectively (*nachträglich*), on the basis of adult experience, that we should approach the supposedly original experiences, tracing the degradations, without ever abandoning intersubjectivity. As long as we remain in the register of psychoanalysis, we must accept the existence of intersubjectivity from the very beginning.'[15] This argument, dating from 1953–4, anticipates Habermas's view, in *Knowledge and Human Interests*, that 'the objective-intentional structure of life history, which is accessible only through self-reflection, is not functionalistic in the normal sense of this term. The elementary events are processes in a drama. . . . That is, the elementary processes appear as parts of a structure of interactions through which a "meaning" is realized' (KHI 259–60).[16] For both Habermas and Lacan, therefore, psychoanalytic aetiology cannot take a purely causal form, since what is at stake is the *meaning* of events, a meaning co-constituted by the responses of significant others and – more broadly – by the culture as a whole.

Because of this shared stress on intersubjectivity, both Lacan and Habermas have, at various points, criticized conceptions of language as consisting in a system of behaviour-co-ordinating signals. Lacan repeatedly illustrates the distinctiveness of language by counterposing animal signalling and communication between human beings. Thus he defines a code in terms of 'the fixed correlation of its signs with the reality they signify', using as an example the 'language of the bees', in which different dance patterns indicate the direction and distance of pollen-bearing flowers. Such forms of information transmission can be reduced to sequences of stimulus and response: we are here operating at the level of behavioural reactions to perceived images and patterns, a level of experience which Lacan categorizes as the 'Imaginary'.[17] In human language, however, communication does not simply convey information; it establishes a relationship of recognition between speaker and hearer. As Lacan states, 'The form in which language is expressed defines in itself subjectivity. . . . In other words, it refers to the discourse of the other. As such it is caught up in the highest function of speech, in as much as speech commits its author by investing the person to whom it is addressed with a new reality.'[18] Parallel views can be found in *On the Logic of the Social Sciences*, where Habermas argues that language cannot be reduced to *behaviour*, since there can be no empirically determinable criteria of the identity of meanings which do not already presuppose knowledge acquired through participation in a linguistic community. He concludes that 'the identity of meanings is not constituted through similar reactions, which an observer could determine as similar, but through the expectation of a certain reaction which the partners in conversation share, in other words through the intersubjectivity of expectations of behaviour' (LSS 65).

IV

In one significant respect, however, it is arguable that Lacan's thinking *anticipated* the 'linguistic turn' which Habermas's work took during the 1970s. In *On the Logic of the Social Sciences* Habermas had argued against behaviourist theories of language primarily in terms of the structure of anticipatory role taking required for communication. He was already resistant to the relativism of the Wittgensteinian version of these insights, arguing that 'Languages themselves contain a potential for reason, which, although expressed in the particularity of a determinate grammar, simultaneously reflects its limits and negates them as particular' (LSS 144). But he was not able to back up this contention with much more than a casual reference to Hegel's 'dialectic of the limit' (LSS 144). It was not until several years later that Habermas began to develop his universal pragmatics, which explicates the nature of this reason implicit in human speech in terms of a system of *validity claims*, and the processes of their redemption.

By contrast, from the early 1950s onwards, Lacan fully appreciated that human language is characterized not only by the *intersubjectivity* of meaning, but by an internal relation between meaning and truth. In his work of the 1950s, Lacan illustrates this point through reference to the patterns of rivalry and courtship, and the accompanying forms of parade and display, to be found in the animal world. There is little doubt, he suggests, that there can occur amongst animals forms of misleading behaviour and deception: animals can lure and intimidate each other, and fool each other as to their subjective intentions, by creating a disjunction between appearance and reality. However, although this is enough to manifest the presence of an animal 'intersubjectivity', it is not sufficient to demonstrate the presence of language in the authentic sense.[19] This is because language only emerges, for Lacan, at the point when a normative expectation of truth telling is established.

Lacan's fundamental argument is that none of the forms of deception found in the animal world, nor indeed the use of a feint or misleading manoeuvre during a battle or a boxing match, can be considered as *mendacious*, since mendacity involves an unjustified claim to *truth*, and it is not in the domain of disjunctions between (physical) appearance and (psychological) reality that the question of truth and falsehood arises. Lacan writes: 'For I can lure my adversary by means of a movement contrary to my actual plan of battle, and this movement will have its deceiving effect only in so far as I produce it in reality and for my adversary. But in the propositions with which I open peace negotiations with him, what my negotiations propose to him is situated in a third locus, which is neither my speech nor my interlocutor.'[20] This locus is the site of a constitutive normativity, or of a 'signifying convention', which is independent of any informative function, or of the 'field of exactitude'. Lacan finds it highlighted by the joke he often retells about an exchange between two Polish Jews on a train: 'Why do you tell me you are going to Cracow so I'll believe you are going to Lvov, when you are really going to Cracow?'[21]

Thus, for Lacan it is only possible for a statement to function as a lie *within* an intersubjective relation structured by a normative background assumption that the purpose of language is to tell the truth. Indeed, what Lacan is highlighting here is a fundamental *asymmetry* between truth and falsehood. A falsehood makes an unjustified claim to truth, whereas a true statement does *not* make an unjustified claim to falsehood, but rather a *justified* claim to truth. Thus, there must be a normative convention that the purpose of language is to tell the truth, whereas no such convention is required for the success of a feint or decoy. As Lacan states: 'it is clear that Speech begins only with the passage from pretence to the order of the signifier, and that the signifier requires another locus – the locus of the Other, the Other witness, the witness Other than any of the partners – for the speech that it supports to be capable of lying, that is to say, of presenting itself as Truth.'[22]

Lacan refers to this witness to the truth as the 'Other' ('le grand Autre'), because such a constitutive requirement of human speech cannot be established by means of an empirical convention between speakers of a language. For, in order for such a convention to be established, the truth-telling function of language would already have to be presupposed. Truth telling is not a norm which we impose by *means of* language; rather, it is a 'transcendental' imperative which language imposes upon us. It will thus already be clear how starkly Lacan's position must be demarcated from that of any form of post-Nietzschean genealogical discourse. For, whereas Nietzsche often seeks to portray truth telling as a coercive, empirically established convention – for example, in his early essay 'On truth and lies in an extra-moral sense'[23] – Lacan argues emphatically that 'even when it communicates nothing, discourse represents the existence of communication; even if it denies the evidence, it affirms that speech constitutes truth; even if it is intended to deceive, discourse speculates on the faith in testimony'.[24]

V

The parallels between Lacan's line of argument and the 'discourse theory of truth' which Habermas begins to develop during the 1970s are unmistakable. Both Lacan and Habermas deny that truth can be reduced to a construct which is relative to a particular language-game or form of life. Truth is, rather, a transcendent claim which, as Habermas puts it, 'bursts every provinciality asunder' (PDM 322). At the same time, however, Lacan does not propose anything resembling a 'theory' of truth. He is content merely to appeal to his notion of the 'Other', which he defines as that which 'even my lie invokes as a guarantor of the truth in which it subsists'.[25]

In this respect, Lacan's position could be said to lie between that of Habermas, on the one hand, and that of one of his more sympathetic critics, Albrecht Wellmer, on the other. In his book *Ethik und Dialog*, Wellmer develops a powerful attack on the ethical and cognitive applicability of the notion of an 'ideal speech situation', as Habermas presents it. He seeks to show that such an idealized situation cannot function as a criterion of truth, since no consensus can be defined as rational in a purely formal manner. Assessments of rationality depend on the assessment of the force of arguments, and – even under ideal conditions – the possibility cannot be ruled out that arguments may subsequently come to appear erroneous or unconvincing, unless the exclusion of such a possibility is tautologically built into the *definition* of ideal conditions.[26] The consequence of Wellmer's criticism, however, is that the specific content of the concept of truth begins to evaporate, since – apart from certain formal structures which have the status of necessary, but not sufficient, conditions – rationality itself becomes largely a matter of judgement. As Wellmer writes, explicating his own position: 'The word "judgement" suggests that, for the "mediation of moments of reason", there are only ever solutions which are right – and this also means groundable – here and now. In this context, "irrationality" would be understood as a partial insensitivity for whole domains of experience and dimensions of validity, and thus as an incapacity to relate the various dimensions of experience and validity to each other in an appropriate way.'[27]

Although powerful in its critical aspect, Wellmer's argument is less convincing in its positive proposals. The notions of 'rightness' and 'appropriateness' which he invokes are vague and elusive, apparently exempt from any more ultimate form of assessment. By reducing the 'ideal speech situation' to the status of 'a quasi-transcendental, a dialectical illusion',[28] Wellmer tends also to defuse any sense of the power of truth, as a validity claim, to *irrupt into* and *explode* the contexts of our life and action – to present itself as a problem. Wellmer argues that, by falling prey to the illusion of ultimate truth, we '*forget* the temporal core (*Zeitkern*) of linguistic meanings and linguistically formulable insights'.[29] But he does not suggest that – in a complementary way – an immersion in locality and temporality can lead to a 'forgetting' of the context-transcending dynamic of truth.

It is precisely this imperious feature of truth, however, which Lacan's conception retains: 'One is never happy making way for a new truth, for it always means making our way into it. It demands that we put ourselves out. We cannot cope simply by getting used to it.'[30] Thus, the Lacanian position preserves a strong sense of the claim of truth – a claim so strong that it can engrave itself on our bodies, in the form of the symptom – without assuming that the nature of this claim can be construed in formal terms, such as those of an ideal speech situation. Unlike the post-structuralists, Lacan is far from celebrating the disintegration of the subject, or rejecting entirely the perspective of reconciliation. He writes: 'The end which Freud's discovery proposes to man, was defined by him at the apogee of his thought in moving terms: *Wo es war, soll ich werden*. . . . This aim is one of reintegration and harmony, I would even say of reconciliation (*Versöhnung*).'[31] At the same time, Lacan cannot be accused of relying – as does the young Hegel, on Habermas's account – on 'mythopoetic' means, which fall below the level of modernity, to articulate the ontological pressure of this drive for integrity and reconciliation. Rather, through an account of the language-constitutive normativity of truth, Lacan locates the transcendent force of a dirempted reason in an Other with which neither the position of a finite human subject, nor that of a Hegelian meta-subject, can ever fully coincide. 'The principles of psychoanalysis', he suggests, 'are nothing other than the dialectic of self-consciousness, such as it was realized between Socrates and Hegel, which begins from the ironic supposition that the rational is real, to be precipitated in the scientific judgement that everything which is real is rational. But Freud's discovery was to show that this verifying process (*procès vérifiant*) only authentically attains the subject by decentering him from the self-consciousness in whose axis Hegel's reconstruction of the phenomenology of spirit maintains him.'[32]

VI

The *alternative* account of intersubjectivity which we have discovered in Lacan may now help to focus an enquiry into the status of Habermas's claim that 'a paradigm-change can render objectless those dilemmas in terms of which Foucault explains the fateful dynamics of a subjectivity that is bent on knowledge and falls prey to pseudo-sciences' (PDM 301). For we must conclude either that there exists more than one paradigm of intersubjectivity, or perhaps that there is a variety of possible positions within such a paradigm. The very existence of such a plurality, however it is construed, already sets a question mark over Habermas's use of the term. This is because Habermas – implicitly at least – makes an extremely strong claim for the consequences of the paradigm shift to communication. This is symptomatically indicated by the fact that he refers to the 'philosophy of consciousness' (*Bewußtseinsphilosophie*), or 'philosophy of the subject' (*Subjektphilosophie*), but to the '*theory* of communicative action'.[33] This contrast between 'philosophy' and 'theory' not only seems to imply the possibility of obtaining stable and generally acknowledged results, but exploits two very different conceptions of the end of the 'metaphysics of the subject' embodied in the previous paradigm. On the one hand, the notion of a theory of communication grounded in formal pragmatics evokes overtones of a 'completion' of philosophy, a resolution of its problems through a reflection on the transcendental pre-conditions of all theoretical enquiry, including this very reflection itself, in the tradition of Fichte's *Wissenschaftslehre*. On the other hand, in the form of what Habermas terms 'rational reconstruction', a theory of communication appears to 'dissolve' philosophy in a more positivist sense, replacing it with *empirical* enquiry, or at least an empirically supported enquiry, which is capable of attaining intersubjectively agreed results. Karl-Otto Apel has taken Habermas to task for equivocating between these two conceptions.[34]

But Habermas's argument is further complicated by the fact that the invocation of a shift to a paradigm of communicative reason also inherits the reconciliatory task of the 'realization' of philosophy, or of what Habermas terms the 'desublimation of reason', initiated by the Left Hegelians. According to Habermas, the philosophy of praxis derived from the Left Hegelians and the early Marx sought 'to conceive of rational practice as reason concretized in history, society, body and language' (PDM 317). While the strength of praxis philosophy derived from its understanding of the dialectical relation of meaning and validity – in contrast with the various tendencies of 'linguistic historicism' – it was unable to exploit this advantage because 'with its paradigm of production it screens out of the validity spectrum of reason every dimension except those of truth and efficiency' (PDM 320). The theory of communicative reason corrects this deficiency, since it can 'affirm the internal connection between meaning and validity for the whole reservoir of meaning – not just for the segment of meaning of linguistic expressions that play a role in assertoric and intentional sentences' (PDM 321).

Habermas's conclusion, directed against an idealizing interpretation of communicative reason, is that 'reason is by its very nature incarnated in contexts of communicative action and in structures of the lifeworld' (PDM 322). Consequently, the violation of this reason is a violation of human solidarity, and hypostatized philosophical conceptions of truth and reason, as well as the inverted materialist assault upon them, can be seen as involving an abstraction from the immanent rationality of the lifeworld. In this sense they are symptomatic of the fracturing of human community (cf. PDM 324). It is in this way, one could argue, that Habermas seeks to preserve the Marxian motif of the 'realization' of philosophy. For a Critical Theory of communicative reason detects the reconciliation of identity with non-identity, which eluded the conceptual nets of metaphysics, in successful everyday communication. It does not seek to substitute for such communication, but rather understands its relation to praxis in terms of fostering and expanding its scope.

VII

If these strong claims are to appear convincing, and if the turmoil of post-Nietzschean philosophy is indeed to be analysed in terms of the 'symptoms of exhaustion' of a paradigm, then Habermas must be able to point to the emergence of an alternative tradition organized around a different paradigm, with appreciable achievements already to its credit. For 'symptoms of exhaustion' can be identified only against the background of plausible theoretical alternatives, and Habermas's claim that the philosophers of modernity have repeatedly taken the 'wrong turning' would look quixotic if another model was not – at least in principle – available. To put it another way, Habermas needs to be able to demonstrate historically that the insights of the philosophy of praxis can be successfully transposed to an intersubjective framework, thereby establishing the outline of the new paradigm to which he wishes us to affiliate.

It is arguable that throughout much of Habermas's career, right up to the discussion of Foucault's 'analytic of finitude' (cf. PDM 266–70), it is the work of George Herbert Mead which has functioned as his basic alternative model. Ever since the 1960s, Habermas has considered American pragmatism as 'the third productive reply to Hegel, after Marx and Kierkegaard, as the radical-democratic branch of Young Hegelianism, so to speak' (AS 151). And, in Habermas's view, it is Mead in particular who first outlines a plausible conception of the reconciliation of social and subjective freedom, who salvages this essential motif of classical German philosophy, without re-establishing what he terms 'an idealism which is incompatible with the naturalistic insights of historical materialism' (PDM 321).

Habermas uses the work of Mead in warding off two opposing challenges. On the one hand, as in *On the Logic of the Social Sciences*, the reference to Mead enables Habermas to counter the reductivist challenge of behaviourist theories of language. In his critical discussion of Charles Morris's theory of signs, for example, Habermas argues – explicitly following Mead – that the identity of linguistic meanings cannot consist merely in a *common* reaction to the same stimulus, but rather must consist in a system of reciprocal expectations of behaviour which are achieved through role taking: 'A symbol has the same meaning content for two individuals, when the speaker can anticipate the reaction of the other no less than the latter can the former's anticipation: the identity of meanings is not constituted through similar reactions, determined by an observer, but in the expectation of a reaction, in which the partners in conversation agree, in other words in the intersubjectivity of expectations of behaviour' (LSS 144). At the same time, at a number of other points, Habermas has used Mead to fend off what he takes to be the exorbitant claims of idealist philosophies of subjectivity. A striking example of this occurs at a crucial turning-point in Habermas's major work of social theory, between the end of volume one and the beginning of volume two of *The Theory of Communicative Action*. Just before this point, Habermas has explored the limits and aporias of the tradition of Critical Theory, whose culminating expression he finds in Adorno's *Negative Dialectics*. He diagnoses these aporias – as he will again shortly afterwards in *The Philosophical Discourse of Modernity* – as symptoms of 'the exhaustion of the paradigm of the philosophy of consciousness'. This argument initiates the transition in the book between the assessment of the tradition of the *critique* of rationalization, which passes from Weber, via Lukács, to the Frankfurt school, and the assessment of the traditions in which Habermas finds the communicative theory of self and society which can provide a reliable *basis* for this critique (cf. TCA1 366–99).

In order to effect this transition, however, Habermas must counter the suggestion that a defence of subjectivity as not being reducible to self-assertion could be mounted within the tradition of the philosophy of the subject. It is for this reason that Habermas attacks Dieter Henrich's 'Fichtean' position, at the end of volume one, before moving on to the critical exposition of Mead at the beginning of volume two. Mead's work clearly functions here as the model achievement which is able to lead beyond subject-centred philosophy in *any* form. This is a move which is reiterated in miniature at the end of Habermas's reply to Henrich's polemic, 'What is metaphysics – What is Modernity?'[35] Here Habermas repeats with some insistence that

the initial Fichtean problem [of self-consciousness] is rendered objectless through a paradigm-change. The self of the self-relation which is instituted through the performative adoption by the speaker of the hearer's perspective on him, is not introduced as an object of knowledge, as it is in the relation of reflection, but as a subject which develops itself through participation in linguistic interaction, and which expresses itself through a capacity for speech and action. . . . For Mead there is no individualization (*Individuierung*) without socialization (*Vergesellschaftung*), and no socialization (*Sozialization*) without individualization (*Vereinzelung*). (PT 25–6)

VIII

But what if other interpretations of Mead's achievement were possible? In this case, the force of Habermas's claim that the paradigm shift to communication can overcome the irresolvable problems of the philosophy of consciousness, effecting a replacement of 'philosophy' by 'theory', might be considerably weakened. It might also turn out that Habermas is still freighting the concept of intersubjectivity with a task of reconciliation which it is not fully able to bear. That there can be such alternative interpretations I shall now attempt to show, by demonstrating that – in certain crucial respects – Mead's work anticipates the insights of Lacan no less than it does the arguments of Habermas.

The aspect of Mead's thought which is crucial here is his distinction between the 'I' and the 'me'. Mead employs the term 'me' to describe the socially constructed self, which is established through processes of identification with the reactions of others, and – at the limit – through an identification with the social process as a whole, in the form which he describes as the 'generalized Other'. Throughout his work, however, Mead also insists that this internalized 'me' does not exhaust the being of the self. Rather, the self is constituted by a dialectic between the 'me' and what Mead designates as the 'I', which embodies the pre-reflectively spontaneous, impulsive and creative dimensions of human agency.

In a major early essay, 'The definition of the psychical' (1903), Mead criticizes various contemporary versions of parallelistic and introspectionist psychology, and seeks to provide an account of the specificity of the psychical domain in terms of its function in enabling the organism to adapt to its environment. Mead here presents the 'I' as the correlative of the temporary state of disintegration and flux brought about by the breakdown of habitual expectations about the world and about others. He argues that the specific object of psychology is 'that phase of experience within which we are immediately conscious of conflicting impulses which rob the object of its character as object-stimulus, leaving us insofar in an attitude of subjectivity; but during which a new object-stimulus appears due to the reconstructive activity which is identified with the subject "I" as distinct from the object "me"'.[36] For Mead it is the 'I' which is the creative agent of repatterning, whereas the 'me' is part of the situation to be restructured:

The reference which is made of this state of subjectivity to the presented self is therefore only in the sense of a statement of the conditions under which the new self is to be organized. In the meantime the experience of this psychical phase is not a presentation, but an immediate and direct experience. That is, this is the self in the disintegration and reconstruction of its universe, the self functioning, the point of immediacy which must exist within a mediate process.[37]

It is clear, at least in the context of this essay, that Mead sets more value on the 'I' than the 'me'. He argues that 'There is nothing that has suffered more thorough loss of dignity of content in modern positivistic psychology than the "I"', and goes on to suggest that 'the greatest loss is the constant drain from the "I" to the "me". No sooner is a content of subjectivity made out than it is at once projected into the object world.'[38] By the late 1920s, however, the period of the lectures on which *Mind, Self, and Society* is based, Mead's position had changed in important respects. Most significantly for our present purposes, he no longer considers there to be any immediate access to the 'I'. Rather, Mead suggests, there is an inevitable lag, an unclosable gap, between the 'I' and the 'me'. This is because 'The "I" of this moment is present in the "me" of the next moment. There again I cannot turn around quick enough to catch myself. I become a "me" insofar as I remember what I said. The "I" can be given, however, this functional relationship. It is because of the "I" that we say we are never fully aware of what we are, that we surprise ourselves by our own action.'[39] But despite this change of view concerning the accessibility of the 'I' to consciousness, Mead still preserves his high evaluation of it. He states: 'The possibilities of the "I" belong to that which is actually going on, taking place, and it is in some sense the most fascinating part of our experience. It is there that novelty arises and it is there that our most important values are located. It is the realization in some sense of this self that we are continually seeking.'[40]

No one familiar with the elements of Lacan's thought could fail to be struck by the parallels between Mead's opposition of the 'me' and the 'I' and Lacan's distinction between 'le moi' (the standard French rendering of Freud's 'das Ich') and 'le je' (understood by Lacan as the 'subject of the unconscious'). Lacan develops the line of thought initiated by Freud in his 'On narcissism: an introduction' (1914), in suggesting that – as for Mead – the ego or 'me' is an 'object' constituted through processes of identification. Furthermore, Lacan insists that the distinction between the 'ego' and the 'subject' is not simply a matter of a corrigible limitation of viewpoint. In his second *Seminar* Lacan states:

There's no doubt that the real I is not the ego. But that isn't enough, for one can always fall into thinking that the ego is only a mistake of the I, a partial point of view, the mere becoming aware of which would be sufficient to broaden the perspective. . . . What's important is the inverse, which must always be borne in mind – the ego isn't the I, isn't a mistake in the sense in which classical doctrine considers error to be a partial truth. It is something else – a particular object within the experience of the subject.[41]

For Lacan, as for the later Mead, we can have no cognitive access to the 'je'. Indeed, Lacan describes the elusiveness of the 'je', its constant 'fading' or transmutation into the 'moi', in a manner strikingly reminiscent of Mead. The fact that the latter speaks in terms of taking the attitude of the other towards one's own acts, whereas Lacan writes of the 'signifier' which the subject must take 'on loan from the Other', should not be allowed to obscure the parallel. Thus, in his seminar on *The Four Fundamental Concepts of Psychoanalysis* Lacan states: 'The signifier, being produced in the field of the Other, makes manifest the subject of its signification. But it functions as a signifier only by reducing the subject in question to being no more than a signifier, by petrifying the subject in the same movement in which it calls upon the subject to function, to speak, as subject.'[42] This is not to imply, of course, that the subject or 'je' could preserve its purity by withdrawing from language into a silent freedom. Rather, it is only through the constant process of 'fading' that the subject comes to be: 'Enunciation that denounces itself, statement that renounces itself, ignorance that dissipates itself, opportunity that loses itself, what remains here if not the trace of that which must be, since it can fall from being?'[43]

IX

Habermas's major essay on Mead, 'Individuation through Socialization: On George Herbert Mead's Theory of Subjectivity', not only confirms the status of Mead's thought for Habermas, as the model achievement which introduces the paradigm shift to communication, but has the special interest of directly addressing the issues which have been raised here (PT 149–204). After an ambitious tracing of the problem of individuality throughout the history of Western philosophy, the essay culminates in an extended discussion of Mead, who is presented as having made a definitive contribution to the solution of this problem, following on from the work of Leibniz, Fichte, Humboldt and others. However, Habermas is aware that if Mead is to be presented as the originator of a theoretical paradigm which – for the first time – renders coherent the reconciliatory ideal of 'individuation through socialization', then Mead's account of the relation between the 'I' and the 'me' must be given an interpretation which does not suggest any stubborn element of irreconcilability.

Habermas's initial response is to reverse the relative valorization of 'I' and 'me' which we have found in Mead. 'At first glance', he argues, 'it is counterintuitive that Mead should ascribe these unconscious powers of spontaneous deviation to an "I" rather than to an "Id", as Freud does, while he conceptualizes the self of the practical self-relation, and thus the identity of the person, the consciousness of concrete duties, as the anonymous product of socializing interactions' (PT 181). A little later, Habermas suggests that Mead's distinction between 'I' and 'me' is problematic: 'For the self of the practical self-relation is not the shadow of memory, which clings to a preceding spontaneity, but a will, which only constitutes itself into an "I will" . . . through socialization.' Correspondingly, 'Those aspects of the personality which both withdraw from and make themselves known to [the practical self] as the unconscious, can scarcely lay claim to the title "I", as a subject of responsible action' (PT 181).

It is clear, however, that a very different interpretation of the relation between the 'I' and the 'me' is possible. Ernst Tugendhat, for example, in his book *Selbstbewusstsein und Selbstbestimmung* goes so far as to equate the Meadian 'me' with the concept of '*das Man*' introduced by Heidegger in *Being and Time*, an interpretation which helps to bring out the connections with Lacan's critical account of the 'ego'. Tugendhat suggests that

The 'Me' includes all the normative expectations that the others have of me. It is the projection of expectations which beam out from society on to me. Clearly, Mead chose this expression, because what is meant by it is what I am as an object of social expectations, or – more simply expressed – how I should be, seen from the standpoint of society – both in my roles, and in the rest of my behaviour. Mead comes very close to Heidegger's description of '*das Man*' when he states: 'The "me" is a conventional, habitual individual. It is always there. It has to have those habits, those responses which everybody has.'[44]

Habermas, of course, is fully aware of the fact that Mead often describes the 'me' in terms suggestive of inauthenticity, and indeed of repression: Mead himself states clearly that 'Social control is the expression of the "me" over against the expression of the "I"'.[45] He therefore develops a second, more comprehensive line of argument, in which the validity – if not the valorization – of the distinction between the 'I' and the 'me' is accepted, but only for a society which has not yet attained the ideal of uncoerced mutual recognition. The discrepancy between 'I' and 'me', in other words, should be interpreted as a *historical*, not a *metaphysical*, feature of the self. This discrepancy reflects the fact that, in all human societies which have hitherto existed, autonomy and spontaneity, self-determination and self-realization, have indeed stood in a relation of tension to each other. As Habermas states: 'The "me" designates an identity-formation, which makes possible responsible action, only at the cost of a blind submission to external social controls, which remain external, despite being taken over as roles' (PT 182).

With this acknowledgement, true individuality is displaced into a futural dimension: both the self of autonomy and the self of self-realization are distorted by the present inegalitarian structure of social relations. However, according to Habermas, the 'post-conventional' identity increasingly demanded by the complexity of modern society requires the individual to *anticipate* a context of reciprocal recognition in which autonomy and self-realization can be reconciled. In the moral sphere (of self-determination), 'the anticipation of an idealized form of communication preserves a moment of unconditionality in the discursive procedure of will-formation' (PT 184). Similarly, in the ethical sphere (of self-realization), 'only the relation to a projected form of society makes it possible to take seriously one's own life history as a principle of individualization – to consider it *as if* it were the product of my own responsible decisions' (PT 186). Interestingly, this anticipation involves a reversal of the usual relation between the 'me' and the 'I'. Whereas formerly it was the 'me' which constantly recuperated the spontaneity of the acting 'I', now it is the 'I' which anticipates the future community which will reflect back a new 'me'. As Habermas puts it, developing Mead: 'The anticipatory production of interactive relations to a circle of addressees is now attributed to the "I" itself, and from their perspective it returns to itself and is able to ascertain itself as an autonomous will and as an individuated being.' In this way '[the self] encounters itself as the alter ego of *all* socialized others, and indeed as a free will in moral self-reflexion, and as a sheerly individuated being in existential self-reflection' (PT 187).

It should be noted, however, that there is a crucial ambiguity in Habermas's presentation here. The anticipatory projection of an ideal community by the 'I' makes it possible for me to regard my own life history as a *principle* of individualization: as Habermas states in *The Theory of Communicative Action*, 'To the ideal communication community there corresponds an *ego* identity, *which makes possible self-realization on the basis of autonomous action*' (TCA2 98; cf. 96–111 for another discussion of the issues raised here). However, the anticipation of such a community cannot answer the question of 'who I am'; it cannot furnish me with the *concrete meaning* of my individual existence. This is because the specific meaning of my life can only be unfolded in *actual* interaction with others. In general, Habermas may not have considered this as a difficulty, because of a tendency in his work – pointed out by Tugendhat – to reduce the concern of the person with his or her *qualitative* identity to a question of individuation as such.[46] In *The Theory of*

Communicative Action, however, Habermas himself points out the problem of Mead's fixation on 'the formal traits of individualism in the domain of personality development' (TCA2 108).

Habermas's answer to this problem introduces a new element. He emphasizes that 'ego-identity' depends upon the ability 'to integrate the sequence of, in part disintegrated, in part superseded, identities into a responsibly assumed life-history', but suggests that this assumption involves an 'existential' decision, an 'indissoluble element of arbitrariness', which is not susceptible to criteria of moral rightness (TCA2 109). At the same time, however, Habermas does not stress that such a decision might be susceptible to other validity criteria, such as those of truth. Yet it can scarcely be denied that the question of who I have been, posed in the light of the question of who I wish to be, concerns the true nature of my past motives, my relations with others, my possibilities and so forth, even though the answer to such questions cannot entirely motivate my decision.[47]

The difficulty for Habermas here is that the truth in question is fundamentally elusive, embedded in the performative structure of the intersubjective relations which characterize the lifeworld which the individual inhabits. Even in an 'ideal speech situation' such a performative structure could not be reflexively retrieved, for reasons which Habermas himself has made clear, in his analysis of the 'double structure of speech' (*Doppelstruktur der Rede*). This structure entails that partners in dialogue must 'unite the communication of a content with a metacommunication concerning the sense of application of the communicated content'. But while the content of the meta-communication, or illocutive act, can itself be objectified in a further constative speech act, this speech act in its turn will have an illocutive component which cannot be simultaneously objectified.[48] It is precisely this distinction between communication and meta-communication, however, which is the concern of both Mead and Lacan. Mead distinguishes not only between the 'I' and the 'me', but also between the '"I" of introspection' and 'the "I" that is implied in the fact that one presents himself as a "me". . . . One presents himself as acting towards others – in this presentation he is presented in indirect discourse as the subject of the action and is still an object, – and the subject of this presentation can never appear immediately in conscious experience.'[49] Similarly, Lacan contrasts the 'subject of the statement' (*sujet de l'énoncé*), comparable to the Meadian 'I' which can be 'presented in indirect discourse', with the 'subject' in his psychoanalytic sense, the 'subject of the utterance' (*sujet de l'énonciation*). In both cases, the self which is the locus of the 'ego' or 'me' and the performative self can never coincide definitively, because of a moment of coagulation which is built into (linguistic) self-presentation as such. Thus the duality of the self cannot be considered as a *merely historical* feature, which would be overcome in a hypothetical society founded on fully mutual recognition.

It is perhaps worth noting in this context that Mead does describe some situations in which the 'I' and the 'me' fuse, but his model cases of this 'fusion' are situations of religious or communal exaltation, where immediate absorption in a common project entails that each participant calls forth by his or her action a similar – not just a complementary – action in the other. These are situations in which the individual is effectively 'lost' in the collective.[50] By contrast, in the highly functionally differentiated state which Mead considers society to be advancing towards, as an ultimate goal, the very degree of social differentiation would entail an endless task of mediating the understandings of individuals. Certainly, even though Mead sometimes entertains the (impossibly) idealized conception of a 'universal discourse' in which meanings would be identical for every social member, he never suggests that in such a society the distinction between 'I' and the 'me' would disappear. Indeed, Mead acknowledges that the question of the relation between the 'I' and the 'me' is ultimately a 'metaphysical' question, and accordingly he denies that it is within his competence as a social psychologist to answer it.[51]

X

We must now return to Habermas's central claim, in *The Philosophical Discourse of Modernity*, that the standpoint of communicative reason can resolve the antinomies of *Subjektphilosophie*, which he finds most cogently analysed in Foucault's *The Order of Things*.[52] In Habermas's account, the recentring of philosophy on 'linguistically generated intersubjectivity' enables us to resolve the three fundamental dilemmas identified by Foucault. First, the perpetual doubling of the subject into empirical and transcendental dimensions can be obviated, since adopting the performative attitude of the other towards oneself in communication is not equivalent to the process of reflective self-objectification of an isolated consciousness, and allows for the reconstruction of our implicit knowledge of formal-pragmatic rules. Secondly, the perpetual retreat of the unconscious from the reflective grasp of the *cogito* need no longer present an impasse, since, although the lifeworld as an encompassing context cannot be retrieved as a whole from the standpoint of a participant, its formal infrastructures can be theorized from the standpoint of a theory of communicative action, and this theory can be connected with individual processes of self-reflection. Thirdly, the perpetual retreat into the past, or advance into the future, of the ground of our own self-conscious activity need no longer present us with the unacceptable choice between history as fate, or *Geschick*, or history as the conscious product of the human species, if we view the lifeworld as reproduced though the assessment of the *criticizable* validity claims raised by participants (PDM 297–301, 316–21).

It should be clear by now, however, that these arguments do not automatically secure Habermas's position. To take the last of the three dilemmas first, it seems that the notion of an irreducible internal duality of the self, in both Mead and Lacan, is not vulnerable to Habermas's attack on the characteristic oscillations of post-Hegelian thought between a demiurgic voluntarism and a hypostatization of the world-disclosing power of language (an oscillation which he finds exemplified in recent social philosophy by Castoriadis). This should be uncontentious in the case of Mead, but it is also true of Lacan, despite the widespread, erroneous early reception of his thought as representing a psychoanalytical 'structuralism'.[53] In his second *Seminar*, for example, Lacan is highly critical of objectivist forms of structuralism, such as that of Lévi-Strauss, while at the same time denying that the linguistically sustained social order – in his terminology, the 'Symbolic' – can be reduced to an externalization of subjectivity. For Lacan, the structuralist treatment of language as a 'machine' is an abstraction, since 'Speech is first of all this object of exchange by means of which mutual recognition takes place. . . . The circulation of speech begins thus, and it expands to the point of constituting the world of symbols which permits algebraic calculations. The machine is the structure as if detached from the activity of the subject.'[54] At the same time, Lacan argues that 'it is insofar as he is caught up in a play of symbols, in a symbolic world, that man is a decentred subject'.[55] Thus Lacan's mature thought hinges on a relation between the subject and the Other – the intersubjectively shared system of meanings – which is *dialectical* without being *reciprocal*, since the Other, as the 'treasure of the signifier', always precedes the subject who must find him or herself within it. In *The Four Fundamental Concepts of Psychoanalysis* Lacan states: 'Here the processes are of course to be articulated as circular between the subject and the Other – from the subject called to the Other, to the subject of that which he has himself seen appear in the field of the Other, of the Other returning. This process is circular, but, of its nature, without reciprocity. Because it is circular, it is disymmetrical.'[56]

This alternative conception of a *dialectic* of subjectivity and intersubjectivity, in which what Mead termed the 'generalized Other' always outweighs the individual subject, as it were, also raises questions about Habermas's solution to the two other antinomies of Foucault's 'analytic of finitude'. Habermas is entirely persuasive in his contention that a fundamental problem of the philosophy of consciousness arises from the fact that reflective self-objectification entails alienation, no matter how worthy the aim it seeks to achieve. What is more dubious is his argument that the paradigm of mutual understanding overcomes this difficulty, because to adopt *the attitude* of the other towards oneself, in the course of interaction, is not tantamount to self-objectification. As Habermas puts it: 'As soon as linguistically generated intersubjectivity gains primacy . . . then ego stands within an interpersonal relationship that allows him to relate to himself as a participant in an inter-action from the perspective of alter' (PDM 297). In Mead and Lacan we have discovered two thinkers who strongly suggest that merely to adopt the attitude of the other constitutes a form of objectification, perhaps even alienation, because any such attitude or cluster of attitudes involves a freez-ing of the fluidity of the pre-reflective or 'unconscious' aspect of the self. In both Mead and Lacan, this aspect of the self is not simply an equivalent of the Freudian 'Id', but is simultaneously both pre- and trans-social, both quasi-natural and yet capable of transcending the given, whether natural or social.[57]

The question of the status of the 'unconscious' – which condenses the issues at stake here – is most explicitly addressed in Habermas's response to the second of Foucault's antinomies, that which condemns reflective sub-jectivity to oscillate between the project of total self-explication and the acknowledgement of an opaque ground of thought. Habermas's answer to this difficulty involves a separation between form and content. While indi-viduals, through self-reflection, can achieve insight only into specific distor-tions and illusions, not into the meaning of a life history or form of life as a whole, formal-pragmatic theory can illuminate the general structures of life-worlds, but not their determinate, qualitative features. However, in Haber-mas's view, these 'two heritages of self-reflection which get beyond the limits of the philosophy of consciousness' can subsequently be brought together within a single theoretical framework. Reviving the argument of *Knowledge and Human Interests*, Habermas proposes psychoanalysis as the model for such a theoretical approach (cf. PDM 300).

Of course, Habermas makes no attempt to suggest that, through such a combined theory, the 'unthought', in the form of the implicit, pre-reflective totality of a life history or of a culture, could ever be brought into consciousness – not even psychoanalysis could make such a claim. But this raises the possibility that the separation of form and content which he describes could be interpreted in a different way. It is conceivable that our awareness of the demand for 'ultimate' grounding, of the context-shattering force of validity claims, which is captured in the formal-pragmatic analysis of communication, combined with an acknowledgement of the impossibility of fulfilling this demand, might bring about a conflict within the modern subject as intractable as any which Foucault describes. Certainly, in Lacan's account of modernity, the lack of any shared symbolic world interpretation, to act as a 'buffer' between the particularity of the individual's existence and the absolute standpoint of the Other, generates such conflicts: 'That the question of his existence bathes the subject, supports him, invades him, tears him apart even, is shown in the tensions, the lapses, the phantasies that the analyst encounters; and, it should be added, by means of elements of the particular discourse in which this question is articulated in the Other.'[58]

XI

There are a number of aspects of Habermas's more recent work which could be said to address this difficulty, in more or less explicit ways. It is notable, for example, that he has tried to play down what Apel has termed the 'transcendental difference' revealed by the demand of philosophy for ultimate grounds. Thus, according to Habermas,

The transcendental gap between the intelligible world and the world of appearances no longer needs to be overcome through a philosophy of nature or history; it is softened into a tension, which has shifted into the lifeworld of those engaged in communicative action, between the unconditionality of context-exploding and context-transcending validity-claims, on the one hand, and the facticity of context-dependent, action-relevant Yes/No attitudes on the other, which generate the current social facts. (PT 142)

Yet why should this tension be considered to be diminished when it is interpreted in this form, rather than – say – in the form proposed by Kant? Why should not the 'Janus face' of validity claims, the fact that 'sociocultural forms of life stand under the restrictions of a communicative reason *at once claimed and denied*' (PDM 322, 325) indicate a rent at the heart of modern consciousness, which can neither simply accept the contingent, nor claim the standpoint of a comprehensively rational world interpretation?

One possible response to such a question would be to suggest that self-understanding, as opposed to 'reconstruction', is an *existential*, not a *philosophical*, issue. It is fascinating to observe, therefore, that Habermas does not take this approach. Rather, his dual conception of philosophy as 'placeholder' and 'interpreter' acknowledges that there is an unavoidable hermeneutic task which falls to philosophy in the lives of individuals and cultures. Habermas admits that philosophy would be risking its own identity if it refused all relation to totality, but this totality should now be seen as implicitly embodied in the lifeworld. Philosophy cannot presume to judge the lifeworld, but it can seek to illuminate it for its participants, by acting as a mediator which retrieves for the lifeworld the one-sided achievements of split-off expert cultures.[59] Because there is a 'moment of unconditionality built into the conditions of action oriented towards understanding' (MCCA 19), it is only philosophy – the discipline which continually enquires into the grounds of grounds – which is ultimately able to fulfil this role. One consequence of Habermas's argument, however, is that such interpretive activity, having renounced the construction of an objective 'philosophy of reason', will always remain in some sense bound to the standpoint of the interpreting individual; as opposed to the achievements of formal pragmatics, we can imagine such hermeneutical elucidations only in the *plural*.

In this context it is worth noting the shift of emphasis in Habermas's attitude to religion in his more recent writings. Earlier, Habermas had tended to suggest that, in advanced societies, the content of religious belief was converging tendentially with the social aspiration towards an undamaged intersubjectivity: 'The idea of God is transformed into the concept of a logos, which determines the community of believers, and thereby the real life-context of a self-emancipating society; God becomes the name of a communicative structure which forces human beings, on pain of loss of their humanity, to overstep their contingent human nature by encountering each other *mediately*, in something which is not themselves' (LC 166). Now, however, Habermas lays more stress on the capacity of religious language to convey dimensions of meaning which elude rational explication: 'As long as religious language conveys inspiring, indeed indispensable semantic contents, which (initially?) elude the expressive power of philosophical language, and resist translation into grounding discourses, philosophy – even in its post-metaphysical forms – will be able neither to replace, nor to repress, religion' (PT 51; cf. also 35, 145).

The acknowledgement, albeit tentative, of this split between religion and philosophy, comparable to the split between the hermeneutic and formal tasks of philosophy itself, once again highlights the questionable character of the achievements which Habermas claims will follow from the paradigm shift from consciousness to communication. For it seems to involve an admission that there can be a dimension of personally experienced meaning which cannot be fully captured in intersubjective, discursive terms. In fact, it may be useful, in conclusion, to recall certain features of paradigm shifts as originally described by Thomas Kuhn, from whom Habermas's usage no doubt ultimately derives. Paradigms, in Kuhn's account, never resolve all the problems posed by their predecessors. Indeed, Kuhn states that 'one of the things a scientific community acquires with a paradigm is a criterion for choosing problems that, while the paradigm is taken for granted, can be assumed to have solutions. . . . Other problems, including many that had previously been standard, are rejected as metaphysical, as the concern of another discipline, or sometimes as just too problematic to be worth the time.'[60]

In this essay, I have expressed concern that such a side-stepping of problems occurs in Habermas's account of the paradigm shift from subject-centred to communicative reason. There can be little doubt that such a shift is indeed one of the crucial developments – if not *the* crucial development – in the history of Western philosophy since Hegel.[61] Nor can it be doubted that a failure to acknowledge the fundamental intersubjectivity of structures of language and human understanding can lead to political consequences incompatible with the essential democratic aspirations of modernity. As we saw at the beginning, both Derrida and Foucault have been obliged – at least implicitly – to acknowledge this. But in philosophy there is no unequivocal criterion of progress which would justify leaving certain problems behind as outmoded. Indeed, it is doubtful whether one philosophical paradigm can be regarded as simply *displacing* its predecessor. Perhaps the 'Other' can be conceived in a manner which does not reduce reason to a puppet of elemental forces. And perhaps it would be a more accurate assessment of our contemporary situation to say that the dilemmas of the philosophy of consciousness have not been entirely dissolved. Rather, they have reappeared in an altered form, as a fundamental tension with which our thinking is confronted – the tension *between* subjectivity and intersubjectivity.

Notes

The translations quoted in this chapter have sometimes been altered.

 1 Cf. Christopher Norris, 'Deconstruction, postmodernism and philosophy: Habermas on Derrida', *Praxis International*, 8/2 (Jan. 1989). The unfairness of this reproach is made clear by the following quotation (one amongst many others): 'In philosophy, in the human sciences, the propositional content of statements is even less to be separated from the rhetorical form of their presentation than in physics. And even here theory is not free from metaphors (as Mary Hesse has shown), by means of which new models, new ways of seeing, new approaches to problems must be made plausible (with recourse to the resources of the pre-understanding implicit in everyday language).' Jürgen Habermas, 'Philosophie und Wissenschaft als Literatur?', in ND 242.
 2 Cf. David Couzens Hoy, 'Splitting the difference: Habermas's critique of Derrida', *Praxis International*, 8/2 (Jan. 1989).

3 Cf. John Rajchman, 'Habermas's complaint', *New German Critique*, 45 (Fall 1988).

4 Cf. Fred Dallmayr, 'The discourse of modernity: Hegel, Nietzsche, Heidegger (and Habermas)', *Praxis International*, 8/2 (Jan. 1989), esp. 397–8; and also David Hoy's remark: 'Models of communicative interaction may be intersubjective instead of subjective, but the appeal to many subjects instead of an isolated subject is still an appeal to subjects.' 'Splitting the Difference', p. 461. Habermas's warning occurs in PDM 337.

5 Jacques Derrida, 'The politics of friendship', *Journal of Philosophy*, 85/2 (Nov. 1988), p. 637.

6 Jacques Derrida, 'Afterword: toward an ethic of discussion', in *Limited Inc.*, ed. Gerald Graff (Evanston, Ill.: Northwestern University Press, 1988), pp. 146, 145.

7 Michel Foucault, 'Truth and power', in *Power/Knowledge: Selected Writings and Interviews 1972–77*, ed. Colin Gordon (Brighton: Harvester Press, 1980), pp. 133, 131.

8 Michel Foucault, 'Polemics, politics, and problematizations', in *The Foucault Reader*, ed. Paul Rabinow (Harmondsworth: Penguin, 1986), p. 381. Cf. also Foucault's comment 'But, when I talk about relations of power and games of truth, I do not mean to say that the games of truth are but relations of power that I would want to conceal – that would be a terrible caricature.' 'The ethic of care for the self as a practice of freedom: an interview', in *The Final Foucault*, ed. James Benauaer and David Rasmussen (Cambridge, Mass.: MIT Press, 1988), p. 16.

9 Cf. Jacques Derrida, *Edmund Husserl's 'Origin of Geometry': An Introduction* (Lincoln and London: University of Nebraska Press, 1989), pp. 76–82. *La Voix et le phénomène* (Paris: PUF, 1967), ch. 3, where Derrida remarks, 'Le rapport à l'autre comme non-présence est donc l'impureté de l'expression' (p. 44). Habermas's critical analysis occurs in PDM 167–72.

10 Michel Foucault, *Discipline and Punish* (Harmondsworth: Penguin, 1979), p. 200.

11 The Slovenian philosopher Slavoj Žižek is one of the few contemporary commentators to emphasize with sufficent clarity that Lacan's thought cannot be assimilated to the outlooks of 'post-structuralism' or 'post-modernism'. 'The Lacanian criticism of the autonomous subject and his power of reflection, of reflexive appropriation of his objective condition, is therefore far from any affirmation of some irrational ground escaping the reach of reason.' Slavoj Žižek, *The Sublime Object of Ideology* (London: Verso, 1989), p. 79. Cf. ibid., pp. 153–5, where Žižek develops a powerful critique of Derrida on Lacanian grounds.

12 Jacques Lacan, *Écrits: A Selection* (henceforth ES) (London: Tavistock, 1971), pp. 52, 50; French original, *Écrits* (henceforth E) (Paris: Seuil, 1966), pp. 261, 259.

13 Jacques Lacan, *Le Séminaire Livre I: Les écrits techniques de Freud* (Paris: Seuil, 1975), p. 20.

14 Cf. ES 86/E 299.

15 Lacan, *Le Séminaire Livre I*, p. 242.

16 The metaphor of history as drama – in other words, as *enacted* – and not merely passively undergone, also occurs in Lacan: 'Events are engendered in a primary

historization. In other words, history is already producing itself on the stage where it will be played out, once it has been written down, both within the subject and outside him' (ES 52 / E 261).

17   Cf. ES 84 / E 297.

18   ES 85 / E 298.

19   Cf. ES 172 / E 524–5.

20   ES 173 / E 525.

21   Ibid. Cf. also E 20, where Lacan contrasts 'le champ de l'exactitude' and 'le registre de la vérité'.

22   ES 305 / E 807.

23   'Dieser Friedensschluss bringt aber etwas mit sich, was wie der erste Schritt zur Erlangung jenes räthselhaften Wahrheitstriebes aussieht. Jetzt wird nämlich das fixirt, was von nun an "Wahrheit" sein soll, das heisst es wird eine gleichmässig gültige und verbindliche Bezeichnung der Dinge erfunden und die Gesetzgebung der Sprache giebt auch die ersten Gesetze der Wahrheit: denn es entsteht hier zum ersten Male, der Contrast von Wahrheit und Lüge.' Friedrich Nietzsche, 'Über Wahrheit und Lüge im aussermoralischen Sinne', in *Sämtliche Werke: Kritische Studienausgabe*, ed. Giorgio Colli and Mazzino Motinari, 15 vols (Berlin/New York: de Gruyter, 1980), vol. 1, p. 877.

24   ES 43 / E 251–2. Most commentators on Lacan, even the most sophisticated, tend to interpret the 'Other' simply as the system of social and linguistic conventions which precedes the existence of the individual subject. The status of the Other as transcendental 'warrant' of truth claims is rarely mentioned, despite its prominence in Lacan's own accounts.

25   ES 172 / E 524.

26   Cf. Albrecht Wellmer, *Ethik und Dialog: Elemente des moralischen Urteils bei Kant und der Diskursethik* (Frankfurt am Main: Suhrkamp, 1986), esp. pp. 69–102.

27   Ibid., p. 169.

28   Ibid., p. 83.

29   Ibid.

30   ES 169 / E 521.

31   ES 171 / E 524.

32   ES 79–80 / E 292. Lacan, of course, refers generically to 'truth', and does not – like Habermas – distinguish systematically between the validity claims of 'truth' (*Wahrheit*), 'rightness' (*Richtigkeit*) and 'truthfulness' (*Wahrhaftigkeit*). However, Habermas himself underlines the extent to which these various dimensions of validity are interwoven in argumentation. Once the notion that different types of claims could in principle be grounded independently, through an ideal consensus, is abandoned, then the distinction between validity claims loses some of its philosophical significance.

33   Cf., for example, PDM 316 (my emphasis).

34   Cf. Karl-Otto Apel, 'Normative Begründung der "Kritischen Theorie" durch Rekurs auf lebensweltliche Sittlichkeit?', in *Zwischenbetrachtungen: Im Prozess der Aufklärung*, ed. Axel Honneth et al. (Frankfurt am Main: Suhrkamp, 1989). I am

indebted to Peter Osborne for his helpful classification of conceptions of the end of philosophy into '1. *its completion* (the fulfillment of its *telos:* philosophical knowledge). 2. its *dissolution* (the demonstration that it was, from the outset, an activity without a legitimate object of its own); 3. its *transformation* (into some other, distinctively different form of intellectual activity . . .); 4. its *overcoming* (its practical, historical, *existential* surpassing through the inauguration of a new form of life, epoch or period of historical development.' Peter Osborne, 'Overcoming philosophy as metaphysics: Rorty and Heidegger', *Oxford Literary Review*, 11/1–2 (1989), p. 75.

35 Cf. Dieter Henrich, 'What is metaphysics – What is modernity? Twelve theses against Jürgen Habermas', in this volume, ch. 10.

36 George Herbert Mead, 'The definition of the psychical', in *Selected Writings*, ed. Andrew J. Reek (Indianapolis/New York: Liberal Arts Press, 1964), p. 55.

37 Ibid., pp. 53–4. The parallels between Mead's account of the emergence of the 'I' through a problem-induced (partial) disintegration of the object world and the artificial procedure of doubt followed by Descartes in the *Meditations* are striking.

38 Ibid., p. 47.

39 George Herbert Mead, *Mind, Self, and Society*, ed. Charles W. Morris (Chicago/London: University of Chicago Press, 1934), p. 174.

40 Ibid., p. 204.

41 Jacques Lacan, *Le Séminaire Livre II: Le moi dans la théorie de Freud et dans la technique de la psychanalyse* (Paris: Seuil, 1978), p. 60.

42 Jacques Lacan, *Le Séminaire Livre XI: Les quatre concepts fondamentaux de la psychanalyse* (Paris: Seuil, 1973), pp. 188–9.

43 ES 300 / E 801.

44 Ernst Tugendhat, *Selbstbewusstsein und Selbstbestimmung* (Frankfurt am Main: Suhrkamp, 1979), pp. 278–9. The quotation is from *Mind, Self, and Society*, p. 197.

45 Mead, *Mind, Self, and Society*, p. 210.

46 Cf. Tugendhat, *Selbstbewusstsein und Selbstbestimmung*, pp. 282–91.

47 Cf. ibid., pp. 239–43, 293–6.

48 Cf. Jürgen Habermas, 'Was heisst Universalpragmatik?', in *Sprachpragmatik und Philosophie*, ed. Karl-Otto Apel (Frankfurt am Main: Suhrkamp, 1982), pp. 22ff.

49 George Herbert Mead, 'The Social Self', in *Selected Writings*, p. 144.

50 Cf. Mead, *Mind, Self, and Society*, pp. 273–81.

51 Ibid., p. 332.

52 Cf. Michel Foucault, *Les Mots et les Choses* (Paris: Gallimard, 1966), ch. 9 (*The Order of Things*, London: Tavistock, 1970, ch. 9).

53 The role of Foucault in encouraging this widespread misapprehension of Lacan's thought should be noted. For example: 'The importance of Lacan derives from the fact that he has shown how – via the discourse of the illness and the symptoms of the neurosis – it is the structures, the system of language itself – and not the subject – which speaks.' Michel Foucault, 'Interview', *La Quinzaine littéraire*, 1–5 May 1966.

54 Lacan, *Le Séminaire Livre II*, p. 63.

55 Ibid., p. 63. These quotations make clear how misleading is Habermas's suggestion that, for Lacan, 'Individuality and creativity of the subject capable of speech
and action, everything which can be attributed to subjectivity as its possession,
are considered as leftovers, which are either neglected or devalued as narcissistic symptoms' (PT 47). Rather, for Lacan, it is precisely the individuality of the
subject which can never be entirely compressed into the reflective ('narcissistic')
structure of the ego.

56 Lacan, *Le Séminaire Livre XI*, p. 188.

57 Thus Mead writes that '[t]he "I" is the transcendental self of Kant, the soul that
James conceived behind the scene holding onto the skirts of an idea to give it
an added increment of emphasis.' 'The mechanism of social consciousness', in
Selected Writings, p. 141. Similarly, Lacan speaks of 'a subject within the subject,
transcendent to the subject' (E 437).

58 ES 194 / E 549.

59 Cf. Jürgen Habermas, 'Philosophy as stand-in and interpreter', in MCCA 18–19.

60 Thomas Kuhn, *The Structure of Scientific Revolutions* (Chicago/London: University of Chicago Press, 1962), p. 37.

61 Vittorio Hösle, *Hegels System* (Hamburg: Felix Meiner, 1987), is highly instructive in this respect.

4

Heidegger's challenge and the future of Critical Theory

Nikolas Kompridis

I Introduction

It is difficult to understand the nature and purpose of Jürgen Habermas's philosophical project unless one sees that it is motivated by the question of how we can self-critically renew our traditions. This question is at work in Habermas's lifelong attempt to bring about a 'new beginning' in Germany's political culture by realigning elements of the German cultural heritage with the liberal-democratic traditions of the West.[1] It also informs his engagement with the less local problem of sustaining the project of modernity and his advocacy of a paradigm change from the 'philosophy of the subject' to the model of linguistic intersubjectivity. Although it is not a philosophical question in the narrow sense, the issue of how we can reflectively renew our traditions is entwined with that other question at the heart of Habermas's enterprise: the question of what reason ought to mean. In what follows, aspects of both questions will be addressed.

The urgency and inescapability of the problem of self-consciously renewing our traditions is a function of what Habermas calls modernity's 'time-consciousness' (PDM 4). This term is used to account for a peculiarly modern historical orientation to the 'novelty of the future' (PDM 5). It is an orientation that keeps perpetually open the promise of a future different from the past – the promise of a break with the past and the promise of a new beginning. An unavoidable consequence of this future-oriented stance is that the present will be subject to historical crises which arise from the disorienting collision of old and new: the more open we are to discontinuity – the more open, that is, to the possibility of beginning anew – the more we will have to wrestle with the problem of continuity. Thus, on each occasion in which modernity's time consciousness intensifies, we are pressed into evaluations and decisions concerning 'the proportion of continuity and discontinuity in the forms of life we pass on' (NC 263).

A further feature of modernity's time consciousness is the way in which the future functions as a source of pressure brought to bear on unsolved problems, on unrealized or unnoticed possibilities. Our open stance towards the future not only places possibility (ontologically) higher than actuality,[2] and thereby renders our traditions permanently vulnerable; it also places an almost unbearable sense of responsibility upon the present. If we are to respond authentically to our consciousness of historical time, we are compelled to take the ethical perspective of a historically accountable 'future present'. From this projected ethical perspective we come to recognize the past as the pre-history of the present, to which the present is connected 'as by the chain of a continual destiny' (PDM 14). Within this reinterpreted historical horizon we bear a special responsibility: we are the ones who must self-consciously renew and correct our forms of life, who must repair what is broken, or break with what seems irreparable. We are the ones who must remake our languages and practices, and make something new out of something old.

I have tried to make explicit the normative implications of Habermas's picture of the reflective renewal of traditions because I want to use it to evaluate the stand which Habermas himself has taken towards one of his own cultural resources – the German philosophical tradition which goes back to Kant and Hegel, and especially that part of it which goes by the name of 'Critical Theory'. The problem of renewing the German philosophical tradition can hardly be taken lightly by someone with Habermas's concerns and outlook, and he has treated it as conscientiously and responsibly as could be expected of anyone. As the principal custodian of Frankfurt School Critical Theory, Habermas has endeavoured to place its insights in the service of reforming the legal and political institutions of liberal democracies. As a rule, Habermas has tried to rescue the Enlightenment elements of the German philosophical tradition, reformulating them in radically democratic terms.

Some elements lend themselves to such reformulation with little, if any, resistance – for example, Habermas's reformulation of Kant's categorical imperative and Hegel's concept of recognition in his theory of moral discourse. But there are all too many elements within the German tradition, it would seem, which strongly resist, if not altogether preclude, reformulation in radically democratic terms – for example, much of what is considered

original in Nietzsche and Heidegger. Therefore, Habermas has understandably erred on the side of caution in just what and just how much of the
German tradition he regards as appropriable. Those ideas, attitudes and presuppositions within the philosophical and related cultural traditions 'that
served to make us blind to the Nazi regime' need a 'critical, indeed, distrustful appropriation'.[3] In so far as Nietzsche and Heidegger are taken to be
the most influential representatives of counter-Enlightenment positions
within the German tradition, a 'critical, indeed, distrustful appropriation' must
always, it appears, govern our relation to their work.

Now, as Habermas himself would be the first to point out, the critical,
even distrustful, appropriation of traditions must itself be re-evaluated, and
when necessary, corrected in light of new, less one-sided or distorted interpretations. In my view, just such a re-evaluation of the German philosophical tradition must now be undertaken when we address the question of the
identity and future of Critical Theory.[4] I believe that what Adorno said about
art in the opening sentences of *Aesthetic Theory* may justifiably be said about
Critical Theory today: it goes without saying that nothing that concerns
Critical Theory goes without saying, let alone without thinking. For all that
it has to recommend it, Habermas's paradigm change has produced a split
between new and old Critical Theory so deep that the identity and future
of Critical Theory are at risk. And that is because the normative gain resulting from the paradigm change to linguistic intersubjectivity is bound up with
interpretations of Critical Theory's sources which have needlessly devalued
and misrepresented their theoretical and critical potential. It is not so much
that these interpretations go undisputed, even when they have acquired the
character of orthodox doctrine; rather, it is that they tend to define the terms
of the dispute within Critical Theory. As I will endeavour to show, they serve
to block off Critical Theory from its own sources in the German tradition.
It is my thesis that the model of Critical Theory which Habermas's paradigm
change has brought about is in need of urgent reassessment if Critical Theory
is to have a future worthy of its past – up to and including the enormously
important work of Habermas himself. The identity and future of Critical
Theory have to be secured under interpretations of its sources in the German
philosophical tradition different from those which have shaped its current
self-understanding. To accept the current interpretations is to risk rendering
oneself insensible to just how much has been lost or given up as theoretically and historically *passé*.

Indeed, for all its theoretical and practical promise, Habermas's paradigm
is beset by intractable problems of its own. Habermas is not unaware of these
problems, but no matter how much theoretical ingenuity he brings to the
task of reconciling them within the terms of his theory, it seems that it is all

in vain: so long as the basic concepts of the theory of communicative action remain unchanged, these problems turn into corrosive agents undermining his paradigm from within. The problems are not only theoretical; they are existential. For they are intertwined with the identity of Critical Theory, and with the meaning and value of the German philosophical tradition. Let me list them briefly:

(1)   Habermas's forceful interpretations of the German tradition from Hegel to Adorno have the advantage of exposing some genuine weaknesses, but the worrisome disadvantage of covering over and inhibiting the renewal of the tradition's critical and theoretical resources – this is particularly true of the tradition from Nietzsche to Heidegger and Adorno.[5] Habermas's propensity to reduce this tradition to 'negative metaphysics', 'aestheticism' and 'irrationalism' brings his position uncomfortably close to Richard Rorty's – namely, that this tradition has no public value, only a private value to those interested in 'self-creation'.

(2)   The shift of paradigm to linguistic intersubjectivity has been accompanied by a dramatic change in Critical Theory's identity. The priority given to questions of justice and the normative order of society has remodelled Critical Theory in the image of liberal theories of justice. While this has produced an important variant of liberal theories of justice, it has severely weakened the identity of Critical Theory and inadvertently initiated its premature dissolution.

(3)   The loss of identity is accelerated by Habermas's current conception of philosophy, which largely restricts the role of philosophy to designing procedures for determining the validity of generalizable, collectively binding norms. By turning Critical Theory into a form of normative theory, he has succeeded in bringing it into the philosophical mainstream – into the normal, international 'business of science'. But there is a price to be paid for turning Critical Theory into a 'normal science': namely, abandoning modernity's time consciousness (for which the fallibilistic consciousness of the sciences is no substitute). Without a constitutive relation to modernity's time consciousness, without an openness to historical experience and without support of the semantic resources of tradition, Critical Theory *qua* normative theory undermines itself.

(4)   By assimilating the liberal position of neutrality towards the good, Habermas's reformulated model of Critical Theory must refrain from critically evaluating and normatively ranking 'totalities, forms of life and cultures, life-contexts and epochs as a whole' (TCA2 383), for such evaluations can make claims to validity only within the traditions, forms of life, etc. from which they issue. Once modernity's time consciousness is abandoned,

and once appeal to ideas of the good is proscribed, Critical Theory effectively blocks itself off from access to the extraordinary, to utopian energies and to its own romantic self-understanding.

(5) Closer inspection shows that the talk of paradigm change is in need of stronger justification than Habermas has provided. On the one hand, Habermas has ignored or denied what his paradigm shares with competing but unacknowledged paradigms of intersubjectivity; on the other hand, he has failed to grant sufficient incommensurability between the issues defining his communicative paradigm and those of the so-called philosophy of the subject. It is no surprise, then, that the shift to the paradigm of linguistic intersubjectivity leaves unaddressed (if not unacknowledged) the problems of normative and cultural change central to the German tradition from Hegel to Heidegger and Adorno.

(6) The most important goal of Habermas's model of communicative rationality is to provide a comprehensive picture of reason that is not vulnerable to the familiar deconstructive critiques of modern reason. Because it is incarnated in mutual understanding in language, in practices of reciprocal recognition, and because it operates with a wider conception of reason, communicative rationality is supposed not to produce an 'other' of reason through what it objectifies, excludes and represses. None the less, communicative rationality produces its own 'other' of reason, because it denies a transformative role for reason, a role it can't help but deny so long as it is narrowly framed in procedural terms.

All these problems coalesce in the Heideggerian problematic of world disclosure, and as the title of my essay suggests, I consider this problematic to represent the most important challenge to Habermas's paradigm. I am also of the view that, if properly understood, this problematic points to less narrow, more capacious conceptions of reason, critique and philosophy than Habermas has been able to supply. That world disclosure is a theme which is itself entangled in the political and moral implications of the thought of Martin Heidegger poses yet another kind of challenge to those who seek to renew Critical Theory through a reinterpretation of the German philosophical tradition.

II World Disclosure in Heidegger

Heidegger's various analyses of the phenomenon of world disclosure – of *In-der-Welt-Sein*, *Lichtung*, *Gestell* and *Ereignis* – represent his central contribution to twentieth-century philosophy. Through these analyses Heidegger developed an original critique of, and an original alternative to, the representationalist epistemology and the naturalistic ontologies of modern philosophy.[6] He marshalled important new arguments (both transcendental and hermeneutic) against mentalistic accounts of intentionality, against views of agency as disembodied and disengaged, and against 'de-worlded' conceptions of objectivity and truth. In *Being and Time* and in *The Basic Problems of Phenomenology*, Heidegger argued that, prior to confronting the world as though it were first and foremost a set of physical objects, or as though it were identical with nature, prior to establishing explicit epistemic relations to the world 'out there', we operate 'always already' with a pre-reflective, holistically structured and grammatically regulated understanding of the world. (So our theoretical understanding of the world always refers back to, as much as it draws upon, a concerned practical involvement with what we encounter in the world.) The notion of world disclosure refers, in part, to this ontological pre-understanding – or understanding of 'being'. Heidegger's investigation of conditions of intelligibility – of how something can show up 'as something' in the first place – took up the radical mode of questioning initiated by Kant's transcendental deduction, but cut much deeper than the epistemologically curtailed and monologically framed question of the conditions of possible experience. One of the hugely important conclusions of his investigation is that if there is to be any understanding of something *as* something at all, 'understanding must itself somehow *see as disclosed, that upon which it projects*'.[7]

The early Heidegger's 'existential analytic' further reveals a reciprocal relation, an interdependence, between world and *Dasein* (human being), between world understanding and self-understanding. *Dasein* is, only in so far as it is in a world; world (not nature!) is, only in so far as *Dasein* exists.[8] In one sense, then, the world is pre-reflectively disclosed to us; yet, in another, the world is disclosed through us: it is we who make its disclosure possible. Disclosure involves both receptivity and activity, both openness to, and engagement with, what is disclosed. And what is disclosed may concern the background structures or conditions of intelligibility necessary to any world or self-understanding – what Heidegger called 'Existenzialien' – or it may concern the ways in which our ontological pre-understanding (let's call it 'first-order' or 'primary disclosure') is opened up and transformed through novel interpretations and cultural practices (let's call them 'second-order' or 'meta-disclosures').

In his later philosophy, Heidegger's account of world disclosure takes a 'linguistic turn', but this turn is made in an ontological rather than a semantic-logical direction. Breaking with the conception of language in *Being and*

Time, where language (*Rede*) opens up or uncovers in a different light something which has already been disclosed independently of language (through concerned involvement with what we encounter in the world), the later Heidegger attributes to language a 'primordial' (*ursprünglich*) world-disclosing function.[9] It is language which first reveals the horizons of meaning in terms of which we make sense of ourselves and the world. Although the notion of linguistic world disclosure has been traced back to Herder's and Humboldt's theories of language, and is certainly implicit in Nietzsche, the challenge contained in this notion is first formulated in its most original and radical terms by Heidegger. Heidegger not only 'linguistifies' disclosure, he historicizes it as well, making possible accounts of the formation and transformation of historical epochs by tracking changes in ontologies (changes in the 'understanding of being').

Much of what is at issue between Habermas and Heidegger, between Habermas and all those who make use of this notion for various critical projects, concerns the ramifications of this later construal of disclosure. Habermas claims that Heidegger and those influenced by him absolutize linguistic world disclosure, robbing human agents of their critical and reflective capacities. He argues that appeal to this notion in order to describe and explain processes of semantic and cultural change involves, among other things, devaluing reason, devaluing the problem-solving and action-co-ordinating functions of language, devaluing everyday practice and devaluing philosophy. And he argues that the appeal of this notion consists in its capacity to provide the sceptical critics of modern reason with a fatalistic or ecstatic 'refuge in something wholly Other' (PT 8). Before I engage directly in analysis and critique of Habermas's response to the challenge of world disclosure, I want first to examine Habermas's claims concerning the internal connections between Heidegger's philosophy and his politics, not in order to go over what is now rather familiar ground, but because implicit in these claims is a political critique of world disclosure that must be addressed. I argue that this critique fails, and fails for reasons which confirm the depth of the problems identified in my six points above.

III Heidegger's Lack: Intersubjective Accountability

In two more or less complementary accounts written in the 1980s, Habermas attempted to uncover the links between Heidegger's philosophy and his stubbornly unrepentant engagement with National Socialism. The first of these appeared in the chapter on Heidegger in *The Philosophical Discourse of Modernity*, the second in the essay 'Work and *Weltanschauung*'. In each of these accounts, Habermas postulates an internal connection between Heidegger's philosophy and his politics. In *The Philosophical Discourse of Modernity*, Habermas argues that the categories of *Being and Time* were rendered fit for duty in the service of National-Socialist revolution simply by a displacing of the accent from their essentially individualistic orientation to a collectivistic one. The empirical support for this claim appears to be quite strong, for that is just what Heidegger did in his political writings of the 1930s. *Dasein*'s own ability to be or not to be itself was given a national-revolutionary reading whereby its horizon of possibilities shifted from the perspective of the first-person singular to that of the first-person plural – from the I to the we. 'Dasein was no longer this poor Kierkegaardian-Sartrean individual hanging in the air, in *Sorge* . . . now Dasein was the Dasein of the people, of the Volk.'[10] To provide further support for this connection, Habermas argues that the transition between Heidegger's early and later philosophy cannot be explained properly as an internally motivated development; rather, it was externally – that is, politically – motivated by Heidegger's much belated realization that National Socialism was not the solution to the problem of nihilism, only its most recent and most extreme symptom. It was this disillusionment with fascism, then, that prompted the transition from the activist impulses of the early philosophy to the fatalism of the late philosophy – from *Being and Time*'s assertive 'decisionism of empty resoluteness' to the 'submissiveness of an equally empty readiness for subjugation' (PDM 141).[11]

In 'Work and *Weltanschauung*', Habermas argues that Heidegger's philosophical thinking assimilated the ideologically tainted *Weltanschauung* of the German mandarins. The mandarin *Weltanschauung*, the subject of a well-known study by the historian Fritz Ringer, consisted of a cluster of ideological motifs that defined a pervasive intellectual and academic mentality which flourished in Germany (and in Europe) in the late nineteenth and early twentieth century: anti-modern, anti-democratic and elitist, it typically expressed itself in a shrill critique of 'mass civilization'. Heidegger appropriated this 'scientifically unfiltered diagnosis of crisis' into his philosophical reconstruction of the historical significance of the present (WW 194). For all the unprecedented and undeniable originality of *Being and Time*, there is no denying, claims Habermas, the 'connections between the mandarin consciousness of the German professor Martin Heidegger and certain limitations from which the argumentation of *Being and Time* cannot free itself' (WW 191). One such limitation shows up in the analysis of *das Man* – the 'one', the 'they', the 'anybody'.[12] According to Habermas, the connection between *Weltanschauung* and work is particularly transparent in this analysis: the mandarin critique of mass civilization and its elitist contempt for the everyday (the communicative infrastructure of the lifeworld) entwines itself with the monological, individualistic (ultimately, solipsistic) premisses of *Being and Time* – premisses from which it is impossible to arrive at the insight that individualization and socialization go hand in hand (PDM 149).

However, the putative links between Heidegger's philosophy and politics that Habermas claims to have established rest on highly debatable, ultimately unpersuasive, interpretations of Heidegger's early and late philosophy. The 'internal' connection postulated in *The Philosophical Discourse of Modernity* supposes the accuracy of Habermas's portrayal of *Being and Time* as a work that is indeed mired in the premisses of the philosophy of consciousness. For all its original insights, the scope of the undertaking is supposedly constrained from within by a methodological solipsism which Heidegger picked up from Husserlian phenomenology and never relinquished. Although I do not have the space to argue for my claim in detail, this interpretation is at best a misreading of *Being and Time*, and at worst, simply inaccurate. And it is strikingly out of tune with the views of significant Heidegger interpreters like Hubert Dreyfus and Charles Taylor, among others, who have refuted persuasively the subjectivistic/monological reading of *Being and Time*.

The arguments of the chapter on Heidegger in *The Philosophical Discourse of Modernity* are based – like so much else in that book – on a very sharp (and often forced) contrast between, on the one hand, purportedly failed attempts to break out of the subject-centred paradigm of modern philosophy and, on the other, Habermas's paradigm of linguistic intersubjectivity. But in the case of Heidegger (as in the clearer case of Hegel), this contrast depends on treating differences between distinct paradigms of intersubjectivity as differences between subject-centred and intersubjective paradigms. Habermas's model of intersubjectivity does not exhaust the possible forms of intersubjectivity.[13] In any case, the salient differences between Heidegger's undertaking in *Being and Time* and Habermas's project do not turn on the difference between subject-centredness and intersubjectivity: 'So far as Dasein is at all, it has being-with one-another as its kind of being' (BT 163 / SZ 125).

Both Habermas and Heidegger are offering paradigms of intersubjectivity, but they focus on different binding media: Heidegger focuses on semantic media, on how something comes to be mutually intelligible; Habermas on justificatory media, on how something comes to be mutually acceptable. At the centre of Heidegger's paradigm of intersubjectivity is the semantic and ontological notion of world disclosure; at the centre of Habermas's is the epistemic and moral notion of non-local justification. A second crucial difference concerns their respective construals of the relation between intersubjectivity and the availability of an objective world shared in common. Whereas for Habermas the world is opened up through relations of intersubjectivity, for Heidegger, relations of intersubjectivity presuppose, rather than bring about, an objective world shared in common.[14] None the less, both Heidegger and Habermas understand themselves to be responding to modern forms of scepticism that issue from the assumptions of the philosophy of consciousness. Heidegger is primarily worried about the threat to the integrity and wholeness (or 'health') of our social practices posed by nihilism – by the disintegration of meaning and the loss of orientation – and so he is preoccupied with the preservation, renewal and creation of intersubjectively binding meaning. Habermas is primarily worried about the threat posed by relativism and contextualism to a universalistic conception of justice – and so he is preoccupied with the context-transcending validity of intersubjectively binding norms. Thus, the third crucial difference between their two paradigms of intersubjectivity concerns the relation of meaning to validity: is this a relation of symmetrical interdependence, or does one have priority over the other? In *The Philosophical Discourse of Modernity*, Habermas argues as though he were committed to the reciprocal interdependence of meaning and validity; but, as I will later show, he is not committed to defending this view outside the context of his book-length dispute with Heidegger and other world-disclosure theorists. He is committed to defending the priority of validity to meaning (truth before disclosure) against the priority of meaning to validity (disclosure before truth): any change of commitment would entail extensive alteration of the basic concepts of the theory of communicative action which suppose as much as they reinforce this priority.

In my view, Habermas has wasted much of his critical energy driving Heidegger's undertaking forcefully, but inaccurately, into the aporias of the philosophy of consciousness: the aporias of Heidegger's thought are not those of the philosophy of consciousness. A more fruitful encounter between Habermas and Heidegger would have to explore the advantages and disadvantages of their respective paradigms of intersubjectivity, paradigms whose respective drawbacks could be corrected through mutual enlargement. If he had treated Heidegger as a proponent of an alternative paradigm of intersubjectivity, Habermas's attempt to probe the shortcomings of Heidegger's early and late philosophy would have yielded more persuasive critical results. He could have argued more effectively in support of his claims concerning the moral and political shortcomings of Heidegger's philosophy if he had identified the most glaring weakness of Heidegger's approach not as the lack of a properly intersubjective starting-point, but as the lack of a sufficiently developed account of intersubjective *accountability* and *recognition*.

Although Heidegger did not entirely neglect the ethical relation between self and other, he paid far too little attention to it. As a result, the ethical dimension of self/other relations remained in a primitive state throughout the changing course of his thought. One can find traces of what might have been in various texts – for example, the discussion intertwining care (*Sorge*) and solicitude (*Fürsorge*) in the first division of *Being and Time*. Here, he draws a contrast between the two extreme possibilities of positive solicitude:

It can as it were, take away 'care' from the other and put itself in his position in concern: it can supplant him (*für ihn einspringen*). This kind of solicitude takes over for the other that with which he is to concern himself . . . In such solicitude the other can become one who is dominated and dependent, even when this domination (*Herrschaft*) is a tacit one and remains hidden from him . . . In contrast to this, there is also the possibility of a kind of solicitude which does not supplant the other, but clears the way for him (*ihm vorausspringt*) in his existentiell ability-to-be, not in order to take away his 'care' but rather to give it back to him authentically as such for the first time . . . it helps the other to become perspicuous (*durchsichtig*) to himself in his care and to become free for it. (BT 158–9 (trs. amended) / SZ 122)

This passage, with its resonances of the dialectic of slavery and domination from Hegel's *Phenomenology*, represents one of those altogether rare occasions on which Heidegger actually contributes insightfully to enlarging our understanding of how our freedom for self-determination – authenticity (*Eigentlichkeit*) in Heidegger's vocabulary – is both dependent upon and facilitated by others.[15] For once in *Being and Time*, the other is not simply an ontologically ineliminable feature of intersubjective structures of intelligibility, of a world which becomes accessible in the first place only in so far as it is a shared world; rather, the other is he or she through whom I learn to realize my freedom, and to whom I am accountable. I can clear the way for the realization of the other's freedom, or I can get in the way; we can learn from each other, or we can fail to learn – in which case we will fail to realize our freedom. But we can only learn from each other when we come to see that mutual recognition and accountability are essential pre-conditions of freedom.

Unfortunately, Heidegger stranded this important insight in the first division of *Being and Time*, and thereby undermined the development of his conception of authenticity in terms of the notion of resoluteness (*Entschlossenheit*). When the meaning of resoluteness is developed in the second division, it is developed not on the model of the relationship between self and other, but exclusively on the model of one's relationship to oneself. The whole construction of resoluteness suffers from this regressive step: each individual *Dasein* must get into the proper relation to itself before it can clear the way for others, before it can become the 'conscience' of others.[16] Consequently, Heidegger cannot win back that ethical dimension of self/other relations essential to freedom.

Heidegger's account of authenticity is certainly one-sided and flawed; but there is something very wrong with the widespread habit of treating every attempt to give normative content to one's relation to oneself as inescapably subjectivistic. Heidegger set out to provide a non-subjectivistic understanding of one's relation to oneself, and thereby to make up for the lack of attention which this relation has received in modern philosophy in spite of (or because of) its subject-centred orientation. The ideal of authenticity articulated in *Being and Time* succeeded partially, if unintentionally, in making explicit the ethical relation to oneself that is the correlate of the moral ideal of autonomy. In this respect – contrary to his own self-understanding – Heidegger did not radically deviate from, so much as enlarge, the Kantian and Hegelian accounts of freedom as self-determination – that is, of positive freedom.

Furthermore, the category of resoluteness is not reducible to a decision procedure, be it arbitrary or not, because resoluteness is a mode of disclosure. More precisely, it is a mode of second-order or meta-disclosure related to and embedded in first-order or primary modes of disclosure, all of which suppose or demand openness and receptivity.[17] Resoluteness involves receptivity to the 'call of conscience', and as such it requires not only openness to, but an active engagement with, what is to be disclosed – in this case, it calls for an active appropriation of one's own ability-to-be (*Selbstseinkönnen*). Neither the active nor the receptive aspects of disclosure are at the disposal of our will: there is nothing *willkürlich* about it. This is as true of the early as it is of the later construal of world disclosure. There can be no disclosure without *Dasein*; on the other hand, neither primary nor meta-disclosure is at the beck and call of *Dasein*. Charles Taylor captures nicely the non-subjectivistic, non-instrumental character of Heidegger's understanding of disclosure: it is *Dasein*-related, but not *Dasein*-centred or *Dasein*-controlled.[18] There is really very little textual evidence in the writings from the period of *Being and Time* to support Habermas's claim that *Dasein* takes over the world-constituting activity of transcendental subjectivity – he could only come to such a conclusion on the basis of a fundamental misunderstanding of the phenomenon of world disclosure.

Habermas's depiction of resoluteness as the 'decisionism of self-assertive Dasein' (WW 198) is another instance of this misunderstanding.[19] By treating resoluteness as a decision procedure, he evinces the degree to which he has missed the receptive aspect of this mode of disclosure and misdescribed its volitional/active aspect. He has been deeply misled by a Sartrean reading of Heidegger that forces the volitional aspect of resoluteness into the decisionistic framework of Sartre's brand of existentialism.[20] Resoluteness certainly involves choosing oneself in light of one's own possibilities. But self-choice doesn't have the subjectivistic meaning that Habermas imposes upon it. As Kierkegaard already showed in the second half of *Either/Or*, self-choice is no arbitrary affair – it takes place within a moral horizon, a horizon within which one self-consciously assumes responsibility for one's life history. Likewise for Heidegger, self-choice can occur only within a horizon (albeit, a morally ambiguous horizon) of significance, a horizon within which *Dasein* is 'always already'. Decisionism and subjectivism suppose precisely what Heidegger's notion of world disclosure denies and seeks to surpass: the idea that meaning and value are instrumental, that they are a function of our will.

Habermas is right to claim that there is a connection between *Being and Time* and Heidegger's political writings of the 1930s. But the connection is much more external than internal. *Being and Time* does not translate as easily into the simplistic, overwrought language of national revolution as Habermas claims, or in the way that Habermas claims. Heidegger could not put to use the categories and analyses of *Being and Time* towards the goal of National-Socialist revolution without violating their normative integrity – without instrumentalizing their meaning. Although well aware of the lengths to which Heidegger would go to manipulate and coerce his thought, in order to bring it into conformity with his self-image, Habermas does not seem to see this very same, apparently inexhaustible personal capacity at work in bringing Heidegger's thought into conformity with his political goals. As a result, the degree to which *Being and Time* resists both its author's manipulations and the goals of National Socialism is drastically underestimated.

Determining the degree to which Heidegger's texts resist their political misuse is of some importance to the question of renewing the critical potential of the German philosophical tradition. It is important to see that the texts possess critical potential *vis-à-vis* Heidegger's life and politics, *vis-à-vis* the instrumental relation he took up towards them. And it is important to see that the 'ethics of authenticity' sketched out in *Being and Time* is not compatible with just any moral and political institutions – that it is not as equally at home in fascism as in a liberal democracy. There is no evidence that the ideal of freedom as self-determination at issue in *Being and Time* is incompatible with the principle of equal respect for all; indeed, it must suppose equal respect for all. For all its deficiencies, Heidegger's ethics none the less expresses an ideal of freedom as self-determination which can be realized (once again, contrary to Heidegger's own self-understanding) only under conditions of liberal democracy; at the same time, such an ethics of authenticity properly developed would contribute to fostering the conditions necessary for a radicalization of democratic forms of life.

Thus far, I have tried to put into question Habermas's subjectivistic and decisionistic interpretation of early Heidegger. If the basic thrust of my analysis is right, it also puts into question Habermas's political explanation for the transition between early and late Heidegger. One can understand Habermas's wish to undermine Heidegger's highly exaggerated (and morally evasive) claims regarding the continuity of his thought; but while there is much less continuity than Heidegger claims, there is somewhat more than Habermas allows. Representing the transition between early and late Heidegger as a wholly external, politically motivated development during which the centre of gravity shifts from the assertive 'decisionism of empty resoluteness' to 'the submissiveness of an equally empty readiness for subjugation', requires, first of all, that resoluteness reduces to decisionism. It does not. Similarly, the transformation of our stance towards 'being', which is the central preoccupation of the later Heidegger, does not reduce to 'submissiveness' or a 'readiness for subjugation'. This is a neat and tidy explanation, but it ignores the continuities between early and later Heidegger's emphasis on openness and receptivity.[21] And this interpretive error is, once again, a function of Habermas's misunderstanding of the phenomenon of world disclosure. It is obvious that the active or volitional aspect of this phenomenon receded in later Heidegger in favour of its receptive aspect, but it did not vanish altogether. In any case, in both the early and the later Heidegger receptivity to sources of meaning outside the self are at the centre of his undertaking. He continues to make use of the 'call' and 'response' form: the shift is from the call of 'conscience' to the call of 'being'. On this view, there is no need to exclude from the account of the transition to the later philosophy the lessons that Heidegger learned from his political misadventure.

The problem which dogs Heidegger's early and later philosophy is also the problem which dogged Heidegger the person. Just as the early work failed to bring together the transformation of one's relation to oneself with a mutual transformation of one's relation to others, the later work failed to bring together the transformation of our relation to 'being' with a mutual transformation of our relation to each other. The problem with the later Heidegger's recommendations *vis-à-vis* our receptivity to 'being' is not the problem of a passive openness to anything that comes along. There is undoubtedly a lack of clear, unambiguous normative criteria regulating such receptivity, but that is not the central problem – in any case, it is not clear that this problem could ever be resolved in a manner that would satisfy Heidegger's critics, if satisfaction would require fixed criteria. The central problem is Heidegger's failure to co-ordinate the stance of receptivity towards 'being' with a corresponding stance of receptivity towards others.

From his very first criticisms of Heidegger, Habermas rightly understood the intrinsically moral nature of this failure: Heidegger preferred to show how we could be 'the neighbour of being', not how we could (and must) be each other's neighbour (WW 199). That this failure shows up in the life as well in the work is surely no coincidence. Between 1933 and 1945 Heidegger turned into a moral cripple, and remained one for the rest of his life. His utter silence on the Holocaust, his denial of individual responsibility for erring greatly, his failure to identify with the victims of Nazi war crimes – in short, his inability to mourn and repent attests to and confirms his morally crippled, melancholic state.[22] Although provided with ample opportunity to respond to the call of others, Heidegger made himself deaf to this call: this moral disability haunts his work and his life. And it is the historical and cultural dissemination of this same moral disability which continues understandably to worry Habermas: 'Heidegger's attitude to his own past after 1945 exemplifies a state of mind that persistently characterized the history of the Federal Republic until well into the sixties. It is a mentality that survives up to the present day, as in the so-called historians' debate about revisionistic interpretations of German war crimes' (WW 189).[23]

In bringing this section of my essay to a close, I would like now to turn to the second internal connection which Habermas claims to have established between Heidegger's philosophy and his politics: the assimilation of the mandarin *Weltanschauung* to the categorial framework of *Being and Time*. Habermas wants us to believe that the analysis of *das Man* in the fourth chapter of *Being and Time* is clear evidence of Heidegger's mandarin contemptuousness towards the everyday, of his failure to recognize that we are individuated as we are socialized, and of his susceptibility to a 'scientifically unfiltered diagnosis of crisis'. But these claims turn out to be as tenuous and unsustainable as the claims made in support of the first internal connection. The account Habermas offers of what's going on in the analysis of *das Man* fails to convey its strengths, and misinterprets its goals. There is no indication whatsoever that Heidegger is saying something importantly new in this analysis, something which represents an advance in our understanding both of the everyday and of the interconnections between socialization and individuation. Even the 'scientifically unfiltered diagnosis of crisis' proves to be of greater value than Habermas is explicitly able to acknowledge. While there is no external evidence to doubt Heidegger's sympathy towards mandarin ideology or his own 'elitist self-understanding', what he has to say in the relevant passages of *Being and Time*, does not conform to, but rather transcends, any elitist critique of the everyday.

In the first place, worries about the 'dictatorship of public opinion' were not exclusive to German mandarins and their ilk; one need only look outside the specific German context of the 1920s and 1930s to find such worries already expressed in Rousseau and, on the other, more democratic side of the ocean, in Emerson and Thoreau. The actual analysis of *das Man* shows no more contempt for 'average everydayness' or the 'who' of everyday *Dasein* than is found in Rousseau's *Second Discourse*, Emerson's 'Self-Reliance', Thoreau's *Walden* or Mill's *On Liberty*.[24] Much more importantly, however, Heidegger does not introduce the analysis of *das Man* simply for the sake of a critique of mass civilization: it no more reduces to a mandarin critique of the everyday than resoluteness reduces to decisionism. The category of *das Man* is an *Existenzial*; it is used to clarify how our ontological pre-understanding enables (discloses) and constrains (disguises and inhibits) the ways in which we take up our relations to the world and others. We acquire this pre-understanding through everyday practices, which practices are the primary source of intelligibility and meaning. Receptivity plays an inelim-inable role here as well, for it is only in virtue of this (pre-theoretical) open-ness to public practices that there is intelligibility and meaning at all. While the everyday practices through which 'being in the world' is first disclosed are socio-historically variable, they are not socio-historically optional or con-tingent. They make possible and enfold the massive background agreement which our speech and action draw upon and presuppose. As Hubert Dreyfus has pointed out, this analysis anticipates the later Wittgenstein's talk about agreement in forms of life, and, as such, it is continuous with Heidegger's attempt to undermine and supplant the subject-centred orientation of modern philosophy.[25]

The 'one' is not some specifically modern constraint against which *Dasein* must heroically assert itself if it is to make legitimate claims to authenticity. The '"one" . . . belongs to Dasein's positive constitution' (BT 167 / SZ129) – which is why mandarin-like exhortations to overcome 'the one' through acts of heroic self-assertion are altogether out of place. Heidegger does not call for anything so conventionally romantic: 'Authentic being-one's-self does not depend upon an extraordinary state (*Ausnahmezustand*) of the subject that is detached from the "one"; rather, it is an existentiell modification of the "one" – of the "one" as an essential existentiale' (BT 168 (tr. amended) / SZ 130). So long as the 'one' belongs to *Dasein's* positive constitution, authenticity depends upon a transformation ('existentiell modification') of the constraints of everyday practice, not upon a heroic escape from them. If the 'one' cannot have the final word on the question of the 'who' of everyday *Dasein* (BT 149 / SZ 114), it is because *Dasein's* activities can modify the very constraints which make its activities possible. Thus, what Heidegger is actually trying to show through the existential-ontological analysis of *das Man* is precisely what Habermas denies he can show: that we are individualized and socialized at one and the same time. Yet Heidegger recognizes, as much as Habermas, that there is a crucial difference between 'institutionalized' or 'obligatory' individuation (authenticity on demand) and a process of individuation which subjects can attribute to their own (spontaneous and reflective) activity.[26] Unlike Habermas, however, he is not advocating an interpretation of authenticity in terms of radical individuality; he is not defining an authentic individual as *einzigartig* (one of a kind) – as 'an individual who distinguishes himself from all others' (PT 190). Heidegger is in fact critical of such modern conceptions of radical individuality, for they entail practices of 'distantiation' (*Abständigkeit*) which he regards – like Rousseau before him – as one of the internal threats to undeformed everyday practices. (It is not difficult to see the extent to which Rousseau's 'amour-propre' is a precursor of Heidegger's 'distantiation'.)

These considerations are meant to shift attention from Habermas's unsuccessful attempt to establish internal links between Heidegger's philosophy and his politics to problems within Habermas's own philosophical project. I have tried to show that his failure to establish these internal links points to larger problems, which are directly connected to the shortcomings of his response to the issue of world disclosure. These problems show up even in Habermas's attempt to support his claim that Heidegger's philosophy was the victim of a 'scientifically unfiltered diagnosis of crisis'. In 'Work and *Weltanschauung*', Habermas everywhere alludes to the 'lasting insights' of Heidegger's critique of reason – to 'critical insights which have not been superseded even today' (WW 292, 195). On the other hand, Habermas claims that in the very period in which Heidegger was producing these 'lasting insights' his thinking had entered into 'a dark alliance with scientifically unexamined diagnoses of the times' (WW 193). Moreover, Habermas argues that the post-1929 Heidegger 'strayed into the regions of a thinking beyond philosophy, beyond argumentation itself' (WW 202); strayed into 'a sublime, primordially operative domain that is removed from all empirical (and ultimately all argumentative) grasp' (WW 193). If this is indeed the case, Habermas leaves totally unclarified how a thinking which has strayed into regions 'beyond philosophy, beyond argumentation', and 'removed from all empirical . . . grasp' can produce insights which 'have not been superseded even today'; he fails to explain not only how Heidegger could produce such insights, but how – given the regions into which his thinking strayed – we came to have access to them; and he throws no light on the status of a critique of reason that is capable of producing 'lasting insights', but which must none the less be viewed with the utmost suspicion on methodological, as well as on moral and political, grounds. This way of interpreting Heidegger's thinking has the undesirable consequence of reinforcing, and unintentionally endorsing, an image of Heidegger very dear to Heidegger himself and to the Heideggerian priesthood: the image of a 'magician', a dark 'genius', with an uncanny power to snatch philosophical gold from the surging waters of the Rhine. This is a conclusion that cannot recommend itself. By exaggerating the discontinuity between earlier and later Heidegger, and by exaggerating the discontinuity between Heidegger and the German philosophical tradition, Habermas adds to, rather than explodes, Heidegger's 'aura'. And it commits him to a position that his own engagement with Heidegger's texts belies: that Heidegger's texts are beyond evaluation and criticism.

However, this unwelcome conclusion does have the advantage of exposing the assumptions governing Habermas's conception of philosophy, argumentation and reason. Heidegger's later philosophy presents a host of difficulties which conventional forms of philosophical presentation and enquiry do not, but these are hardly beyond the reach of standard hermeneutic practices of clarification – otherwise, we would be in no position to talk about insights. So it is not so much that Heidegger's thinking moves into regions beyond philosophy and beyond argumentation; but rather, that it moves beyond Habermas's procedural conception of philosophy and argumentation. There is no room within a procedural conception for practices of critical (meta-) disclosure; and the idea that there can be normative criteria by which to assess such practices will seem rather odd, if not completely unintelligible. That is why Habermas is unable ultimately to distinguish between what is actually insightful and what is merely ideological in Heidegger's fusion of *Zeitdiagnose* with an ontological critique of reason. He is unable do make this distinction because he has failed to address systematically the question of just what makes one *Zeitdiagnose*, one critical meta-disclosure, better than another. Lacking normative criteria for distinguishing between better and worse forms of *Zeitdiagnose*, he is not in a position to justify convincingly his critique of Heidegger's 'scientifically unexamined diagnoses of the times'. Instead, he is left with the unenviable conundrum of how to explain the 'unscientific', non-rational production of lasting insights – a conundrum that arises because of Habermas's reluctance (or refusal) to accept the world-disclosing role of philosophy. For Habermas, such acceptance leads unavoidably to an 'aestheticization' of philosophy, to a philosophical practice which is directed away from 'inner-worldly' problems and disconnected from learning processes initiated by an engagement with the challenges such problems pose.

This brings us to the most fundamental philosophical difference dividing Habermas from Heidegger, a philosophical difference that gets played out in terms of an opposition between reason and world disclosure. As I have already urged elsewhere, we must reject the terms of this opposition.[27] Any conception of reason which cannot recognize the activity of disclosing the world anew as one of its own is not only deeply flawed; it is inescapably self-alienating. It abandons to contingency and to altogether non-rational forces one of modernity's most esteemed ideals: the self-conscious transformation of our practices and self-understanding. But here I am anticipating some of the conclusions of my next section, to which I now turn.

IV Heidegger's Challenge: World Disclosure

Ever since his inaugural lecture at the University of Frankfurt in 1965,[28] Habermas has sought to reinterpret in more plausible terms the comprehensive conception of reason at the heart of German Idealism. Seeking to avoid any relapse into (foundationalist) metaphysics or historicism, he has drawn extensively on the Anglo-American philosophical tradition (especially the philosophy of language, from Frege to Dummett and Davidson, and the pragmatism of Peirce and Mead) and on the social sciences, particularly those described by Habermas as 'reconstructive sciences' (as exemplified by the work of Kohlberg, Piaget and Chomsky). Yet his reinterpretation of reason is confronted by a powerful sceptical challenge that arises from within his own tradition – from that very part of it which demands 'critical, indeed, distrustful appropriation'. Even if I am right to claim that Habermas misrepresented the nature of this challenge, there is no question but that he comprehended its seriousness. On the one hand, it seems to represent a sceptical challenge to his 'postmetaphysical' attempt to recapture the unconditioned or self-determining or context-transcending moment of reason; on the other hand, the force of this sceptical challenge seems to be such that its success would undermine our confidence in the very idea of reason, rendering us unable to reassure ourselves about the rationality or autonomy of our practices and self-understanding. So it is to this challenge that Habermas directed his theoretical and polemical energy.

The Philosophical Discourse of Modernity represents Habermas's most concerted response thereto. No book has publicly defined recent Critical Theory as much as this one, and none has made more explicit Habermas's position vis-à-vis the German philosophical tradition. Whether he is responding directly to Heidegger's conception of world disclosure, or to post-Heideggerian reworkings of this notion in the work of Foucault, Derrida, Castoriadis, Taylor and others, Habermas's argument in The Philosophical Dis-

course of Modernity – bulk of which is directed against this notion – follows a remarkably consistent and (in retrospect) extremely predictable path. It consists of three overlapping strategies: (1) aestheticizing, (2) debunking, and (3) annexing, each of which responds to different aspects of the challenge that world disclosure poses. I shall discuss each of these strategies, showing how and why they fail. I shall also suggest just what a proper response to the challenge of world disclosure demands.

1 *Aestheticizing*

From Nietzsche through Heidegger to Derrida, Habermas detects a series of increasingly radical attempts to aestheticize language, everyday practice and philosophy by assimilating them to the world-opening, world-transforming power of practices of disclosure. Such an assimilation would prejudice and rhetorically overdetermine everyday communicative practice (the 'Yes' and 'No' positions which agents take in relation to criticizable validity claims); it would collapse the difference between logic and rhetoric, between normal and 'poetic' language, between problem solving and meaning creation, and between the everyday and the 'extraordinary' (*das Außeralltägliche*); and it would allow the action-co-ordination function of language to disappear behind its world-transforming function. Rather than allowing world disclosure to aestheticize language, everyday practice and philosophy, Habermas aestheticizes world disclosure. This aestheticizing move involves steering all the virulent talk about the meaning-creating power of world disclosure into the category marked 'art', or the 'aesthetic', the category into which Habermas shoves most of what he considers largely heterogeneous to his validity-based conception of philosophy, reason and everyday practice (the 'existential-ethical', a category of more recent vintage, serves a similar purpose). Thus, the object of this strategy is to contain this aspect of world disclosure within the cultural site (or 'value-sphere') which Habermas argues is 'proper' to it: art and literature. Unconstrained by the justificatory demands internal to proper everyday practices, art and literature can go about creating 'autonomous' worlds of meaning that release subjects from their ordinary routines and from everyday modes of perception and action: validity-based speech and action go on holiday. When housed within its own cultural domicile, where it is both marginalized and domesticated, our contact with the 'extraordinary' can contribute to, but not seriously disturb or threaten, the well-ordered rhythms of everyday practices.

Instead of steering world disclosure into a sphere remote from everyday practice, Critical Theory needs to conceive of everyday practice differently.

The integrity of everyday practice involves considerably more than the linguistic co-ordination of action in relation to 'validity claims geared to intersubjective recognition'; it also involves an enlargement of the realm of meaning and possibility, otherwise everyday practice is not in a position to resist the homogenization and totalization of everyday life which has preoccupied the critics of modernity from Rousseau to Heidegger and Adorno. Moreover, lacking meaning-creating and possibility-disclosing resources, everyday practice is not in a position to solve intractable interpretive problems. For, as Habermas concedes, such problems are symptoms of the need for a new vocabulary, in terms of which problems can be reformulated in a more promising way – or, more radically, in terms of which old problems can be dissolved and entirely new problems generated (PT 106).

We are therefore in need of a much richer conception of everyday practice, and such a conception must begin by rejecting all approaches which immunize the everyday against the extraordinary, just as it will reject all approaches which devalue the everyday in favour of the extraordinary. There is no need to deflate the extraordinary in order to let world disclosure into the realm of everyday practice; but there is a need to retrieve the extraordinary for everyday practice. That we have become accustomed to the opposition between the everyday and the extraordinary is a mark not only of the degree to which we have misunderstood everyday practice, but also of the degree to which our everyday practices have gone awry. Thus, the first challenge which the notion of world disclosure poses to any future Critical Theory is to show how the extraordinary is internal, not inimical, to the integrity of everyday practices.

Habermas's strategy of aestheticizing world disclosure is not meant only to immunize the everyday against the extraordinary; it is also meant to defend his procedural conception of philosophy. In his view, the attempts of philosophers from Nietzsche and Heidegger to Taylor, Derrida and Rorty to justify a world-disclosing role for philosophy would force philosophy to surrender its cognitive claims: 'it would either have to resign itself to the role of aesthetic criticism or itself become aesthetic' (JA 74). If it is to remain a rational enterprise, let alone the guardian of rationality, philosophy must prove its cognitive accomplishments 'through procedural rationality, ultimately through the procedure of argumentation' (PT 38). '[W]hat counts as rational is solving problems successfully through procedurally suitable dealings with reality' (PT 35). Habermas's point supposes, obviously, that cognitive claims cannot be raised in the aesthetic sphere. Just as obviously, his claim is question-beggingly circular; and it is inconsistent with remarks he has previously made concerning the power of aesthetic experience to insightfully alter 'our cognitive interpretations and normative expectations'.[29] In the present context, it is more glaringly inconsistent with what he has rather begrudgingly conceded in his essay on Peirce: that the problem-solving power of a new vocabulary is not reducible to procedural rationality. And, as Habermas must surely understand, there can be no procedures for world disclosure. Either world disclosure is an indispensable facet of a larger conception of rationality than his proceduralism allows, or it is perforce turned into the 'other' of reason, an outcome which undermines, rather than realizes, the aspirations of communicative rationality.

Rather than resolve the tension which his inconsistent positions have created, Habermas's writings persist in reproducing it. In a number of more recent essays, we find him repeatedly claiming that world-disclosure-oriented philosophers (among whom he numbers Wittgenstein and Adorno) seek simply 'to achieve effects which in the first instance resemble aesthetic experiences' (TK 88), and that it is in the very nature of such 'world-clarifying, world-disclosing, world-transforming' activity, that the analyses which issue from it 'are not directed with a view to everyday (*innerweltliche*) practices. It is not directed to actual problems in the world, nor does it initiate learning processes in response to challenges posed by the world' (TK 89). At the same time, when once again Habermas releases the phenomenon of world disclosure from its aesthetic strait-jacket, he claims that the creation of meaning, the enlargement of conditions of possibility, is actually triggered by 'the pressure of accumulating problems'; that, indeed, the actual resolution of such problems points to 'a feedback relation between world-disclosure and epistemological crises' (TK 43).

The incoherence of Habermas's attempt to aestheticize world disclosure deepens yet further when he tries to exclude 'world-disclosing arguments' from the realm of properly philosophical discourse. In reply to Karl-Otto Apel's different interpretation of the scope of discourse ethics, Habermas objects to his colleague's claim that philosophy can not only clarify the 'moral point of view' but also explain 'what it means to be moral' (JA 79). In Habermas's view, this is much too metaphysical a conception of philosophy, demanding of philosophy something 'which cannot be achieved through argumentation'. The desire to be moral can be 'awakened and fostered' in one of two ways: on the one hand, by socialization into a form of life which complements universalistic moral principles; on the other, ' by the world-disclosing power of prophetic speech and in general by those forms of innovative discourse that initiate *better forms of life and more reflective ways of life* – and also the kind of eloquent critique that enables us to discern these indirectly in works of literature and art' (JA 79, my emphasis). Even when such world-disclosing discourses take on an argumentative form, however, they 'are *not essentially philosophical arguments*' (JA 79, my emphasis).

What is interesting about this reply to Apel is Habermas's acknowledge-ment that moral and cognitive progress requires, over and above what can be achieved by arguments that meet the test of procedural rationality, discourses and practices which enable 'us to see things in a radically different light' (JA 79). World-disclosing arguments have the power to initiate 'better forms of life and more reflective ways of life', yet they fall outside the philosophical boundary set by Habermas's procedural conception. Philosophy, thinks Habermas, must refrain from playing this world-disclosing role, even when in doing so it is producing moral and cognitive insight, or the conditions necessary for such insight! This seems to be a clear case of cutting off your nose to spite your face. If applied strictly, Habermas's criterion of what counts as philosophical argument would turn much of what is powerful and com-pelling in the German tradition, and the enquiries of all those from early Critical Theory to Michel Foucault and Charles Taylor, into aesthetics – in his pejorative sense. Habermas's definition of argument is so obviously narrow that it must be rejected if we do not want to reject some of the most significant (if not uncontroversial) argument forms of modern philosophy.[30]

If Critical Theory is to renew itself, it must reject the limitations imposed upon it by a procedural conception of philosophy which would reduce its role, on the one hand, to that of a normative engineer designing the better procedure for testing the validity of generalizable norms, and on the other, to that of a go-between who occasionally makes useful suggestions about what's gone wrong in his little nook of the lifeworld.[31] Therefore, in respond-ing to the first challenge posed by the phenomenon of world disclosure, it must respond to a second: to show that only through its world-disclosing activity is philosophy responsive to modernity's time consciousness, and in contact with the extraordinary. Lacking such contact it could not contribute to the 'discourse of modernity' – to the critique of the deformation of every-day practice (PDM 139). Likewise, it could not contribute to the enlarge-ment of meaning and possibility which may 'initiate better forms of life and more reflective ways of life.'

2 Debunking

Habermas's debunking strategy is formulated in response to the ways in which the notion of world disclosure is used to interpret historical and cul-tural change, and to diagnose the meaning of the present. Heidegger's *Seinsgeschichten* and Foucault's genealogies are critical histories which attempt to deepen our understanding of how we came to have the self-understand-ing, practices, crises and possibilities that we currently do. They are interpretive investigations which seek to understand the formation and transformation of ontological frameworks, world-views, cultural paradigms, epistemes, etc., by determining 'what counts as a thing, what counts as true/false, and what it makes sense to do'.[32] Such investigations not only focus on changes in ontologies; they also suggest how we might understand ourselves as agents of change: of change that doesn't happen to us but rather is facilitated by us.

The debunking strategy focuses largely upon attempts to explain historical and cultural change in terms of ontological change (changes in the 'understanding of being'), and avoids serious discussion of the suggestions concerning how we might facilitate such change. It is a strategy that depends heavily upon exaggerating Heidegger's already exaggerated account of the degree to which changes in ontologies take place behind our backs. According to Habermas, Heidegger's *Seinsgeschichte* assumes that an ontological difference exists between the 'constitutive understanding of the world' disclosed by language and 'what is constituted in the world' (PDM 319). Habermas interprets the ontological difference as an interpretive device that uncouples the 'constitutive understanding of the world' from 'what is constituted in the world'. That makes it easy for him to reduce the results of Heidegger's critical histories to the claim that changes in ontology disclosed by and sedimented in language succeed one another independently of what human beings learn from their interactions with one another and with the world: 'Any interaction between world-disclosing language and learning processes in the world is excluded' (PDM 319). If this were indeed the case, we would of course be unable to make sense of ourselves as agents; and history itself would simply assume the form of predestined fate, unfolding inexorably within the antecedently fixed horizons of meaning set by the most recent (first-order) disclosure of the world. Anyone offering an account of epochal and cultural change that proceeds from the ontological difference would find him- or herself instantly enveloped in self-referential paradoxes. Much of the force of Habermas's argument against world disclosure is due to the success of this debunking strategy, showing how not only Heidegger, but also all those who draw upon his work – Derrida, Foucault and Castoriadis, among others – are inescapably caught in self-referential paradoxes.

While the texts of Heidegger, Foucault, Castoriadis and Derrida lend themselves (sometimes, all too willingly) to Habermas's *reductio ad absurdum*, his interpretation of this aspect of world disclosure is one-sided, occasionally wilful, and inconsistent. Otherwise, he could not ascribe to Heidegger (and to other world-disclosure theorists) such a deterministic view of agency and of history. Heidegger certainly does claim that large-scale (and, for that matter, small-scale) changes in our self-understanding and social practices are not simply at the disposal of our will; and, moreover, that acting on the assumption that they are, envelops us all the more deeply in nihilism (of course, the lessons of his engagement with National Socialism play a decisive role in shaping this view.)[33] But he is far from asserting the self-refuting view that ontological frameworks or primary disclosures of the world determine our self-understanding, our practices and our possibilities independently of what we may (yet) say or do. To say that we cannot make fully explicit and transparent our ontological pre-understanding of the world – to say that we cannot objectify and dominate it, because it is that upon which our theoretical and practical activities depend – is not to say that we are at the mercy of meta-historical transformations of world-views which we can undergo but not resist or initiate ourselves.

Heidegger not only went on (and on) about how our speech and action are constrained and limited, but also about how they are enabled, by our ontological frameworks – just as one would expect of a thinker predisposed to transcendental figures of thought. Habermas concentrates exclusively upon the ways in which meaning horizons, conditions of intelligibility, etc. disclosed by a given understanding of the world are said to limit our social practices, our truth claims and our agency. He has given altogether insufficient attention to Heidegger's attempts to show that its own possible self-transcendence is a necessary condition of any disclosure of the world, any horizon of meaning, any *Lichtung* or 'clearing', any social practice – a necessary feature of its 'opening' and 'concealing' structure. After all, it was Heidegger who claimed that possibility is ontologically higher than actuality. Habermas's objection that Heidegger's view of such change excludes 'any interaction between world-disclosing language and learning processes in the world' is based on a misinterpretation of the ontological difference.[34] The very idea of an isolated, self-enclosing horizon of meaning which fixes in advance what subjects may learn, is incoherent, as incoherent as the very idea of a conceptual scheme.[35] Heidegger was as aware of this as anyone. (The philosopher who provided so much insight into the hermeneutic circle was not the methodological *naïf* that Habermas sometimes makes him out to be.) Yet the debunking strategy must suppose the correctness of this interpretation of the ontological difference in order to dismiss the value of Heidegger's approach to historical and cultural change. And it must unjustifiably disregard the centrality of Heidegger's lifelong preoccupation with the problem of beginning anew, the problem of transforming our inherited ontological frameworks. This is a problem that would dissolve entirely if ontology completely dictated history – if there were no interaction between world disclosure and everyday practice.

Heidegger's early and later writings evince a much more promising attempt to connect world disclosure to the activity of accountable subjects. This attempt is much clearer in the early writings, where Heidegger is elaborating his conception of authentic freedom and self-determination. In both the early and the later writings, agent accountability is not from the start developed in relation to the goal of intersubjective agreement; rather, it is developed in relation to experiences of epistemological crisis, interpretive blocks and communicative breakdown – that is, it is developed in relation to the recognition of the need to begin anew. By comparison with what we normally mean by moral accountability, it seems unhappily situated in rather fuzzy talk about openness and responsiveness. But with a bit of luck, further enquiry will make such talk less fuzzy, and bring about a more comprehensive understanding of accountability.

With their focus on receptivity, the later writings appear to be much more problematic. Often irritating and not without risky implications, the later Heidegger's exploration of receptivity requires critical and open-minded appropriation. It pushes reflections on agency in an unfamiliar direction, not only decentring, but also reconfiguring, what it means to be an agent. I say 'reconfigures', because it is a picture of agency that places a great deal more emphasis on receptivity than we are accustomed to.[36] It does not eliminate activity so much as make receptivity active. The unaccustomed stress on receptivity is what leads sympathetic and unsympathetic interpreters to conclude that, on Heidegger's view, all that is left to human agents is to passively submit to whatever ontological changes befall them. As I have already argued, this conclusion obscures, rather than explains, Heidegger's contributions. The emphasis on receptivity ought to be interpreted in light of the idea that we need to develop a non-instrumental understanding of change, a non-instrumental relation to transformative practice. Reconfiguring agency in terms of the demands of receptivity opens up a different perspective on transformative practice, making it possible to think of ourselves as facilitators, rather than heroic creators, of new disclosures and new beginnings. This suggestion might help free us from the mistaken idea that new disclosures and new beginnings are the work of some artistic 'genius', human or otherwise, and free us from the subjectivistic effects that this idea has had on our conception of agency.

If Critical Theory is to have a future worthy of its past, it must respond to the third challenge of world disclosure: to develop models of historical, cultural and normative change that elucidate – at the level of everyday practice – the ways in which our own agency facilitates such change. If we are to regenerate our confidence and hope, we need to understand much better

than we currently do just how practices which disclose the world anew facilitate 'better forms of life and more reflective forms of life'.

3 Annexing

Of the three strategies shaping Habermas's argument, only the annexing strategy engages constructively with the phenomenon of world disclosure, treating the challenge it poses as an occasion to demonstrate the capaciousness
and flexibility of communicative rationality. The annexing strategy revolves
around the 'reciprocal interaction' thesis which stipulates: (1) that 'world disclosure and proven praxis in the world mutually presuppose one another';
(2) that 'meaning-creating innovations are . . . intermeshed with learning
processes'; and (3) that both meaning-creation and learning processes 'are so
anchored in the general structures of action oriented toward reaching understanding, that the reproduction of a lifeworld always takes place also by virtue
of the productivity of its members' (PDM 335).

These three stipulations are quite clearly in conflict with the intentions
of the aestheticizing and debunking strategies. They preclude an aesthetic
segregation of world disclosure, and undercut the attempt to draw a
sharp distinction between meaning-creation and learning processes. World-
disclosing practices are situated within everyday practice, not on the side
of the 'extraordinary', and are treated as accountable accomplishments
through which agents reflectively reproduce their lifeworld. Thus far, the
implications of the reciprocal interaction thesis point in the same direction
as my own suggestions concerning how the phenomenon of world disclosure ought to be interpreted. They point the way to an enlarged conception
of reason; but this way is blocked by a narrowness with respect to what reason
can mean.

The reciprocal interaction thesis appears to be in conformity with
Habermas's pragmatic theory of meaning, a theory that postulates 'an intrinsic connection between meaning and validity, which nevertheless does not
eliminate the difference between the two' (PDM 320). Understanding and
evaluation are linked in such a way that one understands the meaning of an
utterance (or speech act) when one knows what makes it acceptable (that is,
true or valid). By recasting the relation between disclosure and learning
in terms of his pragmatic theory of meaning, Habermas thinks he avoids
the problems he claims to have identified in Heideggerian and post-
Heideggerian construals of disclosure. Above all, he avoids the problem that
arises when truth is fused with disclosure. Although in a certain way he avoids
this problem, he does not avoid the problems I have already explored in my

analysis of the aestheticizing and debunking strategies. Habermas simply assumes that he can map the reciprocal interaction thesis on to the relation between meaning and validity, as if the former follows unproblematically from the latter. In this he is mistaken. The reciprocal interaction thesis demands a more comprehensive conception of learning processes and everyday practice than is allowed by Habermas's theory of meaning and the procedural interpretation of rationality. Although Habermas grants that our practices and our self-understanding do indeed repose upon a linguistically disclosed pre-understanding of the world, he argues that the idealizations built into action oriented to reaching understanding induce learning processes that transcend 'all local constraints, because experiences and judgements are formed *only* in the light of criticizable validity claims' (PDM 205, my emphasis). But, as we have seen, Habermas concedes that such learning processes break down and are in need of new vocabularies, in need of 'semantic world disclosure', in light of which they can get going again. So the problem I have already thematized remains unresolved: how to grasp as learning – which is to say, as an activity of reason – those accomplishments through which we acquire new tongues with which to say what could not be said and new ears with which to hear what could not be heard; accomplishments through which we overcome stubborn social pathologies, communication breakdowns and partial, one-sided interpretations of ourselves and others; through which we are able to go on learning.

As long as Habermas continues to claim that learning processes are 'formed only in the light of criticizable validity claims', he will be unable to grasp such accomplishments as an activity of reason. And as long as this is the case, the very practices upon which the possibility of 'better forms of life and more reflective ways of life' depend will continue to show up (at best) as superfluous appendages of reason, rather than as essential to the life of reason as practices of critique and justification. If Critical Theory is to have a future worthy of its past, it must respond to the fourth challenge of world disclosure: to reformulate the concept of reason in a way that not only incorporates its transformative (possibility-disclosing) activity, but also co-ordinates the activities of transformation, critique and justification. As in the old Hegel, a regretful tone of resignation shows up in Habermas's recent work: 'Philosophy, working together with the reconstructive sciences, can only throw light on the situations in which we find ourselves. It can contribute to our learning to understand the ambivalences that we come up against as just so many appeals to increasing responsibilities within a contracting space of possibility' (PT 146, tr. altered). It may be that the 'contracting space of possibility' is much more the result of a narrow conception of reason than it is a reflection of the complexity of modern societies.

Notes

1 Jürgen Habermas, 'Historical consciousness and post-traditional identity', in NC 266. The 'new beginning' has been made all the more difficult and complicated since the unification of Germany – a unification wholly unforeseeable at the time Habermas wrote this essay.

2 Martin Heidegger, *Being and Time*, tr. J. Macquarrie and E. Robinson (New York: Harper and Row, 1962), p. 63. German original: *Sein und Zeit* (Tübingen: Max Niemeyer, 1986). Further references to *Being and Time* will appear as BT in parentheses, with the German page reference (SZ) following a slash. I shall be citing from the Macquarrie and Robinson edition, but I have often made substantial alterations to their translation.

3 Jürgen Habermas, 'Martin Heidegger: Work and *Weltanschauung*', in *Heidegger: A Critical Reader*, ed. Hubert Dreyfus and Harrison Hall (Oxford: Blackwell, 1992), p. 189.

4 It will become clearer in the course of my discussion that although I begin with the Frankfurt tradition of Critical Theory, the normative model of Critical Theory I'm working towards is fully pluralistic in its intentions: it is meant to be in partnership, not in competition, with other traditions of critical enquiry. However, it is a conception which remains normatively and theoretically anchored in the German philosophical tradition from Kant and Hegel to Habermas.

5 One can certainly understand the political and philosophical anxieties animating these interpretations: (a) the external, and *possibly* internal, connections between the German tradition and Fascist ideology; (b) the 'provinciality' of the tradition *vis-à-vis* developments in post-war Anglo-American philosophy; (c) its purported 'aestheticism' its 'romanticism' and its focus on the 'extraordinary' at the expense of the everyday. But these anxieties lead to interpretations which distort too much to be accepted without question.

6 For critical assessments of Heidegger's controversial and influential analyses, see the contributions of James Bohman, Martin Seel, Christina Lafont and Nikolas Kompridis to *Thesis Eleven*, 37 (1994). (These contributions appeared originally in a special issue of the *Deutsche Zeitschrift für Philosophie*, 3 (1993).)

7 Martin Heidegger, *The Basic Problems of Phenomenology*, tr. Albert Hofstadter (Bloomington, Ind.: Indiana University Press, 1982), p. 284; tr. slightly altered.

8 Ibid., pp. 169–70.

9 It is this later, rather infamous conception of linguistic world disclosure that has become associated with such remarks as 'language is the house of being' and it is 'language which speaks'. However, Heidegger's view of language must not be taken to refer to language understood in naturalistic terms, least of all because it would reduce his view to a version of linguistic relativism. By 'language' Heidegger means the ontological context necessary for language in the ordinary sense. For clarification, see Frederick Olafson, 'The unity of Heidegger's thought', in *The Cambridge Companion to Heidegger*, ed. Charles Guignon (Cambridge: Cambridge University Press, 1993), pp. 97–121.

10 Jürgen Habermas, 'Life forms, morality, and the task of the philosopher', in *Autonomy and Solidarity: Interviews with Jürgen Habermas*, ed. Peter Dews (London: Verso, 1986), p. 195.

11 '. . . only after this change of attitude did the overcoming of modern subjectivity take on the meaning of an event that is only to be undergone. Until then, the decisionism of self-assertive Dasein, not only in the existential version of Being and Time but also . . . in the national/revolutionary version of the writings from the thirties, had retained a role in disclosing being. Only in the final phase of working through his disillusionment does the concept of the history of being take on a fatalistic form' (WW 198).

12 All these are fairly accurate renderings of *das Man*, but I shall stick to 'the one' for the sake of convenience, and because it captures more fully than either of the other two the meaning which Heidegger attributes to this notion.

13 For a contrast between a Lacanian and a Habermasian account of intersubjectivity, see Peter Dews, 'Communicative paradigms and the question of subjectivity: Habermas, Mead and Lacan', in this volume, ch. 3.

14 'Dasein is equiprimordially being-with others and being-among innerworldly beings. The world within which these latter beings are encountered is . . . always already a world which one shares with others. It is only because Dasein is antecedently constituted as being-in-the-world that one Dasein can existentielly communicate something factically to another; but it is not this factical existentiell communication that first constitutes the possibility that one Dasein shares a world with another Dasein.' Heidegger, *Basic Problems of Phenomenology*, p. 297, tr. altered.

15 Another of those rare occasions can be found in the discussion of 'Mutual understanding and calculation' in the first volume of Heidegger's lectures on Nietzsche, which discussion is cited by Habermas (PDM 137).

16 'Dasein's resoluteness towards itself is what first makes it possible to let the others who are with it "be" in their ownmost potentiality for being, and to co-disclose this potentiality in the solicitude which clears the way and liberates. When Dasein is resolute, it can become the "conscience" of others' (BT 344/SZ 298). In this passage, Heidegger sounds more like an exponent of a 1960s-inspired, Californian 'ethics of fulfilment' than a German mandarin of the 1920s.

17 They are affectedness (*Befindlichkeit*), understanding (*Verstehen*), discourse (*Rede*) and falling (*Verfallen*). Because it is structured by a relation of 'call' and 'response', resoluteness is related to discourse.

18 Charles Taylor, 'Heidegger, language, and ecology', in *Heidegger: A Critical Reader*, p. 259.

19 Heidegger can be charged with an unduly obstinate commitment to (ontological) formalism, but not with decisionism. The formalism of his categories rendered them sufficiently plastic to suit the purposes of his political misadventure. In any case, the entire attempt to correlate purported decisionism with his commitment to Nazi ideology has been pressed (e.g., by Richard Wolin) beyond the point of credibility. As Hans Sluga has shown, it was more typical to defend the

truth of National Socialism by appealing to a theory of 'objective values'. See his 'Metadiscourse: German philosophy and National Socialism', *Social Research*, 56/4 (1989).

20   In an interview with Richard Wolin, Habermas describes the influence of Sartre on his understanding of *Being and Time*. See 'Jürgen Habermas on the legacy of Jean-Paul Sartre', *Political Theory*, 20 (1992), pp. 496–501.

21   For an instructive analysis of the continuities of Heidegger's thought see Olafson, 'Unity of Heidegger's thought'.

22   I am obviously mixing Freudian and Kierkegaardian terminology here. For an insightful discussion of the contemporary relevance of these themes see Gillian Rose, *Mourning Becomes the Law* (Cambridge: Cambridge University Press, 1996).

23   And it is a mentality which continues to survive in ever-renewed forms in post-1989 Germany. For a discussion of the virulent forms of revisionism plaguing the reunified Germany, see Jacob Heilbrunn, 'Germany's New Right', *Foreign Affairs*, 75/6 (Nov.–Dec. 1996).

24   It seems to me that there is no deep division among them on this score. Here's Emerson from 'Self-Reliance' and Heidegger from the relevant section of *Being and Time* in contraposition, followed by Mill from *On Liberty*, just for good measure.

'Man is timid and apologetic. He is no longer upright. He dares not say "I think," "I am," but quotes some saint or sage' (Ralph Waldo Emerson, *Essays* (Dent: London, 1967), p. 43).
'Primarily my "I am" is not that of my own self, but that of the others whose way is that of the "one". It is primarily from the "one" and as the "one" that my "self" is "given" to me' (BT 167 (tr. amended)/SZ 129).
'At present individuals are lost in the crowd' (John Stuart Mill, *On Liberty and other Essays* (Oxford: Oxford University Press, 1991, p. 73).

'Insist on your self, never imitate' (Emerson, *Essays*, p. 52).
'Everyone is the other, and no one is himself' (BT 165/SZ 128).
'Precisely because the tyranny of opinion is such as to make eccentricity a reproach, it is desirable, in order to break through that tyranny, that people should be eccentric . . . That so few now dare to be eccentric, marks the chief danger of the time' (Mill, *On Liberty*, pp. 74–5).

'Our reading is mendicant and sycophantic' (Emerson, *Essays*, p. 40).
'Publicness primarily controls every way in which the world and Dasein get interpreted . . . the way of interpreting the world and being in the world which lies closest' (BT 165, 167/SZ 127, 129).
'Its [the public] ideal of character is to be without any marked character; to maim by compression, like a Chinese lady's foot, every part of human nature which stands out prominently, and tends to make the person markedly dissimilar in outline to commonplace humanity' (Mill, *On Liberty*, p. 77)

As any reader of Stanley Cavell's recent writings will already know, there are also some important affinities between Heidegger and Emerson. Of course, their deepest disagreement would rest on their views of democracy. Still, I think Emerson would agree with Heidegger's *das Man*-ish critique of the 'average everydayness' of currently existing democracy. But, unlike Heidegger, Emerson would hold on to the hope, the possibility, that democratic forms of life could engender more open, less totalizing forms of everyday practice. And so should we.

25 Hubert Dreyfus, *Being in the World* (Cambridge, Mass.: MIT Press, 1991), pp. 141–62. For detailed comparisons of Wittgenstein and Heidegger, see Charles Taylor, '*Lichtung* and *Lebensform*', in *Philosophical Arguments* (Cambridge, Mass.: Harvard University Press, 1995), and Karl-Otto Apel, 'Kritische Wiederholung und Ergänzung eines Vergleichs', in the symposium on Wittgenstein, *Der Löwe spricht . . . und wir können ihn nicht verstehen* (Frankfurt am Main: Suhrkamp, 1991), pp. 27–68.

26 See the opening pages of Habermas, 'Individualization through socialization: on George Herbert Mead's theory of subjectivity', in *Postmetaphysical Thinking*.

27 See N. Kompridis, 'On world disclosure: Heidegger, Habermas, and Dewey', *Thesis Eleven*, 37 (1994).

28 Published in English as the 'Appendix' to *Knowledge and Human Interests* (KHI 301–17).

29 Jürgen Habermas, 'Questions and counter-questions', in *Habermas and Modernity*, ed. Richard Bernstein (Cambridge, Mass.: MIT Press, 1985), p. 202.

30 If followed strictly, Habermas's criterion of what is and what is not a 'philosophical' argument would mean rejecting the philosophical status of some of the most interesting 'arguments' in Kant's three *Critiques*, the *Phenomenology of Spirit*, *The Eighteenth Brumaire*, *The Genealogy of Morals*, *Being and Time*, *Negative Dialectics*, *Philosophical Investigations*, *Truth and Method* and *The Philosophical Discourse of Modernity*, to name just a few significant texts.

31 I'm referring here to Habermas's distinction between philosophy as 'stand-in' and as 'interpreter' (MCCA 17–19).

32 Hubert Dreyfus, 'Being and power: Heidegger and Foucault', *International Journal of Philosophical Studies*, 4/1 (Mar. 1996), p. 4.

33 For an elaboration of this point see, Hubert Dreyfus, 'Heidegger on the connection between nihilism, art, technology and politics', in *Cambridge Companion to Heidegger*, pp. 289–316.

34 The ontological difference offers two *standpoints* from which we can understand cultural change. We can move dialectically back and forth between these two standpoints, but we cannot in principle dissolve the difference between them. These standpoints – the ontological and the ontic – are analogous to the intelligible and empirical standpoints from which, according to Kant, we can understand human freedom. In Habermas's vocabulary, Kant's two standpoints are equivalent to the first-person/participant and third-person/observer perspectives. But the interpretive activity through which accounts of ontological change are

produced moves within, and is subject to, the interpretive constraints of the hermeneutic circle. It cannot be undertaken from the objectifying perspective of the third person without creating problems of self-reference. Successful interpretation results in a 'fusion of horizons' between past and present, us and them, which fusion is possible only because the interpretive constraints in question are *enabling* constraints.

35 Donald Davidson, 'On the very idea of a conceptual scheme', in *Inquiries into Truth and Interpretation* (Oxford: Oxford University Press, 1984), pp. 183–96. See also Hans-Georg Gadamer, *Truth and Method* (New York: Seabury Press, 1989), p. 304.

36 We are accustomed to dismissing or treating disdainfully any conception of agency associated with what are 'feminine' characteristics or capacities.

Part II
Contexts

5

Between radicalism and resignation: democratic theory in Habermas's *Between Facts and Norms*

William E. Scheuerman

A conformist political theory is no theory.   Franz Neumann[1]

In 1962, a relatively unknown scholar published a contribution to democratic theory destined to generate something of a sensation in the still rather staid intellectual universe of post-war Germany. Appearing a mere thirteen years after the re-establishment of liberal democracy in Germany, the 33-year-old Jürgen Habermas's landmark *Structural Transformation of the Public Sphere* focused on precisely those features of contemporary democracy that the young author's more conservative scholarly peers tended to downplay. Influenced significantly by the neo-Marxism of the Frankfurt School, Habermas argued that contemporary democracy exhibited a number of troublesome tendencies: a catastrophic fusion of state and society, unforeseen by classical liberal theory, had resulted in the disintegration of the very core of liberal-democratic politics, a public sphere based on the ideal of free and uncoerced discussion. In Habermas's scathing account, mounting evidence suggested that liberal democracy was evolving towards a new and unprecedented form of authoritarianism, a mass-based plebiscitarianism in which privileged organized interests linked hands (by means of what Habermas polemically described as 'neo-feudal' institutions fusing public and private power) in order to perpetuate social and political domination. Relying on the most advanced American empirical social science, Habermas argued that an ossified and inflexible political system, in which decisions were increasingly 'legitimated' by means of subtle forms of mass persuasion, functioned alongside a profit-hungry mass media that trivialized public life in order to thwart democratic aspirations. The autonomous 'bourgeois public sphere' of the late eighteenth and early nineteenth centuries had been jettisoned for the 'manipulated public sphere' of organized capitalism.

Habermas's study struck a raw nerve in the young German polity. Particularly in the context of a political system in which traditional cleavages seemed increasingly muted – recall Willy Brandt's 1961 comment that 'in a sound and developing democracy it is the norm rather than the exception that the parties put forward similar, even identical demands in a number of fields'[2] – Habermas's analysis of the decline of a critical public sphere seemed prescient. Within a few years, the influence of his work was already manifest in political tracts, sometimes far more radical in character than his own study, written by those who openly identified with Germany's burgeoning New Left.[3]

Thirty years after the publication of his first major work, Habermas's *Between Facts and Norms: Contributions to a Discourse Theory of Law and Democracy* revisits many of the core concerns of his original contribution to democratic theory.[4] Once again, Habermas hopes to offer a conception of *deliberative democracy* capable of providing a guide-post for a revised Critical Theory. Indeed, the analytical framework of his recent contribution to democratic theory is infinitely more subtle than its predecessor, chiefly because Habermas himself has conceded that *The Structural Transformation of the Public Sphere* was seriously flawed.[5] Thus, his recent works articulate a sophisticated neo-Kantian brand of contract theory, in dramatic contrast to the Hegelian Marxism at the core of his original foray into democratic theory. Even more striking, the normative and institutional specifics of the discursive conception of the 'public sphere' introduced, but inadequately developed in Habermas's 1962 work, are elaborated in great detail here. *Between Facts and Norms* also breaks dramatically with what Habermas has recently described as a form of crude 'holism' implicit in traditional democratic socialism, according to which a more or less homogeneous 'macro-subject' ('the people') is assigned the task of establishing a perfectly transparent, democratically planned economy, in order to achieve full autonomy. Habermas now believes that this ideal, which clearly motivated his 1962 enquiry, fails to provide sufficient independence for the 'system imperatives' of modern markets and bureaucracies. For Habermas, radical democracy has to come to grips with the exigencies of social complexity. Failure to do so can prove disastrous, as demonstrated by Soviet-style state socialism.[6] Finally, missing from *Between Facts and Norms* is a problematic feature pivotal to the dramatic texture of his 1962 study: an exaggerated contrast between a stylized, free-wheeling 'bourgeois public sphere', described in a surprisingly sympathetic light, and the bleak reality of contemporary capitalist democracy, described in tones reminiscent of the apocalyptic cultural criticism of the early Frankfurt School. To his credit, Habermas now avoids the oftentimes tortured historical claims that rightly garnered so much criticism for *The Structural Transformation of the Public Sphere*.[7] The democratic theory of *Between Facts and Norms* rests on an impressive attempt at rigorous political and social theorizing, not idiosyncratic myths about a liberal bourgeois 'golden age'.

But my concern here is not with explaining the conceptual advances of Habermas's *Between Facts and Norms* with respect to *The Structural Transformation of the Public Sphere*. Scholars sympathetic to Habermas's project have already done so.[8] Instead, I would like to pursue an alternative line of enquiry. My guess is that Habermas's recent book is unlikely to ignite anything like the scale of the response ignited by his 1962 study. One might simply chalk this up to its immense intellectual complexity: *Between Facts and Norms* is accessible to only a minuscule group of scholarly experts. But it may also point to a profound weakness in Habermas's contemporary democratic theory: namely, its failure to give adequate expression to legitimate unease and anxiety about the fate of representative democracy at the end of the twentieth century. Despite rapidly growing evidence of widespread dissatisfaction with the operations of contemporary capitalist democracy, Habermas's work at times offers a surprisingly moderate and even conciliatory picture of 'real-existing' democracy. In my view, Habermas's justified acknowledgement of the *intellectual* virtues of liberal and democratic thought *à la* Mill or Rawls, and his justified attempt to correct the theoretical failings of his early forays into democratic theory, seems to have generated a troubling side-effect: an inadequately critical assessment of 'real-existing' capitalist democracy.

Let me be more specific. In his eagerness to integrate a mind-boggling array of alternative legal and political theories, *Between Facts and Norms* ultimately offers a deeply ambiguous account of modern democracy. Habermas's democratic theory now lends itself to two competing – but probably incompatible – interpretations, in part because he undertakes to develop his model of deliberative democracy by relying on a series of politically and intellectually inconsistent views. First, *Between Facts and Norms* at times seems to point to the outlines of an *ambitious* radical democratic polity, based on far-reaching social equality, and equipped with wide-ranging capacities for overseeing bureaucratic and market mechanisms. Yet Habermas never adequately develops this line of enquiry. Despite his repeated attempts to overcome a false juxtaposition of normativity and facticity, this model remains at the level of an abstract 'ought'. Second, Habermas simultaneously suggests a *defensive* model of deliberative democracy in which democratic institutions exercise at best an attenuated check on market and administrative processes, and where deliberative publics most of the time tend to remain, as Habermas himself describes it, 'in dormancy' (*im Ruhezustand*) (BFN 379 / FG 458). In my view, this second model risks abandoning the critical impulses that have motivated Habermas's intellectual work throughout his impressive career.

I begin with a brief introduction to the general features of Habermas's model of deliberative democracy (section I) before turning to an analysis of its inconsistent 'critical' (section II) and 'uncritical' (section III) renditions. Finally, I point to the possible sources of this tension in the conceptual structure of *Between Facts and Norms*. In particular, I hope to suggest that Habermas never offers an adequate analysis of the interface between democratic and administrative authority (section IV).

I

For Habermas, the normative core of modern democracy is best captured by the principle that 'Only those juridical statutes may claim legitimate validity that can meet with the agreement of all legal consociates in a discursive law-making procedure that in turn has been legally constituted'.[9] Despite the immense complexity of Habermas's attempt to explicate this (deceptively simple) statement in *Between Facts and Norms*, the broad outlines of his institutional vision of deliberative democracy are relatively straightforward. Habermas develops what he describes as a 'two-track' model of representative democracy, in which an 'organized public' (consisting of legislative bodies and other formal political institutions) functions alongside an 'unorganized public', a broader civil society in which citizens rely on a panoply of devices (including political associations and the mass media) to take part in free-wheeling political debate and exchange. Formal political institutions play a key role by 'focusing' the process of public opinion formation and then codifying the results of this process by giving them a binding legal form, but Habermas's model places special weight on the importance of civil society: it is the free-wheeling character of discourse outside the formal political arena which now takes on the absolutely pivotal role of identifying, thematizing and interpreting political concerns.[10] Indeed, Habermas tends to wax enthusiastic about what he describes as the refreshingly 'chaotic' and even 'anarchic' nature of deliberation in civil society.

Habermas repeatedly describes civil society as 'anonymous' and even 'subjectless', in order to break with a long tradition in political theory that misleadingly conceptualizes 'the people,' in an overly concretistic way, as a unitary, collective sovereign. By more fully acknowledging the profoundly pluralistic and decentred quality of public life in a modern democracy, Habermas hopes thereby to respond to theorists of difference who worry about the potentially anti-pluralistic implications of the tendency, probably most evident in *The Structural Transformation of the Public Sphere*, to privilege a single, homogeneous public sphere engaged in the quest for rational agreement or unanimity.[11] Now, Habermas openly concedes that it makes sense to talk only of a *diversity* of public spheres, and in *Between Facts and Norms* he seems eager to show that complex processes of bargaining and compromise – dramatically distinct from the Rousseauian model of politics that haunted some of his previous work[12] – have a legitimate, and even noble, place to play in modern democracy.

But the anonymous character of civil society by no means renders it impotent. Explicitly building on Hannah Arendt's famous demarcation of power from violence, Habermas describes civil society as the prime generator of what he calls 'communicative power', according to which deliberation and action in concert are essential for understanding the *origins* of political power, though by no means the *exercise* or *use* of power. For Arendt, '[p]ower corresponds to the human ability not just to act but act in concert. Power is never the property of an individual; it belongs to a group and remains in existence only so long as the group keeps together.'[13] In Habermas's view, Arendt thereby identifies the roots of power in uncoerced communication; she grasps the centrality of 'the consensus-achieving power of communication aimed at mutual understanding' (BFN 148/FG 184). Communicative power constitutes a 'scarce good', which state administrators rely on, but are unable to produce on their own (BFN 146–51/FG 182–7). In this model, political power possesses a dualistic structure. Communicative power can be effectively employed in complex modern societies only by means of administrative bodies and forms of decision making which rest on strategic and instrumental-rational forms of action: 'The legitimating ideals of administration are accuracy and efficiency. Administrators are to discover and undertake those actions that will be instrumental to the achievement of specific ends.'[14] Thus, the nature of administrative power conflicts with the logic of communicative power, which is ultimately based – for Habermas, as for Arendt – on relations of mutual recognition and respect.[15] Modern democracy thus seems paradox-ridden to the extent that it requires forms of (administrative) power structurally incommensurable with the very (communicative) power which alone makes democratic deliberation possible in the first place; for Habermas, this is one of the more obvious manifestations of the tension between facticity and validity which he addresses in the extremely demanding theoretical reflections in the work's initial chapters.

For Habermas, in some distinction to Arendt, the medium of *law* plays a central role in transforming communicative power into administrative power. Crucial to *Between Facts and Norms* is the simple idea that law lies at the very intersection of communicative and administrative power; one of the most important implications of this insight is that the fate of representative democracy and the rule of law are intimately linked. In so far as law potentially functions as a successful connecting link, or bridge, between communicative and administrative power, the seeming paradoxes of modern democracy *are* surmountable. Communicative and administrative power should be able to co-operate fruitfully in the service of the plurality of deliberative 'networks' that make up civil society. For Habermas, not only does Arendt fail to acknowledge adequately the autonomous dynamics of administrative power (hence the paucity of legal analysis in her writings), but her republican streak leads her to envision 'power' as a more or less spontaneous expression of a substantive common will.[16] In an extremely complicated discussion that I cannot do justice to here, Habermas tries to counter this view by arguing that communicative power combines otherwise distinct (in his terminology, 'moral', 'ethical' and 'pragmatic') forms of deliberation: politics concerns questions of *moral fairness* guided by a rigorous neo-Kantian criteria of universalizability, questions of *cultural value and identity* concerned with arriving at an 'authentic self-understanding' and which legitimately allow for a loosening of the tough standards of moral discourse, as well as *pragmatic* attempts to reach practical compromises which give equal weight to all relevant interests (BFN 155–6 / FG 193). Thus, political deliberations involve a quest for an uncoerced, reasonable common understanding on normative matters, *as well as* somewhat less pristine processes of mutual bargaining and compromise. In any case, crucial to this process is that we have 'a warranted presupposition that public opinion be formed on the basis of adequate information and relevant reasons, and that those whose interests are involved have an equal and effective opportunity to make their own interests (and the reasons for them) known'.[17] Habermas thus deserves to be grouped among those defending what has come to be described as a 'public reasons' approach in political theory.

II

So much for the bare outlines of Habermas's democratic theory. What, then, is problematic about it?

Initially, *Between Facts and Norms* seems to offer an ambitious interpretation of the idea of a two-track model of deliberative democracy. First,

Habermas emphasizes that *all* manifestations of political power must ultimately derive from communicative power; even if indirectly, administrative
power needs to legitimize itself by reference to discursive processes based in
civil society (BFN 169 / FG 209). In particular, this is guaranteed by the principle of the legality of the administration. The medium of law merely *trans-
fers* or *translates* communicative power into administrative power. The primacy
of deliberatively derived law assures that communicative power effectively
'determines the direction' (BFN 187 / FG 230) of the political system; in
another formulation, Habermas claims that communicative power 'maintains'
or 'asserts' (*behaupten*) itself against administrative and market mechanisms
(BFN 299 / FG 363). Habermas by no means intends thereby to question the
relative autonomy of complex markets and bureaucracies from the integrative force of communicative action. None the less, some formulations in
Between Facts and Norms suggest that their autonomy can legitimately be contained by means of a relatively *far-reaching* set of deliberatively derived democratic checks and controls on their operations. This is arguably a model not
only, as Habermas himself tends to describe it, in which a 'balance' has been
achieved between communicative power, on the one side, and money and
administrative power, on the other, but in which communicative power gains
a pre-eminent position in relation to administrative and market processes
(BFN 150 / FG 187), without thereby unduly impinging on the underlying
dynamics of market and administrative subsystems. Habermas builds on the
work of socialist-feminist theorist Nancy Fraser, who has openly criticized
Habermas's concessions to systems theory *à la* Luhmann, and has often sought
to rework Habermas's theory in a more explicitly anti-capitalist gloss than
Habermas himself.[18] Habermas's most obvious debt to Fraser is his use of her
distinction between 'weak' and 'strong' publics. For Fraser, weak publics are
those unburdened by the immediate task of formal decision making, whereas
strong publics (most importantly, elected legislatures) are those 'whose discourse encompasses both opinion formation and decision making'.[19] In both
chapter 4 and chapter 7 of *Between Facts and Norms*, Habermas reproduces
this formulation: for him, as for Fraser, parliament at times is conceived as an
extension of the deliberative networks constitutive of civil society, as an 'organized middle point or focus of a society-wide network of communication'
(BFN 182 / FG 224). Parliament is merely a technical device necessary in
large, complex societies to 'focus' the process of political debate and exchange,
but this technical feature need not extinguish parliament's own deliberative
attributes.[20] The task of making sure that parliamentary bodies are 'porous'
to civil society, to use Habermas's expression, is thus eminently realistic in
light of the fact that there is nothing *structurally* distinct between weak and
strong publics. In both, communicative power is predominant.

Fraser's original essay never adequately addresses the possibility that strong publics might be forced to realize communicative power in a manner distinct from the 'anarchic' associational life found in civil society. But one can imagine that she might accept Habermas's gloss on her views in certain passages of *Between Facts and Norms*: in parliament, time constraints necessitate that actors are less concerned with the 'discovery and identification than the treatment (*Bearbeitung*)' of problems, 'less with developing a sensibility for new problem positions than with justifying the choice of problems and deciding between competing solutions' (BFN 307 / FG 373). Parliament serves as a site for impressive debate and exchange, even if the imperatives of the formal decision-making process reduce the 'wild' and 'anarchic' features in civil society. Habermas also suggests that 'deciding between competing solutions' is likely to heighten the importance of *compromise* within the 'strong' parliamentary public. But he can be interpreted as arguing that this need not vitiate his (and Fraser's) ambitious view of parliament as a deliberative policy-making body. Here, a compromise is 'fair' if it is in accordance with three conditions: (1) it provides advantages to *each* party; (2) it tolerates no 'free riders'; (3) no one is exploited in such a way as to force them to give up more than they gain by compromise (BFN 165–7 / FG 204–5). As Stephen White has noted, this theory of compromise means that 'it is the privileged agent who is confronted with the choice of . . . demonstrating to what degree his inequality can be discursively justified', of showing that it is in accordance with standards of procedural equality, participation, non-deception and non-manipulation.[21] In this model, the process of reaching and then defending any particular compromise seems unlikely to entail the suppression of deliberation. On the contrary, it seems destined to *encourage* debate in so far as citizens are required by it to consider whether compromise procedures actually compensate for 'asymmetrical power structures' (BFN 177 / FG 218), as Habermas demands they must.

For our purposes, this last condition is most telling. Crucial to Fraser's discussion of weak and strong publics is the insight that 'where societal inequality persists, deliberative processes in public spheres will tend to operate to the advantage of dominant groups and to the disadvantage of subordinates'.[22] Thus, the achievement of a truly free-wheeling civil society, as well as a parliament responsive to its dictates, demands that we radically challenge asymmetries of social power. Habermas's discussion of 'fair' compromise can be interpreted as an illustration of this more general – and implicitly quite ambitious – point. Here again, Habermas reproduces Fraser's explicitly socialist argument: '*All* members of the political community have to be able to take part in discourse, though not necessarily in the same way' (BFN 182 / FG 224). In order for this requirement to gain substance, an egalitarian social environment needs to have been achieved: 'Only on a social basis that has transcended class barriers and thrown off thousands of years of social stratification and exploitation' can we achieve a fully thriving civil society (BFN 308 / FG 374). At another juncture Habermas describes the merits of a civil society 'adequately decoupled' from class structures, and then he adds that 'social power should only manifest itself [in civil society] to the extent that it *enables* and does not *hinder* the exercise of citizenship' (BFN 175 / FG 215).

Deliberative democracy, it seems, *does* in fact need to break with what Marx once described as the 'prehistory' of class society. Although Habermas seems allergic to the conceptual paraphernalia of traditional left-wing political theory, he does imply at many junctures that the socialist tradition's aspiration to destroy illegitimate socio-economic inequality is anything but exhausted. On the contrary, this undertaking arguably takes on *renewed* significance in his work, given the tremendous emphasis placed on civil society in it. To the extent that civil society is especially vulnerable to the pressure of class domination, then, it would seem incumbent on a democratic theory which places special emphasis on the importance of unhindered debate within civil society to salvage something of the socialist critique of the crippling inequalities of capitalist society, even if we now surely need to acknowledge the undeniable virtues of complex markets and bureaucracies in modern society.[23]

Habermas is right to follow Fraser in focusing on the social barriers to deliberative democracy: the idea of a free-wheeling deliberative democracy remains ideological as long as avoidable social inequalities undermine the deliberative capacities of the vast majority of humankind.[24] My concern is merely that *Between Facts and Norms* has nothing adequately *systematic* in character to say about 'social asymmetries of power', let alone how we might go about counteracting them. Habermas points to the need for an account of how (1) capitalist domination undermines democratic deliberation and (2) some egalitarian alternative to existing capitalism alone can allow deliberative democracy to flourish. Alas, no such account is offered in his study. Indeed, matters may be complicated by the strikingly Weberian overtones of Habermas's definition of social power: 'I use the expression "social power" as a measure of an actor's chances to achieve his interests in social relations against the opposition of others' (BFN 191 / FG 235). Does this definition provide the best starting-point for making sense of what Marxists have traditionally described as 'structural' inequalities in economic power? I do not mean to trivialize the difficulty here: in the wake of the demise of Marxist class theory, we still lack an adequate theory of social stratification.[25] Yet, without some analysis of this sort, many of Habermas's more interesting proposals risk representing precisely what he seemed so intent on avoiding in *Between Facts and Norms, normative aspirations* having at best a tangential relationship to the operations of real-existing capitalist democracy (BFN 373 / FG 451).

Many political scientists would, of course, legitimately note that Habermas's model of parliament as a focal point for meaningful debate represents at best an *ideal* of how parliament should operate.[26] Most parliaments today continue to rubber-stamp decisions that have been made elsewhere, by the upper divisions of a state bureaucracy working alongside the representatives of powerful organized social groups, in a manner not altogether unlike that described by the young Habermas in *The Structural Transformation of the Public Sphere* in 1962. Similarly, we would be hard pressed to identify compromises in contemporary democracy that live up to the demanding standards of Habermas's model of just compromises. Amidst the vast economic inequalities of contemporary capitalism, it is inevitable that compromise often means that some group gives up more than it gains: one need only recall the crippling 'compromises' forced upon welfare state 'clients' by neo-liberal governments in recent years.

At worst, Habermas's comments about 'social power' represent little more than a rhetorical left-over from the Hegelian Marxism of *The Structural Transformation of the Public Sphere*. At best, they represent a starting-point for a revised Critical Theory of contemporary capitalism – a Critical Theory which Habermas's *Between Facts and Norms* very much needs.

III

But Habermas's theory of deliberative democracy also lends itself to an alternative reading. Especially in the final chapters of *Between Facts and Norms*, Habermas is intent on showing that his theory has 'empirical referents and represents more than a series of normative postulates' (BFN 373 / FG 451). However understandable, this move generates a real problem for Habermas: it leads him to an interpretation of the two-track model that stands in profound tension to his initial reconstruction of Nancy Fraser's socialist-feminist democratic theory. Moreover, this revised model makes too many concessions to the oftentimes woeful conditions of 'real-existing' capitalist democracy – woeful realities, I should add, with which an ever increasing number of our fellow citizens are rightfully becoming frustrated.[27]

The interpretation of Habermas's model along the potentially radical and socially critical lines indicated above suffers from an obvious flaw. Habermas's comments on the interface between communicative and administrative power are more ambivalent than I have suggested.[28] As I noted, at some junctures he argues that communicative power can rely on the medium of law to *determine* administrative power. Yet, at many other junctures, Habermas offers a more modest view of the scope of communicative power: communicative power 'more or less'(!) programmes, and merely 'influences' and 'counter-steers', administrative power. In any event, communicative power 'itself cannot "rule" (*herrschen*), but only steers the use of administrative power in certain directions' (BFN 300, 444 / FG 364, 535). In this second line of argumentation, the significance of deliberative democratic processes within Habermas's overall model seems substantially reduced. Here, communicative power functions to 'lay siege' in a defensive manner to the exercise of administrative power. But it is utopian to hope that communicative power can gain the upper hand in relation to bureaucratic (and market) mechanisms. In the final section of this chapter, I hope to show that this ambiguity stems from a fundamental conceptual tension within Habermas's argument. For now, let me just suggest that Habermas's institutional gloss on his two-track model of democracy in the concluding chapters of *Between Facts and Norms* takes a substantially less ambitious form than that described above as well.

In chapter 8, Habermas once again elaborates on his two-track model. But now Nancy Fraser's radical democratic socialism fades into the background. In its place, Habermas relies extensively on the work of Bernhard Peters, a German sociologist who has devoted much of his impressive intellectual ability over the course of the past decade or so to developing a critique of precisely those types of radical democratic arguments so important to writers like Fraser. Habermas here relies on a study that Peters himself openly describes as a contribution to a revised version of 'realist' democratic theory, albeit of a 'strongly modified normative' variety.[29] Like Habermas, Peters worries about the normative deficits of systems theory; in contradistinction to writers like Fraser, Peters thinks that Critical Theory remains excessively mired in unrealistic, radical liberal and radical democratic fantasies. In the spirit of Schumpeter, Peters argues that traditional normative interpretations of liberal democracy are essentially mythical in character: the idea of competent deliberative parliaments, deriving their authority from free-wheeling political exchange among autonomous publics and capable of determining administrative action by means of clearly formulated general rules, 'has never even been approximately realized'.[30] Despite its tremendous influence on democratic theory, '[i]t was not even defended as a normative political model – perhaps excepting certain short-lived constitutional doctrines influenced by Rousseau during the French Revolution (Sieyes, the Constitution of 1791).'[31] For Peters, the main source of the limits of every 'idealized model of a democratic cycle of power' (like that described in section I above) is 'the extremely limited capacities for communication and problem resolution', intrinsic to the communicative channels described by it, in relation to the actual decision-making needs of modern representative democracy.[32] Thus, both traditional democratic theory and radical contemporary proposals hoping to salvage its more ambitious normative aspirations must be discarded. In their place we need a model of democracy, a 'very abstract, topological description of the political process', more in tune with the complex dynamics and exigencies of the modern state.[33]

Peters is no conservative in the mode of Schumpeter. To his credit, Peters openly admits that his description of the operations of real-existing democracy may include 'contingent' elements.[34] But the polemical orientation of his book means that he has little to say about such elements. Bent on purging the spectre of radical democracy from Critical Theory, Peters at times seems far more interested in pointing to the 'rational' character of the democratic *status quo* than with elaborating its ills; the burden of proof lies with radical democrats critical of contemporary capitalist democracy. Although this view arguably provides a valuable immunization against irresponsible utopianism, it tends to lead him to downplay worrisome trends in contemporary capitalist democracy – to name just the most obvious: continued declines in participation rates, polls suggesting growing dissatisfaction with traditional legislative devices, and the resurgence of far-right-wing movements pandering to xenophobia and racism.

Alas, Habermas opts to reproduce the core of Peters's realist-inspired model of democratic decision making by simply superimposing it on Fraser's model (BFN 354–6 / FG 429–31). Inevitably, this produces a set of serious tensions in Habermas's argument. The 'two tracks' described by Habermas thus ultimately refer not only to Fraser's distinction between weak and strong publics, but to Peters's idiosyncratic demarcation of the political 'centre' from the 'periphery'. In Peters's model, the 'centre' consists, most importantly, of parliament, the administration and the judiciary. The 'periphery' refers to a host of associations and organizations (1) concerned with 'the definition, aggregation and articulation of interests and demands in relation to the decision-making processes of the centre' or (2) functioning to bring about the 'realization of public functions' within selected spheres of social activity.[35] Autonomous publics and communicative networks make up *part* of the periphery, but Peters seems more interested in those actors emphasized by traditional political science, such as political parties, interest groups and private associations. In order for decisions to take a binding form, they need to pass through the 'channels' (*Schleusen*) of the centre. But, in contrast to traditional liberal democratic models, these channels are located at many different (administrative, legislative and judicial) points within the 'polycentric' decision-making centre found within every modern representative democracy.

Even at this minimal descriptive level, Habermas's use of Peters leads him to modify his initial account of the two-track model. Whereas his original gloss on Fraser made civil society the primary site for the 'perception and thematization' of problems, here Habermas uses the same words to describe parliament's functions (BFN 307, 355 / FG 373, 430). Moreover, now it is the administration which is seen as possessing the most impressive capacity for handling and resolving problems (*Problemverarbeitungskomplexität*); earlier in his study, that quality was attributed to parliament (BFN 307, 355 / FG 373, 430). At first glance, this may seem like a trivial shift. But, in fact, it anticipates a dramatic revision that becomes fully manifest only in the subsequent stages of Habermas's argument: parliament becomes the administration's junior partner in the legislative process, and deliberative civil society is removed an additional step from the actual decision-making process, thereby substantially attenuating its influence over the exercise of political authority. In light of Peters's unabashed attempt to break with traditional 'myths' of parliamentary sovereignty, this move is unsurprising. Given Habermas's purportedly critical aspirations, it is far more surprising.

Peters openly argues that the political centre inevitably gains independent status in relation to the periphery. Habermas accepts this view without showing sufficient concern for its potentially worrisome implications for democratic politics. In the course of what Habermas describes as 'normal' politics, the deliberative periphery inevitably plays a minor role in determining the policy-making process. The autonomization (*Verselbständigung*) of the centre *vis-à-vis* the periphery is inevitable considering the complexity of modern social life (BFN 356–9, 379–91 / FG 431–5, 458–67). Most of the time, 'courts reach decisions, bureaucracies prepare statutes and budgets, party organizations organize electoral campaigns, and clients influence "their" administrators' (BFN 357 / FG 432), and civil society is unavoidably left at the wayside. Indeed, not only civil society, but even those elements of the 'centre' most closely tied to civil society, lose the central place attributed to them in traditional democratic theory: 'the power and initiative to get problems on the agenda and then decide on them lies with the government and administration to a greater extent than the parliamentary complex' during moments of political normalcy (BFN 380 / FG 459). According to Habermas, only in 'exceptional' situations do communicative processes within civil society and parliament again seem to take on a renewed significance for decision making; only during moments of heightened conflict, in periods of crisis, does the legislature finally have 'the last word' and then '*factually determine* the direction' of political decision making (BFN 357 / FG 433).

What concrete evidence does Habermas provide to demonstrate the empirical relevance of this model? (Recall that Habermas wants to show that his vision of deliberative democracy has 'long gained a footing' (BFN 317/ FG 386). This means not only that the self-understanding of modern liberal democracy is best captured by the idea of a two-track deliberative democracy; it also implies that empirical tendencies within contemporary democracy should correspond to his model.) He suggests that the proliferation of autonomous social movements in civil society over the course of the last decades (especially the peace, women's and ecological movements) proves that (1) the periphery of civil society often *can* succeed in thematizing issues ignored by the decision-making centre, and (2) the political centre remains 'porous' to civil society, especially when a 'growing awareness of a relevant societal problem generates a *crisis consciousness* on the periphery' (BFN 382/ FG 461). Habermas's argument here represents an astonishing sleight of hand. Peters never claims that his account is radical-democratic; Habermas seems to think that it is. Nor does Habermas see any problem with synthesizing Fraser's democratic socialism and Peters's cautious brand of democratic realism; I wonder how Fraser and Peters would feel about this. Unsurprisingly, Habermas's model is Janus-faced. At times, he speaks the language of radical democracy, while at other junctures, his defence of what amounts to an administratively dominated 'normal' politics is arguably less ambitious, in crucial respects, than the liberal-democratic models of classical authors like Mill or Tocqueville.[36] The paradoxes here are striking: Habermas began his career as one of the most perceptive critics of 'realist' democratic theory.[37] Is he now willing to engage in a rehabilitation of realist theory, as long as it is packaged in the impressive learning of critical social theory?

Even if we ignore this analytical tension in *Between Facts and Norms*, another problem quickly becomes apparent. In short, this second version of Habermas's two-track model exhibits a number of immanent flaws. No *systematic* empirical argument is offered in support of the claim that it actually corresponds to the workings of contemporary liberal democracy; passing reference to a panoply of left-liberal social movements hardly constitutes adequate evidence for an empirical claim as ambitious as this one. After all, one might legitimately interpret the proliferation of social movements in recent years (as well as the increasingly widespread dependence on civil disobedience, which for Habermas represents the clearest instrument whereby social movements have mobilized public opinion) in a somewhat less positive light. Whatever their undeniable merits, these movements may *also* provide evidence for *worrisome* tendencies within contemporary representative democracy: precisely because the 'centre' has gained exorbitant power in relation to the 'periphery', extra-parliamentary social movements, engaging in illegal action, have emerged to fill the gap left by a formal political system increasingly dominated by ossified parties and organized vested interests. Similarly, civil disobedience often represents what Habermas himself calls 'the final instrument' (BFN 382 / FG 462) whereby political groups hope to *ward off* state action which they consider altogether unbearable; emphasizing this rather *defensive* form of political action hardly seems the best way to demonstrate the continued vitality of civil society in contemporary democracy. In a truly thriving deliberative democracy, one would hope that citizens need not engage too often in peaceful law breaking in order to gain attention.[38]

Habermas's argument here begs a host of unanswered questions. For example, how can we make sure that civil society will reactivate itself during moments of crisis?[39] Habermas refers to the importance of liberal political culture as a pre-condition for this (BFN 382 / FG 462). But, as Ken Baynes has noted, Habermas has very little to say about the specifics of such a culture.[40] Indeed, there may be something downright *un*realistic about the logic of Habermas's borrowing from 'realist' theory: can a 'public in dormancy' (*öffentlickeit im Ruhezustand*) effectively tolerate the exercise of *de facto* political power by isolated political elites without risking its own disintegration (BFN 379 / FG 458)? Tocqueville's warnings about 'democratic despotism' should come immediately to mind here: why would political elites not take advantage of a situation characterized by a 'public in dormancy' in order to exacerbate privatistic tendencies? Habermas claims that a political system temporarily dominated by the 'centre' by no means necessarily means that illegitimate social power has gained undue influence within the political complex (BFN 357 / FG 432). But his explanation here is disappointing, particularly in light of the prescient concerns expressed elsewhere in his work about the dangers of social asymmetries of power for civil society: we can rest assured that social power will not be able to gain illegitimate influence as long as the periphery is able and effective to identify outbreaks of illegitimate social power and then counteract them (BFN 358, 441 / FG 434, 532). But what if social inequality simultaneously distorts the operations of civil society itself?[41]

Sometimes *Between Facts and Norms* presents a refreshingly honest assessment of worrisome trends within contemporary democracy. Habermas offers a clear-headed discussion of capitalist mass media that trivialize public debate and cultivate cultural and political illiteracy; he notes that political parties too rarely serve as a meaningful device for guaranteeing the supremacy of communicative power; he concedes that cynical brands of systems theory have some real empirical correlates in contemporary democracy. In short, he still defends *some* of the critical elements of his empirical account of contemporary democracy in *The Structural Transformation of the Public Sphere*. But Habermas now seems so intent on proving that his own model 'represents more than a set of normative postulates' that he ignores the possibility that his use of Peters's *empirical description* risks forcing him to make unnecessary concessions to the sad state of real-existing capitalist democracy.

IV

For Habermas, law – and, more specifically, legislative bodies like an elected parliament – mediates between communicative and administrative power: law-making bodies depend on communicative power in order to issue norms, which are then rendered binding by the coercive apparatus of the modern state. The ambiguities that I have described in my exegesis above ultimately revolve around the nexus between communicative and administrative power. At some junctures, Habermas seems to point to parliament as the main site for law making; at others, he accepts the 'realist' view that parliamentary sovereignty is little more than a mouldy liberal myth. Sometimes parliament is envisioned as an extension of a deliberative civil society; at other times, parliament's deliberative capacities are demoted, in order to accentuate its pragmatic qualities and to distinguish it from the 'anarchical' processes of deliberation and exchange found within civil society. Habermas tends to emphasize the virtues of a deliberative civil society; at the same time, he is willing to admit that civil society inevitably has little real impact on state action during the course of 'normal' democratic politics. Habermas hopes to show that communicative power can be 'transcribed' into administrative power. But he does not seem altogether sure *exactly* how weak publics, strong publics, and administrative bodies should interact in order to bring about this translation.

The immediate source of this tension is not hard to find. Habermas conceives of his project as an attempt to overcome the one-sidedness of both normative theories allegedly blind to the exigencies of empirical reality (those of Rawls and Dworkin, for example) and social-scientific theories lacking the most minimal normative sensitivity (for example, those of the German systems theorists Luhmann and Willke). In the process, he devotes an enormous amount of energy to an immanent reconstruction of competing views in order to demonstrate (1) how they repeatedly succumb to one of these two flaws, and (2) how, ultimately, their underlying insights can best be integrated into his own thematization of the relationship between *facticity* and *validity*. As a consequence, most of Habermas's own ideas here are formulated by means of an *exegesis and reconstruction of competing theories*. There is no question that Habermas is a masterful practitioner of this craft. But in light of the *fundamental* dissimilarities between the theories discussed by Habermas, there is a real danger that either (1) something essential is lost in the translation of these ideas into Habermas's own, or (2) the integrity of competing theories is preserved, but at the cost of attempting a synthesis of that which probably cannot be synthesized. Indeed, isn't that precisely what we find in Habermas's model of a two-track deliberative democracy, where radical-democratic socialism and democratic 'realism' are oddly transformed into intellectual allies?

In the space remaining, I cannot develop this methodological criticism with adequate care. But it is striking that Habermas's analysis of communicative power is derived from normative theorists (most importantly, Arendt), whereas his discussion of administrative power is drawn from a tradition of social-scientific enquiry oblivious to normative questions (Luhmann). Habermas himself repeatedly emphasizes the incongruities between these two traditions; as he repeatedly shows in *Between Facts and Norms*, each is blind to the merits of the other. In light of this, it should not surprise us that his own attempt to integrate these traditions at times may reproduce something of the original incongruity between them. More specifically, Habermas's description of communicative and administrative power tends at many junctures to posit the existence of a *fundamental* dissimilarity between them. Communicative power rests on action in concert, deliberation oriented towards mutual understanding; it depends on what Hegel famously described as 'mutual recognition'. In stark contrast, administrative action relies on strategic rationality, takes an unavoidably hierarchical form, and is concerned first and foremost with efficiency (BFN 145–51, 186–7 / FG 182–7, 229–30). Given Habermas's insistence on a fundamental difference between these two forms of power, is not the task of translating communicative into administrative power inevitably destined to remain highly enigmatic? Does this undertaking not risk resembling the alchemists' attempts to 'transform' base metals into gold – that is, an inevitably doomed attempt to transform one set of elements into an altogether different set? No wonder Habermas at times stumbles in his description of the interface between communicative and administrative power: he may have defined the task in such a manner as to render it virtually impossible to perform.[42]

Of course, the liberal tradition long provided an easy answer to the question of how communicatively derived legislative power could be successfully transformed into administrative action so as to guarantee that the latter does not infringe on the former: if we insist that legislation take the form of cogent, general norms, then we can make sure that administrative power can be effectively regulated in accordance with the preferences of democratically elected legislative bodies. Although I believe that Habermas is too quick to dismiss the contemporary merits of this traditional argument, he certainly *is* right to suggest that it seems rather anachronistic in light of the proliferation of vague, open-ended legal clauses and concepts in twentieth-century law.[43] For Habermas, the ongoing deformalization of law suggests that we need to reconceive the traditional idea of the separation of powers in such a way as to de-emphasize the orthodox emphasis on generality within legal statutes; this view purportedly rests on an overly 'concretistic' reading of the separation of powers (BFN 187–93, 526–37 / FG 230–7, 526–37).

So Habermas argues in the final pages of *Between Facts and Norms* for a restatement of the idea of a separation between distinct *institutions* (the legislature, judiciary and administrative branch) in terms of a distinction between alternative *forms of communication* and different *ways of making use of reasons and arguments*. Regardless of their *concrete location* within the state apparatus, forms of action deserve to be described as 'legislative', 'administrative,' and 'judicial' to the extent that they make use of forms of argumentation which Habermas sees as capturing the core of what traditional liberal theorists envisioned by means of each of the individual 'instances' of the separation of powers. In turn, such forms of action rightfully deserve to be institutionalized in such a way as to correspond to the logic of the form of communication at hand:

Laws regulate the transformation of communicative power into administrative power in that they come about according to a democratic procedure, ground a legal protection guaranteed by impartially judging courts, and withhold from the implementing administration the sorts of reasons that support legislative resolutions and court decisions. These normative reasons belong to a universe within which legislature and judiciary share the work of justifying and applying norms. An administration limited to pragmatic discourse must disturb anything in this universe by its contributions; at the same time, it draws therefrom the normative premises that have to underlie its own empirically informed, purposive-rational decision making. (BFN 192 / FG 235)[44]

Legislative power is best captured by the idea of communication involving the justification of norms (*Normanwendungsdiskursen*), which – as we have seen – makes use of diverse (moral, ethical and pragmatic) forms of deliberation (BFN 192–3, 439–40 / FG 235–6, 529–30). The gist of Habermas's rather complicated argument here is that we need to consider the possibility of extending communicative forms of this type *whenever* problems at hand require a legislative resolution – for example, when administrators are confronted with a choice of mutually incompatible collective goals in such a way as to explode the boundaries of traditional conceptions of administrative action. In order finally to do justice to a political system in which legislation occurs at many different interstices of the governmental apparatus, central parliaments need to consider the possibility of openly delegating and decentralizing legislative authorities and then organizing them in such a way as to subject them to deliberative democratic procedures (BFN 439–40 / FG 529–30).

Habermas's suggestion here is surely a provocative one. Indeed, if it could be undertaken successfully, it might very well serve as an antidote to some of my criticisms above: if deliberative democratic ideals could be institutionalized within the very *core* of the state bureaucracy, then Habermas's description of an administratively dominated 'normal' politics might begin to seem somewhat less worrisome than I suggested above. Then the 'normal' rule of the 'state administration' need not necessarily entail a realist-inspired corrosion of deliberative democracy.[45]

But his argument here also points to a familiar weakness in *Between Facts and Norms*. Given the immense complexity of Habermas's text, it is easy to miss the tremendous significance of his discussion of a reformed separation of powers for the structure of his overall argument: it is supposed to represent nothing less than an *institutional* solution to the problem of transforming communicative power into administrative power. But, once again, Habermas has far too little to say about the specifics of his agenda here. Even if we are willing to concede the virtue of integrating deliberative democratic elements into the administration, does that necessarily solve the problem of how communicative power is to be effectively *translated* into administrative power? Habermas's proposal is not meant to deny that we still need to acknowledge the autonomous logic of the administrative system; it claims only that what we today describe as the state administration or bureaucracy undertakes legislative tasks that should be organized in accordance with the principles of deliberative democracy. So perhaps this argument simply shifts the *locus* of the interface between communicative and administrative power from the nexus between parliament and the administrative apparatus to *within* the administration itself. If so, we still need an analysis of how deliberative processes can effectively 'steer' and 'bind' decisions within the administration itself. In fairness, Habermas *alludes* to a growing number of experiments (for example, participation by clients in administrative bodies, ombudsmen, administrative hearings) with the 'democratization' of administrative and judicial instances (BFN 440–1 / FG 531). But his examples have now long been established in many administrative practices of the advanced democracies of the West. Does anyone really believe that more ombudsmen or administrative hearings can really protect us from what Habermas himself describes as the 'crisis tendencies' of modern representative democracy?[46] What about more ambitious experiments in political and social democracy? Habermas does not exclude them a priori; he tells us that a careful brand of 'institutional fantasy' is appropriate for the examination of such proposals (BFN 440 / FG 531). Unfortunately, it is just such 'institutional fantasy' that is absent from Habermas's own argument here – notwithstanding its tremendous importance for his own ambitious attempt in *Between Facts and Norms* to reconceive the project of modern representative democracy.

Notes

I would like to thank Iris Young for her helpful comments on an earlier draft of this chapter.

1   Franz L. Neumann, *The Rule of Law under Siege: Selected Essays of Franz L. Neumann and Otto Kirchheimer*, ed. William E. Scheuerman (Berkeley: University of California Press, 1996), p. 197.

2   Cited in Otto Kirchheimer, *Politics, Law, & Social Change: Selected Essays of Otto Kirchheimer*, ed. Frederic S. Burin and Kurt L. Shell (New York: Columbia University Press, 1969), p. 331.

3   See e.g. Johannes Agnoli and Peter Brückner, *Die Transformation der Demokratie* (Frankfurt am Main: EVA, 1968).

4   German original: Jürgen Habermas, *Faktizität und Geltung: Beiträge zur Diskurstheorie des Rechts und des demokratischen Rechtsstaats* (Frankfurt: Suhrkamp, 1992). Unless otherwise noted, all translations are my own. However, I have provided references to the English edition, followed by those in the German edition.

5   Jürgen Habermas, 'Further reflections on the public sphere', in *Habermas and the Public Sphere*, ed. Craig Calhoun (Cambridge, Mass.: MIT Press, 1993), pp. 421–61.

6   See also Jürgen Habermas, 'What does socialism mean today? The rectifying revolution and the need for new thinking on the left', *New Left Review*, 183 (Sept.–Oct. 1990).

7   Wolfgang Jäger, *Öffentlickeit und Parlamentarismus* (Stuttgart: Kohlhammer, 1973), is good on this score: Jäger shows that Habermas's model of the bourgeois public sphere is a myth not unlike that constructed by Carl Schmitt in order to discredit contemporary democracy. Unfortunately, Jäger's work is little known in the English-speaking intellectual world; this may explain the relatively modest character of criticism of the historical structure of Habermas's study. For an interesting discussion of the similarities and dissimilarities of Habermas's and Schmitt's historical accounts of modern democracy, see Hartmuth Becker, *Die Parlamentarismuskritik bei Carl Schmitt und Jürgen Habermas* (Berlin: Duncker and Humblot, 1994).

8   For a helpful brief overview of Habermas's study, see Peter Dews, 'Agreeing what's right', *London Review of Books*, 13 May 1993. More ambitiously: Kenneth Baynes, 'Democracy and the *Rechtsstaat*: Habermas' *Faktizität und Geltung*', in *The Cambridge Companion to Habermas*, ed. Stephen K. White (Cambridge: Cambridge University Press, 1995); James Bohman, 'Complexity, pluralism, and the constitutional state: on Habermas' *Faktizität und Geltung*', *Law and Society Review*, 28/4 (1994); Michel Rosenfeld, 'Law as discourse: bridging the gap between democracy and rights', *Harvard Law Review*, 108/5 (Mar. 1995). These thoughtful discussions address many elements of Habermas's complicated argument that I necessarily leave unexamined here. See also the special issue of *Philosophy and Social Criticism* (20/4 (1994)) devoted to Habermas's legal theory. For a discussion of Habermas that does an excellent job of placing Habermas within (1) debates in twentieth-century German legal thought and (2) jurisprudential debates between positivists and natural lawyers, see David Dyzenhaus, 'The legitimacy of legality', *Archiv für Rechts- und Sozialphilosophie* (forthcoming, 1996).

9   This translation from Habermas (BFN 110 / FG 141) is from Ken Baynes, who offers a fine introductory discussion of the broader complexities of this formulation, including the question of its relationship to Habermas's conception of communicative rationality. For Habermas, communicative rationality refers to the basic idea that communication is not reducible to getting someone to believe something. Instead, it consists (paradigmatically) in reaching an understanding with someone about something, where 'reaching an understanding' draws upon (unavoidable) suppositions constitutive for a weak and fragile (but none the less socially effective) form of mutual recognition. To reach an understanding with someone about something implies that one is also prepared to provide warrants for the claims raised . . . should they be contested, and that one recognizes the other as someone who is free to take a yes/no position with respect to those claims. (Cf. Baynes, 'Democracy and the *Rechtsstaat*', pp. 203, 208.) Here, I have chosen to bracket many of the fundamental questions concerning the normative roots of democratic politics in Habermas's concept of communicative rationality, not because I consider them unimportant, but because I think that an adequate vision of modern democracy ultimately should offer a convincing institutional model, as well as an impressive account of its normative core. In addition, it seems to me that Habermas scholarship too often downgrades 'mere' institutional questions: too often, something of the academic philosopher's traditional snobbishness towards his or her empirically minded cousins in political science can be detected here.

10 Habermas has been influenced here by the important study by Jean Cohen and Andrew Arato, *Civil Society and Political Theory* (Cambridge, Mass.: MIT Press, 1992).

11 Nancy Fraser, 'Rethinking the public sphere: a contribution to a critique of actually existing democracy', in *Habermas and the Public Sphere*, pp. 109–42. In a more general vein, see Iris Young, *Justice and the Politics of Difference* (Princeton: Princeton University Press, 1990). For a discussion of *Between Facts and Norms*

that claims that Habermas's recent work remains inadequate on this count, see Bohman, 'Complexity, pluralism, and the constitutional state,' pp. 920–8.

12 Seyla Benhabib, *Critique, Norm, and Utopia: A Study of the Foundations of Critical Theory* (New York: Columbia University Press, 1986), pp. 309–16. I will discuss Habermas's model of a 'fair compromise' in greater detail below.

13 Hannah Arendt, *On Violence* (New York: Harcourt Brace & Jovanovich, 1970), p. 44. Habermas here downplays elements of Arendt's conception of the public sphere that conflict with his emphasis on uncoerced dialogue. Cf. Seyla Benhabib, 'Models of public space: Hannah Arendt, the liberal tradition, and Jürgen Habermas', in *Habermas and the Public Sphere*. More generally on Arendt and Habermas, see the study by Maurizio Passerin d'Entrèves, *The Political Philosophy of Hannah Arendt* (New York: Routledge, 1994).

14 Jerry Mashaw, *Due Process in the Administrative State* (New Haven, Conn.: Yale University Press, 1985), cited in FG 229.

15 Thus, Habermas argues that radical democracy today must take a 'self-limiting' form: neither administrative bodies nor markets can be *immanently* organized in accordance with the principles of communicative power.

16 See also Habermas, 'Hannah Arendt: On the concept of power', in PPP 171–87.

17 Baynes, 'Democracy and the *Rechtsstaat*', p. 216.

18 Nancy Fraser, *Unruly Practices: Power, Discourse and Gender in Contemporary Social Theory* (Minneapolis: University of Minnesota Press, 1989), pp. 113–90. On the ills of systems theory for Habermas, see also Thomas McCarthy, 'Complexity and democracy: the seducements of systems theory', in *Ideals and Illusions: On Reconstruction and Deconstruction in Contemporary Critical Theory* (Cambridge, Mass.: MIT Press, 1991).

19 Fraser, 'Rethinking the public sphere', p. 134.

20 This comes out most clearly in Habermas's detailed discussion of parliament in chapter 4. There, he explicitly locates different (moral, ethical and pragmatic) forms of political argumentation *within* formal parliamentary bodies, and then suggests that each form of deliberation has particular implications for the institutionalization of deliberative legislative bodies. Pragmatic activities (concerned primarily with reaching compromises) justify a system of fair, equal and secret elections, '[f]or the participation in a fairly organized system of compromise demands the equal representation of all affected' (BFN 181 / FG 222). Ethical debate concerning the 'authentic self-understanding' and 'collective identity' of a particular people requires that '*[a]ll* members of the community . . . take part in discourse'. Thus, deliberations of this type, 'which are only representative in character because of technical reasons', cannot be organized according to a traditional model of an elected representative as a 'stand in' for those represented. Parliamentary debate can constitute only 'the organized middle point or focus of a society-wide network of communication' (BFN 182 / FG 223–4). A similar vision of the legislature as a deliberative *extension* of civil society derives from the nature of moral discourse: 'Here representation can only mean that the choice of representatives should function to guarantee the broadest conceivable

spectrum' of interpretative perspectives, particularly those of marginal groups. For Habermas the strict universalizability requirements of moral discourse demand that the voices even of those groups which may not even make up a particular community (e.g., refugees or resident aliens) need to be heard within the halls of parliament.

21   Stephen K. White, *The Recent Work of Jürgen Habermas: Reason, Justice and Modernity* (Cambridge: Cambridge University Press, 1988), pp. 76–7.

22   Fraser, 'Rethinking the public sphere', pp. 122–3.

23   For an important attempt of this type see Alec Nove, *The Economics of Feasible Socialism* (London: Routledge, 1981). It would be interesting to know Habermas's view of this genre; he utterly ignores it in his written work.

24   For a thoughtful critical analysis of Habermas's theory in light of recent developments in the international capitalist political economy, see Neil Brenner and John P. McCormick, 'Habermas' *Facticity and Validity* and the Historical-Geographical Limits of Contemporary Democratic Theory' (unpublished MS, 1996).

25   Jean Cohen, *Class and Civil Society: The Limits of Marxian Critical Theory* (Amherst, Mass.: University of Massachusetts Press, 1982).

26   The literature here is vast. For a recent summary see E. N. Suleiman (ed.), *Parliaments and Parliamentarians in Democratic Politics* (New York: Holmes and Meier, 1986). For an argument suggesting that even the relatively impressive American Congress exhibits evidence of parliamentary decay, see Theodore Lowi, *The End of Liberalism* (New York: Norton, 1979).

27   What I have in mind here is a massive empirical literature that suggests two different points: first, democratic processes continue to be undermined by social and economic inequalities which too often mean that the voices of the socially vulnerable are inadequately represented in the halls of government. A good deal of the political science literature on this topic suggests that this familiar problem has been exacerbated over the course of the last twenty years, as economic inequality has increased and neo-liberal governments have dismantled welfare state-type decision-making devices that often provided real – though inadequate – representation to socially subordinate groups. Second, growing evidence suggests that contemporary liberal democracy may be experiencing a crisis of legitimacy of sorts: even in the most stable liberal democracies, voting rates are on the decline, and many polls suggest growing unease and dissatisfaction with the workings of parliamentary government. In short, a growing number of citizens are seeking to 'disengage' themselves from the workings of representative democracy, to an extent arguably unprecedented since the Second World War. How serious this crisis will turn out to be in the developed capitalist democracies of Western Europe and North America remains to be seen; in newly democratized countries, this crisis is likely to have far more dire consequences.

28   For a discussion based on similar concerns see Bohman, 'Complexity, pluralism, and the constitutional state'.

29 Bernhard Peters, *Die Integration moderner Gesellschaften* (Frankfurt am Main: Suhrkamp, 1993), p. 352. For a thoughtful discussion and criticism of this work, see James Bohman, 'Review of Bernhard Peters, *Die Integration moderner Gesellschaften*', *Constellations*, 1/3 (1995).

30 Peters, *Die Integration moderner Gesellschaften*, p. 329.

31 Ibid.

32 Ibid., p. 344.

33 Ibid., p. 351.

34 Ibid., p. 345.

35 Ibid., p. 341.

36 For an interpretation of Mill and Tocqueville along such lines, see Carole Pateman, *Participation and Democratic Theory* (Cambridge: Cambridge University Press, 1970). On the surface, Habermas's use of Peters leaves him with a two-track model resembling that of Bruce Ackerman, for whom 'normal' democratic politics is substantially less ambitious in scope than 'exceptional' political moments when the liberal-democratic polity engages in alterations to its fundamental constitutional structure. But Ackerman is arguably more of a radical democrat than Habermas here: Ackerman may not be willing to accept the 'realist' insight that elected democratic legislatures, even during the course of normal liberal-democratic politics, should be satisfied with taking on a secondary role *vis-à-vis* their administrative brethren. Bruce Ackerman, *We the People: Foundations*, vol. 1 (Cambridge, Mass.: Harvard University Press, 1991).

37 Jürgen Habermas, 'Zum Begriff der politischen Beteiligung', in KK 9–60.

38 Ingeborg Maus, *Zur Aufklärung der Demokratietheorie* (Frankfurt am Main: Suhrkamp, 1992). This is not meant as a criticism of Habermas's normative defence of civil disobedience; it *is* meant to suggest that the empirical implications of its proliferation may be quite different from those suggested by him.

39 What exactly, for that matter, is a 'crisis' in this context?

40 Baynes, 'Democracy and *Rechtsstaat*', p. 218.

41 There is a similar ambivalence in Habermas's assorted comments about corporatist decision making here. At times, he repeats a traditional left-wing version of the argument (central to *The Structural Transformation of the Public Sphere*) that corporatist decision making represents a potential threat to popular sovereignty; at other times, he seems willing to concede the unavoidability of corporatism. What protections are there against its ills? He says that '[t]here are no easy recipes. In the final instance, only a suspicious, mobile, alert, and informed public . . . serves as a check against the emergence of illegitimate power' (BFN 441–2 / FG 532). But what if autonomous processes within civil society itself have been undermined by forms of corporatism that privilege the powerful and wealthy?

42 Let me try to be as clear as possible here: I *do* think that Habermas's idea of law as mediating between communicative and administrative power is fruitful. My concern is merely that he has conceptualized this nexus in such a way as to generate a series of tensions within his account that arguably could be avoided.

43 Habermas claims that liberal formal law remains imprisoned in the 'productivistic' assumptions of industrial capitalism (BFN •• / FG 491). Frankly, this seems to me to be rather too simple. As I have tried to show elsewhere, by means of an exegesis of the early Frankfurt school jurists Franz Neumann and Otto Kirchheimer, this view downplays the eminently *democratic* functions of formal law: Scheuerman, *Between the Norm and the Exception: The Frankfurt School and the Rule of Law* (Cambridge, Mass.: MIT Press, 1994). Habermas's position here also shares some surprising similarities with free market jurisprudence, which claims that the traditional liberal rule of law can be preserved only if competitive capitalism is maintained: Scheuerman, 'The rule of law and the welfare state: towards a new synthesis', *Politics and Society*, 22 (1994). For a recent, empirically minded defence of traditional liberal legal forms, see David Schoenbrod, *Power without Responsibility: How Congress Abuses the People through Delegation* (New Haven, Conn.: Yale University Press, 1993).

44 The translation used here is from Baynes, 'Democracy and the *Rechtsstaat*', p. 214. The passage also points out that Habermas sees courts as part of the law-making process (see chs 5 and 6). I have bracketed this complex issue here for two reasons: (1) Habermas tends to see courts as playing at most a secondary role in this process; (2) it would raise complicated jurisprudential issues that I simply cannot do justice to here.

45 Interestingly, he admits that this suggestion may imply that 'my picture of a democratic "state of siege" directed against the apparatus of the state' has been rendered inappropriate (BFN 440/FG 531). It seems to me that this argument potentially moderates Habermas's (in my view, unduly harsh) criticisms of authors like Joshua Cohen, who are more willing to accept a far more ambitious democratization of social and political institutions than Habermas tends to (BFN 304–8/FG 369–73): Joshua Cohen, 'Deliberation and democratic legitimacy', in *The Good Polity*, ed. A. Hamlin and B. Pettit (Oxford: Oxford University Press, 1989).

46 See also the rather modest reform proposals outlined on BFN 442/FG 533: increased possibilities for the exercise of direct democracy, as well as the 'constitutionalization' of the mass media by means of a set of legal procedures counteracting asymmetries of social power.

6

Habermas, feminism and the question of autonomy

Maeve Cooke

Introduction

In the following I investigate the fruitfulness of Habermas's theory from the point of view of a feminist conception of autonomy, understood as a conception congenial to feminists.[1] I begin with an overview of the feminist critique of the ideal of autonomy. I suggest that this critique does not provide compelling reasons for rejecting the very notion of autonomy as a normative ideal, but instead calls for a conception of autonomy that takes account of the relevant objections. I then look at Habermas's theory from this point of view. Although Habermas outlines a model of self-identity, and in particular of ethical agency, that seems potentially attractive to feminists, I argue that his account of autonomy remains unsatisfactory. More precisely, Habermas presents us with two interpretations of individual human autonomy, neither of which is adequate as it stands: on the one hand, a conception of moral autonomy that fails to do justice to important dimensions of human agency; on the other hand, a conception of ethical autonomy that requires clarification and elaboration. I conclude that Habermas's notion of ethical autonomy provides a useful starting-point for feminists concerned to rethink autonomy, but that they must address the problem of ethical validity which remains unclear and underdeveloped in Habermas's theory.

I The Feminist Challenge

Feminist resistance to the ideal of autonomy divides into two main camps.[2] The first camp contains feminists in the fields of moral and political theory. The second contains feminists sympathetic to post-structuralism and post-modernism.

1 Feminist Critique of the Disembedded and Disembodied Self

In the areas of moral and political theory, feminists have long pointed out that the ideal of autonomy as traditionally conceived has been inimical to feminist concerns. In analysing the reasons for this, feminists have criticized the conceptions of self traditionally associated with the ideal. Several feminist critics have drawn attention to the way in which a conception of the self as essentially disembedded underlies both the deontological tradition of moral theory and the contractarian tradition of political theory.[3] As Seyla Benhabib, referring to a formulation by Hobbes, points out, the self is regarded as a mushroom – as though it had sprung up overnight, without history and without connection to other persons.[4] Such a conception of self is unacceptable to feminists for at least two reasons.

First, it fails to acknowledge the self's embeddedness as constitutive of its identity. By 'embeddedness' is meant locatedness in contexts of meaning: for instance, in political arrangements, in contexts of history, in networks of relationships with others, in frameworks of 'strong evaluation'[5] and so forth. While emphasis on the self's embeddedness is neither peculiar to feminism nor shared by all feminists, it seems to tie in with many women's experience of self as relational and contextual.[6]

Second, conceptions of self as disembedded tend to go hand in hand with ideas of self-identity as self-control and self-ownership. Conceptions of self guided by the ideal of self-control stand accused of denying, or at least minimizing, the importance of bodily and affective-emotional needs and desires; the idea of the self as *disembedded* is thus closely linked with the idea of the self as *disembodied*. This latter idea is unacceptable to feminists on account of its suppression of dimensions of subjectivity that historically have been central to many women's experience of self and others; in addition, feminists stress its unwelcome consequences both as far as the socialization of the individual is concerned and with regard to its effects on intersubjective relationships. It is argued that the suppression of bodily and affective-emotional needs and desires gives rise to pathological forms of individual subjectivity, with further, damaging implications for intersubjective relations; it may also produce models of politics that split off the bodily and affective-emotional aspects of human agency from deliberations on law, politics and matters of justice, leading to a problematic privatization of ethical concerns.[7] Conceptions of self guided by the ideal of self-ownership give rise to similar unwelcome relations of the self to itself and between self and others. Furthermore, for many of their adherents they point in the direction of the minimal state, a form of political arrangement regarded by many feminists as destructive of community and the caring values they wish to espouse.

In the areas of moral and political philosophy, therefore, feminists reject the ideal of autonomy on account of the objectionable conceptions of self on which traditional interpretations of autonomy have relied. But it is important to note that what is rejected is not the very ideal of autonomy, but certain historical *interpretations* of it. More precisely, what are rejected are interpretations based on conceptions of self arising from the traditions associated with so-called Enlightenment or modernist thinking. Values closely connected with the ideal of autonomy, such as capacities for critical reflection and for integration of personal experience into a coherent narrative, are not themselves undermined: as a rule, neither the need for critically reflective distance with regard to the contexts of meaning in which selves are embedded, nor the desirability of constructing and accepting responsibility for a coherent life history oriented towards the right or good, is disputed. If it were possible to work out a conception of autonomy that took account of the self's embeddedness and embodiedness, then this first kind of feminist resistance to the ideal of autonomous agency would probably dissipate.

2 The Post-modernist/Post-structuralist Feminist Critique

But feminist challenges to the ideal of autonomy have also come from another direction. Feminists inspired by post-modernism and post-structuralism frequently reject the ideal of autonomy on the grounds that it presupposes a notion of identity that *qua* ideal is repressive and exclusionary.[8] The objection here is not (in the first instance) to the particular interpretations of self-identity that traditionally have been associated with the ideal of autonomy; rather, what is rejected is the very notion of (self-)identity. According to this viewpoint, to postulate the identity of meanings is to effect a closure: a splitting off and exclusion of certain aspects of experience that are perceived as not part of the postulated identity.

Thus, for example, Judith Butler queries the desirability of the category 'woman', on the grounds that it presumes a set of values or dispositions, thereby becoming normative and restrictive in character. In addition, Butler appears to find unattractive the ideal of a unified or integrated self implicit in the construction of categories such as 'woman'. She argues for a notion of the gendered body as radically performative, a body that constantly invents and reinvents its identity and the unity of its life within plural contexts of meaning. Butler's bodies are fluid and fragmented, rather than fixed and coherent, and are constituted through multiple acts that are a function of public and social discourse.[9]

In a similar vein, Jane Flax objects to the term 'the self': on the one hand, because it effects a closure, necessarily attaching importance to certain attributes of subjectivity and dismissing others; on the other hand because of its implicit assumption that subjectivity should aim to be unitary, fixed, homogeneous and teleological.[10] Thus, for writers such as Butler and Flax, the notion of autonomy is problematic from two points of view: first, because it postulates an *ideal* of self, thereby effecting a closure; second, because it affirms the value of attributes such as coherence, resolution and unity at the expense of values such as fragmentation, fluidity and multiplicity.

The difficulties with this kind of feminist challenge to the ideal of autonomy are themselves multiple. One set of difficulties concerns the possibility of feminist politics. Feminist political action or, more generally, feminist struggles to overcome oppression and disadvantage seem to presuppose some notion of reflective, coherent, responsible and goal-directed agency. Both Butler and Flax acknowledge this problem, while disputing that their respective conceptions of subjectivity preclude emancipatory political action. Butler's solution seems to be acceptance of the need for temporary, strategic engagement in identity politics. On occasion – but not consistently – she recognizes the *political* necessity of speaking and acting as and for 'women'; even here, however, she insists on the need simultaneously to deconstruct the subject of feminism.[11] Flax attempts to reconcile her post-modern commitments with a commitment to justice and liberatory political activity through appeal to notions such as 'taking responsibility in a meaningful way';[12] she also speaks of 'better or worse ways of being a person'.[13] However, she neither accounts for nor elaborates these formulations, and they sit uneasily with her conception of fluid, heterogeneous subjectivities.

A fundamental problem with the respective approaches of Butler and Flax is that they treat subjectivity purely as a linguistic effect and, in reducing self-identity to the systems of meaning in and through which it is constituted, leave no room for intentionality. As we shall see, this criticism resurfaces persistently in feminist discussions of post-structuralism and post-modernism; it is one of the main reasons why even feminists favourably disposed to these movements find their positions with regard to emancipatory political action unconvincing.[14]

Another set of difficulties has to do with the capacities and dispositions that post-modernist and post-structuralist feminists regard as valuable. For, notwithstanding their rejection of normative categories, feminists who ally themselves with post-structuralism and post-modernism do not seem to be able to avoid the affirmation of alternative norms. They do not succeed in avoiding normative projections, but merely replace traditional or established normative conceptions of identity with alternative ones. This gives rise to the problem of why feminists should prefer the normative models of selfhood advocated by writers such as Butler and Flax to other available models. Connected with this is the question of the status of their critique: as Linda Alcoff points out, post-structuralist critiques of subjectivity must apply to the construction of *all* subjects, or they apply to none. In her words, 'Why is a right-wing woman's consciousness constructed via social discourse but a feminist's consciousness not?'[15]

Quite apart from problems of justification, however, it is not clear that feminists generally prefer the normative models of selfhood proposed by post-modernist and post-structuralist feminists. Patricia Huntington, for instance, argues that post-structuralist feminists provide too minimalist an account of situated agency, to the extent that they fail to allow equally for women's deliberate involvement in patriarchy and their ability to resist patriarchy. This is because they conflate language and identity, reducing subjectivity to a linguistic effect of the complex knot of signifying practices that comprise its world. They thus deny the possibility of intentional control over personal and social change. Huntington concludes that in leaving women in the position of too great passivity with regard to the construction of their desires and motives, post-structuralist feminism falls prey to the threat of a stoic acquiescence in the face of oppressive signifying practices. Against this, Huntington argues that feminists need to construct a normative conception of autonomy that takes account of the activities whereby individuals cultivate critical consciousness and assume responsibility for their transformations of self and constructions of identity.[16]

Even feminists sympathetic to post-modernism and post-structuralism admit disquiet with regard to the emphasis on fragmentation and the rejection of values such as coherence, reflexivity and directedness.[17] Thus, Susan Bordo associates herself with deconstructionist post-modernism with regard to its critique of disembodied knowledge, while voicing reservations concerning its proposed alternative ideals of knowledge and subjectivity.[18] Bordo argues that feminists who insist on the need for constant, vigilant suspicion of all determinate readings of culture, committing themselves to an aesthetic of ceaseless textual play, succumb to a dangerous (counter-) fantasy, the fantasy of escape from human locatedness – a fantasy, moreover, that echoes the rejected traditional ideals of self as detached and disembodied in disturbing ways. She strongly criticizes the 'new, postmodern . . . dream of being *everywhere*';[19] of 'limitless multiple embodiments, allowing one to dance from place to place and from self to self'.[20]

Or again, Patricia Waugh maintains that feminists can learn from postmodernism, but worries about the rejection of 'modernist' ideals of agency. She holds that the post-modern celebration of radical fragmentation is a collective psychological response to the recognition that Enlightenment ideals of subjectivity as autonomous self-determination are unattainable. Waugh's thesis here seems to be that the Enlightenment ideal of autonomous agency is unattainable to the extent that it presupposes a self defined without reference to history, God, political arrangements or traditional values. We have already encountered feminist critique of this kind of picture of the self. Waugh argues that in rejecting such a conception of dislocated selfhood, postmodernism all too often succumbs to nihilistic nostalgia: the impossible yearning for the lost (imaginary) object of desire issues in the frustrated smashing of the ideal object.[21] She also points out that for feminists the goals of agency, personal autonomy, self-expression and self-determination can neither be taken for granted nor written off as exhausted.[22]

Allison Weir is another feminist who sets out to straddle both sides of the post-modernist/modernist divide. She argues that feminists need a normative account of self-identity that makes space for post-modernist and post-structuralist insights, in particular concerning the multiplicity and fragmentation of identity and its constitution through exclusionary systems of meaning. In the face of post-modernist and post-structuralist antipathy towards certain other dimensions of subjectivity, however, she reminds us that the capacity and responsibility to define one's meanings is both the privilege and the burden of modern subjects. At the same time, she supports the post-modernist and post-structuralist emphasis on multiplicity by pointing out that our increasing need for self-definition is accompanied by an increasing production and differentiation of identity attributes – that is, of possible roles, attachments and affiliations, values, beliefs and so forth – which means that our identities are increasingly multiple and conflicting. In a similar vein, she stresses that struggles to resolve differences and conflicts through an openness to difference are a prerequisite for change and the generation of new meanings. Weir's commitment to certain 'Enlightenment' values thus goes hand in hand with an acknowledgement of the element of truth in postmodernist and post-structuralist accounts of subjectivity.[23]

In short, many feminists wish to take on board some of the insights of post-modernism and post-structuralism without whole-heartedly supporting their emphasis on fragmentation, multiplicity and fluidity, and without wanting to reject outright 'modernist' or 'Enlightenment' ideals of agency.[24] We might conclude that much feminist opposition to the ideal of autonomy can be construed as opposition to the ways in which it has traditionally been interpreted, especially to the pictures of self underlying these interpretations. So, while there do not appear to be compelling reasons for rejecting the very ideal of autonomy, there are good reasons to rethink it. Given the thrust of the feminist criticism encountered in the foregoing, it is clear that the first step in this endeavour is to work out an acceptable conception of self-identity. But this is not sufficient. Conditions of self-identity are not synonymous with conditions of autonomy, although they may be closely linked. The second step, therefore, is to look more closely at the ideal of autonomy, identifying its core elements, and to consider any problems – specifically related to feminism or otherwise – that emerge from this.

II Rethinking the Self

Any attempt to develop an ideal of autonomy that is acceptable to feminists must take on board the main charges that the various strands of feminist critique have levied against traditional interpretations. As we have seen, these are directed primarily against the notions of self underlying these interpretations. The criticisms I have discussed so far remind us that the self develops its identity through being located in a plurality of (frequently shifting and conflicting) contexts of meaning and relationships with others. We are also reminded that the self is embodied, with bodily needs, desires and an affective-emotional constitution that is intimately bound up with its capacities for rational reflection and action. Post-structuralist and post-modernist feminists make the further points that subjectivity is multiple and overdetermined, not just in the sense that it develops within multiple contexts, but also in the sense that it is not unitary but heterogeneous. We can take this, to begin with, as a reminder about the interrelation of reason and desire; however, it also serves as a warning about the possible non-transparency of the self. For, as psychoanalytic approaches from Freud onwards have taught us, there is good reason to suppose that some dimensions of subjectivity will always resist the individual's attempts to retrieve them. However, the aim of transparency is held to be problematic, not only because it is probably unattainable; in addition, it is often seen as constricting in its denial of the importance of the pre-linguistic and non-linguistic dimensions of subjectivity.[25] The idea that subjectivity is fully rationally retrievable is thus a potentially repressive fiction, and, as such, presents a danger that feminist attempts to work out a conception of autonomy must bear in mind.

The post-structuralist and post-modernist thesis that subjectivity is overdetermined overlaps with the thesis that the self is embedded and embodied, although there are two significant differences in emphasis. First, whereas 'embeddedness' suggests rootedness or fixedness, post-structuralists and postmodernists emphasize the processual, fluid and fragmented character of subjectivity. I have already drawn attention to feminist unease as regards this emphasis; none the less, to the extent that the focus on fragmentation, fluidity and processuality *supplements*, rather than undermines, the thesis of embeddedness, I see it as providing a fruitful vantage-point for discussion of subjectivity. However, the thesis of overdetermination has yet another dimension. As we have seen, post-structuralists and post-modernists tend to regard subjectivity as a linguistic effect: as produced by the systems of meaning in which it is formed and over which it has no control. They leave no room for a gap between language and identity, reducing subjectivity to the (multiple) discursive cultural practices in which it is constituted. They thus stand accused of denying the possibility of choice and decision; they cannot account for women's active acceptance of, or resistance towards, prevailing systems of meaning. For this reason, while it is important to acknowledge that subjectivity is constituted in and through various systems of meaning, reduction of subjectivity to these systems is a danger for feminist theories of self-identity and agency.

An initial specification of a reworked conception of autonomy would thus have to take account of the self's locatedness in multiple, possibly conflicting and shifting contexts, its bodily and affective-emotional dimensions, its capacities for fluidity and fragmentation, as well as for critical reflection, coherence, responsibility and value-directed judgement and action, its possible fundamental non-transparency, and its constitution in and through systems of meaning over which it does not have full control. As has been recognized by a number of feminists, Habermas's model of self-identity has the potential to accommodate these various dimensions of subjectivity.[26] It has the advantage that it operates with a relational model of self, thereby acknowledging the self's constitutive connection to others. At the same time, Habermas emphasizes the self's ability to transcend temporarily the contexts of meaning in which it is located at any given time, thus avoiding one of the main dangers of relational models: a failure to acknowledge the negative as well as the positive potentials of relationality as the basis of identity. For, all too often, women's identities have been defined exclusively in terms of their relationships with others, reducing them to their roles as mothers, daughters, wives, sisters, carers and so on.[27] Habermas's guiding framework, the paradigm of communicative action, enables him to interpret the development of the individual human subject in a relational way, while at the same time stressing that subject's capacities for critical reflection and coherent, value-directed action and judgement. According to the paradigm of communicative action, individual human subjects develop and maintain their identity through processes of communication in which validity claims are reciprocally raised and evaluated. Individuals develop their identities as agents through communicative processes in which they come to be seen as accountable for what they say and do. For Habermas, agents are accountable (*zurechnungsfähig*) to the extent that they undertake to provide reasons in support of the validity claims they raise. It is this undertaking – this issuing of a warranty (*Bürgschaft*) – that is recognized in contexts of communicative action: the individual agent's willingness and capacity to provide reasons in support of what he or she says.[28] However, despite his emphasis on rational accountability, Habermas does not reduce the self to this willingness and capacity to engage in argumentation. This is particularly evident in his account of the ethical self.[29]

Habermas identifies two dimensions in which the individual human subject develops its identity. Identity development in the first dimension is referred to as 'self-determination': here the self develops his or her identity as a moral agent. Identity development in the second dimension is called 'self-realization': here the self develops his or her identity as an ethical agent (TCA2 96ff; PT 185ff). We could also speak of a distinction between moral self-identity and ethical self-identity, and, since autonomy is pursued in both dimensions, a corresponding distinction between moral autonomy and ethical autonomy. I shall have more to say about the distinction between moral and ethical autonomy presently. For the moment I want to draw attention, on the one hand, to the locatedness and concrete, bodily-affective identity of the Habermasian ethical self; on the other, to its capacities for integration, coherence and rational reflection.

Habermas's ethical self develops its identity in concrete contexts of interaction, through attempts at self-definition and assignments of meaning and value that imply an orientation toward some vision of the good life. It is a self with a particular bodily-affective constitution – with a concrete, needy, desiring and feeling nature (*Bedürfnisnatur*)[30] – that also has the capacity for integration, coherence and rational reflection.[31] It is a being located in specific webs of relationships with others, a being with specific commitments, convictions, needs and desires that guide its ethical judgements and actions and form the basis for its efforts to shape its own life history; at the same time, it is capable of reflecting on its commitments, convictions, needs and desires, of integrating them into a coherent narrative of self-identity. Furthermore, the ethical self is rationally accountable with respect to the validity claims it raises in its narrative constructions: it must in principle be prepared to defend its self-interpretations and assignments of meaning and value against the critical objections of others.[32] To this extent, rational accountability is also a dimension of ethical self-identity. It is worth stressing, however, that rational accountability does not in the first instance depend on the truth or rightness of the *content* of the self's choices, judgements or actions, but on its issuing of a warranty to provide reasons in defence of these. The advantage of this position is that it secures the connection between subjectivity and intersubjectivity without giving others authority to judge the truth or rightness of what the individual actually believes or does. In addition, it attaches importance to capacities for coherence and integration, while accommodating insights about the non-transparency of the self and its capacities for fluidity and fragmentation. For, according to Habermas's conception of self-realization, the individual human subject merely acts as though its self-definitions and life history were the product of its conscious deliberation (TCA2 99; PT 227). The self's ability to reflect critically, to construct coherent meanings through reference to ideas of the good life, and its willingness to provide reasons in defence of its assignments of meaning and value, neither implies that all dimensions of subjectivity are rationally retrievable nor denies that subjects may be embedded in multiple, conflicting and shifting contexts and may derive pleasure from the experience of fluidity and fragmentation. Admittedly, the latter are not dimensions of subjectivity especially emphasized by Habermas.[33]

From the point of view of our initial discussion, Habermas's model of self-identity, in particular his account of ethical agency, seems attractive to feminist theory on at least two counts: first, in that it avoids the atomistic and disembodied conceptions of self underlying 'modernist' moral and political theory, and the parallel post-modernist and post-structuralist fantasies of dislocation and fragmentation; second, in that it emphasizes the importance of capacities for critical reflection, for assuming responsibility for the coherence of one's identity and life history, and for value-directed judgement and action – capacities that many feminists see as indispensable ingredients of a normative conception of self-identity. These capacities are ones that have a close connection with the ideal of autonomy as it has developed within the evaluative framework of modern Western societies, although – as we shall see – autonomy requires more than this.

I want to argue that Habermas's account of ethical, rather than moral, autonomy provides the most fruitful starting-point for the attempt to work out a feminist conception of autonomy. However, as it stands, Habermas's conception of ethical autonomy is unsatisfactory. Although it relies on a conception of ethical self-identity and agency that is acceptable to feminists, it is weakened by its ambiguous and underdeveloped account of ethical validity. Habermas's model of ethical self-identity assumes that the individual is guided by his or her individually worked-out conceptions of the good. However, he fails adequately to clarify what such an orientation towards the good involves. What is missing here is an account of ethical validity that would make sense of the postulated link between autonomy and subjectively developed yet *non-arbitrary* assignments of meaning and value. However, feminists might ask why they should want to retain this link, either as part of their reworked conception of self or as part of a rethought notion of autonomy. For in this regard, at least two strategies seem open to us. Either we can abandon the postulated connection between autonomy and conceptions of the good, or we can attempt to provide an adequate account of ethical validity. My discussion of autonomy in the following sections tries to make clear why I favour the second option.

III Rethinking Autonomy

The ideal of autonomy is intimately bound up with the understanding of self-identity that has developed within the horizon of Western modernity. Notwithstanding the various ways in which autonomy has been interpreted, and acknowledging that it may be necessary to distinguish between various kinds of autonomy, this ideal appears to contain certain core intuitions. I would like to suggest that the concept of autonomy has three interconnected elements, each of which would have to find a place in any reworked conception of autonomous agency.

We find these core intuitions clearly expressed in common formulations of autonomy such as 'self-determination in accordance with self-imposed laws', 'each person's capacity to determine for himself a view of the good life', or 'the freedom to assess and revise one's existing ends'. Extrapolating, we see that key ingredients of the ideal of autonomy are capacities for critical reflection, for choice and responsibility, and for defining and shaping one's identity and life in accordance with one's own vision of what is right or good. More precisely, it is possible to identify three interconnected aspects of the ideal of autonomy as it has developed within the evaluative framework of Western modernity: first, the ideal highlights the capacities for critical reflection and for coherent, responsible and goal-directed action, without necessarily seeing other dimensions as less important; second, it emphasizes the idea of self-authorship; and third, it asserts a connection between autonomy and a vision of the good life, whereby this is frequently given a moral or an ethical interpretation. The discussion so far has focused on the first of these three aspects. We have seen that Habermas offers a model of self-identity that allows for the self's locatedness in concrete contexts of meaning and value, its constitution within the framework of intersubjective relations of mutual recognition, and its bodily-affective aspects, without losing sight of the self's capacities for coherence, integration and rational accountability. I want now to turn to the other two aspects.

The second central aspect of the ideal of autonomy is closely connected with the first one. This is the dimension of self-authorship. The moral laws to which the self subjects itself must be self-imposed; the notions of the good that guide its actions and judgements must be self-given. To be sure, the idea of self-authorship can be interpreted in various ways.[34] For example, Joseph Raz – in this respect in sympathy with many liberal writers – emphasizes the connection between self-authorship and choice. Starting from the position that there is a special connection between autonomy and self-authorship,[35] Raz argues that self-creation must proceed in part through choice among an adequate range of options, that the individual must be able to choose without coercion and manipulation through others, and that he or she must be aware of the options available and the meaning of his or her choices.[36] By contrast, Habermas's notion of self-authorship focuses primarily on the individual subject's rational accountability: in order to be able to see itself as author of its own life history, the self must undertake to defend its self-interpretations and assignments of meaning and value.[37]

The metaphor of self-authorship should not be taken too literally. Although it implies that the individual must be able to see him or herself as making their own life, it should not be interpreted as the view that the autonomous self is the sole origin of its own will, desire and behaviour, and has complete control over these. The view that the self is its own ultimate origin is, arguably, incoherent. It appears to require that the self's will, desire and behaviour be governable only by itself, such that the governing self is some kind of deeper self, which is in turn governed only by its deeper self, and so on, *ad infinitum*.[38] The metaphor of self-authorship is therefore suspect when it is taken to imply *self-origination*.[39] Equally problematic is the view that the self should have complete control over its will, desire and behaviour, for this ignores the determining influences of heredity and environment and the various ways in which our will, desire and behaviour are determined by forces originating outside ourselves. Furthermore, this view appears to uphold the ideal of the fully transparent self, which, as we have seen, has been called into question by many trends in twentieth-century thought, including Freudian and post-Freudian psychoanalytic theory. The metaphor of self-authorship should thus not be construed in a way that denies the determining influences of heredity, environment and the pre-linguistic and non-linguistic dimensions of human agency.[40]

It should be noted that the idea of self-creation is central to most post-structuralist and post-modernist conceptions of subjectivity. We may recall Judith Butler's rejection of normative categories of self-identity in favour of the notion of a gendered body whose reality is radically performative, inventing and reinventing its identity and the unity of its life. Despite her antipathy to normative categories such as autonomy, however, Butler's ideal of performativity is similar in important ways to Habermas's interpretation of self-authorship, which, as we have seen, neither presupposes the complete transparency of the self nor denies its fluidity and fragmentation: the individual human subject merely acts as though its self-interpretations and assignments of meaning and value were the product of its conscious deliberation. Thus, from the point of view of this second aspect of the concept of autonomy also, Habermas's theory seems potentially attractive to feminists.

The ideal of self-authorship is not only an important aspect of autonomous identity formation, it also comes to the fore in accounts of legitimacy and political will formation, particularly in the traditions of legal and political thinking inspired by Rousseau and Kant. Not surprisingly in view of Habermas's debt to both these figures, the ideal of self-legislation is crucial to his conception of public autonomy, which in turn is fundamental for his normative model of deliberative politics. Indeed, *Between Facts and Norms* can be read as an attempt 'to decipher, in discourse-theoretic terms, the motif of self-legislation according to which the addressees of law are simultaneously the authors of their rights' (BFN 104). It is important to note that Habermas asserts an internal connection between public and private autonomy, seeing these values as co-original and as of equal weight (BFN 408ff). This suggests that any attempt to deal with private autonomy in isolation from public autonomy (or vice versa) is fundamentally misguided. Habermas himself reminds us that feminist theory has especially good reason to wish to bear in mind the dialectical relationship between public and private autonomy, for women's equal right to an autonomous private life depends on a strengthening of their position in the political public sphere (BFN 426). I accept Habermas's thesis that public and private autonomy are internally related, and regard the exploration of this connection as important for feminists in their attempt to develop normative accounts of self-identity and agency. None the less, my focus in this essay is not the conceptual interrelationship between private and public autonomy, but personal autonomy – and moral autonomy in so far as it is relevant to this ideal.[41]

A third important aspect of the ideal of autonomy is its intimate connection with moral validity or ethical validity. This is not an aspect of the notion of autonomy that has featured extensively in feminist discussions up to now, but it is a central one. There are at least two reasons for wanting to affirm a connection between autonomy and moral validity or ethical validity. The first is that it helps to make sense of the common perception that autonomy is a capacity that should be prized and promoted. The second is that the connection has a venerable history. I shall deal with each of these points in turn.

IV The Value of Autonomy

The postulated connection between autonomy and moral validity, or autonomy and ethical validity, helps to make sense of the perception, widespread in Western societies, that autonomy is a value and should, as such, be encouraged. Of course, this perception may not be correct. We can identify at least three possible perspectives on the value of autonomy: first, the view that autonomy is inherently evil or worthless; second, the view that it is inherently good or worthwhile; and third, the view that its value resides in the contribution it makes towards some other goals or ends that are seen as good or worthwhile.

Despite feminist criticisms of autonomy, the discussion so far has not provided any support for the first perspective; it has, however, left open the question of whether the second or the third view is correct. I shall not pursue the first possibility in the following, but confine myself to a brief consideration of the other two.

It is difficult to see how autonomy could be held to have an inherent worth. The capacities associated with autonomy – such as capacities for critical detachment, independent choice or goal-directed action – have no intrinsic value, as can be seen in situations where they are used for purposes that are generally held to be morally bad. For example, if critical detachment is exercised by someone who murders another, we tend to see this as making the deed more, rather than less, morally reprehensible. Similarly, we deplore the capacity for independent choice, and the ability to select goals and pursue them, whenever these are used in morally unacceptable ways. Since we do tend to see such capacities – in particular, when they are combined in the exercise of autonomy – as valuable in many situations, this suggests that their value depends on the value of the purposes to which they are put. The attempt to answer the question of why the capacities associated with autonomy, and autonomy itself, are valuable thus points in the direction of an account of why some goals are more valuable than others. If we are to make sense of the common perception that the value of autonomy and its associated capacities is not reducible to a purely subjectively defined interest and desire (as the murder example suggests), we have to look for some more general account of human motivation. What we require, it appears, is an account of human action in terms of a generally ascribable conception of the good for human beings. Such an account might attribute to human beings a fundamental interest in justice, or in obeying the moral law, or in happiness, or in self-preservation, or in beauty, or in working out for oneself a conception of the good life. In every case, however, it amounts to an account of human beings as fundamentally motivated by some vision of the good life, which, in turn, accounts for the value of autonomy. On this view, autonomy has no inherent value, but rather merely an instrumental one, for it is valuable only to the extent that it contributes towards the realization of an end that is seen as important for human beings.

This perspective on autonomy is supported by writers such as Raz, who stresses that autonomy is valuable only if it is exercised in pursuit of the good,[42] and ultimately to the extent that it contributes to personal well-being.[43] Raz also emphasizes that for those who live in an autonomy-supporting environment, there is no other option but to be autonomous: in such societies, in which well-being is defined in terms of self-authorship, individuals will prosper only if they are autonomous.[44]

On the other hand, the view that autonomy derives its value from the contribution it makes to the good for human beings is challenged by those who wish to separate the question of autonomy from the question of self-identity. Bernard Berofsky, for instance, argues forcefully against the − in his opinion, far too widespread − assumption that autonomy involves 'strong evaluation': second-order reflection on the part of the individual as to whether the goals and ends he or she pursues are worthwhile.[45] Against this, Berofsky makes the case for a conception of autonomy in terms of a variety of intellectual, physical and emotional skills and capacities, combined with purposive rationality and independence. He insists that his account of autonomy does not presuppose any concept of the self or, indeed, of the self's fundamental motivations.[46] Despite the possible advantages of this position,[47] however, it has the disadvantage that it cannot easily account for the value of autonomy; for this, as we have seen, seems to call for some general − formal or substantive − conception of the good for human beings.[48]

It does not follow from the foregoing that this good has to be given either a moral or an ethical interpretation. Making sense of the value of autonomy may require some kind of account of the good for human beings, but this, as already indicated, can be interpreted in a variety of different ways − for instance, as justice or self-realization or self-preservation or aesthetic contemplation. In the following, I focus on the two interpretations of the good for human beings that Habermas offers in his writings, a moral and an ethical one, producing, respectively, a moral and an ethical interpretation of autonomy. While acknowledging that these represent no more than two possible interpretations of the good for human beings, I see them as a useful point of departure for further discussion.[49]

V Autonomy and Validity

The connection between the concept of autonomy and a moral or an ethical interpretation of the good for human beings has a venerable history. Rousseau and Kant, who played a crucial role in formulating the modern understanding of autonomy, did not conceive of it simply as self-direction: they connected autonomous self-government with an objectively conceived moral law. Rousseau's Émile is truly free only when he is virtuous;[50] for Kant, only a will determined by moral insight counts as autonomous.[51] Habermas retains the historical connection between autonomy and moral validity, upholding a notion of moral autonomy. Other contemporary writers, especially those within the liberal tradition, link autonomy to validity in a more general, not strictly moral sense: autonomy is seen as the individual's capacity to work out for him- or herself a conception of the good, as 'the ability of each person to determine for himself or herself a view of the good life'.[52] Whereas the moral view of autonomy binds it to a universally valid moral law, the latter position – which I refer to as the 'ethical view' – connects it to conceptions of the good whose content must be worked out by the individual him- or herself. Habermas also affirms such an ethical view of autonomy, which he sees as complementing the moral conception.

1 Habermas's Conception of Moral Autonomy

Habermas's conception of moral autonomy attempts to retain the idea of objective moral validity while taking on board post-Enlightenment critiques of ahistorical, foundationalist and abstractly utopian notions of reason, truth and justice. One of the most significant tendencies in twentieth-century philosophy has been to cast doubt on the claim that it is possible to uncover objectively valid and timeless normative foundations: on what we might call metaphysical attempts to uphold emphatic, foundationalist, ahistorical conceptions of reason, truth or justice. Habermas describes this as a post-metaphysical impulse,[53] and develops his conception of communicative rationality in response. Communicative rationality is post-metaphysical, yet non-defeatist. It articulates a conception of reason that is formal and procedural rather than substantive, fallibilist rather than foundationalist, situated or contextualized rather than abstract and ahistorical, intersubjectivist rather than monological, complex and plural (allowing for various spheres of validity) rather than fixated on one dimension of validity (theoretical truth). In a similar vein, his communicative ethics provides a 'post-metaphysical' account of moral validity to the extent that it conceives this as the outcome of a discursively achieved consensus on the universalizability of norms and principles. The framework of communicative rationality thus enables Habermas to assert a connection between autonomy and moral validity, while avoiding both moral relativism and metaphysical normative foundations. His post-metaphysical approach seems attractive to feminists who have been sensitized to the problems besetting metaphysical projections. From the point of view of the ideal of autonomy, however, his endeavour runs into difficulties.[54] Habermas's post-metaphysical account of moral validity relies on an idea of moral agency, and a concomitant conception of moral autonomy, that is unacceptable – or of limited usefulness – to feminists.

Habermas defines moral validity in terms of a discursively achieved universal consensus on the acceptability to everyone of certain norms and principles. His principle D states that only those norms can claim to be valid that meet, or could meet, with the approval of all concerned in their capacity as participants in a moral discourse.[55] The internal connection between validity and discursively achieved universal consensus is necessary in order to take account of the idea of general acceptability that is held to be an indispensable ingredient of the idea of objective validity, without succumbing to metaphysical projections. However, the result is a notion of moral validity that is abstractly universalist; it cannot take account of particular commitments, convictions, needs and desires as expressed by specific individuals and groups in concrete contexts.[56] This aspect of Habermas's communicative ethics has been widely criticized, most frequently because its requirement of consensus in the face of contemporary value pluralism would make moral judgements impossible to achieve.[57] Habermas himself admits that the plurality and irreconcilability of value standards in contemporary societies has two significant implications: first, that the norms and principles on which it is possible to reach agreement in discourse will become more and more abstract; second, that the set of questions that can be answered rationally from the moral point of view will become smaller and smaller (JA 90ff). Examples he gives of moral norms are: 'You should not lie,' 'You should not kill,' 'You should keep your promises' (JA 60–9). But norms such as these, precisely because they are abstract enough to be acceptable to everyone, make no reference to the needs and desires of specific individuals and groups in concrete situations.[58] This has implications for Habermas's conception of moral autonomy: autonomy in the sense of self-determination. Habermas asserts a connection between self-determination and moral validity. Agents are autonomous, in the sense of self-determining, to the extent that they judge and act in accordance with morally valid norms and principles that they themselves accept as such. Stressing the cognitive moment inherent in self-determination, Habermas points to the link between autonomy and moral insight: on his view, the autonomous self gives itself only rationally grounded laws (JA 42).

More precisely, the self achieves and maintains its identity as a self-determining being to the extent that it judges and acts in accordance with norms and principles that all could will in common (JA 42); for Habermas, this means in accordance with norms and principles that would be recognized as morally valid by all participants in a moral discourse (PT 193). There is thus a clear connection between Habermas's notion of autonomy, in the sense of self-determination, and discursively interpreted moral validity. However, since moral insight, when conceived in terms of discursively achieved universal consensus, requires the individual to abstract from his or her particular commitments, convictions, needs and desires (for otherwise universal consensus would be impossible), the self achieves moral autonomy (self-determination) only if it undertakes a similar process of abstraction.[59] Habermas does not deny that the self-determining self is embedded in multiple contexts; nor does he deny the bodily and affective-emotional aspects of self-determining agency; however, he insists that achieving and maintaining moral autonomy demands (temporary) abstraction from these multiple contexts and from many of the self's bodily needs and desires.[60] For Habermas, the self's embeddedness in multiple contexts, as well as its bodily and affective-emotional constitution, are relevant aspects of its identity only along the axis of self-realization. In attempting to retain the connection between autonomy and context-transcendent validity, Habermas thus splits off precisely those aspects of self-identity and agency that feminists see as important ingredients. From a feminist point of view, therefore, Habermas's conception of moral autonomy offers – at best – no more than a partial account of human agency, and would have to be supplemented by another account.

2 Habermas's Conception of Ethical Autonomy

Habermas, however, offers not just an account of the morally autonomous self. As already indicated, he describes the process of subjectification as taking place along two axes: the axis of self-determination, or moral autonomy, and the axis of self-realization, or ethical autonomy. Ethical autonomy refers to the self's capacity to work out for him- or herself conceptions of the good, to integrate them into coherent narrative constructions of identity, and to undertake to provide reasons in defence of these conceptions and construc- tions. We have seen that Habermas's account of the ethical self is congenial to feminists in that it acknowledges the self's locatedness and concrete bodily- affective identity, as well as its rational accountability, and allows for the self's fluidity and non-transparency, as well as for its capacities for coherence and integration. However, although Habermas's picture of ethical agency avoids the abstract universalism of his picture of moral agency, as it stands, it is unsat- isfactory. Its main weakness is its inadequate account of ethical validity.

Habermas defines ethical validity in terms of the hermeneutic explication of context-specific value orientations and self-interpretations, together with deliberation on existential questions relating to the successful conduct of life. The norm guiding such hermeneutic explications is authenticity, and the norms guiding discussion of existential questions are happiness and well-being (JA 1–17). The individuals and groups involved must attempt to work out how they should live their lives individually and collectively within the horizon of pre-given forms of life.

Habermas emphasizes that ethical judgements, in contrast to moral judge- ments, are context-specific. This context specificity refers, in the first instance, to the persons and situations to whom ethical judgements apply. Such judge- ments always apply to specific individuals and groups in concrete historical situations: what is right for me (or us, as a group) or you under particular circumstances or in a particular situation may not, of course, be right for me (us) or you under different circumstances or in a different situation. However, the context specificity of ethical judgements says nothing about the basis for their validity. Individual (or group) ethical judgements, as Habermas recog- nizes, refer to individually (or group) held conceptions of the good. But how are we to conceptualize such conceptions of the good? What exactly is involved in holding or pursuing a conception of the good? Are conceptions of the good irreducibly subjective or purely conventional? Or do they, by contrast, have a moment of non-subjectivity and context-transcendence? Not only does Habermas fail to elaborate on what is involved in holding or pur- suing a conception of the good; he equivocates on the question of context transcendence. Sometimes he suggests that ethical judgements are formed through reference to pre-given conceptions of the good; these pre-given ideas of the good require hermeneutic explication, as opposed to critical evalua- tion through appeal to alternative standards.[61] Sometimes he attributes to ethical judgements a moment of universalizability whereby the individual supposes that, under conditions of ideal discourse, everyone would agree with his or her assignments of meaning and value.[62] In the first case, he appears to deny to conceptions of good any inherent non-subjective and non-conventional dimensions; in the second case, he acknowledges these dimensions, but fails to say anything at all about the basis for the anticipated universal agreement.

These problems are not peculiar to Habermas's account of ethical validity. There is a tendency either to construe conceptions of the good as irreducibly subjective or purely conventional, or else to acknowledge their non-subjective and non-conventional dimensions without explaining in what these consist. However, as I shall now show, the former tendency results from a misunderstanding of what it is to hold a conception of the good, and is thus simply erroneous; whereas the latter tendency, by contrast, captures essential features of what it is to hold a conception of the good, although it is frequently connected with an account of ethical validity that is underdeveloped.

3 Conceptions of the Good and Ethical Validity

The very notion of a conception of the good implies a moment of context transcendence. Though the task of specifying the *content* of the good may be left up to each individual, conceptions of the good, even when agnostically defined, have an indispensable non-arbitrary dimension.[63] Otherwise, they would not be conceptions of the good. This is evident, for example, from Charles Taylor's articulation of the various – often implicit – assumptions on which the modern sense of self relies.[64]

Taylor shows that modern self-identity – and, arguably, human agency itself – is constituted through reference to frameworks of value within which human life is seen as meaningful.[65] 'To know who you are is to be oriented in moral space, a space in which questions arise about what is good or bad, what is worth doing and what not, what has meaning and importance for you and what is trivial and secondary.'[66] It follows from Taylor's articulation of the presuppositions of identity that the individual's subjectively worked-out assignments of meaning and value are not just subjective preferences, at least when viewed from the person's own perspective. The very notion of a conception of the good, as Taylor emphasizes, incorporates a crucial set of qualitative distinctions. It involves the sense that some actions or modes of life or modes of feeling are incomparably higher than others that are more readily available to us. The ends or goods that invoke this sense of being incomparably higher are not just more desirable than other, ordinary goods;

rather, they command our awe, respect or admiration. This sense of higher worth implies, on the one hand, that such ends or goods stand independently of our own desires, inclinations and choices, and on the other, that they represent standards by which these desires and choices are judged.[67] For this reason, the view that the individual must work out his or her own conception of the good should not be mistaken for the view that such conceptions are irreducibly subjective. From the individual's own point of view, at least, his or her conceptions of the good have an essential non-arbitrary dimension. The problem is how to interpret this dimension. Does it imply the objectivity in principle of moral or ethical values? If so, in what does this objectivity consist? And how is it to be ascertained? Or does the individual's sense that his or her assignments of meaning and value are non-arbitrary lack any objective justification? Might it not be dismissed as ideological, and criticized as symptomatic of repression?

It is one thing to claim that some kinds of conceptions of the good are ideological and repressive; it is another to claim that this is true for conceptions of the good in general. The latter criticism – if it is to have any force – presupposes the availability of a perspective that does not itself rely on any conception of the good. The crucial question in this regard is whether all kinds of evaluative distinctions can be reduced to the subjective (possibly conventionally imposed) wills and desires of those who wish to uphold their objectivity. Taylor's account of human agency, if correct, suggests that they can not – or, rather, that no perspective is available from which a reduction of this kind would be meaningful. For, as we have seen, Taylor, maintains that human agency requires reference to some kind of framework of value, and that attempts to do without any such framework inevitably substitute alternative frameworks for the rejected ones. However, the strength of Taylor's argument as regards the non-arbitrary nature of conceptions of the good stands in direct relation to its weakness in another area. His argument is most plausible when he leaves open the question of the *content* of these visions of the good. His thesis that human agency presupposes a reference to some kind of framework of value is strongest if the nature of the ends and goods deemed incomparably higher within a given framework is left open. They certainly do not have to be strictly moral conceptions, or even conform to minimal standards of moral acceptability as these have been developed, for example, within the Judaeo-Christian tradition of Western modernity. Thus, although Taylor's picture of human agency undermines subjectivism by defending the non-arbitrary aspect of conceptions of the good, it also raises as many questions as it answers.

Two questions, in particular, require further attention. First, the objective basis for the individual's sense that his or her assignments of meaning and value are non-arbitrary remains to be clarified: Taylor's picture of agency calls for a fuller account of the non-subjective dimensions of conceptions of the good. Taylor himself explains the appeal of conceptions of the good through the sense they make of our intuitions and experience. Visions of the good establish their validity for us by providing terms that allow us to construct the best account we can give of ourselves at any given time.[68] Taylor argues convincingly in favour of a model of practical reasoning that starts from the terms in which people actually live their lives. His guiding standard in this regard is that of the 'best account', which appeals to norms of realism, clairvoyance and insightfulness. He quite rightly insists that such accounts have to be constructed on the basis of people's own experiences. However, although Taylor acknowledges that we sometimes offer accounts of what *other* people are about in their lives, accounts that claim to be more perceptive, shorn of certain delusions or limitations that affect the people themselves,[69] he offers no guide-lines as to how the validity of such third-party claims might be assessed. On what non-subjective basis may our intuitions be criticized as unsound and our interpretations of experience as blinkered, distorted or foreshortened? Taylor has surprisingly little to say on this count. Although he offers a convincing phenomenology of what it is to hold a vision of the good, as well as of the practical reasoning involved,[70] he explicates validity solely from a purely subjective viewpoint – from the first-person perspective of those who are actively engaged in practical reason and concerned to work out (individually or collectively) their own respective conceptions of the good. The question of the extent to which criticism from a third-person perspective is possible and desirable remains in need of closer consideration.

A second question follows directly from this first one. This is the question of whether there are any objective standards available for assessing the moral acceptability of conceptions of the good and of evaluative frameworks. As it stands, Taylor's picture of human agency seems to permit too much. As we have seen, it provides no non-arbitrary basis for discriminating between conceptions of the good, thus leaving open the possibility that these may be supremacist, racist, patriarchal and so on. On the one hand, the strength of Taylor's picture of human agency derives from its complete agnosticism as regards the content of the conceptions of the good that he sees as necessarily guiding human agency. On the other hand, it seems to require supplementation by a moral theory that would filter out morally impermissible conceptions.

Although I have rejected Habermas's account of moral *autonomy* on the grounds of its unacceptable (or, at any rate, limited) picture of moral agency, his theory of moral *validity* may prove useful here. This, as we have seen, provides a post-metaphysical, yet non-arbitrary, basis for adjudicating between moral claims. We also saw that, under conditions of value pluralism, the norms that pass the test of universalizability will be of a highly abstract and general nature, thus limiting the scope of his moral theory. It has been observed that this limited scope causes problems when his moral theory is interpreted simultaneously as a theory of political and legal right.[71] It also, I have argued, gives rise to a conception of moral autonomy that is, at best, of very restricted usefulness. However, for present purposes, the limited scope of Habermas's moral theory is an advantage, rather than a disadvantage. What is required here is neither a theory of political or legal right nor a normative conception of self-identity, but rather a kind of moral filter that will enable us to reject certain kinds of conceptions of the good while allowing for a broad spectrum of possible ones. In order to retain the strengths of Taylor's picture of human agency, while compensating for its weaknesses, we need a non-arbitrary means of sorting out morally unacceptable ends and goods from those that are morally acceptable. Habermas's theory of moral validity provides us with the requisite filter. Drawing on his account of moral validity, we could say that, under conditions of Western modernity,[72] only those conceptions of the good that satisfy the minimal conditions of universalizability as formulated in D are deemed acceptable reference points for individual autonomy. This would eliminate, for instance, conceptions of the good that are inherently supremacist, racist, patriarchal and so on, while permitting ones that are aestheticist, utilitarian, religious, liberal and many more. Thus, Habermas's theory of moral validity, precisely because of its highly abstract and general nature, may help to remedy one of the main weaknesses of Taylor's position.

A second weakness, however, is shared by Habermas and Taylor. Whereas Habermas sometimes acknowledges, and Taylor consistently emphasizes, that conceptions of the good have a non-arbitrary dimension, neither provides much insight into its basis. If an orientation toward subjectively defined, but ultimately neither irreducibly subjective nor purely conventional, conceptions of the good is an indispensable element of individual autonomy, then we need a better account of ethical validity than either Taylor or Habermas provide.

VI Conclusion

My discussion of the feminist critique of autonomy has revealed no compelling reason for abandoning the idea that autonomy is valuable, though it has suggested the need to rethink the conceptions of self-identity on which this idea relies. Here, I have drawn attention to the potential fruitfulness of Habermas's framework of communicative action and, in particular, of his account of ethical agency. I then argued that feminists concerned to rethink autonomy should attempt to identify its central elements, considering them from the point of view of feminist concerns. One of these central elements turns out to be far from straightforward: autonomy's connection with some or other picture of the good for human beings. Although this element cannot easily be dispensed with, it gives rise to a number of problems. These problems occur even when the good for human beings is defined in a way that highlights the individual's self-authorship rather than the content of the goals towards which this self-authorship is directed. Such a view of the human good, referred to by Habermas as ethical agency or autonomy, focuses on the individual's *capacity to work out for him or herself* a conception of the good life. Particularly as it is incorporated within Habermas's theoretical framework, this view of (a fundamental motivation of) the self is likely to be congenial to feminists. This is because it is readily compatible with feminist emphasis on the locatedness and embodiedness of subjectivity, and on the historical, relational and non-linguistic aspects of self-identity, but does not jettison capacities for critical reflection, independent thinking and coherent, goal-directed action. Moreover, in leaving the question of the content of the good to individuals themselves, it appears to avoid the problem of finding a non-arbitrary basis for the validity of individually held conceptions of the good. It only *appears* to avoid the problem, however. Although it is not evident from Habermas's account of ethical agency, ethical autonomy, properly understood, appeals to the idea of a non-arbitrary conception of the good. Ethical autonomy thus relies on an idea of validity that, at one and the same time, is subjectively defined and not irreducibly subjective. What exactly is involved here? In particular, what is the basis for the individual's sense that his or her assignments of meaning and value have a non-arbitrary dimension? On what grounds may criticism of individual ethical judgements be carried out? Habermas offers little insight into the concept of ethical validity. Even Taylor, who provides a less ambiguous and phenomenologically richer account, fails to provide enlightenment as regards the possibilities of non-subjective and non-conventional ethical critique. If, as I have proposed, feminists concerned with autonomy look to Habermas for inspiration, then they will have to look more closely at the question of ethical validity and the non-arbitrary basis for judgement that it implies.

I want to conclude by rendering the question more specific. Drawing on Habermas's model of ethical agency, I have made a case for a conception of autonomous self-authorship that entails an orientation towards individually

worked-out ideas of the good, suggesting that such a conception is congenial to feminists. A first step towards clarifying the non-arbitrary dimensions
of this orientation towards the good might be to consider the relation
between autonomy and *intersubjectivity*. Taylor stresses that the individual who
holds certain ideas of the good does so because he or she finds them to make
best sense of his or her intuitions and experiences. However, although such a
starting-point is inescapably subjective, in seeing certain ends and goods as
'incomparably higher' and as commanding awe and respect, the individual
describes them in terms that are non-subjective and that, in fact, suggest an
analogy with truth. He or she sees the ends pursued and the conceptions of
the good adopted as 'true', in the sense that they offer the best available
account of how he or she should live his or her life. Habermas follows
Charles S. Peirce, who asserts a connection between truth and general agreement: 'The opinion which is fated to be ultimately agreed to by all who investigate is what we mean by truth.'[73] We have already seen that Habermas's
discourse ethics draws on this view of truth, although his principle D stresses
the *discursive achievement* of truth as much as the idea of an ultimate consensus. Even if we leave open the way in which the ultimate consensus is reached
(allowing for non-discursive as well as discursive methods), truth on this view
has an inherent intersubjective dimension. However, the postulated connection between truth and universal agreement is in the first instance merely
conceptual: it explicates (part of) the meaning of the concept of truth.

None the less, even such a conceptual link between truth and universal
agreement may be relevant to our discussion of ethical validity. If this link
obtains, the notion of universal agreement or recognition functions as a regulative ideal that forbids us to reject other people's opinions on a given matter
as *in principle* false or irrelevant. Although in a concrete instance, it may turn
out that there are good reasons for dismissing the opinions of others with
regard to a matter under discussion, the concern with truth requires us, initially at least, to take them seriously. The conceptual connection between
ethical validity and universal recognition thus has implications for the possibility of rational critique. The link, if it obtains, implies that the individual's
development as an autonomous agent is impaired when he or she suppresses
the intersubjective dimension of his or her evaluative judgements by sealing
them off from the critical approbation of others.[74] If this is so, we gain a basis
for criticizing those modes of identity formation in which individuals, when
working out for themselves their conceptions of the good, deny the relevance in principle of other people's opinions and judgements, thereby withdrawing into an impermeable private space. Furthermore, criticism of this
kind of disorder of identity (which is also a failure of autonomy) simultaneously permits criticism of the reifying and alienating social forces that frequently create the need for the individual to retreat from the critical opinions

of others.[75] Thus, even a merely conceptual link between ethical validity and intersubjective recognition has possible implications for social and political critique.

In addition, however, the intersubjective dimension of ethical judgements can be given a stronger interpretation that goes beyond a mere conceptual argument. On this interpretation, the individual seeks public – and possibly even political – recognition for the validity of his or her ethical judgements, and for the conceptions of the good on which these are based. If, for example, homosexuals are permitted to live the life-style of their choice only so long as they do so privately or in carefully delimited enclaves, they are denied the public affirmation of identity and their assignments of meaning and value that is afforded to those who adopt conventionally accepted, heterosexual life-styles. The same argument holds for the innovative self-inventions espoused by feminists such as Judith Butler, and to the self-definitions, life choices and conceptions of the good held by individuals and groups on the margins of society. Arguably, the freedom to have a public identity – and this means a publicly affirmed identity – is fundamental to individual human flourishing. It has been said that the 'freedom to have impact on others – to make the "statement" implicit in a public identity – is central to any adequate conception of the self'.[76] If this is so, autonomy is not only linked conceptually with intersubjective recognition; it is also connected with public – and possibly political – recognition in ways that require further exploration and discussion.

Drawing on the work of Habermas, the thrust of my discussion has been to propose a conception of autonomy as a component of self-identity which would be compatible with feminist concerns. I have tried to identify some of the problems arising from this, spending most time on the question of ethical validity. I have done so because it is an issue that feminist discussions of autonomy have not yet addressed. But it is, in my view, a central one. For it is only by clarifying the notion of ethical validity that feminists will be able to make autonomy, which presupposes a capacity for insight into the validity of one's values and convictions, compatible with an appropriately embedded notion of the self.

Notes

1 I leave open the question of whether the project of a feminist conception of autonomy can be understood in a stronger or more substantive sense.

2 Clearly, this schema cannot do justice to the many variations in the positions held within the two camps. It may also fail to do justice to the complex positions of 'French' feminists such as Julia Kristeva and Hélène Cixous. Kristeva can

be read as proposing an idea of the 'feminine' as an alternative to the 'masculine' symbolic order, Cixous as proposing one that is subversive of it. Arguably, however, Kristeva does not reject the 'masculine' value of autonomy, but sees it as in need of supplementation through the 'feminine' dimensions of subjectivity. Furthermore, although Cixous's notion of the 'feminine' does seem to undermine the ideal of autonomy, it runs into difficulties similar to those encountered by post-structuralist and post-modern critics (see below).

3 See, e.g., Susan Moller Okin, 'Reason and feeling in thinking about justice', in *Feminism and Political Theory*, ed. Cass Sunstein (Chicago: University of Chicago Press, 1990), pp. 15–35; Seyla Benhabib, 'The generalized and the concrete other', in *Feminism as Critique*, ed. S. Benhabib and D. Cornell (Minneapolis: University of Minnesota Press, 1987), pp. 77–95.

4 Benhabib, 'Generalized and the concrete other', p. 84.

5 Here I follow a central thesis of Charles Taylor. Cf. his *Philosophical Papers*, vol. 2 (Cambridge: Cambridge University Press, 1985), and *Sources of the Self* (Cambridge: Cambridge University Press, 1989).

6 Cf. Carol Gilligan, *In a Different Voice* (Cambridge, Mass.: Harvard University Press, 1982).

7 Cf. Maeve Cooke, 'Are ethical conflicts irreconcilable?', *Philosophy and Social Criticism*, 23/2 (1997), pp. 1–19.

8 This is not true for all feminists who associate themselves with post-structuralism and post-modernism. Drucilla Cornell, for instance, draws heavily on Derridian post-structuralism without wanting to reject normative conceptions of self-identity as such. She argues rather for a particular normative conception of self-identity – one that takes account of difference as an inevitable part of conceptual thought, and that recovers the affective and 'natural' dimensions of moral agency. Cf. D. Cornell, *The Philosophy of the Limit* (New York: Routledge, 1992); also D. Cornell and A. Thurschwell, 'Feminism, negativity, intersubjectivity', in *Feminism as Critique*, pp. 143–62.

9 Judith Butler, 'Gender trouble, feminist theory and psychoanalytic discourse', in *Feminism/Postmodernism*, ed. L. Nicholson (New York: Routledge, 1990), pp. 324–40.

10 Jane Flax, *Disputed Subjects* (New York: Routledge, 1993), pp. 93ff.

11 Judith Butler, 'Contingent foundations: feminism and the question of postmodernism', in *Feminists Theorize the Political*, ed. J. Butler and J. Scott (New York: Routledge, 1992), pp. 3–21, at p. 15.

12 Cf. Flax, *Disputed Subjects*, pp. 32, 108, 127.

13 Ibid., p. 101.

14 Cf., e.g., Linda Alcoff, 'Cultural feminism versus poststructuralism: the identity crisis in feminist theory', in *Feminist Theory in Practice and Process*, ed. M. Malson et al. (Chicago: University of Chicago Press, 1989); and Allison Weir, 'Toward a model of self-identity: Habermas and Kristeva', in *Feminists Read Habermas*, ed. J. Meehan (New York: Routledge, 1995), pp. 263–82.

15 Alcoff, 'Cultural feminism', p. 309.

16 Patricia Huntington, 'Toward a dialectical concept of autonomy', *Philosophy and Social Criticism*, 21/1 (1995), pp. 37–55.

17 To be sure, Flax states explicitly that she is not advocating fragmentation as the only possible or desirable alternative to a false sense of unity (*Disputed Subjects*, p. 102); furthermore, she shows convincingly that 'lacking the ability to sustain coherence, one slides into the endless terror, emptiness, desolate loneliness, and fear of annihilation that pervade borderline subjectivity' (ibid., pp. 102–3). What are needed, in her view, are better ways of organizing subjectivities. But it is far from clear on what basis subjectivities are to be organized and how such normatively guided organization of subjectivity fits with her outright rejection of 'Enlightenment' values such as autonomy, self-determination and individuality.

18 Susan Bordo, *Unbearable Weight: Feminism, Western Culture and the Body* (Berkeley: University of California Press, 1993), pp. 225ff.

19 Ibid., p. 227.

20 Ibid., pp. 228ff.

21 Patricia Waugh, 'Modernism, postmodernism, feminism: gender and autonomy theory', in *Postmodernism: A Reader*, ed. Patricia Waugh (London: Edward Arnold, 1992), pp. 189–204, at pp. 191–2.

22 Ibid., p. 194.

23 Weir, 'Toward a model of self-identity'.

24 Michèle Barrett, for instance, argues that we need a better conception of agency and identity than has been available in either (anti-humanist) post-structuralist thought or its (humanist) modernist predecessors. She calls for an imaginative reopening of the issue of humanism: Barrett, 'Words and things', in *Destabilizing Theory*, ed. M. Barrett and A. Phillips (Cambridge: Polity Press, 1992), pp. 201–19, at p. 216. This call is echoed by Judith Grant, who advocates a feminist humanist vision: a new and improved post-Enlightenment humanism: Grant, *Fundamental Feminism* (New York: Routledge, 1993), p. 183.

25 For instance, the aim of full, rational retrievability would be seen as repressive according to the model of subjectivity developed by Julia Kristeva, which attaches central importance to the pre-linguistic (and proto-linguistic) 'semiotic' realm. Cf. J. Kristeva, 'The system and the speaking subject' and other essays, in *The Kristeva Reader*, ed. Toril Moi (New York: Columbia University Press, 1986).

26 The potential usefulness of Habermas's basic theoretical framework for thinking about questions of self and agency is recognized in the articles by Benhabib, Waugh and Weir already cited; despite serious reservations, it is also recognized by Iris Marion Young (cf. 'Impartiality and the civic public', in *Feminism as Critique*, pp. 57–76).

27 Patricia Waugh (cf. 'Modernism, postmodernism, feminism', p. 204) sees Virginia Woolf's work as particularly important for feminists, in that she offers a critique of the exclusive identification with relational modes of identity as they have functioned within patriarchy.

28 Cf. Maeve Cooke, *Language and Reason: A Study of Habermas's Pragmatics* (Cambridge, Mass.: MIT Press, 1994), pp. 158ff.

29   The model of self-identity proposed by Habermas does not reduce agency to rational accountability. However, problems arise due to the fact that Habermas splits agency into moral agency and ethical agency. I argue that his account of moral agency, although it does not deny bodily and affective-emotional dimensions, dismisses them as fundamentally irrelevant to its exercise. His account of ethical agency, by contrast, takes these dimensions as its starting-point (without, admittedly, discussing them in any detail).

30   The bodily dimensions of subjectivity are presupposed but not especially emphasized in Habermas's account of ethical agency. Habermas has most to say about these aspects of subjectivity in his formal-pragmatic analyses of processes of everyday communication, where they form part of the subjective world of experiences to which the individual subject has privileged access (cf. CES 67f and TCA1 312ff; for his account of identity and individuation through reference to G. H. Mead see TCA2 96ff and PT 149–204).

31   Cf. TCA2 74f.

32   Cf. PT 187f; also JA 11.

33   Young (cf. 'Impartiality and the civic public') argues that Habermas ignores the expressive and bodily aspects of communication, thereby reproducing an opposition between reason and desire and feeling. It seems to me, however, that Young's thesis is too strong. Habermas often seems to disregard the expressive and bodily aspects of communication because of his focus on forms of communicative action (in particular, moral discourses) in which these aspects are held to be irrelevant. As I have argued, his account of ethical self-identity does acknowledge these dimensions. This is not to deny that Young's basic intuition is correct. Habermas's lack of interest in the bodily-affective aspects of subjectivity has a number of serious implications: in particular, a conception of justice that gives a foreshortened account of human suffering (cf. A. Honneth, 'The other of justice: Habermas and the ethical challenge of postmodernism', in *The Cambridge Companion to Habermas*, ed. S. K. White (New York: Cambridge University Press, 1995), pp. 289–323). Weir's contrast between Habermas, who presents the development of linguistic competence in terms of response to a threat, and Kristeva, who sees it as a pleasurable process, should also be noted in this regard (cf. Weir, 'Toward a model of self-identity').

34   In Maeve Cooke, 'Questioning autonomy: the feminist challenge and the challenge for feminism', in *Questioning Ethics*, ed. R. Kearney (London: Routledge, 1998), I propose an interpretation of the metaphor of self-authorship in terms of capacities for accountability and responsibility, independence, purposive rationality and strong evaluation.

35   Joseph Raz, *The Morality of Freedom* (Oxford: Blackwell, 1986), p. 370.

36   Ibid., pp. 389f.

37   This is not to deny that Habermas also connects self-realization with choice. He refers to the self's capacity for existential decisions, and speaks of the radical choice of self (cf. JA 9). Even here, however, Habermas emphasizes the self's commitment to its existential decisions (*Entschlußkraft*) more than its capacity to select from a variety of options.

38 Susan Wolf makes this point in her critique of the autonomy view of the self in her *Freedom within Reason* (New York: Oxford University Press, 1990), pp. 10–14.

39 Since Wolf interprets the idea of self-direction only as self-origination, she ends up rejecting the ideal of autonomy completely. Bernard Berofsky's rejection of the view that autonomy is self-direction is also based on an interpretation of self-direction as self-origination: see his *Liberation from Self: A Theory of Personal Autonomy* (New York: Cambridge University Press, 1995), pp. 1ff.

40 In 'Questioning autonomy' I show how the requirements of responsibility and accountability mean that the self must take issue with the external and internal forces that influence its life, and must query their inevitability and justifiability. Some influencing factors are purely contingent or, possibly, so deeply rooted in culture or biology that the self has no option but to accept them as given; others can be criticized on normative grounds (as exploitative, reifying, alienating, unjust, pathological and so on), and resisted in various ways, and with more or less success.

41 For Habermas, private autonomy is not synonymous with personal (ethical) autonomy. According to his account of legal autonomy as presented in BFN (cf. 450–1), personal autonomy is just one of two aspects included in the notion of private autonomy: in addition to personal (ethical) autonomy, which is oriented towards the idea of the good life (and seems to be just another formulation for 'self-realization'), private autonomy encompasses the negative freedom to pursue our goals without interference from others (BFN 399–400). I attempt to disentangle the ambiguities and complexities of Habermas's notion of private autonomy in my, 'A space of one's own: autonomy, privacy, liberty', *Philosophy and Social Criticism*, 25/1 (1999), pp. 23–53. A further aspect of Habermas's account of legal autonomy that requires elaboration is the role played by moral autonomy.

42 Raz, *Morality of Freedom*, p. 381.

43 Ibid., pp. 289ff and 391ff.

44 Ibid., pp. 391ff.

45 See Berofsky, *Liberation from Self*, esp. ch. 5 and ch. 9, pp. 226ff.

46 Ibid., ch. 9.

47 Berofsky maintains that it frees us to pursue questions about the nature of the self without having to worry that our views on autonomy will be profoundly affected (ibid., pp. 236–7).

48 Despite his explicit acknowledgement of the question of the value of autonomy, as testified to by the title of his final chapter, Berofsky in fact seems to take its value as self-evident.

49 If my argument is correct, the value of autonomy stands in relation to its contribution to some or other conception of the good for human beings. If this is so, any attempt to rethink autonomy while retaining it as a value will have to acknowledge its reliance on a picture of the good life for human beings. Clearly, it makes sense to start by looking closely at some of the existing suggestions. Given that Habermas's theory of communicative action produces an account of

self-identity that in some important respects is congenial to feminist concerns, feminists rethinking autonomy have good reason to look more closely at Habermas's account of agency – and specifically, at his accounts of moral agency and ethical agency – in terms of their underlying visions of the good for human beings.

50	J. J. Rousseau, *Émile*, tr. B. Foxley (London: Dent, 1974), p. 408.

51	I. Kant, *The Moral Law*, tr. and ed. H. J. Paton (London: Hutchinson, 1948), pp. 94–5.

52	This is the view of autonomy that Taylor (in my view, correctly) attributes to liberalism (cf. C. Taylor, 'The politics of recognition', in *Multiculturalism and the 'Politics of Recognition'*, ed. A. Gutmann (Princeton: Princeton University Press, 1992), p. 57).

53	Cf. PT, esp. chs 1–3 and 6.

54	There may be other problems connected with Habermas's post-metaphysical interpretation of truth. It could be argued that one price he pays is the loss of a vital ingredient of the idea of truth: its imperative character. Peter Dews draws attention to the power of truth, as a validity claim, to irrupt into and explode the contexts of our life and action (cf. P. Dews, 'Communicative paradigms and the question of subjectivity: Habermas, Mead and Lacan', in this volume, ch. 3). Although I cannot develop this argument here, I think it could be shown that Habermas's post-metaphysical, discourse-theoretical account of truth fails to convey a sense of the imperious power of truth.

55	Strictly speaking, this is Habermas's formulation of his discourse principle as opposed to his universalization principle, which he regards as the specifically moral principle. In my view, however, Habermas's fundamental intuition is captured just as well by D as by U, and the former has the advantage that it avoids a number of difficulties that U incurs through its reference to consequences and side-effects. I thus concur with Seyla Benhabib who argues 'that "U" is actually redundant in Habermas's theory and that it adds little but consequentialist confusion to the basic premise of discourse ethics' (in her 'Afterword' to *The Communicative Ethics Controversy*, ed. S. Benhabib and F. Dallmayr (Cambridge, Mass.: MIT Press, 1990), pp. 330–69, at p. 344).

56	The abstract universalism of Habermas's idea of moral validity has been criticized from a basically sympathetic feminist perspective by Seyla Benhabib, *Situating the Self*. (New York: Routledge, 1992) and Young, 'Impartiality and the civic public'.

57	Cf. Albrecht Wellmer, 'Ethics and dialogue: elements of moral judgement in Kant and discourse ethics', in *The Persistence of Modernity: Essays on Aesthetics, Ethics and Postmodernism*, tr. D. Midgley (Cambridge, Mass.: MIT Press, 1991), pp. 113–231; Benhabib, *Situating the Self*; Thomas McCarthy, *Ideals and Illusions* (Cambridge, Mass.: MIT Press, 1991), esp. pp. 181–99.

58	General norms such as these require interpretation and application in concrete situations before they can do so: a point that Habermas himself acknowledges (cf. JA 35–9); see also next note.

59 Habermas acknowledges that morally valid norms and principles have to be applied in concrete situations in light of all their relevant specific features. This requires context-sensitive judgement guided by the norm of appropriateness. However, he also admits that, like moral discourses, discourses of application are a purely cognitive undertaking, and cannot compensate for the uncoupling of moral judgements from the concrete (affective-emotional) motives that inform them (cf. JA 14).

60 Jürgen Habermas, 'Reply to my critics', in *Habermas: Critical Debates*, ed. J. B. Thompson and D. Held (London: Macmillan, 1982), p. 255.

61 I discuss this in more detail in Cooke, 'Realizing the post-conventional self', *Philosophy and Social Criticism*, 20/1,2 (1994) pp. 87–101. Habermas is, of course, right to say that we cannot reflectively agree to the shape of our life histories and the forms of life into which we have been socialized in the same way as we can reflectively agree to a norm of whose validity we have convinced ourselves (cf. TCA2 109). The kind of abstraction that is required in the case of universalizable moral norms and principles is neither possible nor desirable in the case of ethical judgements. However, Habermas tends to move from this to the highly questionable position that ethical judgements are guided only by non-universalizable standards of happiness and well-being (TCA2 110). He thus frequently presents ethical validity claims as context-specific in a double sense (cf. TCA1 43 and JA 1–17).

62 On occasion, Habermas does suggest that ethical validity claims are context-specific only in the first of the two senses I have outlined, seemingly concurring with Mead, who connects ethical judgements with universal recognition (cf. PT, esp. 187 and 193; also TCA2 98ff).

63 Cf., e.g., W. Kymlicka, *Multicultural Citizenship* (Oxford: Clarendon Press, 1995), pp. 80ff; J. Rawls, *A Theory of Justice* (Oxford: Oxford University Press, 1971), p. 544.

64 Taylor, *Sources of the Self*, esp. chs 1–4.

65 The status of Taylor's claim with regard to frameworks of value is not quite clear. Although his primary concern in *Sources of the Self* is to explore facets of modern identity, he argues that not just modern identity, but human identity in general, requires reference to frameworks of value and, consequently, an orientation to some vision or visions of the good. It is not clear, however, in what sense this reference and orientation is 'inescapable'. The title of his first chapter is 'Inescapable frameworks', where he stresses that it is a mistake to think that it is possible to act without any framework of value (e.g. pp. 21, 27, 29). Sometimes, however, he appears to advance the weaker thesis that an orientation towards a vision of the good is the best available way to make sense of our moral life, thereby seeming to allow for other possibilities (p. 71).

66 Taylor, *Sources of the Self*, p. 28.

67 Ibid., pp. 19–20.

68 Ibid., pp. 57ff.

69 Ibid., p. 58.

70 Ibid., pp. 71ff.

71 This is the gist of the respective critiques of McCarthy, Benhabib and Wellmer, as mentioned in n. 57 above. Habermas has taken on board this criticism by introducing an explicit distinction between moral validity, on the one hand, and legal and political validity, on the other, in his recent work (cf. esp. BFN, ch. 4).

72 Habermas himself does not restrict his theory of moral validity to the evaluative horizon of Western modernity, but rather sees it as holding good universally. Against this, I argue that its core ideas are unavoidable presuppositions of communication only in certain sorts of society (see my *Language and Reason*, ch. 2).

73 Charles S. Peirce, *Collected Papers of Charles Sanders Peirce*, ed. C. Hartshorne and P. Weiss (6 vols, Cambridge, Mass.: Harvard University Press, 1965), vol. 5, sec. 407.

74 I outline such an argument in 'A space of one's own'.

75 Ibid.

76 F. Michelman, 'Laws's Republic', *Yale Law Journal*, 97/8 (1988), pp. 1493–1537, at p. 1534, quoting Law, 'Homosexuality and the social meaning of gender', *Wisconsin Law Review*, 1/15 (1988).

7

Jürgen Habermas and the antinomies of the intellectual

Max Pensky

I

From an outsider perspective, to a non-German, it would seem an exemplary instance of the work of public intellectuals. Martin Walser, distinguished novelist, essayist and visible public intellectual, had been chosen to deliver the address on the occasion of the awarding of the Geschwister-Scholl Prize for Civic Virtue to the late German-Jewish writer Victor Klemperer. Klemperer's diaries, recounting in voluminous detail his wartime survival spent in and near his home in a suburb of Dresden, had recently been published to wide acclaim in Germany. And, like virtually all public events in the Federal Republic, the diaries generated what Habermas would term an 'ethical discourse' in the domain of Germany's inexhaustible memorial politics.

As Amos Elon, Henryk Broder and others have noted, Klemperer's wartime diaries elicited a complex and not altogether coherent range of reactions among their German readers. On the one hand, Klemperer's clear-eyed understanding of the internal link between National Socialism and genocide, and his awareness of the operation of the death camps at Auschwitz and Birkenau from his extreme isolation during the war, added more fuel to the argument that knowledge of the Holocaust must have been widespread amongst 'normal' Germans – yet another round in the interminable German discourse on the nature and extent of collective guilt and responsibility. On the other hand, for the German reading public, perhaps the most remarkable aspect of Klemperer's wartime diaries was the depth of his devotion to German culture, to the 'good' Germany of Goethe, Schiller and Kant, a store of cultural goods that was threatened by what Klemperer insisted was an aberrant and profoundly un-German National-Socialist dictatorship.[1] The unquestioned value that Klemperer saw in the store of German cultural tradition, like his obstinate self-identification as a cultured German, seemed to many a small sign that the nightmarish past of German nationalism, even of German–Jewish relations, might still be able to bring forth some resources for recovering a renewed and invigorated positive sense of Germanness.

This, in any case, seemed to be the direction that Martin Walser took in his address. Praising the (distinctively German) 'principle of precision' (*Prinzip der Genauigkeit*) with which Klemperer was able to mobilize such a fantastic psychic and moral resistance to his tormentors, Walser went on to suggest that the tenacity with which Klemperer clung to his Germanness even as the conditions for its possibility lay in ruins, far from exhibiting the tragic paradoxes and nightmarish outcome of the failed experiment of German–Jewish relations, could serve as a powerful literary and historical resource for the recovery of the blighted history of the German Jews and, with them, of German nationhood as well. In this sense, Klemperer appears to Walser as 'the ideal human figure in the German memory-conflict'.[2]

Seen through the historical lens of Auschwitz, Walser argued, Klemperer's life, like the entire history of the German-Jewish experiment, could appear only as tragedy and calamity, and his defence of his German identity a fatal self-delusion. But Walser insists on the possibility of removing this lens, or at least changing its focus. It should be possible, he insists, to look at Klemperer's assimilationist vision of German cultural greatness and national belonging *as if* Auschwitz had not been its unavoidable outcome. And here Walser extends a claim that stands at the centre of his argument, a claim that – not surprisingly – provoked an angry response from Jürgen Habermas, a member of the audience. 'Was it inevitable', Walser asked,

that the collective life of Germans and Jews, had it continued to develop under normal, civilized conditions, would lead to nothing other than this most horrible catastrophe? Certainly not. There is very little occasion for this sort of wishful thinking, but Klemperer's work, in which eighty years of this collective life is clung to and retold, compels an after-the-fact wishful thinking of this sort. And I give myself up to it gladly. Much more so than to what became reality later. Whoever regards everything as a single path that could have ended only at Auschwitz makes the German–Jewish relationship into a fated catastrophe under all conceivable conditions. This seems to me absurd. Quite apart from the fact that [were this the case] there would be no German-Jewish flourishing in the present and the future. But this is contradicted by immigration statistics. Germany is, even if the purveyors of the image of the hated German don't want to admit it, also an immigration country, even for Jews.[3]

Of course, what Walser refers to here as 'after-the-fact wishful thinking' could also be called 'moral revisionism of the past', and his argument here should be roughly familiar to anyone who remembers the terms and strategies of the 'Historians' Debate' (Historikerstreit) from the mid-1980s. Indeed, Walser's position should be seen as one aspect in a broad transformation of Germany's familiar intellectual scene, the revising of familiar distinctions between Left and Right, between progressive and neo-conservative, and a deep change in the grammar of political-cultural debate. This transformation began with the conservative political reorientation, the Tendenzwende of the early 1980s, and culminated (if in a rather fortuitous way) in the unification of the two Germanies in 1990. A former supporter of the German Communist Party and staunchly left-wing writer and intellectual for decades, Walser has steadily drifted into a characteristically neo-conservative position on questions of national identity and the moral-political negotiability of the recent German past. This places him in the company of many leading figures in the literary and political public sphere of the former Federal Republic.[4]

Despite many fears, German unification has not led to any dramatic rebirth of a particularist and exclusionary German nationalism, in large measure because the unification process has been generally regarded in economic and administrative terms, rather than as the epochal rebirth of a sovereign German nation. Yet, at the level of Germany's intellectual elites, the question of nationalism and national consciousness, their symbols, sources, effects and legitimacy, has sharpened considerably in the new landscape of the 'expanded Federal Republic'. Intellectuals have been obliged to re-examine what had been an unquestionable cultural consensus, according to which any overt expressions of 'Germanness' or national pride violated a political taboo of the Left, and insufficiently strenuous remorse over Germany's Fascist past was a telegraph of right-wing sympathies. One by one, they have been compelled to reorient themselves in a transformed political landscape, in which unification (which up until the very day of the unexpected event itself had operated for years as little more than a shopworn bit of political rhetoric of the national conservative parties) seemed to offer the intoxicating chance of self-transformation and re-creation, of a release of decade-long tensions. The reacquisition of Germany's national sovereignty, if seen as the 'break', or transitional moment, in the more gradual process of a return to 'normal' nationhood, and with it a normalizing ambition toward matters of collective memory and national feeling, has also put Germany's 'traditional' left-wing intelligentsia sharply on the defensive. It has obliged them to justify in public a rejection of nationhood and national identity that had been taken for granted for decades. And leftist intellectuals such as Habermas who still insist on this position – who insist that a reclaimed German particularism is an unacceptable prospect in terms both of world and domestic policy and of collective morality – are finding themselves increasingly isolated and increasingly few.

These broad underlying circumstances help to explain Habermas's response to Walser's Geschwister-Scholl Prize address. In a blistering attack published in the *Frankfurter Rundschau* a few days after Walser's speech, Habermas accused Walser of deliberately downplaying the tragic dimension of Klemperer's story – the sheer fact that Klemperer's dependence on the strength of the better Germany was in the end desperately wrong – as part of a broader strategy of reappropriating pre-war German traditions: 'That this dimension can disappear behind the self-satisfied self-congratulation of an obscenely harmonized German-Jewish culture . . . is a symptom of a transformed state of consciousness.'[5] From Habermas's point of view, Walser's strategy is clear: with a German Jew representing the still undamaged heritage of the German intellectual tradition, and Hitler and his followers dismissed in the same breath as an un-German aberration, the way stands open for a reappropriation of that German intellectual inheritance that until now had to pass the over-demanding critical litmus test of Auschwitz. In a peculiarly neo-conservative strategy that Habermas has called attention to over and over again, the argument subtly shifts the sense of 'normalcy' of German nationhood: once unproblematically retrieved, a particular set of traditions, attitudes and values constituting a unique form of 'Germanness' now forms a continuity, interrupted by an aberrant period beginning in 1933 and ending only with German unification in 1990. Hence the Federal Republic, and the painstakingly slow and generally successful cultivation of a republican and post-conventional political culture that made the Federal Republic possible, now appear, retrospectively, as simply an episode in a now concluded era of the *Sonderweg*, that distinctively German path of national and social development.

II

This brief public argument, which flared up quickly in the autumn of 1995 and was just as quickly forgotten, is entirely typical of the public political climate of post-unification Germany, and hence of the atmosphere in which Jürgen Habermas operates as an intellectual, in at least three distinct senses.

First, it illustrates the back-and-forth between contextual problems of collective tradition and their critical reception in the mediatized arena of ethical discourse that makes up the habitat of the public intellectual. Secondly, the exchange with Walser shows the extraordinary continuity of Habermas's political writing, a consistency stretching back over forty years and composed of an arrestingly small number of basic themes. Third, Habermas's rejection of Walser's argument points to some aspects of his role as a public intellectual that are themselves open to critical questioning. By exploring these three interlocking themes I will argue that the culturally and historically particular conception of the role of the intellectual in Germany, and above all the manner in which this conception developed in relation to the image of the conservative academic mandarin, has been definitive for Habermas's own self-understanding as a public intellectual. The influence of this conception has in large measure determined both the content and the character of his political writings, and this fact marks out both their critical strength and their distinctive shortcomings.

On an initial level, we may ask about the *role of the intellectual* generally and its specific place in Habermas's own understanding of his work. The exchange between Walser and Habermas shows the sort of tangled, context-dependent issues that public intellectuals take as their natural territory: ethical-political discourses carried out in a political public sphere, concerning deeply troubled, problematic collective traditions and identities. Both Walser and Habermas operate as *private citizens* – that is, as discursive participants who represent neither the interests of an administrative body nor (though, as Habermas had argued as early as *The Structural Transformation of the Public Sphere*, this second aspect remains rather dubious) their own direct interest: the intellectual is, pre-eminently, a creature of a bourgeois political public sphere.[6] As free participants in discussion, intellectuals effectively transfer talents and capacities pertinent to their professional roles – often as scholars or professional academicians or writers – in an attempt to influence the process of collective will formation. They find their subject-matter in contentious claims – say, those arising from a text such as Klemperer's diaries, a film, a historical text – which are raised out of their 'normal' professional interpretive context and provide material for ethical discourse in the narrow space *between* professional discourses and political institutions. '[T]he intellectual', as Habermas writes,

commits himself on behalf of public interests as a sideline, so to speak, (something that distinguishes him from both journalists and dilettantes), without giving up his professional involvement in contexts of meaning that have an autonomous logic of their own, but also without being swallowed up by the organizational forms of political activity. From the point of view of the intellectual, art and scholarship remain autonomous, certainly, but not altogether esoteric; for him, political will-formation is certainly related to the system dominated by professional politicians, but this is not controlled exclusively by it. (NC 87–8)

This rather casual, structural definition of the intellectual plays a small but crucial role in Habermas's own self-understand of his political writings, a body of work which, despite its obvious importance to him (one need only glance at Habermas's published output), he often dismisses as a side occupation, or *Nebenrolle*, in comparison to the serious work of theory building.[7] But Habermas clearly has a far more substantial, indeed deeply normative, historical and politically partisan understanding of the role and purpose of the public intellectual as well, in which the intellectual is seen not just as a participant in ethical discourse, but as a discourse agent whose activity appeals to the *moral* or context-transcendent normative dimension of public discourse; as a tradition-smashing agent of Enlightenment modernity, a supporter of principles of universal justice and right, of critical debate and democratic rule, with a deep suspicion concerning conventional identities and traditions of all kinds.

The definition is clear: when intellectuals, using arguments sharpened by rhetoric, intervene on behalf of rights that have been violated and truths that have been suppressed, they address themselves to a public sphere that is capable of response, alert and informed. They count on a recognition of universalist values; they rely on a half-way functional constitutional state and on a democracy that, for its part, survives only by virtue of the involvement of citizens who are as suspicious as they are combative. In terms of its normative self-understanding, this type belongs to a world in which politics has not shrunk to state activity; in the world of the intellectual, a political culture of opposition complements the institutions of state (NC 73).

This notion of the intellectual, as appealing to universal procedures or interests *within* the thicket of context-dependent practical discourse, certainly differs from descriptions of the intellectual role we might have encountered in the context of French debates.[8] Habermas is indeed far removed from a rather characteristically French notion of the supreme capacity of the intellectual to mediate public disputes and generate abstract forms of rational solidarity by appeal to universal values, a version that found its extreme formulation in Benda's *The Treason of the Clerks*. On the other hand, while avoiding this 'representative function' of rational universalism (which is at best naïve, ultimately incompatible with open political dialogue and therefore self-contradictory), Habermas's position is still essentially a universalist one. Ethical discourses are *completely* embedded in the historical contextuality of particular lifeworlds; moral discourse is always the episodic and counterfactual, procedural transcendence of a *specific* set of unique circumstances. But appeals to universalism, while always occurring within a determinate historical and cultural context, are nevertheless not diminished *as* universal. The intellectual's claims insist on a dialectic of universality and contextual situation, and it is the tension of this context (the open, inter-institutional version of the juridical tension that Habermas explores in *Between Facts and Norms*) that provides the critical edge for intellectual interventions.[9]

If the intellectual, for Habermas, enacts or appeals to universal orientations within the context of ethical discourses concerning traditions which have become problematic, this would certainly provide a powerful interpretation of the *Streit* over German identity and Jewish memory, pitting Habermas against (in this case) Walser. Their disagreement is one that can be traced genealogically, at least in its grand themes, to the political constellation in which the very term 'intellectual' first arose, the Dreyfus Affair, and its effects on the German discussion of the status of the intellectual. In 1898, 'les intellectuels' had rallied to the defence of an assimilated Jew, seeing the case of the unjustly accused captain as a referendum on two issues that by century's end had in effect coalesced into a single problem. On the one hand, there was the question of how political universalism and the 'ideas of '89' should be appropriated in a climate of cultural reaction and new nationalistic impulses. On the other hand, there was the question of the status of Jews, and the meaning of anti-Semitism, and thus also of anti-anti-Semitism, within states nominally under a democratic rule of law. In the case of Viktor Klemperer, though, it is the retrospective *recovery* of the normative content of Jewish assimilation that is at issue — a normative content that now, oddly, is appealed to in the name of a recovered sense of conventional, nationally rooted cultural identity, rather than the universalism and commitment to universal right and recognition.

The historian and sociologist Dietz Bering has reconstructed the mournful history of the role of the intellectual in Germany by tracing the genealogy of the word itself, which appears as the 'history of a term of abuse' in the German discourse.[10] In France, 'les intellectuels' emerged first as a term of disparagement for the left-leaning, rule-of-law defenders of Captain Dreyfus; Bering documents how 'intellectual' was thus immediately brought into a constellation of nationalist political aspirations and anti-Semitic conspiracy theories. The intellectual, for French proto-Fascists such as Barrès, was 'abstract and instinctless', 'anti-national', Jewish by birth or by attitude and 'decadent'.[11] This constellation of negative connotations was eagerly adopted in the German discourse at the turn of the century, but with a signal difference. In France, left-wing intellectuals had successfully countered their attackers by insisting on the internal connection between 'intellect' and political *raisonnement*, by showing that their demands for justice for the wrongly accused captain were grounded in Enlightenment notions of public reason. The French Right thus found itself obliged to challenge the Left for this *positive* notion of public intellectual. Hence a dialectic of positive and negative connotations – rootless versus rational, parasitic versus universalistic, anti-national versus cosmopolitan – was sustained (and still is) within the tensions of the familiar terms of French political culture.

The absence of a similar dialectic in Germany resulted in a statically negative image of the intellectual and the adoption of essentially irrationalist political orientations by both the Left and the Right. This foreshortening of the political spectrum could be seen most clearly in the Weimar Republic, where both Fascist and Marxist alike rejected the image of the intellectual as 'useless', 'parasitic', 'hostile to life', 'decadent' and as posing a grave danger to the health of the body politic. As biological anti-Semitism augmented the older list of sins, the image of the intellectual and that of the Jew became inextricably bound up with one another. In Germany, the discourse of the intellectual thus became *definitively* linked with that of anti-Semitism.

In terms of the development of Germany's political culture, the signal difference from other European countries, however, was the enormous influence exerted by the so-called German mandarins, the anti-democratic, anti-modern and reactionary professorate that had established itself as an elite, supposedly apolitical guardian of national culture since the middle of the nineteenth century. In their deep hostility to the dynamic of cultural and social modernization, German mandarins played a central role in the characteristic vilification of the image of the intellectual in Germany following the Dreyfus Affair. The resulting typology developed the opposing poles of *Intellekt* and *Geist*, a contrast that encapsulated an entire range of mutually hostile cultural and political values. Fritz Ringer's reference to a mandarinate meant to convey something of the deeply entrenched cultural elitism of an illiberal professorate that for generations constituted a central mechanism for the uncritical continuation of particularist national traditions, providing high-cultural legitimation for anti-Semitism, and effectively blocking the institutionalization of the free political writer in Germany for generations.[12]

Ringer's familiar thesis is that modernization processes brought about the gradual decline of the German mandarins by 1933. In a 1971 review of Ringer's book, Habermas drew on his own personal experience to provide a stinging refutation of Ringer's argument: to the immeasurable harm of German democracy, the mandarins in fact did not 'decline' in the first decades of the twentieth century. In fact, they did not even vanish following the Second World War.[13] As a young university student in the 1950s, Habermas discovered to his horror that a core group of anti-Enlightenment academic philosophers, many of them open and unrepentant Nazis, collaborators or sympathizers, survived until well into the early decades of the Federal Republic, and even when barred from further academic duties (as in the case of Carl Schmitt) had an enormous influence on the subsequent development of West German political culture. In effect, they provided a reservoir of anti-modern, anti-democratic attitudes, and a bridge to pre-war traditions of German greatness and destiny that survive to the present day.[14]

This initial shock at finding the worst pre-war attitudes surviving unreconstructed into the post-war decades, when the formation of a new Federal Republic and a new federal university system were to have launched West Germans on the path to a democratic *Rechtsstaat*, figures frequently in Habermas's own reconstruction of his intellectual development. It appears so often that we should regard it, along with the trauma of the moral catastrophe of the Holocaust itself, as part of the rock-bottom experiential foundation for Habermas's oldest and most unshakeable convictions. In the present context, Habermas's argument is that the German intellectual was able to acquire a degree of institutional visibility – in some role other than scapegoat, intriguer and contaminant other – only in a Federal Republic in which the German mandarins and all they stood for had been self-consciously negated. Only the catastrophe of war and genocide provided the conditions for the emergence of a political culture in which the social role of the intellectual could find something like a secure, institutionalized place. Conversely, it was only after the war that German academics were able to bypass the influence of mandarin culture and its deeply anti-Semitic strains in order to reappropriate marginalized or suppressed elements of the German tradition. Only in its opening to the West, in other words, could Germany open for itself its own pre-1933 traditions of cultural and intellectual modernism and radicalism, and only via this path could Germans critically rediscover the lost tradition of radical Enlightenment thought. This tradition lay buried for decades beneath the mandarins' peculiarly opaque cultural edifice, constructed of equal parts of *Geist*, irrationalist longing for authenticity, unreflective love of place, mystification of national destiny and hatred of difference.[15] Habermas is willing to argue this point in arrestingly strong terms: it took Germany's catastrophe to introduce Germans to those elements of their own cultural heritage that resisted catastrophe; it took the Holocaust to exile Germans from their own nationalist traditions in a way analogous to the physical exile of generations of German intellectuals from Heine to Benjamin and Tucholsky, to force them finally to see the internal connection between irrationalist conceptions of national fate and the horror of moral catastrophe.

Only the revelations of the Nazi crimes have opened our eyes to the monstrous and sinister things that Heine saw brooding in our best, our most cherished traditions. . . . Only after 1945 were we able to transform the spatial distance that lay between Heine and the arena in which he intended his work to have its effect into a historical distance, into a reflexively disrupted relationship to the traditions and intellectual forms that have shaped our identity. Now what is most our own, once become problematic, no longer needs to be shielded from the estranging intellectual gaze. (NC 92)

This extraordinary argument – which one could certainly object to on a number of levels – has its positive pole as well: the post-war institutionalization of the role of the intellectual was made possible only by moving beyond and resolving the frozen cultural antinomy between intellectual and mandarin. And such a resolution could be figured only as part of a larger transformation of German culture. The estrangement from pre-war traditions had to be matched by the establishment of democratic rule of law and institutions of collective will formation, of a half-way functional public sphere, of a range of collective mentalities and expectations that enabled practical discourse to take place. A university system had to arise in which an ideology of cultural hegemony and elitism could be gradually replaced by an egalitarian pedagogy, and where a broader cultural programme, a learning process, could find an institutional anchor. Crucially, universities had to provide a secure institutional framework for individual scholars to engage simultaneously, and without prejudice or restriction, in both critical reflection on matters of public concern and political engagement within a lifeworld context. Universities allowed the antinomy of intellectual and mandarin to resolve itself *in the persons of* a critical, politically active professorate, in which teaching, research and involvement in the political public sphere could all tolerably coincide. There thus emerged a broader democratic vision of a *Volkspädagogik*, a 'popular pedagogy', of the sort that Adorno was urging Germans to take up throughout the 1950s. Indeed, thinking of this 'resolution' as a collective, political task, rather than an interpretation of personal idiosyncrasies, sheds a rather different light on the role of the first-generation Critical Theorists, above all Horkheimer and Adorno, who so quickly returned to Germany after the war, to assume prominent and highly visible academic positions in the post-war universities.[16] (That this resolution of intellectual and mandarin in the form of a distinctively post-war ideal of activist-scholar remains a deeply problematic one, even for Habermas, can be seen in his own somewhat conflicted views of the exemplars of this ideal type from the 1960s: Jaspers and, above all, Adorno.[17])

But equally crucial is Habermas's conviction that the mandarins and their mentality did not go away. Germany's catastrophe may have been the condition for the possibility of a collective learning process, in which the historical fact of moral collapse provides something like a collective barrier to the uncritical reappropriation of particularist, national traditions – such, at any rate, was the essence of Habermas's claim in the historians' debate. But Habermas always accompanies this claim with the reminder that the survival of the mandarins (and their essentially, literally conservative post-war role in providing a bridge to pre-war traditions) could not be squared with this learning process in its basic orientation, and was in fact openly hostile to it. As the last of the mandarins themselves finally faded away, in the course of the 1970s, they provided the impetus for a renewed critique of the left-wing intellectuals as a reaction to the excesses of the student revolts of 1967 and 1968. In the process, the last of the mandarins underwrote the return of a specifically German version of neo-conservatism that was instrumental in bringing about the *Tendenzwende* at the federal level in 1983. They provided models and inspiration for the political rhetoric of the German Right and its odd, piecemeal, often maladroit rehabilitation of the symbols and rituals of nationalism from the mid-1980s onward. And for Habermas, they live on in the intellectual climate in which Walser, at the end of his own political reinvention, can transform the older, jagged process of *Vergangenheitsbewältigung* (coming to terms with the past) into a source of comfort to nationalist sentiments.

III

This discussion of the history of mandarin and intellectual in Germany is intended to help us understand a basic aspect of Habermas's political writings. They are – without exception – related to a deep anxiety concerning the continuing influence of the mandarin mentality on the future of the political culture of the Federal Republic. Habermas's 'Four Horsemen' – Heidegger, Schmitt, Jünger and Gehlen – appear again and again in his political writings, with such frequency and regularity that one is tempted to speak in terms of a response to trauma. They are the ineffaceable figures of unease in any discussion of cracks in the foundations of German democracy, the ghosts of the bad past that seemingly cannot be exorcized. They pop up in otherwise distant literary and cultural contexts; their effects (the 'great influence', as Habermas has put it in reference to Heidegger) permeate the practice of political debate down to the tiniest capillaries of argument.

Heidegger's paeans to German destiny still mould the terms of debate in Nolte's irrationalist reactions in the historians' debate; Gehlen's critique of intellectuals as undermining traditional sources of solidarity and sapping the strength of the nation reappears in the debates over German unification; Schmitt's irrationalist jurisprudence is revealed to have influenced an entire generation of otherwise respectable jurists in the form of secret seminars and tutorials lasting for decades;[18] Jünger's 'Young Conservatism' reappears in the guise of post-modernism.

Here we find a crucial point of tension between Habermas's theoretical and political writings: in his theoretical work, most notably *Legitimation Crisis* and *The Theory of Communicative Action*, Habermas argues that the normative core of democratic institutions and practices – the forms of mutual recognition and the context-transcendent aspects of communicative conduct which are encoded both in the structures of everyday interaction and in the basic insights and principles of deliberative democracy – are threatened chiefly by the degradation of communicative reason endemic to rationalized Western societies in general. The communicative structures and potentialities of the lifeworld come increasingly under pressure from non-communicative economic and administrative steering media. From the point of view of theory, this diagnosis of an inner colonization of the lifeworld applies to a transnational phenomenon of modernization and rationalization, and is largely indifferent to specific differences amongst national political cultures and traditions. Habermas's social theory is largely silent concerning the culturally specific forms of reaction, evasion, legitimation and accommodation that arise as strategies to compensate for the loss of traditional meaning in modern societies. Rationalization devalues *all* national traditions, regardless of location or content. From a theoretical point of view, then, all traditions that retain a meaning-giving force in a post-conventional social milieu do so either as a result of some half-way successful process of collective self-reflection or as the result of a failed or missing discourse, by structural failure or strategic manipulation.

Habermas's political writings, on the other hand, all address themselves essentially to this final possibility; to the reappropriation of pre-modern national traditions as the specific form that compensation for the loss of tradition has taken in his own country. For Habermas, in fact, it is this *nationally and culturally specific form of compensation* for the depradations of social modernity, rather than the more fundamental, but less visible, erosion of communicative structures, that forms the deepest threat to the continued health of German democracy. As Habermas has frequently put it, for the *Rechtsstaat* of the post-war Federal Republic, the chief danger lies in the return of the past as future.

The unwavering consistency of Habermas's political writings can therefore be regarded as one aspect of a seemingly uneradicable anxiety about the specific *content* of national traditions, as well as the effects of their postmodern survival: the irrationalist-romantic, particularist and nationalist 'undercurrent' of the German tradition, a pre-modern creature that has somehow managed to survive until the present day, re-emerging to ruin the Federal Republic's delicate forty-year learning process on the way to a truly 'post-metaphysical' and post-national republicanism. This anxiety over the bad German past is, of course, a basic component of political culture of the Federal Republic, and gives rise to many, if not most, of its characteristics, from the fundamental political principles articulated in the German Basic Law to an entire spectrum of distinctive attitudes and values. Yet few have matched Habermas in his sense that the *intellectual* heritage of German irrationalism – its ghostly survival in an era that should have definitively rejected it – remains a deeply threatening force within everyday political culture. The constant threat of relapse – whether pictured as the literal repetition of the crisis in a collapse of democratic procedure, or as the more inchoate but more foreboding spectre of a gradual erosion of universalist and democratic orientations under the weight of particularist cultural traditions – is Habermas's basic strategy for understanding the continuing interest in intellectual figures such as Heidegger, Gehlen, Schmitt, Jünger and Schelsky. Conversely, Habermas's readings of these Weimar-era luminaries has for forty years remained his basic model for understanding the allure of pre-war German particularisms and the contemporary uncritical appropriation of them.

Another way of sharpening this point is to say, simply, that *The Theory of Communicative Action* offers no account of Fascist horror or genocidal violence. Nor can it, without reducing Auschwitz to one moment in a spectrum of pathological side-effects of a generally asymmetrical rationalization of lifeworlds – a result that no theoretician could wish for. For this reason, too, Habermas's social theory remains silent on the question of whether postwar Germany constitutes a special case as a modern society, both in terms of its unparalleled moral catastrophe and in the way that the political culture and institutions of the Federal Republic responded to it. Similarly, within the deontological framework of Habermas's moral theory, the demand that moral discourse be carried out under context-transcendent conditions specified by a principle of universalization (U) cannot address the question of the moral uniqueness of Auschwitz. (This is true even though Habermas, in his insistence on the moral equivalence and interdependence of demands for justice for individuals and solidarity for intersubjective forms, clearly imposes demands upon deontological moral theory that trace back to the moral catastrophe of the Holocaust.) Theoretically, at least, Habermas cannot argue for a German *Sonderweg*, even though it is just this 'special path' that forms the crucial context for Habermas's work, both theoretical and political. Theory thus finds itself unable to give an account of the event of its origin. And in fact, it is tempting to offer just this predicament as a definitive characteristic of theory itself.

Just for this reason, Habermas's political writings are in effect 'about' nothing else than this originating event, both in their motivation and their content. Yet, given the divide between theory and non-theory that structures Habermas's work so powerfully, the political writings address themselves to the moral catastrophe only in so far as they insist on the status of the Holocaust as the non-negotiable filter of ethical self-reflection through which all national traditions must pass. Hence these writings bear witness to the continuing effects of the Holocaust upon the lifeworld of which Habermas is a member, tracing the ethical and political causality of the event, while disavowing any attempt to link this causality back into the theoretical reconstruction of the modern, rationalized lifeworlds of occidental civilization. Like theory, then, political writing too is prohibited from directly addressing its own 'foundational' event, thus making the event itself – the Holocaust – yet again a way of figuring the antinomical relation between theoretical and political writing. Indeed, it is the uneffaceability and the unapproachability of the Holocaust as an object of writing that forms the point around which the antinomy between these two carefully distinguished sides of Habermas's work revolves – an antinomy that keeps them apart, but provides them with their unceasing productivity. In this sense, it is in essence a misreading of Habermas's career as a politically engaged intellectual to divide his political writings into this or that 'debate' – the student debate, the historians' debate, the asylum debate and so forth. In fact, there has been a *single*, continuous debate with a single objective and a single, if constantly multiplying, opposition.

IV

In his 1953 review, in the *Frankfurter Allgemeine Zeitung*, of Heidegger's newly reissued *Einführung in die Metaphysik*, the 24-year-old Habermas focused specifically on Heidegger's involvement in the Nazi Party and the clear affinities between Heidegger's thought and his politics from the early 1930s onward – themes that of course recur in all of Habermas's rather numerous treatments of Heidegger since. More significant, however, is Habermas's view that the republication of the Heidegger lecture was an illustration of the moral-political failings of the Adenauer years, a politically motivated attempt to reclaim some sense of mandarin greatness amidst the bleak cultural landscape of post-war recovery. Moreover, Habermas insisted that the repopularization of Heidegger, in the context of a political culture founded on a collective flight from responsibility, served up the language of ontology 'to inculcate today's students with the identical values that led to catastrophe', as Robert Holub has put it.[19] This sense of an unreconstructed intellectual heritage returning, spectrally, to kill off the first tenuous roots of a republican political culture edges into a continuum of a basically unrelievable anxiety over the possibility of a slip back into fascism, which even by 1953 was not especially likely.

Another major theme of Habermas's journalistic work in the 1950s and 1960s was the movement toward curricular reform in Germany's state system of secondary and university education. While it is not possible to summarize these articles here, we can say without over-simplification that they all are structured around one controlling theme: Habermas's claim that the educational system in general, and the state-supported university system in particular, had taken on a special moral-political responsibility in the post-war era as a resource for the universalist and republican political norms that mark the decisive break separating the Federal Republic from the German past. This claim implies a demand for curricular reform that addresses not just the task of training a highly skilled work-force, but above all the mission of developing a unified national curriculum to prepare German citizens for the complex challenges of collective life within a democratic society. Clearly the political writings of Jaspers and Adorno during the 1950s played a central role in the development of Habermas's views on the 'self-understanding' of the post-war university and secondary educational systems. The development of a truly democratic *Volkspädagogik* was, in the spirit of Adorno, a task of 'education after Auschwitz'. In the critical mode, Habermas's arguments for the centrality of educational reform were directed against the 'conservative spirit' of Schelsky, whose pessimistic philosophical anthropology, like that of Gehlen, remained deeply sceptical of the egalitarian and democratic ambitions of a national curriculum. Here, once again, the underlying issue at stake was the manner in which a new generation would have access to its national traditions, and whether a critical pedagogy would be able to supplant an essentially conservative (in the literal sense) curriculum.[20] And Habermas's debates with members of the student movement in the last years of the 1960s – including his infamous (and later retracted) denunciation of the 'left-wing fascism' of Rudi Dutschke – should be read as an attempt to convince radical students *not* to appeal to any form of pre-war political mentality. They should not allow the intoxication of action to overwhelm their better political judgement, not let notions of world-transforming praxis, an activist aesthetics of the deed, or visions of revolutionary intoxication, supplant the duller but sounder practices of fallibilistic negotiation and reasonable discussion that make gradualist reform possible.

Interventions of this kind show Habermas's sensitivity to the often unconscious appeal to bankrupt traditions as a means of interpreting and responding to new political problems and crises. His writings after the mid-1970s, especially from the *Tendenzwende* of 1982 onward, are marked by his conviction of the *deliberate* and *strategic* appropriation of tradition in the rise of a neo-conservative political rhetoric.

The constellation of themes raised in the historians' debate of the mid-1980s is by now widely familiar, as is its basically aporetic outcome. From our present perspective, it is useful to regard it as a generational dispute within German academic culture; the swan-song of the last generation of mandarins and their ideological allies against an attack, levelled by Habermas, against the very notion of mandarin detachment. Nolte, Hillgruber and other 'conservative historians' were in general old enough to have experienced the war as adults; their younger allies (Michael Stürmer, for example) belong to a generation of disillusioned '68ers who emerged as neo-conservative intellectuals following the *Tendenzwende*.[21]

Habermas's principal objection to the works of Nolte and Hillgruber was that the 'moral revision' of the Nazi period was a form of politicking masquerading behind the myth of the apolitical mandarinate; he thus saw a broad collaboration between the (traditionally conservative) professorate and the (newly conservative) federal government, both engaged in a wide-reaching programme of detoxification of the recent past, in the interests of a renormalization of German history and a recovery of an unproblematic German nationalism.

Rightly or wrongly, Habermas has insisted that the question of the new status of the unified Federal Republic cannot be separated from the essentially ethical question of the *normalization* of Germany's relation with its recent past; hence desirable *versus* undesirable conceptions of political normality have come to dominate his outlook on the current political situation in Germany. While never opposing German unification outright, Habermas was sharply critical of the essentially non- or anti-communicative *mode* in which unification was carried out – as a bureaucratic and administrative procedure which took place over the heads of the citizens, who were never offered (and, it must be said, never expressed a deep interest in) a collective ethical discourse concerning their own future. Hence Habermas has presented a dual argument against conventional nationhood for Germany. It is morally inadmissible to look beyond the historical wall of Auschwitz to revive a sense of continuity that would uncritically connect the German state to its (mostly fictive) pre-war versions; at the same time, German nationhood is, from a practical point of view, already an antiquated conception in light of the growing globalization of economies, technologies, migrations and their corresponding crises. German nationhood, if considered to be anything more substantial than a democratic *Rechtsstaat* unified by an abstract, formal solidity, is thus both morally wrong and geopolitically unwise.[22]

In his writing on the question of political asylum, Habermas insisted that the legal wrangling surrounding the contentious rewriting of the guarantee of political asylum in the old West German Basic Law amounted to a cynical dismantling of the principles of constitutional democracy in the short-sighted interest of a re-established sense of national sovereignty, defined negatively as a resistance to the non-German immigrant. Hence the internal link between nationalism and xenophobia re-emerges on the level of national politics in the image of a German nation protected from the outside, a hollow historical echo of the older nationalist ambition of a state as a racially homogenous *Volksgemeinschaft*.

Which brings us, finally, back to Martin Walser and Victor Klemperer. Habermas's denunciation of the 'obscenely harmonized' history of German–Jewish relations in Walser's speech appeared at the end of a short article in which Habermas was responding to a question posed by the editors of the liberal daily, the *Frankfurter Rundschau*: are there new political mentalities emerging in Germany in the face of the growing globalization of national economies and cultures? Habermas's answer is blunt: yes, there are new mentalities, and they are the old ones. In the light of growing tendencies toward globalization, the old, catastrophic ambition of a German *Volksgemeinschaft*, now discredited on all sides, is making its final bid for validity. The exhaustion of the project of the social welfare state, now a necessity given the unalterable move toward global interdependencies and a borderless state, is still able to give a last bit of impetus to a German particularism that defines itself primarily in terms of all those whom it is still capable of excluding. Hence, between two equally fascinating, equally unacceptable alternatives of a future Germany, the one a cyber-nation of mastered market forces and universally permeating subsystems of information exchange, the other a nation-state struggling for its identity by policing its physical and cultural borders ever more fiercely, the only viable alternative is, finally, the utterly unexciting prospect of an open republic. Without national enthusiasm and without national destiny, a post-metaphysical Germany must try to manage its many problems, along with the rest of the world, under the new conditions in which matters of consequence for the developed democratic nations can no longer coherently be regarded as matters for sovereign nation-states

to address unilaterally. The co-operative enterprise of a politically, economically, environmentally and technologically viable *Weltinnenpolitik*, a 'global
domestic policy' transcending and often ignoring questions of the identity of
sovereign nations, puts the question of cultural politics in a very different
light. It releases culture from its association with the nation, and makes
the question of cultural identity and cultural survival into a transnational
question.

Regarding the cultural archive that a globalized Germany will be able to
appeal to in order to clarify its own sense of identity, the answer is the old
one: from the cultural as well as the geopolitical point of view, there is no
alternative to the *Westorientierung* of the Federal Republic. Reactions such as
Walser's are indeed the 'past as future' in one relevant sense: as the last gasp
of a fund of cultural traditions that are being rendered increasingly irrelevant,
they now point less to the danger of a relapse into an old-style Fascist threat
than to the spectre of a general degradation of the discourse about the
German past.[23]

V

In closing, I would like to indicate some potential problems that emerge from
the extraordinary consistency of Habermas's career as a public intellectual. I
will focus upon (a) the suspicion that Habermas's concerns as a public intellectual cover an overly narrow range; (b) the potential conflict between a discourse theory grounded in the implicit possibility of consensus and an
argumentative praxis that assumes the essentially strategic posture of the
opponent; and (c) the question of consistency of theory and practice.

(a)   The general nature of this first problem will be clear enough from the
preceding reconstruction. Generated from a rather narrow conception of the
nature of tradition and the special character and responsibility of the intellectual in the German context, Habermas's political writings have confined
themselves to the national question and the question of problematized
national traditions. He has remained so deeply convinced of the threat to the
post-war political culture of the Federal Republic posed by the continued
influence of the old academic mandarinate that he has concentrated on the
German question to the exclusion of other problems and areas – the effects
of global rationalization on the Third World, for example, or questions of
gender inequality, class, social movements and possibilities for resistance
outside Germany's borders – that might have greatly benefited from the

critical perspective of discourse theory. I have argued above that this over-estimation of the threat of pre-war traditions and their agents arises from a conception of the ethical obligation of writing that relates, while keeping separate, Habermas's theoretical and political writings.

Habermas has consistently espoused the values of political universalism, but, in doing so, has insisted on remaining rooted in the particular ethical discourse of Germany. As I have written elsewhere, the ironic result of this position is that Habermas has in effect become the most influential and most widely read German intellectual precisely by virtue of his insistent attack on the traditional sources of German collective identity.[24] Meanwhile, outside the German context, his theoretical achievements have won wide recognition, but his role as an intellectual has, until quite recently, had virtually no effect. (Habermas's most recent writings on questions of multi-culturalism and citizenship, and his interventions regarding the question of the relation between the two Koreas, may indicate a rather large-scale change in this regard.) Does this justify a criticism that Habermas ought to expand his range of intellectual causes beyond the German question?

In a sense, of course, such criticism would be wide of the mark. If it is true that intellectuals operate within the horizon of a particular ethical context, if they are always as deeply situated in a communicative lifeworld as discourse theory suggests – and Habermas's rather moderate notion of the hermeneutics of lifeworld contexts is a deeply convincing aspect of his theory – then it is ultimately not up to the intellectual to choose which sorts of cultural conflicts to address. Moral questions only *become visible* within local contexts, which cannot be discarded or adopted at will. On the other hand, it is also true that lifeworld contexts are ultimately just that – contexts, with respect to which a great many interpretive moves are possible, including moves toward different contexts. In fact, the same processes of simultaneous globalization and fragmentation that render the question of German nation-hood increasingly moot also tend to expand the cultural horizon of the intellectual, such that, in a multi-cultural society, 'ethical discourses' increasingly come to concern *other people's* lifeworlds and the problems of identity, tradition and critical appropriation that arise at the shifting frontiers of cultural *mis*understanding within a single social setting. Increasingly, as the ethical discourses of Western democracies come to focus upon the critical appropriation of previously foreign traditions (which are brought to presence now from a geographical rather than a temporal distance), the crucial questions concern how collectives can be constituted at all in the face of a tapestry of traditions that may often be in open conflict. In other words, following the very dialectic of universalism and situation leads *out* of a particular cultural context, and compels an increasingly expanded understanding of cultural identity. In his most recent work on the implications of multi-culturalism, Habermas has been sensitive to this circumstance, while insisting that it is only via the category of abstract solidarity in structures of mutual recognition that the problem of multi-culturalism can be reconceived. It must be seen as a question of the expanded and deepened understanding of citizenship in a democratic constitutional state. Following this insight, we can expect that the major concern of Habermas's intellectual work – German identity – will lead out of itself through its own dynamic. The antinomies of the intellectual – in which appeals to morality are necessarily rooted within particularisms that both contextually ground abstract justice and solidarity and make them counterfactual – dissolve into a global contextualism in which the intellectual must look increasingly to different cultural contexts in order to understand the struggles for identity and tradition occurring in his or her own home. In the expanding crazy-quilt of cultural traditions within a single society, it is the same dynamic of practical discourse that increasingly expands the range necessary to conduct *ethical* debates coherently, even for the intellectual who insists on staying home. Habermas's political writings, with their unswerving concentration on the dialectic of universality and context, can be seen as a powerful corrective to an unreflective defence of cultural traditions, which are often embraced *because* they are threatened in a multi-cultural society. To engage fully with this multi-cultural context, however, Habermas would need to expand considerably beyond the range of ethical problems that he has so far been willing to devote his attention to. In this sense, the ongoing threat of Heidegger and Schmitt seems less pertinent than the promise of a truly multi-cultural democratic society. Habermas's decision to append his lectures on citizenship and asylum rights to his *Between Facts and Norms* may signal just such an expansion.

(b)   In another respect, however, the very forcefulness of Habermas's critiques of his neo-conservative opponents over the years has resulted in a curiously skewed relationship to his own theory. Part of the consistency of Habermas's political writings is the *uncompromising* nature of his opposition to *any* legitimate expression of German nationalism. The insistence that *only* a constitutional patriotism would survive a critical public examination of German national traditions has provoked a wide range of objections, most of them protesting the unsuitability of constitutional patriotism, or abstract solidarity, to provide any substantial sense of collective identity at all – solving the national problem too well.[25]

We might be inclined to dismiss this sort of objection to an excessive rigidity: strong positions require strong arguments; there are certain political positions that one does not compromise. But the inflexibility of Habermas's defence of constitutional patriotism, and his attacks on anything deviating from it, do raise a rather more structural problem concerning how well the argumentative procedure of his political writings squares with his defence of rational consensus in his discourse theory. It is not entirely clear whether Habermas is actually *arguing* with his opponents at all.

Since the conservative *Tendenzwende* of the early 1980s, Habermas has insisted on understanding the role of pre-war German particularist traditions in explicitly strategic terms, as part of a grand political-cultural strategy that Habermas laid out in his essay on 'Neoconservative cultural criticism in the United States and West Germany'. In the contemporary Federal Republic, the 'survival' of the bad old traditions of *Deutschtum* is to be explained chiefly by the practical need to compensate for the legitimation crises of a highly rationalized social system – hence Habermas's own conviction that the 'strategic' (or 'cynical') deployment of national traditions is roughly synonymous with the 'uncritical' reappropriation of them. It is the *usefulness* of such traditions in shoring up weakened structures of motivation and identification, and of avoiding potentially disruptive processes of collective discourse on needs, that makes them such good candidates for reappropriation. An *uncritical* appropriation of tradition is thus one that fails, by design or not, to open problematic traditions to the forum of public discussion.[26] A *critical* appropriation of particularist, nationalist traditions, by contrast, presumably entails submitting them – their content, their context, their possible effects – in the form of problematized norms to the 'normal' procedures of public discussion within the institutional horizons of a democratic political public sphere. Hence a critical encounter with tradition, for Habermas, is a necessary condition for a collective to open itself to its own history in a learning process. Learning processes for collectives are structured by crisis; they are driven by the recognition of the *failure* of a traditional source of meaning to clarify or interpret a new experience.[27] Revision and negation are the basic patterns for the critical 'reception' of tradition; 'learning' in this sense basically entails *rejecting* traditions.

Crucially, therefore, Habermas tends to assume that a critical encounter with tradition, in the context of the Federal Republic and its unique structure of collective memory and collective 'accountability' for the catastrophe of war and genocide, would, if left undistorted by strategic interventions of one sort or another, effectively filter out just those elements of German tradition that are incompatible with the normative content of European Enlightenment. That is, Habermas's political writings all implicitly assume that his own position concerning German traditions is the one that constitutes a real learning process, and that would win approval in a public ethical discourse. There is certainly nothing remarkable about this – we argue our positions because we regard them as convincing, ideally, and not vice versa. Conversely, however, Habermas presumes that the positions of his various opponents, whether old-conservative or neo-conservative, gain whatever public influence they do only in so far as they do not encounter traditions critically. A *strategic* encounter with tradition is thus part of a general pattern of avoiding, frustrating or subverting the process of public discussion, tapping into deep-seated anxieties, fears and aspirations, a sense of lack and loss, yearnings for strength and visibility, resentment and anger.

Yet, in the very scope and power of Habermas's indictment of his neo-conservative opposition, one can detect a rather characteristic problem thrown up by the conflict between Habermas's theoretical commitments to a public, proceduralistic, consensus-based notion of truth and his role in public intellectual debates. From the theoretical point of view, we must necessarily assume that discursive practice is the sole procedure that can grant validity to any contested claim. Practical discourse depends on the participants' context-transcendent presumptions concerning the openness of the discursive situation, and hence their (counterfactual) attributions of good faith or sincerity to discourse participants, even if only in order to find these attributions disappointed in practice. In this sense, if it is the case that Habermas *presumes* the merely strategic stance of his opponents in an ethical-political discourse, this would constitute a serious inconsistency between discourse theory and the performative aspect of political engagement. The *presumption* of a strategic attitude rules out in advance that the opponent's argument could count as articulating authentic interests and positions, and would therefore tend to make one's own argument effectively irrefutable. On the basis of such a presumption, no real practical discourse is possible.

(c)   Anyone who has read with attention Habermas's theoretical and political writings cannot fail to notice the high level of consistency which they display. Theory and practice (by which I mean public speaking and writing as an engaged intellectual) fit seamlessly together. While far, indeed, from providing a theory that would provide some guarantee of correct praxis, Habermas's theoretical and political writings move in a calibrated back-and-forth in which theory may always have the first and last word, but political experience is capable of informing it as well.

Yet, one can wonder whether there is not also a strength to be found in inconsistency. There are certain sorts of political experiences and convictions that are highly resistant to theoretical formulation, but remain central to one's self-understanding as a politically active citizen. There are certain ways in which theory can most effectively inform practice through the very inapplicability of one to the other. This sense of the possibility of a gap or rupture between theory and practice being a source of strength seems to me to be what Habermas must have meant when, in a recent interview, he came back once more to the figure of Adorno. Asked whether, as a politically engaged academic, he shared Adorno's and Heidegger's dark prognoses of the fate of contemporary technological civilization, he dismissed the question in order to focus on its formulation. Adorno and Heidegger could not be compared as intellectual figures, since Adorno, no matter how bleak his *theoretical* prognoses became, nevertheless remained a practically engaged defender of the Enlightenment as an *intellectual*:

Adorno understood that the most radical form of the critique of reason still takes its direction from a power for negation that springs from reason itself. Unlike Heidegger, he never became an anti-Enlightenment critic. He was therefore inconsistent enough to speak and act as a public intellectual quite differently than one would have expected from the theoretician of the 'totally administered society'. Despite his theoretical pessimism, he conducted himself in relation to the wider public precisely in terms of a *Volkspädagogik*. (KPSVIII 65)

Was the excessive bleakness of Adorno's theory (of a 'total context of domination') a practical ploy in order to render calls for a collective process of moral re-education, by contrast, plausible? Or were such calls ruled out in advance by the theory, making them highly impractical, hence counterfactual moral demands, whose very impossibility of fulfilment marked out an ethical comportment, while at the same time critically illuminating the extent of the 'totally administered society' more clearly than any theory could have?

If Adorno's inconsistency arises from the collision of a pessimistic theory with an attitude of democratic pedagogy that contradicts the theory, something new — a tension, a gap and a possibility — sustains itself within just such an inconsistency. Were the relation between theory and practice in Habermas's thought to harbour such an inconsistency, I suspect it might be the other way around, something closer to Kant than Adorno: the theory, so implicitly positive and progressivist in its deontology, in its faith in the possibility of development, and in its explicit vision of a domination-free relation lying at the heart of everyday communicative practices, might encounter in practice a moment of doubt or lack. This would reveal the strengths of the theory all the more clearly for having illuminated its limits and weaknesses, its inconsistency with itself.

It seems to me that two such moments, such inconsistencies, actually lie somewhere near the heart of Habermas's work as a public intellectual. The first is his conviction that the historical fact of Auschwitz provides the *definitive*, non-negotiable barrier to any uncritical reappropriation of pre-war

German traditions, a conviction that can neither be grounded in any possible discourse-theoretical perspective, nor one that Habermas's political position can do without. The second is Habermas's notion that the fact of intersubjective 'accountability' among all Germans grounds a collective responsibility to practise a counterfactual, 'anamnestic solidarity' with the victims of the Nazi horror. This explains Habermas's moral indignation at attempts, such as those of conservative historians or Walser, to tinker with the process of collective remembrance, in order to move closer to an artificial closure. No discourse theory can accommodate the moral relationship to the dead, which both arises as a foundational commitment in Habermas's political arguments and tends to undo the theory of universal communication that tries to support it.[28] Without this inconsistency, Habermas's position would lose what in hindsight appears to be its outstanding strength: he is still willing to consider that he might be responsible for Klemperer's violated solidarity, and that the injury done him still requires restitution.

Notes

1   See Viktor Klemperer, *'Ich will Zeugnis ablegen, bis zum letzten': Tagebücher 1933–45* (Berlin: Aufbau, 1995).
2   Martin Walser, *Das Prinzip Genanigkeit. Laudatio auf Victor Klemperer* (Frankfurt am Main: Suhrkamp, 1996), p. 21.
3   Walser, p. 35.
4   For a signal moment in Walser's transformation see his essay 'Deutsche Sorgen', in *Der Spiegel*, 26 (1993).
5   Jürgen Habermas, 'Aufgeklärte Ratlosigkeit. Warum die Politik ohne Perspectiven ist. Thesen zu einer Diskussion', *Frankfurter Rundschau*, 30 Nov. 1995.
6   See STPS 51ff. It is certainly possible for intellectuals to exist without a public sphere. As Habermas has argued in the case of Heine, they can serve as forerunners and irritants whose work calls attention to the absence of political or cultural conditions for a public sphere; moreover, in historical terms, political public spheres develop only out of predominantly literary ones. More recently, David Bathrick has shown in the case of the former East Germany that a literary public sphere can flourish in the absence of a political public sphere, without necessarily serving as the harbinger of the latter, until it runs into structural limits: David Bathrick, *The Powers of Speech: The Politics of Culture in the GDR* (Lincoln, Nebr., and London: University of Nebraska Press, 1995). However, it is entirely possible, with the rise of essentially anonymous forms of immediate global communication, that public spheres may be able to do without intellectuals.

7   See, e.g., Habermas's comments in 'Keine Normalisierung der Vergangenheit', in KPSVI 17.

8   As Peter Hohendahl has written, 'Clearly, for Habermas, modern democracy is unthinkable without intellectuals, not because they are endowed with a form of higher truth or special powers, but because their task is to influence public debate through arguments and criticism. This definition undercuts the recent distinction between universal and special intellectuals introduced by Michel Foucault in his critique of Jean-Paul Sartre. While Habermas seems to uphold a more emphatic understanding of the role of the intellectual than does Foucault, he carefully avoids the representative function that the French tradition had claimed for the intellectual.' Peter Hohendahl, 'Foreword,' to PF, pp. ix–x.

9   I have discussed this at some length in my essay, 'Universalism and the situated critic', in *The Cambridge Companion to Habermas*, ed. Stephen K. White (Cambridge: Cambridge University Press, 1995), pp. 67–96.

10 Dietz Bering, *Die Intellektuellen: Geschichte eines Schimpfwortes* (Stuttgart: Klett-Cotta, 1978).

11 Ibid., p. 324.

12 See Hauke Brunkhorst, *Der Intellektuelle im Land der Mandarine* (Frankfurt am Main: Suhrkamp, 1987).

13 See Habermas, 'Die deutsche Mandarine', in PhPP 458–68.

14 See Habermas's comments on the survival of the German mandarins in AS 74ff.

15 See Habermas, 'Zur Entwicklung der Sozial- und Geisteswissenschaften in der Bundesrepublik', in TK 209ff, and 'The German idealism of the Jewish philosophers', in PPP 21ff.

16 For an illuminating discussion of this matter see Peter Hohendahl, 'Education after the Holocaust', in *Prismatic Thought: Theodor W. Adorno* (Lincoln, Nebr., and London: University of Nebraska Press, 1995), pp. 45ff.

17 In fact, one could trace out something like a miniature history of Habermas's notion of the scholar-intellectual in his thoughts on Adorno, from the early (1959) essay 'Theodor W. Adorno: ein philosophierender Intellektueller' (later reprinted in PhPP, but mysteriously omitted from its English translation) to the recent essay 'Das Falsche im Eigenen, Zu Benjamin and Adorno', in which Habermas comes back once again to Adorno's exemplary status as a personal mediation between mandarin and intellectual – with the implication that, as with all *Aufhebungen*, moments of the old mandarin consciousness remained very much intact. See KPSVIII 130ff.

18 See Habermas, 'Carl Schmitt in der politischen Geistesgeschichte der Bundesrepublik', in KPSVIII 118ff.

19 Robert C. Holub, *Jürgen Habermas: Critic in the Public Sphere* (London and New York: Routledge, 1991), p. 16.

20 See Habermas, 'Konservativer Geist – und die modernistischen Folgen', in KPSI–IV 41ff.

21 This generational arithmetic is actually central for understanding the constellation of arguments in the historians' debate; born in 1929, Habermas belongs to

a precise generational cohort of those who were old enough to have experienced the normalcy of the everyday life of National Socialism, and who experienced the collapse of the regime as self-aware adolescents, but who were too young (just) to have participated in the regime and the war as adults. This underlies, to a considerable degree, the sharpness of disagreements between Habermas and such figures as Hillgruber, a few crucial years older, and in general marks a 'great divide' in generational experiences of collective guilt or collective accountability.

22   For the most recent version of this dual argument, see Habermas, '1989 im Schatten von 1945: Zur Normalität einer künftigen Berliner Republik', in KPSVIII 168ff.

23   As if to make this point, the interest in Victor Klemperer's diaries was roughly simultaneous with another event in German culture that must count as a milestone of sorts: by the spring of 1996, *Hogan's Heroes* had become one of the most popular programmes on German television, drawing nearly a million viewers per day. This success, the *Wall Street Journal* reports, was due in large measure to a brilliant stroke of innovation on the part of the German producers, who rewrote large portions of the original sound-track and re-dubbed the programme into a sort of Dada word salad of non-sequitorial jokes and context-free raunchy dialogue, in order to make it unambiguously a comedy. Many Germans nevertheless regard the popularity of the programme as a sign that Germans are finally able to laugh at themselves; Werner Klemperer, a German Jew who fled his native Cologne before the war and went on to play Colonel Klink in the programme, is reportedly pleased by its new success in the country of his birth. Greg Steinmetz, 'Some Germans find Hogan a new hero', *Wall Street Journal*, 31 May 1996.

24   Pensky, 'Universalism and the situated critic', pp. 68–9.

25   One interesting variant of this complaint is that of Karl-Heinz Bohrer, who objects to Habermas's conception of constitutional patriotism in this way: 'If I have understood Habermas's concept correctly, it does not mean, of course, simply the anemic presence of democratic loyalty, drummed in with pedagogical rigor, to the "free state on German soil." Far more than this, Habermas's concept includes a specific awareness of Germany's recent history, which, above all, makes the remembrance of the fascist period into a moral-political law for any German national consciousness. When I look more closely into Habermas's protestant argument, I find hidden within it a kind of negative chiliasm, the idea of the one overriding event in our history: it is called the Holocaust. The Holocaust is the great, unavoidable fact of our modern history, and any hermeneutic of a new German self-understanding has to be developed from it. In this respect the demand for a Federal German constitutional patriotism gains, in fact, a kind of emphatic power which – should it indeed succeed as a national project – ought, in a hundred years, to be seen as the spiritual turning point of the modern nation: as a successful spiritual-political innovation after the catastrophe, as an enlightened myth of the victory of reason against nationalism' (Karl-Heinz

Bohrer, 'Why we are not a nation – and why we should become one', in *When the Wall Came Down: Reactions to German Unification*, ed. Harold James and Marla Stone (New York: Routledge, 1992), p. 69). Bohrer's point – that constitutional patriotism, growing from the 'negative chiliasm' of the hypostatized event of the Holocaust, is every bit as much of a national mythology as the irrationalist versions it seeks to replace – is worth considering; but Bohrer completely ignores the argument that political myths do not operate according to categories of public will formation, the premiss of Habermas's conception.

26 See Habermas, 'Neoconservative cultural criticism in the United States and West Germany', in NC 22–47.

27 See Habermas, 'Aus der Geschichte lernen?', in KPSVIII 15ff.

28 I have explored this in 'On the use and abuse of memory: Habermas, anamnestic solidarity, and the *Historikerstreit*', *Philosophy and Social Criticism*, 15 (1989), pp. 351–80.

Part III

Contemporaries

8

Society and history: a critique of Critical Theory

Michael Theunissen

The initial historical points of reference for the thought of Michael Theunissen are remarkably similar to those of Habermas. Theunissen, too,
begins from the philosophy of Hegel, and from the new relation between
theory and existential and social practice initiated by post-Hegelian thinkers
such as Marx and Kierkegaard. What Theunissen criticizes in Habermas,
however, is the attempt to understand the achievement of community
purely in terms of a realization of subjective human capacities. For Theunissen the crucial philosophical divide is not between subjectivity and
intersubjectivity. Rather it is between all forms of modern domination, and
the acknowledgement of a transcendence to which we are called to
respond, and whose privileged site of disclosure is the intersubjective
encounter. Unless intersubjectivity is recognized as such a site, then it
stands for no more than an enlarged subjectivism. The present essay by
Theunissen was first published in 1969, in response to *Knowledge
and Human Interests*, but it remains a classic essay on Habermas's place
in the tradition of the Frankfurt School. For it critically investigates a
crucial turning point in Habermas's thought: his attempt to escape dependence on the philosophy of history, by establishing a reflective, 'quasi-
transcendental' justification of the norms of social critique.

According to Theunissen, Habermas's quasi-transcendental grounding
strategy results in a 'naturalization' and immobilization of structures which
are then mistakenly assumed to be immune to historicity. The result is a
danger of falling prey to ideological illusion, and a limiting of the possibilities of real historical transformation. By contrast, Theunissen wants both

to hold on to a more radical conception of historicity, which leaves not even philosophical knowledge beyond its scope, and to retain the notion that history must be conceived as moving towards the domination-free dialogue of all with all, or what he later calls 'communicative freedom'. Theunissen willingly admits that this circle can be squared only if one acknowledges the inevitability of a theological dimension to the philosophy of history: subjectively (or intersubjectively) based theories alone cannot preserve the objectivity of historical meaning.

This reliance on theological premises is, of course, open to obvious criticisms. Thus, in his *Festschrift* essay for Theunissen, Habermas writes: 'But when God remains the *only* guarantee in history that a break-out from the ceaseless, remorseless, nature-bound cycle of a history dominated by the past is still possible, then the concept of the absolute presupposed in every act of successful understanding is left without an adequate philosophical explanation.'* In his response to such objections, Theunissen's strategy is to show *philosophically* that certain phenomena ultimately elude philosophical explanation. In Theunissen's view, for example, the emergence of self-conscious subjectivity cannot be explained – as Habermas tries to explain it – in terms of an internalization of the standpoint of the other. For this presupposes a viable interpretation of what it means to encounter the *other* in the first place. In general, any attempt to account for subjectivity will presuppose intersubjectivity, and vice versa – the other, it seems, cannot be encountered as an object of knowledge, and cannot be presupposed immediately either. As with the Kierkegaardian paradoxes of selfhood, which Theunissen agrees can only be resolved through faith in the absolute power which sustains us, the philosophical deadlock of intersubjectivity points towards the primordial, underivable notion of the 'between' (*das Zwischen*). The 'between' is the dimension which enables self and other to meet, the irruption into the present of the future kingdom of God.†

I Aim and Subject-Matter of the Investigation

Jürgen Habermas's *Knowledge and Human Interests*, which is intended as a 'prolegomenon' to the Critical Theory of society, is a good barometer of the current state of this theoretical tradition.[1] Habermas's investigations in this work developed out of his inaugural lecture at Frankfurt University (TWI 146–8). The declared aim of the lecture was to build on Max Horkheimer's essay 'Traditional and Critical Theory', in which, more than a generation earlier, in 1937, the concept of Critical Theory was first formulated.[2] The following reflections are an attempt to grasp the general contours of the Critical Theory of society, and they restrict themselves to the task of linking up its relative beginning in Horkheimer's early essays with its provisional culmination in the work of Habermas,[3] Herbert Marcuse and T. W. Adorno. However, I will refer explicitly to Marcuse (who made an important contribution to the debate concerning 'Traditional and Critical Theory' as early as 1937[4]), to Adorno (who in 1944 co-wrote the *Dialectic of Enlightenment* with Horkheimer[5]) and to Horkheimer's later work, the *Critique of Instrumental Reason*, only when their thought bears directly on the matter at hand.

The thesis concerning Critical Theory which I develop here is itself critical, and is therefore appropriate to its object. Meaningful critique, however, presupposes more than just distance. For, strictly speaking, one can only criticize what one in principle accepts. In the reflections that follow I express an agreement that transcends this critical distance. To begin with, in section II, I outline the programme of Critical Theory, the underlying intentions of which I endorse. Then, in section III, I describe how the Theory's line of development has diverged from the original intentions of the programme. Finally, I attempt to uncover what I take to be the reasons for these deviations, and suggest certain corrections, which are intended, if not to close, then at least to narrow the gap between what Critical Theory intended to be and what it has in fact become (section IV).

II The Correct Intention of the Programme

1 The Distinction between Critical and Classical Theory

The programmatic intentions of Horkheimer and his followers can be brought to light most clearly by comparing the concept of Critical Theory with the concept of Platonic-Aristotelian *theoria*. The first thing this comparison reveals is a stark opposition. *Theoria* immerses itself in a cosmos, a natural universe, which appears as divine by virtue of the changelessness of its eternally recurring movements. Critical Theory deals with the historically shifting human world which the Greeks regarded as an object unworthy of theoretical knowledge, on the grounds of its mutability.[6] Critical Theory thus understands itself as a philosophy of history, in the sense that nothing lies beyond its grasp.[7] While classical theory accepts the eternal cycle of the natural cosmos as the whole within which the historically shifting human world fades into insignificance,[8] Critical Theory sees history as the ultimate horizon against which even the natural sciences must be measured. This gap becomes all the more significant in view of the fact that Critical Theory understands history in precisely the same way as classical theory, in the very way which devalued it in the eyes of the Greeks: as the ever-present happening, which once was not yet and which soon will be no more. Critical Theory is one with the philosophy of history in being a critical diagnosis of actual historical reality, the determinacy of which, at each moment, prescribes what Critical Theory itself has to do *qua* 'determinate negation'. The historical present, not the unchanging course of the world, is the totality which puts everything in its place. Yet Critical Theory also attempts to grasp the actually occurring temporal process as a totality,[9] and it is this attempt that justifies its claim to be philosophy, not just a form of specialized science.[10]

Because this opposition between the historical and the natural-metaphysical world-view is so fundamental, it can also seem to be so self-evident that Critical Theorists need not reflect on it at all. Reflection begins only when critique begins, the critique of what Habermas calls the 'onto-logical illusion of pure theory' (TWI 154). Pure theory is supposed to be mere illusion, because it rests on an underlying ontology of nature which ultimately reveals itself to be an illusion. The significance of pure theory for life consists in the fact that the soul reflects the harmony of the cosmos. However, Habermas argues, the idea of this kind of imitative formation of the self (*nachbildenden Bildung*) is based on the false assumption that the cosmos to be imitated is given to us as a prior, internally structured reality. The untruth of pure theory stems from the untruth of the objectivism inherent in this prior ontology of nature (TWI 150, 152ff, 154, 159, 165ff). Although such a criticism is highly dubious, as can easily be shown, it none the less provides a clear indication of the intention behind Critical Theory.[11] The subject of Critical Theory knows that it cannot be separated from its object; consequently, it also knows that it could not fulfil its claim to comprehend the whole of the current historical process if it did not think itself along with its object. Hence the subject includes itself as part of the object which it investigates.[12] Of course, the subject of Critical Theory is aware that even the most general concepts it employs are ones which originally emerged from historical reality, and which are thus not just imposed, retrospectively as it were, on an apparently separate experiential content.[13] What Horkheimer once called 'the intention aiming at the whole'[14] includes within itself the consciousness of its own historicity: the whole is not the whole without the subject that turns towards it. The early Horkheimer in particular takes the fact that his thought is bound to its time very seriously. He concludes that his thought is constantly in need of revision, and he makes the lesson that theoretical changes are determined by historical change an integral part of his theory.[15]

The opposition between classical and Critical Theory described so far also lies at the root of their different relations to praxis. *Theoria* denotes neither praxis (*praxis*) in the narrow, strict sense, which means more than just activity (*energeia*), nor thinking that strives towards practical realization. Whether or not the charge of objectivism stands, the fact that *theoria* stands at a second remove from praxis stems largely from a second fact: that being, which is always already complete in itself, and which owes its own autarky to its independence, lacks nothing. In so far as *theoria* is a vision (*Schau*) of being in its completion, it takes the form of a retro-spective (*Rückschau*) rather than prospective insight (*Vorschau*); it is not an insight into a future lying beyond the life of the human subject who has this insight, a future which might be mastered through practical engagement. By contrast, the unity of theory and praxis called for by Critical Theory follows from its involvement in an ongoing historical process. Critical Theory forms a unity with praxis in two ways. First, in so far as it participates in the historical process which it takes as its object – that is, as a moment of the history which it advances through its knowledge – Critical Theory is itself praxis.[16] Secondly, Critical Theory forms a unity with praxis in so far as it is interested in praxis as a future event of world history. The early Horkheimer defines his philosophy of history, in a way which is valid for the whole Frankfurt School, as 'the Critical Theory of existing society, a theory that is imbued with an interest in future conditions',[17] and he indicates that his intention is to furnish 'an analysis of the course of history which is guided fundamentally by an interest in the future'.[18] In opposition to the retrospective viewpoint that characterizes classical theory, a viewpoint which corresponds to the closure of its object, Critical Theory orients itself in terms of its essential interest in the future.[19]

2 The Unity of Critical and Classical Theory

Later on, we will need to question the adherents of Critical Theory regarding the determinate content of this praxis. But at this point, where we are concerned only with outlining its formal structure, we are faced with another task. We must significantly narrow the opposition between classical and Critical Theory which we noted above. For the opposition can be seen as sublated in a kind of unity. That this unity has not hitherto been paid the same attention as the opposition is at least partly the fault of Horkheimer and Habermas themselves. The current opinion that the two conceptions of theory form an abstract, unmediated opposition may have been given currency by Horkheimer. For it was he who separated off Critical Theory from 'traditional' theory, which he understood as embracing the entire tradition, when in fact it represents only a model of specialized science which emerged within bourgeois society, a model which was formally reflected in Cartesian philosophy and further distorted by neo-Kantianism. So, when Habermas claims that the object of Horkheimer's investigation is the difference between Critical Theory and theory in the Greek sense (TWI 147), this can have only one effect – to deepen a misunderstanding which is already extremely destructive. For it is possible to capture the unity of Critical Theory and Greek theory with the help of a concept which is common to both: that of the *end-in-itself.*

It is true that the quality of being an end-in-itself is not quite the same in Critical Theory as it is in Aristotle; in Critical Theory it is sublated (*aufgehoben*) in the precise sense that it is cancelled, yet preserved under altered conditions. This is already implied by the dialectic which Horkheimer himself describes between critical and traditional theory. On the one hand, the traditional theory of modern organized science imagines itself to be autonomous, but is in fact enmeshed in the functional context of existing society; Critical Theory, on the other hand, acknowledges its functional dependence, but in fact possesses the 'independence'[20] that belongs to 'self-determination'.[21] According to Horkheimer, both the illusory autonomy of traditional theory and the actual autonomy of Critical Theory stem from their respective functions. For the illusory autonomy with which the specialized sciences endow themselves is produced by abstracting from the narrow confines within which a society deeply marked by the principle of the division of labour keeps even professional scientific work.[22] Yet, the function of Critical Theory is not a service that is performed in and on a pre-given whole, but the transformation of the totality itself, the 'transformation of the social whole'.[23] Such a transformation presupposes that what Horkheimer calls the 'critical attitude' stands over against the social whole. Therefore it forms no part of what exists, and, furthermore, does not depend on society as a part depends on the whole. 'Although the critical attitude arises from the social structure, its role is not to try and make something within the social structure function better; this is neither what Critical Theory consciously intends nor what it objectively means.'[24] In other words, the critical attitude lacks 'the pragmatic character, which traditional thinking has, by virtue of being a kind of useful vocational labour'.[25] What this means, positively speaking, is that the critical attitude is autonomous with respect to its specific function. Horkheimer ascribes to critique the same kind of uselessness to which Aristotle also refers in negatively designating the quality that theoretical knowledge has: that of being an end-in-itself. Against this, it might be claimed that Critical Theory can at most be useless with respect to existing society, but not with respect to a future one, since Critical Theory is essentially interested in the future. However, the objection fails. For, to be useless for Aristotle means first and foremost to serve no *alien* purposes;[26] and Critical Theory, even in its relationship to the future, will certainly be useless in the sense that it will serve no alien or external purposes. What the interests of Critical Theory are directed towards is not something alien to it, because Critical Theory is itself always a moment of the praxis it intends. The unity of the historical process to which its act belongs, and in which it finds its *telos*, makes this *telos* into an end-in-itself. It is this thought that is captured by the affirmation that interests are not external to knowledge whose aim is enlightenment, but emerge from its very ground.[27] However, in discussing Critical Theory's close relation to the praxis with which it is concerned, we must not forget the temporal distance between the present of its act and the future of its aim. This temporal distinction within the unity of the encompassing historical process is what also marks the difference between critical and Greek knowledge of ends-in-themselves, within their overarching identity. It is a difference which stems from such knowledge being reconceived in terms of the philosophy of history. *Theoria* serves no alien purposes, since it does not point beyond itself into the future at all. Critical Theory serves no alien purposes, because the praxis towards which it points is only the fruition of the praxis that is Critical Theory itself.

The dignity of being an end-in-itself, however, belongs not just to the act, but also to the object of Critical Theory. From its very inception Critical Theory distinguished itself sharply from instrumental thought, which merely seeks the means that suit the attainment of pre-set ends.[28] Critical Theory wants to determine the end for itself, and indeed the final end in the Aristotelian sense – an end which cannot be a means to anything else. Following Aristotle, Critical Theory calls this end the 'good life' (*eu zen*).[29] The definition of the good life as the final end is supposed to guide the historical present on its journey into the future. Instrumental reason, which only thinks about means, makes itself into a means for the 'reproduction',[30] or for the preservation and intensification, of the whole into which it is integrated. By contrast, Critical Theory attempts to determine the good life anew, by reflecting on the form of society itself, on the social system.

Accordingly, this sublation of Aristotelian thought into a radical, universal philosophy of history ultimately consists in a kind of intensification of an insight, already introduced by Aristotle, into the objective characteristics of the end-in-itself. For Aristotle already thinks of the good life as belonging not just to individuals, but also, and indeed primarily, to the community of the *polis* within which alone the individual can be what the individual is. The nature and tendency of the radicalization that this idea undergoes can be seen most clearly from the new orientation provided by the theory of science. For Aristotle the determination of the good life of society was not a matter for theoretical science, which had to do with trans-historical and eternal things. The task of determining the good life for man was a matter for less strict forms of enquiry, which took their points of orientation not from *theoria* but from practical wisdom, or *phronesis* (TuP 14, 31). Habermas, however, brings the task of determining the good life back within the purview of theoretical science. His comprehensive conception of Critical Theory, the nature of which we have yet to investigate, deals with the supposedly strict scientific conception of social philosophy, one which, since Hobbes, has sought to guarantee its scientific status by retranslating authentic political practice into the technical task of making means fit ends. In particular, Habermas wants to revise and correct this modern conception of social theory from the perspective 'from which the classical doctrine of politics was once able to understand itself as the prudent direction of practice' (TuP 49).

III How Critical Theory Abandoned its Intention

1 *The Overburdening of the Subject and the Apotheosis of Nature*

It is essential to the guiding intention of the programme outlined above to rehabilitate the ancient idea of knowledge as an end-in-itself, under the altered conditions of a universal dependence on factual history. According to this intention, what is important is not so much the rehabilitation of the idea, as the fact that the idea is assigned a place within the all-encompassing horizon of history, and is thus not attained at the price which Aristotle is supposed to have paid – the hypostatization of an underlying, all-encompassing natural cosmos. Yet, if we look at the way in which Critical Theory actually develops, we notice that it tends to break out of the framework of a universal, radical philosophy of history. Failing to fulfil its intention, Critical Theory threatens to collapse back into what it originally sought to overcome, into an ontology of nature which is now indeed unquestionably objectivistic. At the very least, it threatens to collapse back into a kind of thinking that prioritizes nature over history, and which inflates the former into an absolute origin. Furthermore, it is easy to show that this apotheosis of nature lies at the end of an avenue of thought which begins with a certain overburdening of the empirical subject – or, more precisely, of the human species as the totality of empirical subjects. This overburdening of the subject inverts dialectically into the inflation of a natural facticity that is no longer grounded subjectively.

This claim implies an objection which is so important that we cannot do without substantiating it with reference to the relevant material. I shall therefore attempt to justify it in two steps: first through an exposition of Horkheimer, then through an analysis of Habermas's attempted new beginning.

2 The Rupture in Horkheimer's Thinking

What I call the 'overburdening of subjectivity' occurs when the various representatives of Critical Theory try – to put it in terms of the history of philosophy – to repeat the post-Hegelian repetition of Kant. This project was originally undertaken by the Left Hegelians, on the historical ground that Hegel had prepared. In concrete terms, the overburdening of the empirical subject results from the transposition of the authority which Kant invests in 'consciousness in general' to a human species whose real unity is still only anticipated. According to the young Horkheimer, Kant's notion of consciousness in general is the image of an authentically productive future society, although Kant himself was not aware of this.[31] On this view, a future society would be able to bring about concretely what consciousness could achieve only formally: the ceaseless transformation of chaos into the spontaneously created order of the understanding. In the programmatic document 'Traditional and Critical Theory' this anticipated culmination of Critical Theory is expressed in the form of a utopia from which all contingency has been eliminated.[32] But the projection of a world in which there is in principle no more contingency simply overloads the capacities of freedom. The aim is to reduce to a minimum the realm of nature that escapes freedom, and the essay on 'Traditional and Critical Theory' ventures the prognosis that even objects of sense perception, when they come under social 'control', will lose their 'character of pure factuality'.[33] It is labour that is supposed to extend the compass of our power over nature in this way. Indeed, Horkheimer defines the whole sphere of social-historical praxis, of which Critical Theory itself forms a part, as labour. Critical Theory functions as a 'non-independent moment within the labour process'.[34] The process aims at a kind of freedom that is 'identical with the mastery of internal and external nature through rational decision'.[35] In Horkheimer's view it is simply and solely the domination of nature which guarantees 'rational organisation',[36] the completely rational planning of a world which, because it is totally social, can be totally shaped by society.

The young Horkheimer criticizes the economic chaos of a late capitalism haunted by economic crises. This chaos represents the complete opposite of such social planning. But the cure he so warmly recommends, the technology-guided mastery of nature, becomes the object of criticism in the later works.[37] The 'critique of instrumental reason' applies to the claim to total mastery over nature just as much as the critique of a one-dimensional Enlightenment that Horkheimer co-wrote with Adorno. Around 1944 Horkheimer and Adorno agreed that scientific and technological progress based on labour threatens to rebound in a catastrophic regression, and, in a certain sense, has always represented such a regression.[38] The mastery of nature now reveals its dialectic: the attempt to liquidate a nature which evades calculating control leads to a 'liquidation of the subject',[39] to the domination of human beings. For, in order to be able to control nature, human beings must adapt to nature. Man is reduced to an exact reflection of the reality he wants to control. 'Subjectivisation, which inflates the subject, thereby also condemns it.'[40]

In so far as Horkheimer himself once gave unqualified praise to what he now regards as regressive, it is fair to say that his thought develops from an initially dominant, explicitly asserted optimism, to a kind of pessimism that culminates in a thoroughgoing resignation about the very possibility of progress.[41] In May 1967 such resignation prompted him to wonder 'whether the realm of freedom, once realised, would necessarily prove to be its opposite, the automatization of both society and human behaviour'.[42] Certainly, Horkheimer was right to claim, restrospectively, that a certain pessimism deriving from Schopenhauer[43] had always been an element of his thinking.[44] It is true that as early as the Thirties he emphasized the 'pessimistic features'[45] of materialism, its 'melancholy'[46] and 'metaphysical sadness',[47] which he defends against the confidence of Christianity and of post-Christian ersatz religions.[48] The truth of this claim lies in the fact that the over-optimistic appeal to the faculty of freedom, once the impossibility of its demand is admitted, already implies its inevitable transformation into its opposite, a pessimism which then only needs to become explicit.

Conversely, the pessimism implied by the critique of instrumental reason also tends to oscillate between itself and its opposite. Horkheimer's attitude to the history of regression is ambivalent. On the one hand, he holds the single remaining task of philosophy to be that of describing the regressive course of the scientization of the world and spelling out its consequences.[49] On the other hand, he calls on philosophy to reconcile instrumental reason with the kind of reason which once mistook itself for 'absolute objectivity'.[50]

But this reconciliation surreptitiously turns into a 'reconciliation with nature'.[51] Reason is supposed to wrest itself free from the bad dialectic between the mastery of nature and the relapse into nature, by giving itself over to the good dialectic, in which reason's own liberation is granted in return for the liberation of nature. But if nature is to be liberated dialectically, it cannot be liberated immediately; it can only be liberated through mediation, that is, by making reason admit to its principle of domination. Horkheimer and Adorno follow up their famous sentence, 'the relapse into nature consists in the mastery of nature, without which spirit does not exist', with the line: 'By the humbling admission, in which spirit concedes that it is domination and withdraws into nature, its hegemonic claim, which enslaved it to nature, dissolves.'[52] The point is this: spirit is supposed to renounce domination by admitting to it. The authors of *Dialectic of Enlightenment* call upon spirit 'finally to renounce its power'.[53] However, the view that in this renunciation nature somehow comes to itself presupposes what Habermas would call an 'objectivistic ontology', one that entails that nature has a selfhood independent of subjectivity. Here we find unmistakable resonances of Heidegger's thinking of Being, which for Adorno stands in for 'ontology' as such.[54] The critique of knowledge, regarded as technological in its essence,[55] converges with Heidegger's critique of subjectivity as soon as it breaks loose from the critique of specifically capitalist forms of domination and returns towards originary ground of Western humanity.[56] The only difference is that, where Heidegger recommends 'openness to Being', Horkheimer and Adorno advocate 'humility in face of nature'.[57] Adorno's indictment of Heidegger's thinking of Being for demeaning itself before a *factum brutum* is a charge that could be much more plausibly levelled at his own practice, when he commits his thought to an ethos of pious nature worship.

To aver that spirit should 'withdraw into nature' simply amounts to the disempowering of history. History has not only to surrender its domineering role to nature; it must also evacuate the realm of value and truth which it once occupied.[58] It is clear that the 'critique of instrumental reason' is guided by a dualism of the real and the ideal,[59] of actuality and truth.[60] Thus it sunders the concrete unity within which, according to the original project of Critical Theory, a determinate historical reality had to be mediated with its determinate historical truth.[61] When the philosophy of history atrophies to such an extent, Critical Theory is played out. Horkheimer reluctantly departs from Critical Theory when he claims that the 'fundamental distinction between the ideal and the real' is the same as that between 'theory and practice',[62] and then finally announces that the Marxist insistence on the unity of theory and praxis is a feature it shares with Scholasticism.[63] In place of Critical Theory, and consistent with the rehabilitation of an objectivistic

ontology of nature, we have *theoria*. Horkheimer thus relapses into pure contemplation, since he does no more than recollect an inexorable decline.
However, where he entrusts himself with the *activity* of preparing for the
reconciliation with nature, *theoria* nevertheless still has a place in the field of
his enquiry, the place beside traditional theory which was formerly occupied
by Critical Theory. But the methodological ambivalence of Critical Theory
is reflected in its theme. By limiting itself to retrospection, it ends up restricting the kind of thinking 'that Aristotle describes as theoretical contemplation'[64] to a lost paradise. Yet theoretical contemplation emerges, as Critical
Theory's original intentions develop into the project of a reconciliation with
nature, as the promise of that future in which, according to ancient theological tradition, the *vita contemplativa* is supposed to culminate – although of
course the future has now descended to the here-below. The only thing that
is capable of breaking the spell of resignation, is the feeble hope that 'the
earth could become a realm of contemplation and happiness'.[65]

3 Habermas's New Approach

Habermas claims to have detected this regression of Critical Theory. In his
critique of Herbert Marcuse, he takes the opportunity to point out that, along
with Marcuse, Bloch and Benjamin, even Horkheimer and Adorno – like the
young Marx – cling to the mystical hope of a 'resurrection of fallen nature',
and secretly hope that nature, which was condemned by Idealism to be the
other (*das Andere*) of the human subject, will finally reveal itself as the other
subject.[66] Habermas, however, avoids this error by means of two basic measures. On the one hand he breaks the monopoly of labour by renewing Aristotle's distinction between *poiesis*, or *techne*, and *praxis*. He translates Aristotle's
concept of *poiesis* into the concept of 'labour' or 'instrumental action', which
is interested in technical mastery, and he translates Aristotle's concept of *praxis*
into that of 'interaction' or 'communicative action'.[67] Just as he accuses Marx
of falsely deriving interaction from labour (TWI 45ff), so his own Marxism
aims, through the correction of this reduction, to clarify Horkheimer's vague
yet necessary concept of 'social praxis', with the help of the distinction
between instrumental and communicative action. Habermas also reinterprets
Marx's object of enquiry, the relation between the forces and the relations of
production, in terms of the more abstract but historically more relevant distinction between labour and interaction (TWI 92). All his efforts are directed
towards two aims: making clear the contemporary relevance of this distinction, which threatens to vanish from human consciousness, along with the
progress represented by the increasing technical exploitation of means (TuP

232ff); and awakening the insight that technical-scientific progress in no way entails the progressive development of communicative action (TuP 251; TWI 46ff). This particular focus is significant in at least two ways. First, it preserves Habermas's approach from the fate of Horkheimer's. For, since Habermas does not subscribe to the prior reduction of social praxis to labour, he is not forced to give up the whole notion of social praxis when it begins to manifest its obverse side in the predominance of labour-based and technically exploitable sciences. Secondly, Habermas ensures himself against the danger of simply objectifying nature by interpreting the dimension of interests in which labour and interaction are located in Kantian terms, as an 'achievement of the transcendental subject'.[68] For there can be no place for an objectivistic ontology of nature in a picture which portrays the being of every entity as constituted by a transcendental subject.

According to Habermas, the eschatological concept of nature that is taken up by Benjamin, Bloch, Marcuse, Adorno and Horkheimer, and which guides the young Marx's demand for a naturalization of human beings and a humanization of nature,[69] is incompatible with a theoretically informed Marxism.[70] The later Marx, Habermas contends, has three concepts of nature: objective nature, which emerges only within the social labour process; subjective nature – that is, the nature of the socialized individual; and nature 'in itself', which is supposed to ground human history in much the same way as Kant's 'thing in itself' is supposed to ground appearances (EI 37, 42, 45ff, 57). It is only here that Habermas properly identifies the mistaken conception of nature which Horkheimer and Adorno fail to overcome. Without doubt Benjamin, Bloch and Marcuse all take up the eschatological conception of nature of Marx's *Paris Manuscripts*. By contrast, the new objectivism of Horkheimer and Adorno, in spite of its eschatological significance, really only refers to objective nature, to a nature which is already there and not 'yet to come'. Marcuse in fact completely departs from the ground of the Hegelian dialectic[71] – with his concept of an 'other dimension' and of a 'qualitative difference' from the existing world, he idealizes the Marxian confrontation of bourgeois and classless society into a Platonic two-worlds doctrine, reminiscent of Kierkegaard's Platonizing critique of Hegel.[72] In Horkheimer and Adorno, however, nature tends to remain within the dialectic of the equiprimordial moments of subject and object. The 'critique of instrumental reason' transposes the Hegelian concept of a unity of unity and difference into its ideal of a 'reconciliation with nature': spirit and nature are meant to stand opposed, yet in such a way that each is at the same time reflected in the other.[73] But by differentiating Marx's conception of nature into more specific and supposedly less specific concepts, Habermas not only develops the systematic framework within which he can account for the kind of naturalization encountered in Bloch,

Benjamin and Marcuse, on the one hand, and striven for by Horkheimer and Adorno, on the other; he also indicates the places where he himself concedes to nature a predominance that suppresses history.

4 The Return of the Subjectivizing and Naturalizing Tendency in Habermas's Thought

Habermas himself tends to absolutize both subjective nature and nature in itself. When he claims that 'The achievements of the transcendental subject have their basis in the natural history of the human species' (TWI 161), he solidifies nature in itself, a concept of nature which betrays itself through its name alone, into the being that grounds the subject. Of course, Habermas defends himself against the naturalistic misunderstanding of this thesis (TWI 161; EI 351). Yet he stands accused by the very defence he offers. For he claims that labour and interaction go beyond the natural principle of self-preservation in which they are grounded (TWI 16ff). But mere transcendence is powerless to free human beings from the grasp of nature. The very negativity of the concept, which is supposed to indicate something more than mere nature, testifies to nature as the positive moment beneath it.

Furthermore, nature creeps upward into the subject from its base, eventually objectifying it from inside, as it were. Nature penetrates the very activities of consciousness, and petrifies the transcendental horizon of world constitution into what Habermas so often refers to as a 'frame of reference', which is inherently something static, as the very concept clearly suggests. The frames of reference provided by labour and interaction resemble the environmental housings (Umweltgehäusen) which were the object of Uexküll's enquiries, and which man carries around with him, like a snail its shell. It is no accident that Habermas invokes Gehlen against Marcuse (TWI 55ff). The authority of biological anthropology supports the premises on which Habermas bases his critique. He attacks Marcuse's notion that the project of present-day science, the mere exploitation of nature through technology, could one day be transformed into a project of protecting and fostering nature. Habermas's counter-argument against Marcuse is that the different attitudes to nature which the latter conceives as historical projections are in fact suspended in the transcendental frames of reference of labour and interaction. The supposed sequentiality of epochs turns out to be the simultaneity of invariant structures (TWI 55–8). In face of these anthropologically fixed structures, argues Habermas, there can be no question of a historicity that is at work in the cultural determination of human beings. No historical event could break through the bell-jar that encloses the traffic between humans and things. No encounter could ever exert sufficient force to break the rules according to which human beings communicate with one another.

Like Horkheimer, Habermas starts by overburdening the empirical subject and ends by renaturalizing it. And as with the former, the latter's overburdening of the subject is based on the trick of equating the transcendental subject with the human species.[74] Moreover, Habermas presents us with a further subjectivization of his own. For he later inserts a third feature into his initial conception, which divides up social praxis into labour and interaction – that of self-reflection, which, he claims, is what Hegel called experience (*Erfahrung*) in the *Phenomenology of Spirit* (EI 27, 81). Experience frees 'the subject from the dependence on hypostatized forces' (TWI 159), and does so by dissolving all false objectifications and revealing them to be products of the subject's own activity. Up till now, however, Habermas has conspicuously failed to provide an adequate characterization of the relation between self-reflection and interaction. At times he subsumes self-reflection under communicative action; at others he separates the two. The subsumption rests on the prejudice, as yet unexplained, that intersubjectivity always vouchsafes the truth which the individual alone cannot find. On the basis of this prejudice, Habermas is able to assert apodictically that self-reflection is 'not a solitary movement; it is bound to the intersubjectivity of linguistic communication with another person'.[75] Why, then, does he divide self-reflection off from communicative action? One answer to this question is to be found in his comment that the 'interest in speech' (let us leave aside the issue of what this means) strives not only for 'the maintenance of the intersubjectivity of mutual understanding, but also for the production of communication free from domination' (TWI 91). Normal interaction is supposed to aim at preserving intersubjective agreement, while action that moves the other person to self-reflection is supposed to aim at the production of communication free from domination. So it must be the difference in the direction of these two interests which prompted Habermas to make self-reflection independent of communicative action. Self-reflection and interaction tend in different directions, because the one pursues a revolutionary interest, and the other a conservative one. Reform, which includes both the preservation and the extension of the realm of tradition in which we reach understanding with one another, also belongs to the conservatism of interaction, which is regulated by obligatory norms and sanctions (TWI 62f). One reason why Habermas might try to describe communicative action in this way is that, in defining the lifeworld basis of the historical-hermeneutic sciences, he relies on Gadamer's hermeneutics to such an extent that he undermines his own critique of Gadamer's position.[76] But however this may be, the reduction of the revolutionary interest to self-reflection is a logical consequence of this description. In this manner Habermas subjectivizes revolution, and this subjectivization obscures the gulf between the praxis of Critical Theory and the praxis that it intends to bring about. What is ultimately lost from the picture is the historical process itself. On Habermas's view, self-reflection is 'knowledge for the sake of knowledge'.[77] The idea of the end-in-itself, which Horkheimer earlier reconceived in terms of the philosophy of history, is returned again to the ahistorical level of the Aristotelian conception of theory. The pure theory that Aristotle discusses can be easily understood as an end-in-itself, in the sense of being knowledge for the sake of knowledge. By contrast, and according to its own criteria, Critical Theory is developed for the sake of a praxis that historically transcends it, a praxis which can only be the theory's own end-in-itself in so far as the critical attitude already participates in it. Habermas cuts out this historical transcendence, by expressly averring that the emancipatory interest aims 'for the pursuit of reflection as such' (TWI 164) and for this 'alone' (ZLS 193). Thus the history of the formation of the individual and the species turns out to be the main theme of Critical Theory, a theme that entails the erasure of the future by the present in which the act of reflection takes place, and which presupposes the retrospective viewpoint of Aristotelian theory. The subject emancipates itself, Habermas argues, 'to the extent that it becomes transparent to itself in the history of its genesis' (EI 243ff). And the 'end-point' at which the self-reflection of the subject aims is supposedly reached when this subject 'remembers' the reflexively dissolved objectivations 'as the paths along which it has constituted itself' (EI 317). The power of tradition, under the influence of which Habermas translates *poiesis* into 'labour' and *praxis* into 'interaction' reaches further than he realizes: this power also collapses self-reflection into *theoria*, which Aristotle distinguishes from both *praxis* and *poiesis*.

IV The Reasons for the Failure of Critical Theory

1 The Elimination of 'Absolute Objectivity' from History

We have just surveyed the material which documents the way in which Critical Theory departed from its original intention. This material calls for a hypothesis concerning the reasons for the deviation. These reasons can be found, first, in the basic tenets of the programme of Critical Theory and, secondly, in one of its presuppositions. This presupposition is not externally related to the elementary implications of the programme; it counts as the most important principle of Critical Theory as a whole. The systematic and seemingly contrived distinction between the programme as it was originally devised, and the standpoint it reaches on the basis of this presupposition (which we have yet to examine), reproduces a tension within the subject-matter itself. The same tension reigns between Hegel and Marx, or, more precisely, between the use that Critical Theory makes of Hegel and the use it makes of Marx. The concept of a theory which is an end-in-itself, yet also its own self-realization in practice, by virtue of being a hermeneutics of its own historical epoch, resembles Hegel's concept of philosophy.[78] Essentially, Critical Theory radicalizes Hegel's already radically historical approach in four basic steps. I shall limit myself merely to mentioning the first two here; the final two we have already touched on.

1   Critical Theory gives up the theologically motivated belief, present in Hegel as well as in Kant, that progress, however conceived, is guaranteed.[79] Giving up this belief leads to an intensification of historical thinking, because the guarantee of progress gives history a kind of 'naturalness' (Naturwüchsigkeit) which places it beyond the decisions of historically acting subjects.

2   Critical Theory distances itself from the conception of a universal history,[80] because such a conception has to deny that thinking is exposed to factual history, in order to be able to survey history as if it were a naturally given universe.

3   Critical Theory states explicitly what Hegel scarcely dared to acknowledge as being a consequence of his approach: that philosophy which is nothing but 'its time comprehended in thought' owes even its most general concepts to factual history.

4   Critical Theory subjects itself to the law of historical relativism, from which Hegel exempted only his own philosophy (at least, so the representatives of Critical Theory claim). Viewed from the standpoint of the history of philosophy, the inadequate self-realization of Critical Theory threatens to undermine the guiding intention of the whole programme. It puts at risk the whole attempt of the Theory to move beyond Hegel by means of the originally Hegelian insight into the historicity of its own principles and the acknowledgement of their historical mutability.[81]

Insofar as this danger does not arise directly from the programme we outlined at the beginning, it arises from Critical Theory's reception of Marx. One can divide the founding presuppositions which Critical Theory derives from Marx into two levels: the level at which its deepest roots lie buried, and a second level, which we have already examined, which represents a development from these roots. We have already seen that Critical Theory leaves the ground of Hegel's philosophy of history, in its role as fundamental philosophy, by appropriating Marx's doctrine of the natural basis of history (cf. EI 36–59). This is not the place to decide whether Marx himself severs pre-historical nature (albeit a nature he himself admits to be knowable only from the perspective of history) irreparably from history, so that the term 'nature in itself' is warranted. However, we can state with some certainty that contemporary Critical Theory removes nature from under the aegis of history. For Critical Theory, external nature ranks not below, but beside, human history. Yet contemporary social theory could not have reached the point at which it now actually ranks nature above history, had it not remained true to its Marxian presuppositions in claiming that there is no 'absolute objectivity' in history, to use Horkheimer's terms, no objectivity that reaches beyond intersubjectivity and is the subject's ultimate ground. Hegel can make his attempt to found nature in history only because he presupposes an absolute objectivity which is intrinsically historical. The most essential pre-supposition of Critical Theory is the denial of Hegel's presupposition, and thus the removal of absolute objectivity from history. This denial goes hand in hand with the acceptance of Marx's demand that the human species, already ordained as the sole subject of history, should realize itself as this subject, and finally make the history, of which it has always in fact been sole author, voluntarily and consciously.[82] By means of this denial, history is equated with society. From the perspective of Critical Theory, the only true objectivity consists either in the natural objectivity of internal and external nature or in the historical objectivity of social intersubjectivity. Besides these, all that remains is the illusory objectivity of 'apparently natural' objectivations, through which intersubjectivity attains a kind of quasi-naturalness to the extent that it fails to assume the role of the sole ruler of history. In spite of the 'positivism dispute', Critical Theory agrees with the modern logic of science in its enormous overestimation of the truth-value of intersubjectivity. This overestimation needs to be corrected with the truism that intersubjectivity, even when realized in the form of the human species, is only an extension of subjectivity. The expansion of subjectivity into intersubjectivity by no means justifies the dignity of the 'Absolute', which Critical Theory confers on it. That this is a false absolute is indicated by its catastrophic reversal into the equally false absolute of nature. The suspicion here is that nature functions as a surrogate for an historical absolute, whose tasks cannot be carried out by the individuals who have been mystified into the 'overarching subject'[83] of the human species.

This worrying supposition forms part of our more comprehensive thesis that the dynamic which causes Critical Theory to depart from the guiding intention of its programme is set in train by the elimination of absolute objectivity from history. This hypothesis implies the further the suspicion that the basic presupposition of Critical Theory, which is bound up with the interest in the prevention of dogmatism, is itself dogmatically introduced. The reversal of the intentions of Critical Theory that we have just observed seems to arise from a process that is at work at the very root of Critical Theory, transforming criticism into dogmatism. Other indications support this view. One is the fact that the whole Frankfurt School breaks off the dialectical method, which it explicitly embraces,[84] at the precise point where this method is supposed to elucidate once and for all the grounding of the subject through absolute objectivity. For Hegel there are two dialectics: first, the dialectic which intertwines subjective and objective spirit; and second, the dialectic which entrusts absolute spirit to the human subject, yet without depriving it of its priority. Critical theorists unfold the dialectic between subject and object as equiprimordial moments, none with more virtuosity than Adorno; but they revert to an undialectical logic whenever they have to explain the dialectic of the absolute grounding of the subject. They ignore the thought that has persisted from Eckhart to Buber, that God delivers up his world-historical fate to human freedom, but does not thereby fully abandon himself to this freedom. Horkheimer writes: 'Mysticism began by making God just as dependent on man, as man is on God, and ended with the news of the death of God.'[85] Habermas assures us of the logic of this move. For he understands the Marxian postulate which endows the human species with the rights of a subject that rules history as a consistent outcome of the mystical-idealist doctrine which portrays the Creator designating his creature as a partner of potentially equal status, as an *alter deus*. According to Habermas, Marx deciphers the God who, despite his omnipotence, is limited by the independent sovereignty of free will, 'for his part as the alter ego of humanity' (TuP 137); Marx realizes 'that humanity has encrypted in the figure of God the implicit awareness of its own power over history, which nevertheless always seems to elude it'.[86]

However, the dogmatism which apodictically declares the abstract independence of the subject to be the truth of any attempt to ground the subject absolutely has far-reaching consequences. First and foremost, it makes such crucial concepts as 'emancipation' and 'responsibility' deeply ambivalent. Liberation from nature and from the apparently natural compulsion of social relations appears self-evidently to be a liberation of man from any power that is imagined to lie beyond the human. Because of this, the aim of emancipation, 'autonomy and responsibility' (*Mündigkeit*), oscillates between the unproblematic notion of responsibility for oneself and that of the freedom of human beings from everything which they have hitherto set higher than themselves, a freedom whose reality has in no sense been demonstrated. Finally, and more worryingly, this critique which flips over into dogmatism leads to a doctrinaire intolerance. Although the critique has already become astonishingly academic, refraining from polemic in all other respects, it none the less puts any philosophy which differs from it to the test of its 'annihilating judgement' (EI 86). With this invocation of the magical powers of annihilation, critique falls victim to the fate that Horkheimer and Adorno prophesied for an Enlightenment which ceases to be dialectical: it becomes 'totalitarian'.[87]

2 Unresolved Problems and Possible Solutions

Of course, even assuming that the thesis proposed here is true, we would not be entitled to assert dogmatically that there can be an absolute objectivity that is also historical. But how would things stand if Critical Theory, by dogmatically exorcizing the absolute from history, not only failed to meet its own standards, but turned out to be determined in its original form by the fact that it secretly clung to a conception of historically absolute objectivity? A re-examination of the reasons for the departure of Critical Theory from its original programme, reasons that lie within the programme itself, pushes us towards at least considering this question. There are two problems here. The first is contained in the following question: How can Critical Theory have the present totality in view, and none the less participate in the current historical process? Critical Theory can only have the totality in view if it remains outside of this totality, yet it can only become a moment of the historical-social process if it moves within the totality. The sentence in which Horkheimer's programmatic essay formulates this contradiction is supposed also to indicate its sublation. 'Theory as a moment of a praxis that aims towards new social forms is not, however, a cog in an already existent mechanism.'[88] Horkheimer resolves the contradiction by distinguishing within the present social totality between the praxis of emancipatory labour and the workings of the machinery of alienation that opposes it. On this view, Critical Theory is situated within existing society as a moment of the labour process, yet outside this process to the extent that it remains unaffected by the bad praxis of the *status quo*. In particular, Critical Theory remains free from the ideological distortion of existing norms; it lacks 'confidence in the criterion which social life, in its present form, places in everybody's hand'.[89] However, the possibility of such a freedom existing in reality is not philosophically explained. Here we encounter a dogmatic belief, one which transforms the admission of historical relativity into an assertion of absoluteness which can be precisely defined. Critical Theory's specific claim to absoluteness is indicated by the early Horkheimer. According to his study 'On the problem of truth', the theory may need to be revised in line with the future course of the world, but it always delivers absolutely valid knowledge for its own time, thanks to its freedom from ideological distortion. No other theory can be assumed to be valid at the same time.[90]

Habermas, by contrast, offers the remarkable spectacle of someone who formally appeals to Critical Theory to become aware of its own implication in the criticized object (TuP 181), yet, as a result of his systematic approach, all too readily raises the claim to absoluteness to a height reminiscent of Hegel's absolute knowledge, albeit in the altered guise of critique. Only here does Habermas reveal what he means by the 'end-point' of self-reflection: since self-reflection is the experience that is described in the *Phenomenology of Spirit*, then this 'end-point' can be none other than the absolute knowing in which this experience culminates. Habermas pursues reflection both as the preferred object and as the vehicle of his Critical Theory, 'up to the point at which the self-consciousness of the human species, having become critique, has wholly freed itself from ideological distortion' (EI 76ff). Since it thereby reaches completion, self-consciousness is also absolute, since instead of being content with criticizing, it has turned into critique, just as the idealist, according to Kierkegaard, turns into 'pure speculation'. Habermas's underlying systematic approach replicates the Hegelian system. For Hegel's system claims to do without presuppositions, not in the manner intended by Husserlian phenomenology, by virtue of the absolute evidence of the beginning, but through its promise to recuperate the presuppositions from which it started at the end of the process. In Habermas work this figure recurs as the thought that self-reflection can 'recuperate' its own interests (TWI 163ff). Completed self-reflection lays claim to absoluteness, in so far as it insists on the complete transparency of its interests.

By contrast, it seems sensible to me to hold open at least the possibility of an unilluminated remainder of interests, a remainder in which the effects of the ideologically distorted norms of existing society find expression. Only thus could the admission of historical relativity be given its full due, and only thus could Habermas meet his own demand that critique must always also be self-critique.[91] This would in no way blunt the edge of Critical Theory. On the contrary, it would eliminate its dogmatic and consequently uncritical aspect. It is as dogmatic to assure oneself that one has completely liberated oneself from ideological illusion as it is to refuse to liberate oneself and others from ideological illusion. The dogmatism of both positions lies in the stubbornness of the insistence. And it makes no difference whether the 'end-point' of complete freedom from opaque, unreflected interests is supposed to lie in the present or in the future. Even the future-oriented position proclaims the possibility that history can come to a standstill. If one wants to be truly critical, it is not enough simply to initiate the process of liberating oneself from hypostatized forces; one must relentlessly keep this critical process in motion.

The second problem posed by the programme of Critical Theory arises out of the decision which Critical Theory hopes will resolve the first problem: namely, the refusal to be guided by the criteria of existing society. One may doubt that it is possible to remain permanently independent of these criteria, but this is in no way to deny the necessity of following other norms than those offered by existing society. Thus the question arises: from where, if not from existing society, is Critical Theory to derive its standards of judgement? It can do so neither from a transcendent realm of values, the existence of which it disputes; nor from nature, for nature contains no norms, a point on which Horkheimer and Habermas rightly agree.[92] According to its own programme, Critical Theory is supposed to derive its criteria from the anticipation of a future society.[93] The idea of the 'good life' against which Critical Theory measures society, is the reality of a future society that is anticipated in thought (TWI 164). This assumes, of course, that the necessarily abstract conception of freedom to which the abstract character of bourgeois society gives rise can define the 'good life' for man, once it is grasped more concretely. This anticipation is held to be distinguishable from that of a utopia beyond all scientific control, because it can point to the objective tendency toward freedom that exists in a reality that is already given.[94] Labour, for Horkheimer, is such a reality, and fulfils this function. On his conception of Critical Theory, it is labour that safeguards within the bad existing society the hidden reality of the good life, on which Critical Theory can rely for the empirical verification of its anticipation: 'The perspectives, which Critical Theory derives from historical analysis, above all the idea of a rationally organised society that meets universal needs, are immanent to human labour.'[95] But this interpretation of labour as emancipation is not an immediately evident item of knowledge, independent of history. It was only the ideal of subservience to authority conveyed by Lutheranism which transformed labour from a curse into a blessing. Marcuse and the later Horkheimer prove that labour can just as well be understood as unfreedom, and freedom be understood as freedom from labour. But it would be simply naïve to argue that what holds true of the interpretation of labour in the horizon of freedom does not also hold true of the interpretation of interaction and self-reflection. Habermas's claim that the standards of self-reflection are 'theoretically certain' and can 'be known a priori'[96] cannot be seen as anything other than a manoeuvre that tries to cover over the historicality of these standards. This manoeuvre is clearly related to his tendency to naturalize the frames of reference of knowledge-guiding interests, and thus to turn them into invariant structures and to remove them from the reach of history.

By contrast, we should hold on to the original intention of Critical Theory in this respect too, and reflect on the dependency of even the highest principles on factual history. Such reflection can make use of the concept of anticipation, which Habermas, in spite of his tendency to naturalize interests, captures in the following sentence: 'We must comprehend the process of Enlightenment . . . as the attempt to test the limits of the realizability of the utopian content of cultural tradition under given conditions' (EI 344). Behind this sentence stands a conviction that Horkheimer and Habermas share with Ernst Bloch, that the critical philosophy of history preserves the heritage of the Christian theology from which it sprang.[97] The care with which Habermas preserves this heritage can be seen from his conception of freedom, according to which history is heading towards the 'dialogue of all with all that is free from domination' (TWI 164). But if the method of Critical Theory – namely, anticipation – is an experiment which tests the Christian idea of freedom for its feasibility, then we must suppose that the philosophy of history has not only emerged from theology, but is, and always has been, possible only *as* theology. In our historical situation the only serious alternative to a Critical Theory which has internalized an awareness of its theological presuppositions is a Popperian 'critical rationalism'.[98] Such a rationalism proceeds consistently from the elimination of absolute objectivity to the removal of objective meaning from history, and restricts critical activity to the responsibility of individuals for their subjective interpretations.

Notes

*   Jürgen Habermas, 'Kommunikative Freiheit und negative Theologie: Fragen an Michael Theunissen', in *Vom sinnlichen Eindruck zum symbolischen Ausdruck* (Frankfurt am Main: Suhrkamp, 1997), pp. 122; 'Communicative Freedom and Negative Theology', trs. Martin J. Matuštík and Patricia J. Huntingdon, in M. Matuštík and M. Westphal, eds, *Kierkegaard in Post/Modernity* (Bloomington and Indianapolis: Indiana University Press, 1995), pp. 182–98.

†   See Michael Theunissen, *Der Begriff Verzweiflung: Korrekturen an Kierkegaard* (Frankfurt am Main: Suhrkamp, 1993), and *Der Andere: Studien zur Sozialontologie der Gegenwart*, 2nd edn (Berlin/New York: Walter de Gruyter, 1997), esp. pp. 483–507.

1   Albrecht Wellmer reflects thoughtfully on the most recent changes in social theory in his *Kritische Theorie der Gesellschaft und Positivismus* (Frankfurt am Main: Suhrkamp, 1969), a work which is heavily influenced by the Frankfurt School. Wellmer's study focuses, like the present one, on the problem of the unity of

theory and praxis that critical social theory strives to bring about, and it too begins with an analysis of Horkheimer's early work as a basis for an evaluation of Habermas's methodologically oriented new beginning. The first essay in the volume (pp. 7–68) corresponds to sections I–V in the essay 'Kritische und Analytische Theorie' which Wellmer published in *Marxismusstudien*, 6th series (Tübingen: Mohr, 1969), pp. 187–239.

2   Max Horkheimer, 'Traditionelle und Kritische Theorie' (henceforth 'TkT'), *Zeitschrift für Sozialforschung* (henceforth ZfS), 6 (1937), pp. 245–92; repr. in Horkheimer's *Kritische Theorie* (henceforth KTI and KTII) (2 vols, Frankfurt am Main: Suhrkamp, 1968), vol. 2, pp. 137–91. ('Traditional and Critical Theory', tr. M. O'Connell et al., in *Critical Theory* (henceforth CT) (New York: Seabury Press, 1974), pp. 188–243.)

3   Cf. in general G. E. Rusconi, *La teoria critica della società* (Bologna: Il Mulino, 1968), particularly sec. III. On Horkheimer's relation to the whole school see Alfred Schmidt in the 'Afterword' to the reprint of Horkheimer's early work (KTII 333–58). On Habermas see Harald Pilot's trenchant view from the standpoint of the analytic theory of science: 'Jürgen Habermas' empirisch falsifizierbare Geschichtsphilosophie', in *Der Positivismusstreit in der deutschen Soziologie* (Berlin and Neuwied: Luchterhand, 1969), pp. 258–87' (*The Positivist Dispute in German Sociology*, tr. G. Adey and D. Frisby (New York: Harper, 1976)). Among the now growing literature on Marcuse are two outstanding works: Hans Holz, *Utopie und Anarchismus – Zur Kritik der Kritischen Theorie Herbert Marcuses* (Cologne: Pahl-Rugenstein, 1968); and *Antworte auf Herbert Marcuse*, ed. J. Habermas (Frankfurt am Main: Suhrkamp, 1968).

4   'Philosophy and Critical Theory' (with a supplementary word by Horkheimer), ZfS 6 pp. 625–47. Marcuse's contribution is included in the collection entitled *Kultur und Gesellschaft*, vol.1 (Frankfurt am Main: Suhrkamp, 1965). Horkheimer's response is reprinted as the postscript to 'TKT', in KTII 192–200 (Marcuse, 'Philosophy and Critical Theory' (1937), in CT 58–74; Horkheimer, 'Postscript to TCT', in CT 244–52).

5   Max Horkheimer and Theodor Adorno, *Dialektik der Aufklärung* (Amsterdam: Querido, 1947) (henceforth DdA).

6   Theory in the Greek sense refers, according to Habermas, 'to the immutable essence of things, beyond mutable realms of human attributes' ('Technischer Fortschritt und soziale Lebenswelt' (1965), in TWI 109). His main source is George Picht, 'Der Sinn der Unterscheidung von Theorie und Praxis in der griechischen Philosophie', in *Zeitschrift für Evangelische Ethik*, 8 (1964), pp. 321–42. Cf. J. Ritter, 'Die Lehre vom Ursprung und Sinn der Theorie bei Aristoteles', in *Veröffentlichungen der Arbeitgemeinschaft für Forschung des Landes Nordrhein Westfalen, Abt. Geisteswissenschaften*, vol. 1 (Cologne and Opladen, 1953), pp. 32–52. Here I can only mention the distinction between theory as a form of life and theory as science that Ritter develops.

7   Horkheimer, 'Geschichte und Psychologie' (henceforth 'GP'), in KTI 9, 29; 'Die Gesellschaftliche Funktion der Philosophie' (henceforth 'GFP'), in KTII 303; Habermas, TuP 172, 179.

8 See the late works of Karl Löwith. The reception of Löwith's work of relevance to this study is Habermas's 'Karl Löwith's stoic retreat from historical consciousness' (1963), repr. in PhPP.

9 Horkheimer, 'Zum Problem der Wahrheit' (henceforth 'PW'), in KTI 253, 258ff cf. Jürgen Habermas, 'Zwischen Philosophie und Wissen schaft: Marxismus als Kritik', and 'Dogmatismus, Vernunft und Entscheidung: Zu Theorie und Praxis in der verwissenschaftlichten Zivilisation', in TuP. Habermas, TP 172 and 239: 'grand theories attempt to reflect the context of life as a whole'; see also his 'Analytische Wissenschaftstheorie und Dialektik', in *Zeugnisse: Festschrift für Theodor W. Adorno* (Frankfurt am Main: Suhrkamp, 1963), pp. 473–501, also published in *Logik der Sozialwissenschaften*, ed. Topitsch (Cologne/Berlin: Kiepenheuer und Witsch, 1965), pp. 291–311.

10 Horkheimer, 'Nachtrag', in KTII 195.

11 Here I can only allude to the fact that Habermas can construct such an abstract opposition between the contemplation of objects in Greek theory and the self-reflection of Critical Theory only because he obscures the theological dimension. In so far as it is originally God who beholds himself in the contemplation of the cosmos, theory, in Aristotle's sense, also has the character of self-reflection. I leave aside the hermeneutic problem of whether concepts such as 'objectivism' and 'objectivistic' adequately capture the Greek comprehension of being.

12 Horkheimer, 'Materialismus und Metaphysik' (henceforth MuM), in KTI 49; 'Zum Problem der Voraussage in den Sozialwissenschaften' (henceforth PVS), in KTI 111; Habermas, TuP 177; see also his 'Analytische Wissenschaftstheorie und Dialektik', in *Logik der Sozialwissenschaften*, pp. 291, 293: 'Theories of this more mobile type reflectively acknowledge, even in the subjective arrangement of the scientific apparatus, that they remain themselves a moment of the objective context which they subject to analysis.'

13 Horkheimer, 'TkT'; see also *idem*, 'Zu Bergson's Metaphysik der Zeit', in KTI 178, 186, and 'Autorität und Familie', in KTI 279.

14 Horkheimer, 'Nachtrag', in KTII 197.

15 Cf. in particular Horkheimer, 'TkT', KTII 182–7.

16 Horkheimer points to this most expressly in his early works: e.g., 'Materialismus und Moral' (henceforth 'MuMo'), in KTI 91; 'PW', in KTI 255; 'TkT' in KTII 160, 161, 164, 182.

17 Horkheimer, 'TkT', in KTII 147; O'Connell uses 'dominated by' where we use 'imbued with' – trs.

18 Ibid., p. 174.

19 Thus Horkheimer at the 11th International Congress of Sociologists in Geneva, 1933, articulated the position of Critical Theory with the following thought: that 'the aim of the discipline is the knowledge of processes to which the dimension of the future necessarily belongs' ('PVS', in KTI 111).

20 Horkheimer, 'Nachtrag', in KTII 199.

21 Ibid., p. 191. Cf. 'Bemerkungen über Wissenschaft und Krise' (1932), in KTI 1–8.

22 Horkheimer, 'TkT', in KTII 146.

23 Ibid., p. 168.

24　Ibid., p. 156.

25　Ibid., p. 157. Cf. 'Die Gesellschaftliche funktion der Philosophie' (henceforth 'FPh', in KTII 300: 'Philosophy, in contrast to other disciplines, has no sharply defined field of operation within the given order. This order of life with its hierarchy of values is itself a problem for philosophy'.

26　Aristotle, *Metaphysics* I. ii. 982b24.

27　Horkheimer, 'TkT', in KTII 162, 172, 190; Habermas, TuP 231. Cf. the fourth thesis of the essay 'Knowledge and human interests': 'in the power of self-reflection knowledge and interest are one' (TWI 164).

28　The whole study that comprises Horkheimer's *Zur Kritik der Instrumentellen Vernunft* (Frankfurt: Suhrkamp, 1967) (henceforth KIV) (*Critique of Instrumental Reason*, tr. M. O'Connell et al. (New York: Seabury Press, 1974), which in its original edition in America was called *The Eclipse of Reason* (New York: Continuum, 1947), is devoted to these two ways of thinking.

29　TuP 13f; TWI 162; EI 350. Cf. Horkheimer, 'FPh', in KTII 306ff. Aristotle famously anticipated 'happiness' (*eudaimonia*) only from the 'good life'. But *eudaimonia* has a Janus face: on the one hand, it is realized as *praxis* in the bounds of the *polis*; on the other hand, in book 10 of the *Nicomachean Ethics* it is shown to be the *theoria* that is rooted in, but which wrests loose from, the political community, and in which (originally divine) reason, beholding the rationally ordered cosmos, intuits itself. This is why Horkheimer is right to say that 'The self-intuition of reason, which forms the highest level of happiness for ancient philosophy, has, in modern thought, been transposed into the materialist concept of a free, self-determining society' ('Nachtrag', in KTII 196).

30　Horkheimer, ibid.: 'Theory in the traditional Cartesian sense, which we see operative in the professional activities of the specialised sciences, organises experience on the basis of questions which arise from the reproduction of life within existing society.'

31　Horkheimer, 'TkT', in KTII 148–53.

32　Ibid., pp. 56, 158f, 166: 'In the future the relation between rational labour and its realisation will take the place that the enigmatic harmony between thinking and being, understanding and sensibility, human needs and their satisfaction enjoys in today's chaotic economy, a harmony, which in the bourgeois epoch appears to be a contingent.' Cf. 'MuMo', in KTI 78.

33　Horkheimer, 'TkT', in KTII 158.

34　Ibid., p. 161.

35　Horkheimer, 'PVS', in KTI 117.

36　Horkheimer, 'Nachtrag', in KTII 193; 'FPh', in KTI 306.

37　See, e.g., KIV 147.

38　Ibid., pp. 63, 129, 238; DdA 9f, 50.

39　KIV 94.

40　Ibid.

41　Compare the conclusion of the letter to the publisher S. Fischer, 3 June 1965, in which Horkheimer justifies his request to postpone a plan to reprint his early writings. 'My hesitation stems from the difficulty of expressing my former ideas again, which were not independent of their time, without harming what I now believe to be true: that we must renounce the belief that the ideas of Western civilisation are about to be realised, and yet defend these ideas – without the concept of providence, and indeed against the progress which is attributed to providence' (KTI p. xi). On the early optimism see 'TkT', in KTII 168; 'FPh', in KTII 309.

42 KIV 9 (Foreword). Cf. the letter to the publisher: 'My faith of the thirties in progressive activity, a faith that was based on an analysis of society, is now changing into fear of a new disaster, of the domination of an all-encompassing administration' (KTII p. ix).

43 Cf. Horkheimer, 'Die Aktualität Schopenauers' (1961), in KIV 248–68.

44 Horkheimer, KTI p. xiii (foreword to the new edn).

45 Horkheimer, 'MuM', in KTI 47.

46 Horkheimer, 'On Theodor Haecker's *Christ and History*' (1936), in KTI 373.

47 Ibid., p. 372. Cf. 'Bemerkungen zur Philosophischen Anthropologie', in KTI 295.

48 Horkheimer, 'Gedanken zur Religion' (1935), in KTI 376.

49 Horkheimer, KIV 155, 165. Cf. 'Religion und Philosophie' (1966), in ibid., p. 238: 'The service which philosophy can still perform for the transitory present, is to explain what is happening and its consequences.'

50 Ibid., p. 18.

51 Ibid., p. 123.

52 DdA 54.

53 Ibid., p. 57.

54 T. W. Adorno, *Negative Dialektik* (Frankfurt am Main: Suhrkamp, 1966), pt 1, pp. 65–134.

55 DdA 14.

56 Cf. above all the discussion of the phrase that 'myth is already Enlightenment' (DdA 18ff), and also Marcuse's statement that Aristotle's logic is a logic of domination ('Philosophy and Critical Theory', p. 33).

57 KIV 120.

58 'MuMo', in KTI 192ff: 'There is no eternal realm of values.' On the historicity of truth see 'PW', in KTI 228–76. The young Horkheimer praised the Hegelian maxim that a dialectical theory judged 'not according to what is above time, but what is in time' ('Nachtrag', in KTII 198).

59 KIV 171.

60 Ibid., p. 120.

61 How little such historicity still figures can be illustrated by the sentence: 'A concept cannot be accepted as the measure of truth, when the ideal of truth which it serves presupposes social processes which do not allow to thinking an ultimately decisive role' (KIV 84). In the same vein Horkheimer attacks positivistic pragmatism: 'Because science is an element of the social process, its appointment to the role of *arbiter veritatis* would itself subject truth to changing social standards' (KIV 76). The truth which underlies 'all genuine philosophy',

and to which philosophy lays claim, is quite traditionally defined, indeed with explicit reference to 'Platonism' as 'correspondence of name with thing', of 'speech with reality' (KIV 168).

62 Ibid., p. 171.

63 Horkheimer, 'Theismus-Atheismus' (1963), in KIV 219.

64 KIV, p. 102.

65 Ibid., p. 145. Cf. the talk of 'the joy of insight' and of 'the self-forgetting of thought' in DdA 14, 43.

66 TWI 54–7. [The German language can make a simple distinction between the other thing (das Andere) and the other person (der Andere) with the gender of the definite article – trs.]

67 TuP 13–51. Later Habermas finds this distinction between work and interaction in the Jena Hegel. Cf. TWI 9–47.

68 TWI 161. Habermas also speaks Kant's language when he differentiates knowledge-guiding interests from particular and group-specific interests, which distort reality, characterizing the former as 'the conditions of possible objectivity' (TWI 160; cf. EI 351).

69 Cf. 'Dialektischer Idealismus im Übergang zum Materialismus – Geschichtsphilosophie Folgerungen aus Schellings Idee einer Contraction Gottes' (henceforth 'DIM'), in TuP 152; 'Ein marxistischer Schelling – Zu Ernst Blochs spekulativen Materialismus' (1960), in TuP 336–51.

70 EI 45; cf. Alfred Schmidt, Der Begriff der Natur in der Lehre von Karl Marx (Frankfurt am Main: Suhrkamp, 1962), pp. 136ff.

71 Cf. Herbert Marcuse, Der eindimensionale Mensch (Berlin: Neuwied, 1967), p. 104. When Marcuse speaks of a 'two-dimensional dialectical mode of thought', it could not be clearer that he is no longer speaking of dialectics in the Hegelian sense.

72 Ibid., pp. 41, 84, 98, 107, 116. Kierkegaard not only employed the term 'qualitative difference' but also made extensive use of the term 'that which currently exists' (das Bestehende), regarding Hegel as the very embodiment of this. The theological motivation of Kierkegaard's critique of Hegel returns in concealed form in Marcuse. Just as Kierkegaard's 'Christian' aim is to entice human beings 'in a Christian way' beyond this world and to awaken in them the consciousness of sin, without which they would not accept divine grace, so Marcuse's intention is to make those who are totally integrated into the dominant social system, even in their apparently most intimate needs, and who are thus incapable of picturing a 'qualitatively different universe', conscious of the 'hell of the society' in which they actually live (ibid., p. 44).

73 KIV 158, 160. Hegelian idealism even resides in the critical remark that reason 'made Nature into a mere object and failed to find the trace of itself in such objectivation' (ibid., p. 165; my emphasis). The later Horkheimer turns explicitly against the view that the 'fetishism of nature' enables the 'great unity to speak' (KIV 223).

74 Habermas contends that knowledge-guiding interests make objective knowledge possible, because they overcome the bad subjectivity of the individual and the

group in the intersubjectivity of the species. They are supposed – and herein lies the Left Hegelian correction of Kant – to be transcendental achievements which are none the less, because of the contingency of the human species, of empirical origin (EI 240, 249).

75 EI 290 n. 56. Habermas admits that he imports a whole set of assumptions here: 'Given materialist assumptions, the interest in reason . . . can no longer be conceived as an autarkic self-explication of reason' (EI 349).

76 Cf. the dispute with Gadamer in ZLS 149–80, but then the recourse to Gadamer's *Wahrheit und Methode* (Tübingen: Siebeck and Mohr, 1965) in the description of the historical-hermeneutic sciences (TWI 157f).

77 TWI 164: 'In self-reflection knowledge for the sake of knowledge attains congruence with the interest in autonomy and responsibility (*Mündigkeit*).' Habermas reiterates this sentence word for word in his book of the same name (EI 244).

78 Cf. Hans Friedrich Fulda, *Das Recht der Philosophie in Hegel's Philosophie des Rechts* (Frankfurt am Main: Suhrkamp, 1968). I give a more detailed justification of this thesis in *Hegels Philosophie des Absoluten Geistes als theologisch-politischer Traktat* (Berlin: Walter de Gruyter, 1970).

79 Horkheimer, 'GP', in KTI 17; 'MuMo', in KTI 105; Habermas, 'Kritische und konservative Aufgaben der Soziologie', in TuP 218; EI 346.

80 Horkheimer, 'MuM', in KTI 42, 46, 48, 50; see his 'Zum Rationalismusstreit in der gegenwärtigen Philosophie' (1934), in KTI 125; Habermas, TuP 214.

81 It is inherent in the problematic outlined here that the critique of the idea of guaranteed progress, just like the critique of universal history, falls into a strange ambiguity. Before Horkheimer came close to the idea of a guaranteed historical regression, he was 'wedded to the conception that reality necessarily produces, if not the good itself, then at least the forces which could realise it' (letter to the Fischer publishing company, in KTII 176). Cf. the explication of the concept of 'meaningful' necessity in 'TkT', in KTII 176–9. Habermas is right to challenge the necessity of progress in the emancipation of consciousness (EI 343), but he cannot avoid viewing progress in the technological exploitation of objectified processes as guaranteed. The same ambivalence is apparent in their attitude to the notion of universal history. Horkheimer calls for a 'comprehensive theory of history' ('FPh', in KTII 303), and Habermas finds missing in Gadamer's hermeneutics 'the transition from the transcendental conditions of historicity to the universal history in which these conditions are constituted' (ZLS 180).

82 Horkheimer, 'MuMo', in KTI 78; 'PVS', in KTI 116; 'TkT' in KTII 181, 189; Habermas, 'DIM', in TuP 154, and 'Zwischen Philosophie und Wissenschaft: Marxismus als Kritik' (henceforth 'PhW'), in TuP 211ff.

83 'TkT', in KTII 189.

84 Critical Theory's modifications of the Hegelian concept of dialectic reflect the tendency to radicalization adumbrated above. For Horkheimer dialectic is synonymous with the implication of knowing in the historical process which is known ('MuM', in KTI, 51, 54; letter to Fischer publishing house, KTII p. xi.). For Habermas dialectic means objectively the 'coercive context' of a history not

yet made with will and consciousness, and not yet liberated into dialogue (TuP 159, 256) and, subjectively, the constitution of thought which reflects on the above process, that 'takes the historical traces of suppressed dialogue and reconstructs what has been suppressed' (TWI 164). Although Horkheimer's concept of dialectic is positive, and Habermas's negative, they agree on one point, for both are worked out with Hegel against Hegel. Where the one points to the historicity that Hegel did not thematize, the other wants to unmask what Hegel thematized as historicity as prior to the beginning of true history.

85 KIV 73.

86 TuP 185; cf. the whole section 'Critique and crisis: mythological genesis and scientific structure of an empirical philosophy of history with a practical intention' (TuP 179–88), and also the Schelling essay, in particular the following two sections: 'The consequences of the idea of a contraction of God for the philosophy of history' (TuP 130–7), and 'The secret materialism of the philosophy of "The ages of the world": Schelling and Marx' (TuP 152–6). On the relation of Schelling to the Left Hegelians see also Habermas's dissertation *Das Absolute und die Geschichte: Von der Zwiespältigkeit in Schellings Denken* (Bonn, 1954).

87 DdA 16.

88 Horkheimer, 'TkT', in KTII 165. Of course, this is a problem faced by Marxism as a whole. Marx already connects a critique unaffected by the object of criticism to the conditions of a standpoint which lies outside the totality and which, in his opinion, only the outcast position of the immiserated proletariat can offer. Even according to Habermas's interpretation of Marx, 'the objective position of the proletariat in the process of production allows one to reach a standpoint beyond this process, a perspective from which one can grasp the system critically as a whole and pass sentence on its historical contingency' (TuP 212). Cf. the particularly cogent repetition of this thesis in Georg Lukács, *Geschichte und Klassenbewußtsein* (1923) (Berlin: Neuwied, 1968), p. 161.

89 Horkheimer, 'TkT', in KTII 156; cf. 'FPh', in KTII 295: 'social praxis vouchsafes no standards to philosophy.'

90 This is what Horkheimer means when he says that Critical Theory overcomes the opposition between dogmatism and relativism. It overcomes this opposition, on his view, by being relatively valid in relation to history as a whole, but absolutely valid with respect to the present ('PW', in KTI 228–76).

91 TWI 84: 'The knowing subject must also direct the critique of ideology at itself.'

92 Horkheimer 'MuM', in KTI 40; Habermas, 'Die Klassische Lehre von der Politik in ihrem Verhältnis zur Sozialphilosophie', in TuP 32–7.

93 Horkheimer, 'PW', in KTI 269; Habermas, 'PhW', in TuP 214; 'Dogmatismus, Vernunft und Entscheidung – Zu Theorie und Praxis in der verwissenschaftlichten Zivilisation', in TuP 239; ZLS 194f.

94 Horkheimer, 'MuMo', in KTI 85f; 'TkT', in KTII 168; 'FPh', in KTII 309.

95 Horkheimer, 'TkT', in KTII 162.

96 TWI 163. Habermas attempts to justify this with the following argument: 'What raises us out of nature is the only thing whose nature we can know: *language*. Through its structure autonomy and responsibility are posited for us. Our first sentence expresses unequivocally the intention of universal and unconstrained consensus.' But instead of a justification, all we have here is a series of new assertions.

97 Horkheimer, 'Zu Theodor Haeckers *Der Christ und die Geschichte*', in KTI 371; 'Gedanke zur Religion' in KTI 374; 'Montaigne und die Funktion der Skepsis' (1938), in KTII 254; 'Zum Begriff des Menschen' (1957), in KIV 181; 'Religion und Philosophie', in KIV 229. Habermas, 'PhW', in TuP 180, 207. Horkheimer, whose present interest is mainly in the problems of the philosophy of religion, has recognized in his later years that the philosophical concept of absolute objectivity, however this might be more precisely articulated, is 'modelled on the absoluteness of religious revelation' (KIV 27). Furthermore, the loss of this concept has become ever more obvious and painful to him. Cf. 'Theismus-Atheismus', in KIV 227: 'To seek to salvage an unconditional meaning without God is futile. However independent, differentiated or inwardly necessitated a particular expression in some cultural sphere, art or religion, might be, it must also give up, along with any theistic belief, the claim to be objectively something higher than any practical action.' Furthermore, in recent years Horkheimer has reached the insight that a nature stylized into an all-encompassing horizon is nothing but a surrogate for historically absolute objectivity (KIV 223).

98 Karl Popper, *The Open Society and its Enemies*, vol. 2: *The High Tide of Prophecy* (London: Routledge and Kegan Paul, 1945); *idem, The Poverty of Historicism* (London: Routledge and Kegan Paul, 1960).

9

Openly strategic uses of language: a transcendental-pragmatic perspective (a second attempt to think with Habermas against Habermas)[1]

Karl-Otto Apel

Karl-Otto Apel is a long-standing friend and colleague of Habermas, and his philosophical development has in many respects followed a parallel path. During the 1960s both philosophers developed a theory of knowledge-constitutive interests, in opposition both to positivism and to Heideggerian hermeneutics. They have since worked on a discourse theory of morality, which locates the justification of moral norms in an ideal intersubjective agreement. It is perhaps precisely because of these deep affinities that the debate between Apel and Habermas has – in recent years – become so acute.

In summary, we could say that Apel is unconvinced by Habermas's programme for the 'desublimation of reason'. He insists that the most general norms of argumentation, which we implicitly acknowledge whenever we enter into discussion, cannot themselves be established though a form of enquiry vulnerable to empirical evidence (such as Habermas regards 'reconstruction' to be), since even the assessment of empirical evidence and its theoretical impact already presupposes the validity of the fundamental norms of discussion. To avoid such difficulties, Apel proposes a strategy of 'Letztbegründung' – or ultimate justification – of the constitutive norms of discussion, through a process of 'strict reflection' which grasps them as necessary preconditions of any possible truth claim we can make. Indeed, Apel is convinced that any attempt to avoid the need for such a *Letztbe-*

gründung ultimately leads to radical incoherence. Thus, to assert that the principle of fallibilism (the general principle – to which Habermas subscribes – that any truth claim is in principle revisable) is itself fallible would amount to admitting the *possibility* of absolute truth, and hence contradict the very principle. Such are the consequences, in Apel's view, of collapsing the 'transcendental difference' between the results of strict reflection and all other truth claims.

In the essay translated here, Apel focuses his critique on one specific point: namely, Habermas's account of openly strategic uses of language. Habermas defends the view that openly strategic uses of language (for example, the use of violent threats to extract compliance) are parasitic on the uses of language oriented towards achieving consensus (which, he is deeply convinced, are fundamental). But since he also wishes to eschew a purely 'transcendental' or 'reflexive' justification of the norms of discourse, he is obliged to suggest that, even here, there is some implicit empirical norm or residual relation of authority (in other words, some minimal consent or consensus) which is being violated. Apel seeks to show that this is very often not the case – indeed, that strategic uses of language without normative backing are a common feature of our social world. If Habermas is to defend his basic intuition that strategic uses of language violate the immanent orientation of language towards the *telos* of agreement, then he must climb off the fence, and accept that the norms of discourse do indeed have an unequivocally transcendental status. This status can only be shown conclusively through the self-reflexive discourse of philosophy itself.

In what follows I would like to present my views on a problem which first emerged clearly in the discussions around Habermas's work *The Theory of Communicative Action*. The problem in question, as the title of my essay indicates, is that of the 'openly strategic use of language' (henceforth, OSUL). According to *The Theory of Communicative Action*, this use of language should be understood as an alternative to the 'concealed strategic use of language' (CSUL), and therefore as a variant of the 'instrumental use of language' (IUL), which stands in contrast to the 'use of language oriented to mutual understanding' (ULOMU).[2]

But in what sense has the reception of *The Theory of Communicative Action* revealed a specific problem concerning OSUL? And what is the rationale for analysing this problem from the perspective of *transcendental pragmatics*?

At the beginning of this essay I can indicate my answers to these two questions only in a provisional way, since I have yet to develop a more precise analysis. This applies particularly to the terminological distinctions, which I have simply taken over from Habermas in the first instance.

In *The Theory of Communicative Action* and, more generally, in his 'universal' or 'formal pragmatics', Habermas starts from the assumption that the 'telos of [strategically unconstrained] understanding is internal to language'.[3] Accordingly, he is concerned to show that the 'strategic' use of language (in other words, a use which is primarily oriented towards 'success', not 'understanding') stands in a relation of *parasitic dependency* to the primordial, 'understanding-oriented' use of language (ULOMU). In *The Theory of Communicative Action* Habermas was able to show this quite convincingly for the 'concealed strategic use of language' (CSUL), and indeed in a *purely descriptive* way – in other words, without appealing to controversial assumptions concerning the norms of language use.

Let us take the case of someone wishing to achieve a 'perlocutionary' effect in a manipulative way when speaking to another, so that the conversation partner has no opportunity first to *understand* the speech act (*illocutionary effect*), and then either to accept it not accept it, on the basis of the *validity claims* which it raises. If the speaker wishes to do this, he must not allow the other to become aware that this is his aim. In other words, he must use language in such a way as to create the *illusion* that he wishes to give the other the opportunity to 'reach agreement about validity claims' which is in fact being withheld. To put it in a nutshell: whoever wishes to *talk someone into* doing something must pretend that they wish to *convince* them. This *description* of the relevant phenomenon already shows that anyone who employs language in a concealed strategic manner already knows, or has implicitly acknowledged, that CSUL is 'parasitically' dependent on ULOMU.

Can we also show in this way that OSUL is parasitically dependent on ULOMU? This was, and remains, Habermas's goal. But in *The Theory of Communicative Action*, and even in the ensuing discussion, he has proved unable to demonstrate this parasitic dependency, at least in my view and that of many other critics. Why is this?

In OSUL – for example, according to Habermas, in the case of imperatives such as 'Hands up (or I'll shoot)!' or 'Hand over the money (or this will go off)!' – the speakers need not engage in any pretence if their threat is seriously meant. In no sense do they indicate that they recognize the parasitic dependence of their language use on a use of language which presupposes an agreement about validity claims. Indeed, at first glance it is difficult to see in what sense the bank robber's use of language is not oriented towards 'understanding'. After all, the robber gives the cashier the chance to *understand* his intentions and then – admittedly at lightning speed – to *consider* whether there are *good* (*rational*) reasons of self-interest to accept the robber's demand. Is this not also an 'understanding' achieved through language?

Of course, in this case there are no *validity claims* concerning whose justification an agreement would have to be, or could be, reached. There is only a claim to *power* or *violence* on the part of the bank robber. And the grounds which a speaker normally puts forward to support his claims in a discussion aimed at mutual understanding are in this case replaced by the direct *threat of sanctions*, as the robber's waving of his pistol makes clear. But this threat of disadvantage, if I can put it like that, is a good reason for the addressee to accept the speech act.

From a moral standpoint such talk might be regarded a cynical. But how could one show that the speech act of the bank robber always already presupposes *in principle* a different kind of language use, on which it is parasitically dependent? And how could one show that this primordial use of language always already presupposes 'mutual understanding', in the sense of a justification and acceptance of validity claims – such as claims to *truth, sincerity* and *normative rightness*?

I will state my position briefly in a preliminary way here. I am basically convinced that Habermas's fundamental intuition is profound, and indeed correct. But I am also of the view that Habermas's attempts to justify his parasitism thesis in relation to OSUL have failed, and indeed could not help but fail. The reason for this is that, in the case of OSUL, it is impossible in principle to decide which use of language – the *strategically rational* or the *consensually communicatively rational* – is more fundamental, without appealing to controversial *philosophical* presuppositions concerning the rational norms of language. Indeed, it is impossible to decide whether there is a *fundamental* use of language at all.

This means that the question cannot be decided on the basis of a *formal pragmatics*, which ultimately aims to demonstrate the presuppositions of language use in an *empirical-descriptive* manner.[5] However, my thesis is that the question can be decided on the basis of a *universal pragmatics* which understands itself as a *transcendental pragmatics* of language. Such a transcendental pragmatics does not back away from the problem of an *ultimate reflexive justification of rationality* – so it is also able to address the problem of the relations of dependence between different types of rationality.

Of course, to back up my thesis, I must first of all investigate in more detail what I regard as the aporia of Habermas's attempts to solve the problem. But this requires me to look more closely at the rather idiosyncratic *terminological* presuppositions of *The Theory of Communicative Action*. These presuppositions, which deviate considerably from the usual terminology of linguistic analysis – for example, that of speech-act theory – cannot be understood unless one grasps the speculative (and this means philosophically controversial) assumptions of Habermas's formal pragmatics. The discussion up till now has been deficient in this regard. For example, if one begins from the assumption that language is a neutral instrument or a medium of human purposive-rational action, as do the majority of linguists and empiricist philosophers in the analytic tradition, there is no possibility of doing Habermas's argument justice, either hermeneutically or critically.

The first, and by far the most important, terminological presupposition of *The Theory of Communicative Action* concerns the use of the words 'understanding' (*Verständigung*) and 'oriented towards understanding' (*Verständigungsorientiert*). Habermas has obviously been inspired by a systematically ambiguous use of language, which, as far as I know, is only available in German – at any rate, not in French or English. For he uses these two terms not just in the narrower sense of an *understanding of meaning* made possible by linguistic communication, but also in a broader sense. This second sense refers to the *achievement of a consensus concerning validity claims* (truth, truthfulness and normative rightness), which can be connected with three relations to the world and three *functions of language* (in the sense of Karl Bühler). These functions are *representation of the object world*, *expression of the subjective inner world* and appeal to the *normative order of the social world*.

This implies that the mode of intersubjective understanding, which Habermas takes to be primordial for the 'co-ordination of action' (in contrast to strategic communication), does not aim simply at the sharing of *public meanings*. Beyond that, it aims at an *agreement* on the basis of the *acceptance of validity claims* in speech, or – in the case of (argumentative) discourse – of the *grounds* which are brought forward to back up these claims. More specifically, Habermas presupposes an *internal* relation between understanding (*Verstehen*) (in Austin's terms: 'uptake' as an 'illocutionary effect') and the possible *acceptance* of speech acts. And he understands this internal relation not just in the way which is usual among analytical philosophers – in the sense (which is *value-free*, as it were) of a relation between intelligible meanings and *possible* conditions of redemption for validity claims (for example, possible truth conditions). Rather, he understands this relation in the sense that the *telos* of understanding intrinsic to language can be fulfilled only through a consensus.[6]

In this way our problem, which concerns whether OSUL or ULOMu has priority, is actually already resolved as far as Habermas is concerned – by means of a terminological *petitio principii* as it were. For from the standpoint of an analytical semantics and pragmatics of language, Habermas has already loaded the concept of understanding normatively, so that a consensual-communicative solution to the problem of rational communication, and thus to the problem of linguistic understanding in the broadest sense, tends to be anticipated. Indeed, the whole point of discourse ethics is already anticipated in this way. But can this solution to the normative problem of the rationality of understanding, which is anticipated in the term 'understanding', be grounded by means of the pragmatics of language? This is the crucial point, since if it can't be, Habermas's theory is based on a *petitio principii*.

But first a little more about the speculatively laden terminology of *The Theory of Communicative Action*. In line with the emphatic use of the term 'understanding', which I have just commented on, Habermas also uses the contrasting term 'oriented to success' (*erfolgsorientiert*) in a very specific sense. First of all, he does not use this term to refer to those 'innocent' perlocutionary intentions, aimed at success, which Austin regards as connected with normal 'illocutionary' acts by the 'conventions' of language use. Thus, an intention to inform is connected with 'statements', while an intention to convince is connected with arguments.

Departing from Austin's approach,[7] and from that of the speech-act theory developed after him,[8] Habermas does not call these normal intentions aiming at success 'perlocutionary', but counts them, as intentions to gain an *acceptance* achieved through an understanding concerning validity claims, as part of the 'illocutionary' intentions or effects. (See TKH1 391.) According to Habermas, these would include another effect besides 'uptake' (mere *understanding*), one which first arises (or fails to arise) through the communication partner's assessment of what has been understood. (For example, I cannot say 'I hereby convince you that the situation is such and such'; since the effect of convincing someone depends on the judgement of the partner.)

Of course, Habermas's terminological innovation contradicts the 'I hereby'-criterion of illocutionary acts, since this criterion cannot be applied to speech acts aiming at consensus (such as 'I convince . . .'). This contradiction is serious from the point of view of the analytical philosophy of language. For it is precisely this criterion which expresses a prohibition on anticipating a 'success' of the speech act which goes beyond 'illocutionary' success in Austin's sense (the mere 'understanding' of meaning). In short, the terminological innovation, which adapts the meaning of 'illocutionary' to the emphatic meaning of 'understanding', has almost no chance of being accepted by the representatives of analytical philosophy. In my view, it is also unnecessary for Habermas's approach, as I will show later. Yet it should be clear that this terminological innovation expresses the speculative tendency to connect the understanding of meaning internally not just with the mere *possibility* of *acceptance* or *non-acceptance*, but with the achievement of the (ideal) consensus.

Accordingly, in *The Theory of Communicative Action*, Habermas does not apply the term 'oriented to success' to normal speech acts at all (which, after all, are presumed to aim for success in the sense of a 'co-ordination of action'). He applies it exclusively to those speech acts which seek to achieve success not via 'language use oriented towards understanding', but *directly*, as it were. But this stipulation must obviously be applicable not just to manipulative speech acts (CSUL), but also to what Habermas terms *openly strategic speech acts* (OSUL). But here we find ourselves once more confronted with the unresolved problem mentioned at the beginning. Where are the difficulties for Habermas?

In my view, an initial difficulty arises because Habermas, in *The Theory of Communicative Action*, takes only limiting cases or marginal phenomena as examples of OSUL; he considers only what he calls 'simple imperatives' such as 'Hands up!' or 'Hand over the money!' (See TKH1 403ff, 408ff.) I will seek to show that the structure of these apparently exceptional examples of speech acts makes them no more than extreme cases within a broad domain of normal language use. A sociologically ambitious theory of communication, such as *The Theory of Communicative Action*, should actually give them a central position.

I believe the reason why Habermas scarcely discusses the type of normal language use which I mean in *The Theory of Communicative Action* is that he has not thought enough about the fact that his emphatic employment of the term 'understanding' implies a speculative anticipation of a *consensus theory of understanding*. However, it is possible, and sometimes even necessary, to interpret 'understanding' in a value-neutral sense as mere 'understanding of meaning' – in complete abstraction from all actual achievement of consensus concerning validity claims. If one seriously considers this possibility of linguistic understanding, then it is easy to see that – in the context of the normal use of language in everyday life – there is also *understanding of meaning in the service of strategic purposive rationality* – and not just in the service of achieving consensus regarding validity claims. I am thinking here of the wide field of language and interaction represented by negotiations or bargaining. Shouldn't these be the real paradigm of OSUL? And wouldn't one have to begin here, in order to pose the question of the priority of the strategic or consensual-communicative rationality of language use with the appropriate radicality?

I am going to leave this suggestion aside for now, and turn my attention to the controversy between Habermas and his critics regarding the evaluation of so-called 'simple imperatives. Here, in contrast to orders or legitimate demands or wishes, validity claims and their virtual justifications are supplanted by threats of the use of force.

In *The Theory of Communicative Action* Habermas tries to solve the problem by way of the 'parasitism' argument, presenting OSUL as consisting of *deficient* speech acts. In the case of speech acts in the full sense (where speech displays the *telos* of understanding internal to it), a 'normative authorization' must be added to the 'mere claim to power', and 'conditions imposed by sanctions' must be replaced by the 'rationally motivating conditions for the acceptance of a criticizable validity-claim'. Since, according to Habermas, these rationally motivating conditions 'can be derived from the illocutionary role itself, a normal demand has an autonomy which the simple imperative lacks'.

This fact makes clear once again, according to Habermas, 'that only speech acts with which the speaker connects a criticizable validity-claim can bring a hearer to accept the speech act, and thus be effective as a mechanism for co-ordinating action through their own force, as it were' (TKH1 409ff).

As I have already remarked, the basic intuition expressed here seems to me to be entirely correct, if one presupposes the *emphatic concept of understanding*. And, as I also indicated at the beginning, I endorse the emphatic concept of linguistic understanding at the level of intuition. But in my view we have still not reached the real *justification* of the underlying conception – for example, the justification for the view that OSUL can provide *rationally motivating* conditions for the acceptance of a suggestion just as well as ULOMu.

However, the following discussion takes off from another difficulty. In *The Theory of Communicative Action*, Habermas distinguishes OSUL from CSUL, since it consists of *illocutionarily intelligible speech acts* (TKH1 410). But he also distinguishes them from ULOMu, since he regards them as *strategic*, or 'success-oriented', acts. But this seems to suggest that OSUL is simultaneously – and in the same respect (with reference to its perlocutionary aims) – 'oriented to success' *and* 'oriented to understanding' (and thus both 'parasitic' and 'non-parasitic'). This argument has been brought against *The Theory of Communicative Action* by the Norwegian philosopher Skjei.[9]

I would like to state straightaway that I regard this contradiction as merely apparent, since it is simply a matter of unclarified terminology. OSUL is of course not 'oriented to understanding' in the same *respect* in which it is 'oriented to success'. For it brackets out *understanding concerning validity claims*, and stakes everything on the successful implementation of a claim to power (I will say more about this later!).

But the worst thing is that Habermas has *acknowledged* the apparent contradiction which Skjei has indicated,[10] and has now begun to develop a new solution. Unfortunately, this new solution is totally misleading, because it completely loses sight of the original *philosophical* problem (the need for a compelling philosophical justification of the priority of ULOMU over OSUL). Why is this?

In his new attempt at a solution, Habermas consistently follows his worrying tendency to look to the social sciences for *descriptive-empirical* answers to problems of justification in the pragmatics of language. In this particular case, the result is that he revokes the intuition of *The Theory of Communicative Action* (which I believe is profound and correct). He no longer maintains that imperatives accompanied by the threat of sanctions, such as 'Hand over the money (or I shoot)!' are *(openly) strategic speech acts*, which are different in principle from ULOMU. But he still insists that they are *parasitically dependent* on ULOMU. How are we to make sense of this?

Habermas would now like to portray the disputed imperatives as *empirical marginal cases of normal acts of command*, in which the sanctions which are threatened in the case of non-compliance are *normatively backed up* (as are orders or regulations within a constitutional state). Habermas puts this in the following way:

It is certainly correct that, in the case of simple imperatives, the binding effect that co-ordinates actions is provided via a claim to power and not a claim to validity; but it is wrong to analyse the way in which this power claim works by using the strategic influencing of an opponent as one's model. It is only in *extreme* cases that compliance with an imperative expression of will occurs on the basis of naked subjection to the threat of sanction. In the *normal* case simple imperatives function entirely *within the frame* of communicative action, because the position of power on which the claim made by the speaker's imperative is based is one that the addressee acknowledges – *even when this position rests on a purely habitual power relation* and not one with an explicit normative authorization. The most promising approach, I think, is to argue *that the sharp distinction between normatively authorized and simple imperatives cannot be sustained*; that, *rather, there is a continuum between habitual power and power that has been transposed into normative authority.* Then *all* imperatives to which we can ascribe illocutionary force *can be analysed according to the paradigm of normatively authorized requests.* What I wrongly took to be a categorical distinction has dwindled to a mere matter of degree: *claims to power are often linked with fairly remote normative contexts and with diffuse claims to normative validity* that are difficult to identify.[11]

Here the *philosophically* deep and insightful, and – above all – *ethically crucial* distinction is simply conjured away. I mean the distinction between those speech acts which, as 'oriented to understanding', base their 'socially binding force' on discursively redeemable validity claims, and those whose 'socially binding force' (possible acceptance) consists in coerced submission to the power-backed will of the agent. Furthermore, this move is made by replacing a philosophically relevant analysis of the phenomena with a – philosophically irrelevant – *empirical explanation* (reduction) of the really interesting phenomenon. Habermas confirms this change of method (in my view, an entirely implausible one) in the 'Response' to his critics in *Communicative Action*, where he states:

As a sociologist I should have known that there is a continuum between power which is merely factually habitual, and power which has been transformed into normative authority. For this reason, *all* imperatives to which we ascribe an illocutionary force can be analysed *on the model of normatively authorized demands*. What I wrongly regarded as a categorial distinction collapses into a gradual one. The demand of the bank robber which is backed up with a 'Hands up!' is one of those limiting cases of a manifestly strategic use of language, where the absent illocutionary force [exactly! – K.-O. A.] is replaced by an appeal to *potential sanctions*.[12]

Clearly, here the *parasitism* is supposed to be established by the fact that an appeal to sanctions makes an understanding of the speech act on the part of the addressees possible. And this understanding is to a certain extent borrowed from illocutionary acts where the potential for sanctions is normatively legitimated, as in the case of authorized orders in a constitutional state. But is this really plausible? More specifically, can the case be made, on empirical-hermeneutic grounds, that the understanding of OSUL is dependent on a borrowing of normative backing for the possible sanctions connected with it? Can it be shown that such language use is based on a parasitic relation of dependency, within a continuum of more or less normatively backed illocutionary acts?

Can we not show that there are cases of OSUL where we can assume a clear understanding of the meaning of the speech acts (and, furthermore, the *possibility of their acceptance*), and yet there is *no normative backing* – no backing endowed with *illocutionary force* and *socially binding force*? I will be returning to this point later.

Habermas's false solution to the problem – an empiricist and harmonistic one – cannot have left him feeling comfortable. We can see this from the following passages from *Nachmetaphysisches Denken*:

Such acts, which are autonomous from a perlocutionary standpoint [such as 'threats' – K.-O. A.], are *in no sense illocutionary acts*, since they do not aim for the rationally motivated response of an addressee.[13]

And:

Imperatives or threats which are deployed in a purely strategic way, without any normative validity claim, are in no sense illocutionary acts, in other words acts directed towards understanding.[14]

These passages offer no solution to our problem, but their underlying tendency corresponds to the original intuition of *The Theory of Communicative*

Action, which I regard as deeper. In order to develop them consistently – in other words, to think with Habermas against Habermas – I would now like to attempt a *transcendental-pragmatic* analysis of OSUL.

First of all, I would like to play devil's advocate and put the emphatic concept of 'understanding' (which I actually share with Habermas!) out of bounds. I will adopt the position of the majority of analytical philosophers, who regard the understanding achieved through illocutionary acts as simply the *understanding of meaning*. From this standpoint, this function of language appears as neutral in the face of additional *normative* claims to *consensus* or *agreement regarding validity claims*.

With this methodical step I also return definitively to the position of Austin and the majority of speech-act theorists, according to which the *acceptance* of speech acts (apart from the acceptance of the claim to communicate an intelligible meaning implied by mere *understanding*) can in no sense be regarded as an *illocutionary* effect. Rather, it belongs to the – conventionally normal – type of *perlocutionary* effects. (Apart from this type, there must of course be at least two other types of perlocutionary effects: those – foreseen by Austin – which occur *accidentally*, and *strategically intended* perlocutionary effects of the kind implied by Strawson's concept of 'perlocutionary acts', which are also at issue in CSUL and Habermas's notion of OSUL.)

Let us make the assumption that *understanding* by means of illocutionary acts means in the first instance simply the *understanding of meaning*, and that all *acceptance* of normative validity claims has *perlocutionary* status. We are now in a position to reveal a broad range of OSUL – or rather, of *openly strategic language-games* – in which simple imperatives such as 'Hands up!' and 'Hand over the money!' feature simply as *limiting cases*. Now, however, they are not limiting cases of *normatively* backed speech acts, covered by *legitimate sanctions*; rather, they are limiting cases within a wide domain of *openly strategic communication*.

What I am referring to here are the language-games of *interest-driven strategic bargaining*, which I have already mentioned. I am not including here those *moral* or *legal institutions* – for example, binding treaties – by means of which strategic bargaining – for example, political and economic agreements – had already been domesticated in archaic times, and which are especially widespread in the contemporary world. (It is highly interesting and significant for the understanding of cultural evolution that strategic negotiations can be contained by means of a *non-strategic understanding* (*consensus*) and can be – potentially – made to serve the common welfare. Such is the case with the free rein given to the strategic behaviour of actors in a *market economy*.) Rather, I am referring in what follows to *purely strategic bargaining* – in other words, language-games which essentially consist of two types of speech acts: *offers of co-operation* (and often *advantage*) and *threats of disadvantage*. Often these two kinds of speech acts are so closely interconnected that either the *offers* or the *threats* are accentuated, while the complementary acts are merely implied.

At this point it will be obvious that even *simple imperatives* such as 'Hand over the money (or I'll shoot)!' or 'Hands up (or I'll shoot)!' display this *structure of complementarity*. But at the same time it becomes clear that, in the broader context of strategic negotiations, further functional conditions of these strategic language-games are essential. These conditions show that we are not here confronted with an extreme and rare marginal phenomenon of language, which is essentially dependent on understanding regarding validity claims, but with an autonomous *central phenomenon of lifeworld communication*. What are at issue are *agreements* (a kind of *accord* or *consensus* [Apel uses the English words as a gloss here – tr.]) which are achieved through the *grounded acceptance* of speech acts, if not *validity claims*. This already implies that it is wrong to assume, with Habermas, that the speech acts which are constitutive for strategic negotiations – including OSUL in the sense already discussed – have no 'socially binding force', or do not aim at 'the rationally motivated response of an addressee'.

For it seems clear that the *possible rational motivation of the addressees*, on which the *socially binding force* of OSUL is based in the framework of negotiations, is precisely the *strategic rationality* of *maximizing advantage* and *minimizing disadvantage* which is analysed in *strategic game theory*. Of course, such an analysis relies on the widely shared assumption that what is at issue is *human rationality* as such. (But this conception was shared, for example, by Martin Luther and Thomas Hobbes.)

If we now pose the question of the reciprocal relations between *strategic* rationality and Habermas's *communicative* type of rationality, and in particular the question of priority between them, it becomes clear that Habermas's assumption that OSUL 'does not aim at the rationally motivated response of an addressee' is based on a *petitio principii*. It simply turns upside down what is today the standard evaluation of the relation between 'rational choice' (in the purposive-rational/strategic sense) and irrational ethical decisions, in favour of ultimate values or norms. So far I have not offered any *philosophically rational* decision in this domain either. This is what the aporia of OSUL has revealed.

From a *transcendental-pragmatic* perspective it is necessary to approach the question of the possible *parasitism* of OSUL in an entirely new way. In this context I would first like to discuss the relationship between three presumed types of communicative rationality (in the widest sense):

1   The rationality of lifeworld communication and interaction
2   The rationality of strategic negotiations
3   The rationality of the *argumentative discourses* of science and philosophy (including, finally, the discourse of the *philosophical theory of rationality*).

I would now like to put forward the following theses with respect to the relation between these:

(1)   *Lifeworld communication and interaction* is not characterized by a unitary type of rationality; rather, both *strategic rationality* and *communicative rationality* (in Habermas's sense) are embedded in it. And up until now – as I will explain and justify later – they have functioned in a relation of reciprocal mediation, one which is dependent on context and on the *judgement* (*phronesis?*) of the actors concerned. There are, of course, *indications* that over the long term this relation of mediation can be altered in favour of *communicative* rationality (in Habermas's sense), and that this latter could therefore achieve systematic priority.

This possibility is connected with the fact that there could be no human society in which people successfully reached agreement *solely* on the basis of CSUL or of OSUL (for example, in the sense of Thomas Hobbes's *recta ratio* or of strategic game theory). Children in such a society could not learn language, and thereby communication and interaction. But, in principle, a society *would* be possible that was based solely on ULOMu – in other words, *communicative rationality* in Habermas's sense. But this possibility, which is given in principle, is not realizable in the reality of the lifeworld today – for reasons which I have yet to explain. And even the question of the logical *priority* of strategic or communicative rationality cannot be decided at the level of the analysis of the use of language in the lifeworld. For even the appropriate interpretation of the *indications* I have mentioned – and its convincing defence against possible objections from those who regard instrumental-strategic rationality as the only possible rationality of co-operation – cannot be achieved through a broadly *empirical* analysis of lifeworld communication (for example, linguistic or sociological analyses). This is possible, as I shall show, only from the transcendental-pragmatic perspective of a *self-reflexive rationality of discourse*, which is capable of *self-grounding* and *ultimate grounding*. But before I turn to this ultimate grounding, I must introduce a second thesis, in which I defend the relative autonomy of *strategic rationality*.

(2)   The *relation of compromise between strategic and communicative rationality* which functions in the framework of traditional forms of life (of 'unconstrained substantial *Sittlichkeit*', in Hegel's sense) has entered a crisis during

the eras of enlightenment in world history up till now (first of all, during the so-called axial era of the emergence of high cultures). What occurred was that, simultaneously, *purely strategic negotiations* and *argumentative discourses concerning validity claims* separated out, and were consciously practised as rival models of *rational* conflict resolution.[15] For example, this happened in Greece during the age of the Sophists or the philosophical enlightenment. An example of *purely strategic negotiations*, which can be interpreted in the context of the Greek enlightenment, can be found in the famous dialogue between the Athenians and the Melians which Thucydides has handed down in book V of the *History of the Peloponnesian War*.

What is characteristic of these negotiations is that they are carried out on both sides at a high intellectual level, yet obviously with full awareness of their *strategic* structure. But this does not at all imply that the opponents put no value on the 'rationally motivated' positions of the other side. On the contrary, they try to bring about such positions by placing themselves – almost to the point of self-alienation, it seems – in the strategic position of the other (the contextually determined constellation of possible advantages and disadvantages). Of course, in the last instance this is done from the *dominant perspective of one's own interest* or of the *perlocutionary goals* which follow from this interest. And this means that the 'arguments' (if we can use this term) of the opponents are not related to rationally redeemable or criticizable *validity claims* (not even to *truth claims*). There is, however, an interesting exception: the following – *meta-communicative* – exchange at the beginning of the dialogue, in which the Athenians nevertheless make clear that they have no wish to enter into a discussion concerning normative validity claims.

The Melians begin as follows:

The quiet interchange of explanations is a reasonable thing, and we do not object to that. But your warlike movements, which are present not only to our fears but to our eyes, seem to belie your words. We see that, although you may reason with us, you mean to be our judges; and that at the end of the discussion, if the justice of our cause prevail and we therefore refuse to yield, we may expect war; if we are convinced by you, slavery. (Thucydides, V. 86)

But the Athenians have no intention of entering into a 'domination-free' or 'violence-free' discourse concerning 'justice'. They point out that the Melians should consider how to preserve their city, 'looking your circumstances in the face', and then give the following – quasi-philosophical – explanation, which was possibly inspired by the latest theses of the Athenian Sophists:

Well, then, we Athenians will use no fine words; we will not go out of our way to prove at length that we have a right to rule, because we overthrew the Persians; or that we attack you now because we are suffering any injury at your hands. We should not convince you if we did; nor must you expect to convince us by arguing that, although a colony of the Lacedaemonians, you have taken no part in their expeditions, or that you have never done us any wrong. But you and we should say what we really think, and aim only at what is possible, for we both alike know that into the discussion of human affairs the question of justice only enters where there is equal power to enforce it, and that the powerful exact what they can, and the weak grant what they must. (Ibid., V. 89)

The Melians then accept their situation – 'But we admit that this conference has met to consider the question of our preservation; and therefore let the argument proceed in the manner which you propose' (ibid., V. 88) – and themselves switch over to strategic 'argumentation':

Well, then, since you set aside justice and invite us to speak of expediency, in our judgement it is certainly expedient that you should respect a principle which is for the common good; that to every man when in peril a reasonable claim should be accounted a claim of right, and that any plea which he is disposed to urge, even if failing of the point a little, should help his cause. Your interest in this principle is quite as great as ours, inasmuch as you, if you fall, will incur the heaviest vengeance, and will be the most terrible example to mankind. (Ibid., V. 90)

What follows is then simply a matter of the Melians arguing strategically for their independence, while the Athenians offer the Melians the alternative of annihilation or entry into the Attic League with – often cynical-sounding – 'arguments' of this kind: 'To you the gain will be that by submission you will avert the worst; and we shall be all the richer for your preservation' (ibid., V. 93). And: 'for you are not fighting against equals to whom you cannot yield without disgrace, but you are taking counsel whether or no you shall resist an overwhelming force.' And:

Many men with their eyes still open to the consequences . . . have suffered a mere name to lure them on, until it has drawn down upon them real and irretrievable calamities; through their own folly they have incurred a worse dishonour than fortune would have inflicted on them. If you are wise you will not run this risk; you ought to see that there can be no disgrace in yielding to a great city which invites you to become her ally on reasonable terms, keeping your own land, and merely paying tribute; and that you will certainly gain no honour if, having to choose between two alternatives, safety and war, you obstinately prefer the worse. (Ibid., V. 111)

The terrible outcome of the negotiations, in which the Melians preferred the risk of defending their independence – and thus their honour as relations of the Spartans – to accepting subjugation, is well known. In this context I wanted only to offer an example of one of the first pure discourses of negotiation to be handed down. Here the *rationality of openly strategic speech* appears as consciously differentiated, and to a large extent emancipated from traditional reservations (arising from belief in the gods and in an absolute notion of right). We have an early example of a type of discourse which has not lost its significance even today – especially in the arena of relations between states, which is still largely exempt from legal regulation. This example is surely sufficient to make clear that there can be no question of parasitically dependent *limiting or extreme cases of normatively backed speech acts*, and just as little of a type of 'discourse' which would be devoid of rationally motivating and socially binding power.

To be more precise, this evaluation holds as long as one sticks to an *external, value-neutral* – an *empirical-descriptive* and *empirically testable* – analysis of language-games and the related types of rationality, which are pre-reflectively given, as it were. My thesis concerning the *openly strategic rationality of language use and the form of action co-ordination which it achieves* must accordingly run as follows: the difference between an *openly strategic* and a Habermasian *understanding-oriented* rationality of action can certainly be established by means of the usual forms of linguistically or sociologically oriented analysis of language and communication. But nothing concerning the *priority* of one or the other type can be decided in this way. For the subjects of strategic rationality in no sense reveal through their strategic use of language that this is parasitically dependent on an 'understanding-oriented' use of language, in Habermas's sense of an understanding concerning validity claims. On the contrary: just like the Athenians in the time of Thucydides, even today the defenders of the monopoly of *instrumental* or *strategic* rationality (or of the practice of the *will-to-power* as the appropriate rationality of discourse) do not conceal their belief that every appeal to a rationality relevant to normative grounding (for example, in ethics) can be shown to be illusory. Such appeals are regarded as ideological and dogmatic; and this is true even at the meta-communicative (in the last instance, philosophical) level of discourse.

But in my view this account cannot be correct, in a sense which is yet to be explained. And here I come to my *third thesis*: the specifically *transcendental-pragmatic thesis concerning the unavoidable primacy of the self-reflexive rationality of philosophical discourse* (and this means the *rationality of the theory of rationality* itself).

(3)   Let us return to Thucydides, and let us imagine that the Athenians, in the course of their meta-communicative introduction to the negotiations with the Melians, have accepted a continuation of this meta-communication in the sense of an open philosophical discussion. They would then have had to enter into a discussion of normative legal claims. And this means an argumentative discourse between parties who, in principle, have equal rights. For one cannot seriously *discuss* whether the bracketing-out of claims based on right from the dialogue is permissible without granting the partners in discussion – in abstraction from the relations of power obtaining – the same right to bring forward claims based on right (by contrast, the Athenians impose this bracketing-out by diktat). But, with this step, the breakthrough to a discourse concerning validity claims which would be open in principle, and thereby also to a *recognition of its priority over strategic-rational constraints on the rationality of negotiation*, would be achieved.

For one would at least have to acknowledge the following point. If the partner in communication is to regard the proposal of a bracketing-out of claims based on right in favour of a purely strategic negotiation as *intersubjectively valid* on rational grounds, and not just be forced to accept it on rational grounds (for example, grounds of advantage), then the suggestion itself cannot be grounded through strategic negotiations. It can only be grounded through an argumentative discourse concerning validity claims. It is here that we find a recognition of the *priority* of the consensual-communicative rationality of argumentative discourse.

In other words, the fact that the normatively unrestricted *rationality of understanding* is actually the 'original mode' (Habermas) of communicative rationality cannot be shown through the description and comparison of the rationality of different types of speech act at the level of lifeworld communication and interaction. It can only be shown through *strict reflection on the type of rationality which is presupposed and must be employed by a philosophical theory of rationality itself.* Furthermore, this priority is priority not just over *strategic* rationality, but also over the normatively neutral rationality of the simple *meaning comprehension*, which makes even OSUL, and thus the language-game of strategic negotiations, possible.

For let us imagine someone who did not wish to appeal to a rationality based on *understanding concerning validity claims* (in other words, their possible redemption or critique) at the level of the self-reflexive rationality of philosophical discourse, or who was unwilling to distinguish this type of rationality as *the* definitive human form of rationality. Such a person would find himself caught in a contradiction with the rationality of the discourse he is actually making use of: in other words, a performative self-contradiction. He would thereby show that every type of rationality which is appealed to as, or declared to be a substitute for, the rationality of discourse is in fact *parasitically dependent on discursive rationality*. To this extent, Habermas's basic intuition – as outlined in *The Theory of Communicative Action* – can be salvaged. For it has in fact turned out that only *rationality oriented to understanding in the emphatic sense* – and not, for example, a rationality which completes the normatively neutral comprehension of meaning only with claims to power or appeals to the force of interests – can be adequate to the autonomy of the self-reflexive *logos* of language. Thus it can be shown that the '*telos* of understanding' does indeed inhabit language. But this demonstration can only be achieved via the strictly reflexive 'detour' of an answer to the question of the *transcendental-pragmatic conditions of the possibility of valid argumentation in general* – and not through an *ontology* in the pre-Kantian sense (which talk of a *telos* internal to language suggests). Even less can it be achieved through a *quasi-empirical theory of communication* or a *sociology of communication*.

At this point, after a long, painstaking passage through the new and controversial problematic of the relation between the *strategic* and the *communicative rationality* of action, we have at last reached the apex – or, perhaps better, the basis – of a possible *transcendental-pragmatic theory of types of rationality*. This is the point at which a possible philosophical theory of rationality reflexively retrieves its own rationality, as it were, and reveals it to be *untranscendable*. It is clear that here – *in the self-reflection of discursive rationality* – we reach a point of priority, in terms of validity, not only in relation to the *strategic rationality* of communication and interaction, but also in relation to any conceivable type of rationality which can be discursively analysed, and whose validity can be grounded. We thus also reach the transcendental-pragmatic point of departure for a *self-differentiation of reason* through *reflection on various abstractive limitations of its potential*, limitations which take the form of a differentiation of types of rationality.[16]

Notes

1 See my contribution to *Zwischenbetrachtungen im Prozess der Aufkärung*, ed. Axel Honneth et al. (Frankfurt am Main: Suhrkamp, 1989), pp. 15–65.
2 See TKH1, ch. 3.
3 TKH1 387; ND 75.
4 TKH1 395ff. See my critique of Habermas's terminology, which deviates from that of speech-act theory, in what follows.
5 I refer here to Habermas's thesis that 'formal pragmatics' as a 'reconstructive science' must test its observations – even those concerning 'necessary presuppositions of argumentation' – against as many different empirical examples as pos-

sible (just like Chomsky's linguistics). To put it more sharply: Habermas's thesis is that there is ultimately no difference between the method of testing hypotheses in linguistics and the method of *internal* (discursively reflexive) testing of transcendental-pragmatic arguments concerning (amongst other things) the normative conditions of possibility of the argumentative testing of hypotheses; no difference, that is, in the sense of the *transcendental difference* between empirical science and philosophy. See Karl-Otto Apel, 'Fallibilismus, Konsenstheorie der Wahrheit und Letztbegründung', in *Philosophie und Begründung*, ed. Forum für Philosophie Bad Homburg (Frankfurt am Main: Suhrkamp, 1987), pp. 116–211, esp. 207ff, n. 84.

6   On this point, which in my view Habermas does not fully clarify, see my discussion in *Zwischenbetrachtungen*, pp. 23ff, 35ff, 40ff.

7   See J. L. Austin, *How to Do Things with Words* (Oxford: Oxford University Press, 1962), pp. 115ff.

8   It is true that Peter Strawson has explicated Austin's term 'perlocutionary act' in the sense of CSUL (of speech acts, whose practical aim cannot be openly declared or admitted); see his 'Intention and convention in speech acts', *Philosophical Review* (1964), pp. 439ff). But Strawson does not draw the conclusion that successful take-ups which are openly striven for – in the case of warnings or arguments, for example – are not 'perlocutionary' but 'illocutionary'.

9   See E. Skjei, 'A comment on performative, subject and proposition in Habermas's theory of communication', *Inquiry*, 28 (1985), pp. 87ff. See also D. Köveker, 'Zur Kategorisierbarkeit "verdeckt" und "offen strategischen Sprachgebrauchs": Das Parasitismus-Argument von Jürgen Habermas', *Journal for General Philosophy of Science*, 23 (1992), pp. 289–311.

10 See Jürgen Habermas, 'Reply to Skjei', *Inquiry*, 28 (1985), pp. 105ff, esp. p. 112, where Habermas admits the contradiction.

11 Ibid., p. 112. On this, see D. Köveker's insightful critique, 'Zur Kategorisierbarkeit', pp. 292ff in the same issue.

12 Jürgen Habermas, 'Entgegnungen', in Axel Honneth and Hans Joas, eds, *Kommunikatives Handeln* (Frankfurt am Main: Suhrkamp, 1998), pp. 361–2.

13 See Jürgen Habermas, 'Handlungen, Sprechakte, sprachlich vermittelte Interaktionen und Lebenswelt', in ND 74.

14 See Jürgen Habermas, 'Zur Kritik der Bedeutungstheorie', in ND 135.

15 On this see Karl-Otto Apel, 'Weshalb benötigt der Mensch Ethik?', in *Funkkolleg Praktische Philosophie/Ethik, Dialoge*, ed. K.-O. Apel, D. Böhler and G. Kadelbach (Frankfurt am Main: Fischer, 1984), pp. 49–137, and in *Studientexte* (Weinheim/Basel: Beltz, 1984), pp. 13–156.

16 See Karl-Otto Apel, 'Die Herausforderung der totalen Vernunftkritik und das Programm einer philosophischen Theorie der Rationalitätstypen', in *Pragmatische Rationalität*, ed. G. Meggle and A. Wüstehube (Würzburg: Königshausen and Neumann, 1995), pp. 29–64.

10

What is metaphysics – What is modernity? Twelve theses against Jürgen Habermas

Dieter Henrich

Despite their often strenuous dispute over methods of grounding, Habermas and Apel are agreed that contemporary philosophy must be 'post-metaphysical', abandoning speculation about the essential nature of the world. Furthermore, they both believe that the post-metaphysical turn involves abandoning the 'philosophy of the subject', or the primacy of the experiencing consciousness, in favour of a communicative and intersubjective paradigm or basic philosophical model. It is this conviction of the historical necessity and effectiveness of a 'paradigm shift', the assumption that the problems of metaphysics are generated only by the superannuated standpoint of self-consciousness, which Dieter Henrich contests. Like Apel, Henrich defends the autonomy of the most general forms of philosophical enquiry, and their qualitative difference from the enquiries of the specialized sciences. But, unlike Apel, he remains committed to some of the fundamental insights of German Idealism. This leads him to contest Habermas's claim that the conscious self can be explained philosophically as generated out of an intersubjective context of communication. Once this irreducibility of self-consciousness is granted, then metaphysics no longer appears outmoded. It remains essential to modernity, as a necessarily tentative exploration of, and struggle to reconcile, the contradictory experiences which our status as beings who live self-consciously opens up to us.

In the polemical essay translated here Henrich is in fact replying to a critical review of his book *Fluchtlinien* by Habermas, who provocatively associated Henrich's defense of metaphysics with the 'conservative' turn in German politics and culture during the 1980s.* Here Henrich not only outlines his defence of metaphysics as an integral part of the philosophical endeavour of modernity; he also contests the naturalism which Habermas associates with the intersubjective and communicative turn. Far from leaving illusory problems of metaphysics behind, Henrich argues, Habermas's thought is in fact riven by a classic metaphysical conflict between naturalism and anti-naturalism. His readiness to draw on both the resources of the phenomenological tradition – for example, in making crucial use of the concept of the 'lifeworld' – and the analytical tradition in the philosophy of language reveals this. For it suggests that Habermas would like the ideological benefits of naturalism, without paying the philosophical price which analytical thinkers are in many cases more than willing to pay.

'Metaphysics' could only function as the name of a special philosophical discipline as long as philosophy viewed itself as a body of doctrine established on a firm ground plan. It is well known, however, that the prehistory of metaphysics is highly ambiguous, just as the history of its reception is a series of embarrassments. Originally 'metaphysics' was simply the name for a collection of lectures by Aristotle, which were placed after the lectures on physics in his collected works. 'Metaphysics' is thus only a stopgap designation for a kind of investigation which has remained without a proper title to this day. Much has been associated with it and continues to invite such association. For this very reason it is easy to taint anyone who does not simply criticize whatever stands under this non-title *par excellence*, but still links unresolved tasks for our thinking with it, with all kinds of shady connections. Yet this non-title also evokes the memory of fundamental extensions of our understanding – and not just empty profundity or misguided efforts to escape the stream of history.

Jürgen Habermas placed a question mark at the end of the title of an essay in which he discussed tendencies towards a return to metaphysics in recent German philosophy.[1] The question mark is intended to indicate that such tendencies should be regarded as obsolete, and that in any case they serve only to distract us from the project of modernity, whose continuation Habermas advocates with legitimate insistence. The following series of theses constitutes an answer to his essay. They are meant to clarify a concept of metaphysics which is essentially bound up with the project of modernity. They also aim to show that Habermas is wrong to think that his own theoretical enterprise can do without figures of thought for which – even today – we have no better title than 'metaphysics'.

I The Place of Metaphysics

In times when the doctrinal system of philosophy remained stable, there was at least a table of contents to be added to this non-title. This took the form of a list of investigations, although the reasons for the inclusion of specific enquiries could not be gleaned from the list itself. There were, for example, investigations into what makes a thing self-sufficient, into possibility and necessity, the nature of mind, the concept of a world, and into the underlying ground of both forms and their alterations. Why enquiry should begin at these points is easy to see, although why they are gathered together under this non-title is more obscure.

This is why we find the non-title also connected with a long series of attempts to trace the origin of this nameless tangle of questions, and thus to put the series of enquiries which it assembles in correct order, and free it from inclusions which in fact deal with problems which are either confused or irresolvable, or belong elsewhere. For us, the most significant of these attempts was that of Immanuel Kant. Anyone for whom the non-title still evokes the prospect of thoughts which could have a demonstrable validity, must establish a more than merely conventional relation with Kant's attempt to throw light on the inner constitution of the enterprise derived from Aristotle. This applies just as much to the critic who appeals to Kant, but in fact merely takes up a reproach of futility against the metaphysical enterprise, and the hopes bound up with it, which is far older than Kant.

Kant divided the enquiries which require a metaphysics into two groups, and based this division on a classification. On the one side are investigations concerned with the fundamental operations of our intelligence. These are 'metaphysical' to the extent that they do not analyse merely the constitution of these operations themselves, but also the presuppositions on which such operations rely with respect to the content which they disclose. Thus a metaphysics can arise in connection with object-determining knowledge, if it can be shown that such knowledge implies presuppositions concerning the basic constitution of all objects which cannot be derived from experience and methodical investigation. And there can be a metaphysics of 'morals', if it can be shown that the distinction between 'good' and 'bad' does not simply rely on normative propositions, but implies assumptions regarding their conditions of validity, and thus regarding agents – in other words, persons – and the possible motivations for their actions.

The other group of enquiries consists of themes and trains of reflection which have an entirely different place and value. They do not belong to the domain in which object-determining and normative statements originate, and where they find their initial anchoring point. They are not elementary thoughts, but thoughts of a resolving closure (*Abschluß*). Bound up with these thoughts of resolving closure is an interest in metaphysics which is not professional, but, rather, is a latent interest of every human being. Such thoughts are unavoidable, for two reasons which presuppose each other: (1) The basic forms of knowledge lead to essentially incomplete results, which – furthermore – contradict each other. (2) Neither reason, nor a life oriented towards reason, can simply remain in this state of incompletion and in such contradictions. The metaphysics of resolving closure is thus not an enterprise which is dependent on the disposition which generates our programmes of theoretical enquiry. As such it is neither a concern of the sciences – in other words, a product of theoretical curiosity – nor does it arise from our capacity for construction in the service of vital needs. It is a concern of reason, and as such concern of humanity. By virtue of this origin, the rationality which is claimed by the metaphysics of resolving closure is not constrained to generate only thoughts which can be supported by scientific forms of demonstration. Reason can also be said to be at work when we consider what is the best – in other words, the most comprehensive and internally consistent – answer to a perplexing situation, one in which various domains of problems intersect, each requiring the use of a different method, none of which is subsumable under any more general concept of method. Reason, in its fullest sense, includes forms of understanding and interpretation which lie beyond what can be ascertained by means of proofs, no less than it does demonstration and critique. Only if the discussion of thoughts of resolving closure is entirely insulated from critique, and from a comprehensive evaluation of what speaks for and against a particular thesis, does it become an enterprise dominated merely by arbitrariness and absurd pretentions.

II Hyper-theory or Scepticism?

It is important to realize that Kant's thoroughly modern redefinition of 'metaphysics' arose from solidarity with a kind of thinking which every human being engages in. It is a kind of thinking which aims at self-understanding, but which goes hand in hand with – and indeed cannot be separated from – the attempt to give form to our life, so that it does not merely 'happen', but is consciously 'lived'. With this connection in mind, we can say that metaphysics emerges from 'conscious life', or – as Kant would say – from its 'spontaneity'. Solidarity with such a form of life is already characteristic for the beginnings of metaphysics in Plato, as also for the redefinition of its essence in modern philosophy. 'Metaphysics' takes shape in the spontaneous thinking of every human being, long before its eventual formulation in the language of theory. Philosophy has the task of understanding the fundamental assumptions of such thinking (in a metaphysics of the elementary), as well as its exploratory extension (*Ausgriff*) (in a metaphysics of resolving closure). It has to defend them against hyper-theories which would deform our life if they became effective within it. For such theories emerge from a basic scientific outlook which pre-empts all real thought, and which confronts and opposes the spontaneous life of reason in the form of an opaque, rigid and alien institutionalization of a certain use of concepts. In this respect, Habermas misses the mark when he raises the objection that metaphysics, understood in this way, would violate the principle of fallibility which the modern understanding of science can no longer abandon. For every theory of the series of natural numbers is fallible. But this is no argument against the spontaneous generation of the series itself. Accordingly, the justification of metaphysics does not require the claim to possess an infallible theory, or the right to speak *ex cathedra*, on the part of the person who seeks to evaluate of the viability of ultimate thoughts (*letzte Gedanken*).

Anyone seeking to impose such false conclusions on the whole of European metaphysics of the pre-modern era will soon make another move, in order at least to separate the explorations of the metaphysics of resolving closure from the spontaneity of conscious life. Since such explorations cannot be assigned any truth-value, it must also be possible to abandon them, and to give one's life a fundamental orientation which is more modest in its aims. This objection is also as old as metaphysics itself in all its forms. It is bound up with that scepticism which appears as a suspension of judgement, and which is intended not just as a critique of theory, but in the first place as the recommendation of a certain way of life and a certain attitude to life. It is thus useful to recall that modern philosophy emerged far more out of a defence against this kind of scepticism than out of a defence against professionalized hyper-theories. It is the successful battle of modern philosophy on both these fronts which explains its development, its innermost tendencies and its historical consequences.

Anyone who thinks the second – sceptical – move can easily be countered should recall the position of Kant, who had to defend his work in an age which, far from being intoxicated with hyper-theories, had rather turned away from metaphysics and sought refuge in irony and mockery. For Kant, it was Voltaire, rather than Leibniz, who set the contemporary tone. And Voltaire represents the view that, under the conditions of modernity, the kinds of enquiry which are essential for human beings can afford to ignore any enterprise connected with the non-title 'metaphysics'. Kant's decisive objection to this view, one which is inseparable from the basic conviction which gave rise to his philosophy, runs as follows: 'Those supposed indifferentists, however much they try to make themselves unrecognizable through the alteration of the language of the schools, inevitably fall back, to the extent that they think anything at all, into the very metaphysical assertions for which they displayed such contempt.'[2] We shall soon discover that this statement is just as applicable to Habermas's theory as to the style of thinking which Kant attributed to his contemporaries 200 years ago.

III Self-descriptions

But why does Kant believe that an apparently relaxed indifference will inevitably undermine itself through an implicit metaphysics, as soon as any effort is made to think about truly fundamental problems? A lecture which has only recently been published gives us an indication of his basic reasons: 'We cannot force the understanding to abandon these questions, they are woven into the nature of reason to such an extent that we cannot get free of them. Even the despisers of metaphysics, including Voltaire, who would have liked to present themselves as carefree fellows, had their own metaphysics. For everyone must have some view regarding his own soul.'[3] Talk of the 'soul' is here only a placeholder for all the answers to questions which reason forces us to pose with respect to ourselves: How do you think about yourself, when – taking account of everything you know and everything you are able to distinguish – you try to give an account of who and what you truly are? That is precisely the question into which Kant, in words which have become part of our cultural heritage, compressed all the questions of philosophy. But this question acquires a non-trivial meaning only when it is taken up as a synthesis of preceding questions and of preliminary efforts at answering them: 'What is man?' (*Was ist der Mensch?*) Given a suitable reformulation, this question can also be posed in the semantically oriented theoretical language of our time. It would then read: What self-description of the being who is capable of rational speech holds good in the face of everything which we know about him, and about the necessary pre-conditions of different self-descriptions?

If the synthetic meaning of this question is missed, we can easily be fobbed off with old and partly trivial answers: The human being is a living being, capable of laughing and thinking; he is *homo faber*, the inventor of his own

conditions of existence; he is a responsible agent; he is social, and thus inter-
acts with others in institutions; he is a fellow human being (*Mitmensch*), an
ego always in relation to another, and thus capable of sympathy (*mit-leidend*);
and he is (here comes the triviality which is claimed, from the standpoint of
semantics, to be an advance over the previous answers) a speaker. All these
answers can of course be connected with the perspectives of particular theories. And in this way they can acquire a philosophical profile. However, if
they are offered point-blank, they all share a feature which makes them miss
the meaning of the question. They fail to see that the explosive force of the
question arises from the fact that it aims at a synthesis, while they seek to
provide their reply at the first level, in relation to only one layer of self-
description. Because of this, they portray human beings in a one-dimensional
way which is remote from our real self-understanding. And precisely for this
reason, they cut themselves off from the thinking which is in fact always at
work in self-understanding. It is for this thinking that the non-title 'metaphysics', in accord with its modern redefinition, must hold open a space in
theory. The title word itself has no significance. It can be replaced – and the
most significant thinkers who came after Kant avoided it.

IV Beginning in Conflict

So far we have defined only negatively the point of departure for the questions posed with respect to metaphysics, when philosophy set out to help
modern consciousness articulate itself and reach clarity about itself. Philosophy did not dismiss as mere illusion or confusion the discovery that the self-
understanding of human beings leads to conflicts between equally convincing
self-descriptions. These self-descriptions apply to a being who – either by
way of unavoidable presuppositions or through spontaneous reflection –
arrives at concepts which can be applied to himself. We are in each case
assumed to be, or addressed as something *other* – depending on whether we
are testing the grounds for the truth of an assertion; not simply acknowledging, but taking as criteria for our actions, norms which cannot be derived
from the interest in survival; or not merely honestly communicating ourselves
to another, but revealing ourselves in a relation of trust. These different self-
descriptions already cause us to come into conflict with ourselves. For it
seems clear that we cannot avoid acknowledging norms for which we can
offer no compelling grounds. And the intimacy with which one life is bound
up with another makes it difficult, in certain crucial situations, to view the
relationship from the standpoint of strictly universal norms. These conflicts

force us to seek some more comprehensive dimension in which these conflicts could finally be resolved, one which would make possible a self-description which reconciled the primary self-descriptions. This exploration is in fact always taking place wherever human beings have to live their lives consciously. A thinking which commits itself to this exploration, and to evaluating the kinds of grounds which would be most compelling in this domain, is under no obligation to show from the very beginning that its considerations could be supported by a definitive theory of a scientific kind.

The three self-descriptions which I have just mentioned, and which belong to a much larger group of such primary self-descriptions, can indeed be differentiated in terms of speech acts and the validity claims built into them. However, to conclude – as Habermas does – that the mere analysis of these speech acts opens a perspective, and reveals a dimension, in which the self-descriptions of conscious life are harmoniously combined, would be to commit oneself to an approach closed off to insight into conflicts and the manner in which they arise. It would be to ignore the fact that these conflicts have been encountered by all of us in our lives, long before the intervention of theory. And this would mean taking one's distance from the consciousness of modernity, and the forms of theory which characterize its philosophical discourse.

'Lifeworld' is a term which has this avoidance written into its profile. For it declares the essential point of departure for all speech acts to be a totality which is in principle harmonious. In fact, even Habermas, by using this term, would like to hold on to the heritage of the basic system-founding notions of modern philosophy, to the extent that modern philosophy has not dissipated itself in the illusions of hyper-theory. But the term was given currency by the renegades of a long lost immediacy. And the deficiencies stemming from this origin cannot be repaired by theoretical measures which are essentially directed towards the possibility of a social theory. Habermas's thought has remained under the influence of the intellectual style of his first teacher, Erich Rothacker – despite all the efforts and achievements which have taken him beyond it.

V Distance and Synthesis

'Reflection', however it might be more closely defined, is a fundamental term in modern thought. It brings together at least two activities of the mind – first of all, an awareness of the differences between the forms of understanding which develop spontaneously in conscious life. Whoever reflects has already understood that he is at home not only in one world, and that he cannot merge seamlessly with the world. 'Reflection' also means, secondly, taking a distance from the primary tendencies which underlie our forms of understanding and self-descriptions as a whole. This distancing opens up two possibilities for finding a stable attitude to our conscious life, one which is based not merely on abstinence with respect to ultimate thoughts. Either the primary forms of knowledge and of action guided by insight, and in particular the concepts of the world which they imply, can be brought together, even while their differences are acknowledged, which requires an integrating conception which is not available at any of the primary levels; or whatever orients the primary discourses, and whatever is presupposed by them, can be seen through as illusory – deceptive with respect to everything on which their claims to correctness, and in particular to definitiveness, are based. These two alternatives are strictly opposed to each other. But it is just as true of both that reflection in the second sense must make us unwilling to regard the convictions connected with the primary discourses as complete and definitive. There must be a readiness either to transform and transpose them to a different context, where they can be preserved, or to put them completely at a distance, and to suspend their validity in a form of knowledge opposed to them. Modern thought in all its essential variants emerged from this problematic situation. However, a theoretical language such as that of Habermas avoids this situation, since it opts – albeit unwillingly – for immediacy. It regards the resources of the lifeworld, without further enquiry, as ultimately reliable and valid.

It is important to realize that even the alternatives which emerge from reflection in the second sense are not forced upon conscious life by the theories of the philosophy profession, or by the progress of the sciences. Even these alternatives unfold spontaneously within a consciousness which runs ahead of all theories and interpretations. Modern philosophy has done no more than put itself in the position of this consciousness, and thereby subordinate itself to that of which it speaks.

It is also important to keep in mind that it is precisely those theoretical achievements of modernity which appear most emphatically metaphysical which have responded to this situation. Modern metaphysics is a series of attempts to resolve the problems arising from reflection on conditions of validity and conflicts of validity, by moving in the direction of the first of the two alternatives. Thus Leibniz's system is nothing other than an attempt to produce a theoretical synthesis in which the different world concepts implied by the material, the organic, the mental and the formal world could be brought together in a unified ontology. Through this synthesis of world concepts the various self-descriptions of human beings were to be freed from conflict and placed in a continuum. To take an even clearer example, the aim of Spinoza's metaphysics is to interpret and ground the fundamental anthropological concept of self-preservation (*Selbsterhaltung*), which served as the basis for Hobbes's political theory, in such a way that it would no longer come into irresolvable conflict with the concept of a pure knowledge in which the self is dissolved. It is from such projects that the basic metaphysical conceptions of classical German philosophy emerged. These conceptions helped to shape and sustain the consciousness of a whole era. Every contemporary mode of thought – regardless of whether or not it bears the non-title 'metaphysics' – which connects up with these conceptions across the history of their many transformations finds itself confronted with the same task to fulfil. Yet Jürgen Habermas perceives in these modes of thought only an expression of the misguided and hypertrophied knowledge claims of an elitist marginal group. Here we should bear in mind that the non-title 'metaphysics' can show both modern philosophy and modern existence a way to reach life-orienting ultimate conceptions only when it appeals to criteria of legitimacy different from those which are at work in the progress of the sciences. It is indeed true that the clarification of a task by no means ensures that it can be carried out. And it is also true that anyone wishing to defend a mode of thought which differs in its rationality from the specific rationality of the sciences is under an obligation to justify distinct criteria of legitimacy. Furthermore, these criteria must be set in relation to the rationality of the sciences, a relation which can itself be justified. Only in this way can the unity of our sense of reason be preserved, a unity which modern metaphysics has committed itself to – and which stands in contrast to uncontrolled and emphatic modes of speech. However, there is also a way of presenting the aim and scope of metaphysics so that both these tasks inevitably appear devoid of any prospect of success, indeed as pure presumptiousness. This is Habermas's procedure. But such misjudgement and foreshortening can be countered by recalling the way in which the metaphysical projects of modernity are constructed.

It is clear that all the subsequent theories which derived from Kant's thought aimed to serve the spontaneously emerging thinking, and resolve the conflicts, of a form of life oriented by reason, and that they acknowledged the tasks of justification just mentioned. What made them so impressive, and gave them their superiority, was not an abstract notion of the Absolute as a supersynthesis. It was rather the way in which they were able to disclose the dynamics of conscious life and to render it more transparent to itself – a life which has to begin amidst conflicts which are irresolvable at the first level.

Although they took their inspiration from Kant, they also incorporated impulses deriving from Rousseau, the theorist of conflict *par excellence*. And they also wanted their procedures, no matter what method of construction was brought into play, to satisfy Jacobi's demand that philosophy not erect self-sufficient edifices. The authentic task of philosophy was to 'reveal being' (*Dasein zu offenbaren*). All these impulses were brought together and worked out not only in Hegel's *Phenomenology of Spirit*, but also in Hölderlin's poetry, which is guided by metaphysical conceptions, and, in a different (and more Kantian) way, in the music of Beethoven.

Hegel's *Phenomenology* illuminates the inner construction of forms of discourse by incorporating the self-descriptions which are built into them, and which take shape prior to any explicit theory. Despite the similarities, its theoretical approach is not that of a developmental theory such as those proposed by Piaget and Kohlberg. This is because it deals with forms of discourse which are all at the disposal of adult consciousness, and which thus coexist and find themselves in conflict with one another. For this reason they overlap and exert pressure towards discursive syntheses, which – as Hegel tries to show – require the development of complex conceptions of the world. These deviate from our primary, familiar world conceptions, and are therefore both metaphysical and 'speculative' in their procedures. Many later theories which have played a significant role in the development of modern consciousness have been guided by the basic model of this type of theory. Kierkegaard, Heidegger and Sartre are the most obvious examples.

VI Naturalism in the Last Instance?

However, it is the other possibility opened by taking a reflective distance from the primary tendencies of life which laid down the approach which has been decisive for the subsequent history of modernity. This approach involves the dissolution of primary conflicts through insight into the illusions on which they entirely – or in large part – depend; in other words, through a naturalistic description of the world. This dissolution finds support in a self-description of human beings which is not based on forms of discourse and their validity claims, but receives a powerful impetus from everyday human experience – from the facts of procreation and death, of heredity and sickness, from observations of the continuity of species, which includes the human species, and also from a knowledge of our phylogenesis, and of the long prehistory of high cultures, which was first acquired in the nineteenth century. Naturalism, as a form of theory able to reconcile these experiences with the facts which, ever since Plato, have blocked a naturalism such as that of Democritus, has only developed in the second half of our own century. This naturalism is a creation of the new regional cultures which arose in the former colonial territories of Europe. But it can be understood only as an inverted response to those attempts, of which Hegel's *Phenomenology* stands as a prime example, to discover the authentic explanation and ultimate synthesis of the elementary forms of discourse.

This naturalism exploits the means of analysing forms of discourse which have been made available by the theory of the use of signs – itself an achievement of the late nineteenth century. In this respect naturalism, as a perspective to be reckoned with, is built into the theoretical insights into language which contemporary philosophy employs as indispensable tools for the clarification of fundamental problems. This naturalism analyses the primary forms of discourse as different forms of the rule-governed use of signs. The presuppositions concerning human beings and the world which inform these discourses are reduced to no more than the conditions for the use of linguistic signs. In this way it seems possible to explain the use of signs via a theory of linguistic behaviour, which in turn can be reduced to the laws governing the occupation of successive time–space points in the material world. The assumptions bound up with primary discourses, which presuppose grounds of validity and an immanent rationality of the use of language, are thus suspended through a multi-levelled demonstration procedure. Primary discourses are well-functioning forms of interaction; but once they have been analysed, their claims to knowledge and to a self-sufficient intelligibility cannot be sustained.

The most powerful formulations of this kind of naturalism derive from the work of Quine. His theses, and the naturalistic perspective which informs them, have long since saturated the domain of problems specific to the philosophy of language, and radically transformed it in comparison with its origins in Wittgenstein and Frege. Thus the widespread discussion concerning the best way to understand the nature of linguistic meaning, and the conventions which underpin it, is dominated by the background question of the legitimacy or illegitimacy of the naturalistic reduction.

Until recently, the reception of the methods of the philosophy of language in Germany suffered from a basic deficiency – namely, an indifference towards the pressure of the problem of naturalism. This indifference can be observed in the fact that basic 'semantic' terms, such as 'meaning', 'truth' and the 'object reference' of linguistic expressions, are employed as if they were entirely unproblematic and self-explanatory. This naïve self-confidence is highly characteristic for Habermas's theory of communicative action. It enables him to give the methods employed for the semantic clarification of speech acts a directly universal scope, even though these methods should be used only with caution and with appropriate reservations. In this way Habermas can introduce the concept of the lifeworld, as that which ultimately sustains a communication community, and employ it without any further attempt at clarification or justification. This indifference also means that Habermas is unconcerned by his own extensive reliance on Austin's theory of speech acts. Austin's theory was developed in a conservative milieu, one immunized against naturalism. Even John Searle, who has systematized this theory in a form which Habermas has found very convenient, has more recently been unable to avoid giving an account of the sense in which intentionality is bound up with speech acts. He has had to defend himself before the forum of those who have been brought up within the naturalistic perspective and are convinced of its correctness.

VII The Alternatives

However, there is an amply justified sense in which this naturalism can itself be termed a metaphysics. For metaphysics as such is not synonymous with anti-naturalism, as the examples of Aristotle, Spinoza and Nietzsche make clear. It is of course something different from a scientific theory. Yet this naturalism ties itself to the results of physics, and confirms the view which is usually found in conjunction with physical theory, that such theory gives us an accurate description of reality, and is not merely an instrument for the mastery of the data provided by experience. Nevertheless, this naturalism is the result of extrapolation, and in its internal structure it is a synthesis of scientific disciplines, a synthesis which cannot itself be a result of empirical research. In this sense it broadly corresponds to Kant's account of a metaphysics of resolving closure. It also accords with the modern understanding of metaphysics, in the sense that it strives for a definitive understanding of the connection between different forms of discourse and modes of experience.

However, there is a fundamental feature which separates this naturalism from the modern project of metaphysics, a feature which is in fact constitutive. It strives for the self-distanciation of conscious life. It does not transform conscious life into a mode of experience, one in which such a life can know itself as gathered together and preserved, rather than denied; it has no recourse to ultimate conceptions – in other words, 'Ideas'. Rather, the dynamic which is triggered by the conflicts and conflicting validity claims of conscious life is regarded as having only one resolution which is capable of

justification and testing: the knowledge of the unity and all-inclusiveness of
the laws of nature. The life of human beings is viewed as a process of acting
and interacting by means of sounds and signs, one which is entirely determined by these laws. And once this insight is achieved, we can immerse ourselves, cheerful and at ease, within this life – without making claims to step
beyond the limits of the world, and resolutely resistant to the seduction of
such claims, whenever they are raised. In this way naturalism also has its own
political consequences, regardless of its refusal of ultimate conceptions.

We must therefore distinguish naturalism within metaphysics from an
authentically modern, reductive naturalism. To these can be added a third
form: a common-sense naturalism which raises no clearly formulated theoretical claims. However, anyone who is simply indifferent towards the
specifically modern form of naturalism (from Holbach to Quine), and yet
proposes a theoretical universalism which is justified by philosophical means,
remains tangential to the contemporary situation of thinking, and is incapable
of taking up and developing the project of modernity in a credible way.
Habermas pays no attention to the ambiguous basis of his argumentation, to
the fact that it is the very theory of language which most favours naturalism that provides him with his arguments for universalism. Perhaps the sly
smiles of those who pose as 'post-modern' would bring this home to him,
were they to realize what powerful unwitting allies they could find in this
quarter.

One could of course advocate another version of 'post-modernism', one
marked by a theoretical reticence which limits itself – as Montaigne once
did – to undeniable partial truths and to the necessary tasks of life. But in
this case the universalistic claims of the theory would have to go. Once could
also give primacy to social theory, and provide it with the best available con-
ceptualizations of social forms and processes. But this would result only in a
modern specialized theory, with a degree of generality comparable to that of
physics or economics, but also with the baggage of unresolved problems of
classification and justification which characterize these disciplines, and which
would have to remain untouched. But then the fusion of philosophical and
sociological problems which is characteristic of Habermas's work would have
to be dropped.

This does not mean that Habermas's universalism has already been undermined, any more than have his efforts to take over the best methods of philosophical enlightenment. But it should be clear by now that the task of
grounding this universalism requires more wide-ranging exertions. And the
fact that Habermas entirely excludes naturalism – the inverted mirror-image
counterpart of modern metaphysics – from his reflections throws light on
the casual way in which he puts the metaphysics of modernity under suspi-

cion, and removes it from the domain of rational consideration. There is clearly a complementary relationship between this incrimination and the repression of naturalism. One could also show that the best chances for naturalism are to be found in a mode of justification drawing on the philosophy of language, and that this combination has produced a perspective which can no longer simply be left out of account. This is not to say, of course, that its entry on to the philosophical stage also gives its the last word. But if it does not have the last word, this is because a perspective based precisely on metaphysics can be opposed to it, a perspective which thus cannot in any sense be separated from the project of philosophical modernity.

It will already be clear that the enterprise of developing ultimate, and thus reconciling, conceptions, in which conscious life can come to an understanding of itself, in no way tries to outdo the sciences by their own means. It does not seek to establish foundational theories, and is not oriented towards the setting up of a 'world behind the world' (*Hinterwelt*). To this series of negative criteria others can be added – such as that the success of the enterprise does not depend on whether realism with respect to our knowledge of the 'external world' can be justified. Nor does it depend on finding an ultimate basis in the knowledge of things in themselves. 'Substance', 'freedom', 'life' and 'mind' were once the basic concepts of a modern metaphysics. Their acceptance is entirely dependent on a thesis concerning reality, but this is a thesis which, from the very beginning, includes the process of discourse within what it regards as real. The true world of the modern metaphysician is thus neither a *Hinterwelt*, nor a world characterized by an objectivity which is left standing uninterpreted over against knowledge itself.

How such concepts of the world might be more specifically defined and justified, and what correlations they might find in contemporary thought, are questions which can scarcely be pursued here. This is to be regretted, and is a serious deficiency in this series of theses. For the best reply to those who would contest the justification and possibility of any thinking continuous with the modern tradition of metaphysics would be a demonstration of its actual survival. Such a demonstration also functions as a decisive refutation of similar claims in legal procedure. It would have to be shown that such thinking does in fact emerge, and is carried out in the forms which are distinctive to it. But in the face of the abstract and general theses in which Habermas formulates his objection, apology and polemic are also required. These imply a different atmosphere and different space constraints, within which the reflections typical of such thinking cannot develop their own distinctive movement.

The situating of modern metaphysics which has been proposed so far might give the impression that any conception of resolving closure could only be a projection or a Baconian idol. Such conceptions would always already have been undermined by reflection on their conditions, which in turn become the real source of legitimacy. For this reason, I must sketch at least the formal outline of the structure of a possible justification for ultimate conceptions. In a first step, the internal lack of homogeneity in, and the conflicts between, the primary world conceptions and self-descriptions has to be shown, so that they can then be translated into synthesizing second-stage conceptions. In a second step it would be necessary to show that such conceptions of resolving closure are not simply fictions, but are capable of truth, by all the criteria of demonstrability which apply in this domain.[4] In a third step the whole sequence of demonstrations would have to be reconstructed from its end-point, so that what first appeared merely as a conclusion could also be grasped as a point of departure. In this way a theory which begins as an analysis of the dynamic of our discourses can be transformed into a thinking which also starts out from conceptions of resolving closure and their contents. It thereby becomes a thinking *about* our discourses as a whole, a thinking which even subordinates itself to the contents which were initially disclosed as conceptions of resolving closure. Such a way of thinking is outlined for the first time in the structure of Kant's system. This way of thinking can only remain contemporary, however, when it is separated from claims to a form of knowledge which once described itself as 'absolute'. It must connect up with definitions of the meaning of 'knowledge' which – under entirely different presuppositions – have become influential via the work of Wittgenstein and Heidegger.[5]

Perhaps this will suffice to overcome the impression that any definition of modern metaphysics cannot help but become entangled, from the very beginning, in an approach which could never break out of the parentheses of a suspected fictionality. However, such abstract commentaries are not very informative. Here I have been able to clarify adequately only the concept of modern metaphysics itself, the situation to which it corresponds, and a few conditions of the possibility of such a metaphysics.

VIII A Change of Paradigm?

We have now reached the point where our elucidation of the nature of metaphysics in the context of modern thought must venture some account of the problem of 'self-consciousness'. Habermas blames the hypertrophy of which he convicts all metaphysics, which supposedly leaves such thinking in an awkward relation to the project of modernity, on a fixation with self-consciousness as the domain of investigation and as the means of solving problems. With this diagnosis of a distorted development he adds his voice to the critique of earlier Critical Theory. For its part, earlier Critical Theory was inspired by Heidegger's account of a historical decline of thought, which is taken to have reach its final crisis in a universalization of the self-relation of consciousness. Certain theorems of Fichte appear to be the most obvious proof of this pathology of modernity. But, in contrast to his sources, Habermas has no wish to see the crisis overcome by means of a shift into a totally new mode of thought. He is content partly to note, and partly to foster, a change of theoretical 'paradigm'. After this change, the problems which the classical thinkers of modernity, in their orientation to self-consciousness, could approach only by means of hopeless over-dramatizations of the power of thought, can be brought to a simple and successful resolution.

This new paradigm results from a basic reorientation of theory towards linguistic communication. Habermas is convinced that this could already have been carried out by the classical thinkers of modernity. In this respect he still holds fast to his old aim, inspired by Benjamin, of recovering the traces of path-breaking thoughts which remained lost and repressed in Hegel's early works. Habermas regards language, and the forms of interaction which take place through language, as the point of convergence of all authentically modern theoretical developments. Thus language and interaction can provide the basis for his theory of modernity as a whole, a modernity whose project he wishes to save and whose discourse he wishes to continue, despite the fact that they only became accessible to distinct methods of investigation around 1900.[6] Habermas is therefore obliged to argue that, in the early history of modernity, a form of thought which had not yet reached sufficient clarity about itself disengaged the entirely dependent moment of self-consciousness from the network of linguistic interactions. Self-consciousness was inflated into an autonomous, solitary point of reference, and this move was then undermined by the anti-modernists. It is in this way that Habermas, aided by the rise of an old but repressed insight to the status of a paradigm, aims to open the prospect of a rescue and renewal of modern thought.

It is worth pointing out, in the first place, that this pattern of argumentation, which explains a revolutionary change of paradigm in terms of a response to theoretical failure, does not throw much light on the dynamics of the history of modern theory. One would at least like to know what theoretical achievements of their own suggested to the classical thinkers of modernity that they should not subject themselves to the new paradigm, which was already available. Since these thinkers, as we have already seen, were concerned to illuminate the fundamental tendencies of the life of rational beings, tendencies which lay concealed in the language of pre-modern theory, the obvious explanation seems to be that they were rightly unable to see how the analysis of language and interaction could help to make transparent and reconcile the plurality of primary world conceptions and the self-descriptions presupposed by them.

Of course, we need not be reluctant to admit that the theory of the use of signs, and in particular semantics (the theory of meanings), have provided new ways of clarifying long-standing fundamental questions and theoretical tasks of philosophy. The question is only whether this theoretical shift should be interpreted as a historical shift of paradigm. Did such a shift really offer salvation to a self-consciousness which had been manoeuvred into a position of exaggerated theoretical status, which had furthermore become groundless and despairing as a form of life, by opening it up to the communicative community within a shared lifeworld?

IX Self-consciousness and Linguistic Form

In investigating this question, a further reminder is first of all appropriate. Although it is Kant who was responsible for the fact that theoretical hopes were hung on the idea of connecting up with a principle of 'self-consciousness', it was far from being his intention to present this self-consciousness as self-sufficient or solitary. He did indeed make theoretical use of it as a principle, but only as one functioning within a broader frame of reference. Neither the fundamental logical forms, nor the justifications of science and metaphysics, nor the fundamental norms of action, can be derived from it as direct implications. Self-consciousness precedes them only in the sense that they would lose their meaning and systematic use – and the legitimate basis for these – if the existence of self-conscious beings could not be presupposed by them. In this specific sense, self-consciousness is the anchoring point for every use of reason, and also the guarantee for the validity of norms, and not merely their addressee.

All this would need more precise explication. But the decisive point can be presented in the following way: even if self-consciousness is not put forward as a self-sufficient universal ground, the theoretical hopes which were pinned to it have not become obsolete simply because it turns out that the semantics of the form of propositions and norms requires elucidation within the framework of a theory of linguistic meaning. Everything depends on whether it is possible to ground the far stronger thesis that self-consciousness can be reduced to linguistic interactions – in other words, can be entirely derived from them.

This is, of course, the thesis on which the success of a semantically grounded naturalism depends, one which stands in the forefront of its strategy of legitimation. And it is against precisely this thesis that I tried to argue long ago, when the theory of language was still bound by the constraints of a theory of sign-mediated interaction. Of course, in this context we also encounter the further problem of how self-conciousness can be suitably described, and perhaps conceptualized. But this primarily theoretical problem is directly connected with that other problem which conscious life represents for itself. For such a life is dependent on the possibility of finding a stable description of itself. This also explains the context in which the prospect of a metaphysics, which is intrinsic to modernity, becomes connected with the problems of a theory of self-consciousness.

If there are signs today of a 'turn' in the style of philosophy and in the state of discussion, this is not because an all-embracing change of paradigm can be announced. And we should certainly not allow Habermas, ever-resourceful in tracking down conservatisms, to manoeuvre into a corner every shift in the theoretical situation, and thus every change in the theoretical climate, which does not favour his theory of interaction – a corner where it can be dismissed as presaging political complacency and cultural confusion.

I have already explained elsewhere that the developments I find encouraging are at the centre of current discussion in the Anglo-Saxon world.[7] It is no longer the case that the problems of self-ascription, and thus of self-consciousness, can be decided in advance in favour of linguistic interactionism – and thus in a way which is of vital theoretical interest to that modern naturalism which follows, and will continue to follow, modern metaphysics like its shadow. It would be inappropriate to go into the details here, but a few indications can be given. Thomas Nagel tried to show early on that 'subjectivity' requires a different explanation from that which study of the use of the first-person singular in language can offer. The semantics of demonstratives and modalities then led to the self-relation implied by the use of predicates being given a key role in the elucidation of all language use (H. N. Castañeda, John Perry, David Lewis, etc.). This insight belongs to the same constellation as another realization – that the relation to an object (termed 'reference') presupposes a distinctive form of self-ascription, and thus also of self-consciousness (Sidney Shoemaker). To this constellation belongs also the further insight that the fully developed use of the concept of truth includes the possibility of a self-relation. For when I claim that something is true, I imply that things do not simply appear to *me* to be such and such a way (Roderick Chisholm, etc.).

Of course, one cannot simply regard these theorems as truths which have been ascertained for all time. It is difficult enough to link them correctly with each other, within a field of problems whose peculiar difficulty is once more being acknowledged. It is of course possible that they could be taken up and integrated into the framework of a naturalistic doctrine of appropriate refinement. Although the combined emergence of these theorems has already led to a rehabilitation of the most speculative of metaphysicians (E. Anscombe, with reservations, for Descartes, and R. Nozick for Fichte), their explosive potential does not give us licence to develop a metaphysics from them without further ado. It lies rather in the disruption of the dogma of the self-sufficient priority of linguistic interaction in relation to self-consciousness. Along with other signs of a loosening up in the theoretical situation, they point to the fact that forms of conceptual elaboration and explanation which take up the themes of modern metaphysics can no longer be dismissed as outdated before they have even appeared.[8]

Every new, fruitful method tends to encourage those who employ it to believe that they have found something like the philosopher's stone. It is easy to find oneself expecting that what formerly resisted conceptualization can now be captured within a universal theory. Habermas connects this hope, which has meanwhile become outdated in semantics, with his theory of society – a theory which he actually began to construct far earlier, and indeed 'with practical intent'.[9] But all such far-reaching expectations soon fall prey to other reservations. These reservations do not necessarily defeat the impulse which gave rise to the new methodological approach. But they cannot help but disrupt a premature self-confidence, the belief that a straight path leads from an apparently revolutionary paradigm to a universal theory. This situation allows us to understand the project of modernity, and to continue its unfolding, far better than the theoretical approaches advocated by Habermas. He believes that these approaches could have placed the theory of language and society in the position of a fundamental science, a position vacated by their predecessors, had they been pursued consistently at an earlier date. But the thinkers of modernity avoided this path for good reasons – even if they were not fully able to explain them. Often, as in the case of Hegel, they explicitly refused it.

X Communication instead of Subjectivity?

Habermas is ready to welcome anyone as a witness against the rumours of a survival of metaphysics, provided they are willing to endorse the primacy of the community of interaction emphatically enough, and to delimit and shield themselves from the 'philosophy of subjectivity' and metaphysics with sufficient determination. Habermas has not only made his whole work dependent on this thesis. It springs from the underlying, and undoubtedly deeply personal, motives which brought him to philosophy in the first place, and turned him into a theorist.[10] Thus the question of its tenability does not bear merely on the issue of whether a paradigm shift to the priority of communicative action over all forms of subjectivity really does draw a decisive line under an epoch. On one side of this line are placed the footsore, unable to keep up with an advancing modernity, along with all variants of conservative thought; on the other, Habermas's band of witnesses. In this community it is even permissible to speak of an 'absolute', as long as one also makes hostile remarks about the subject and about the term 'metaphysics'. The drawing of this line also raises the question of whether Habermas relies on adequate or inadequate assumptions regarding a life which has to be led in the light of reason. Anyone who has a relation to his work of some kind must try to get clear about this issue.

I have already given some indication of the many factors which have brought the theme of 'self-consciousness' back into the analysis of language. The manner of this return already gives us a basis on which to answer the question. For it turns out that the functioning of linguistic communication presupposes a self-relation on the part of the 'speaker' – as one of its constitutive pre-conditions, one which is no less fundamental than the subject–predicate form of the proposition. To say this is not to repeat the thesis which Habermas merely imputes to the 'philosophy of the subject': namely, that communication can only arise when solitary subjects enter into communication with each other. Such a view would be merely the inversion of the hypothesis which Habermas finds convincing, and which he pursues: namely, that the linguistically organized lifeworld, which for its part is self-sufficient, can generate self-relations – and hence the identity of speakers – out of itself. Furthermore, it would be incapable of describing or understanding language and communication.

We should therefore say, rather, that the capacity for language can only develop *along with* the spontaneous emergence of a self-relation. This emergence in turn requires explanation. And this would require us to speak of an implicit self-relation, which already appears or functions at the most elementary level of language acquisition. For it is clear that the capacity to use the grammatical first-person singular (the pronoun 'I') is acquired only at a late stage in the process of language acquisition. If the existence of a self-relation were dependent on, and determined by, the acquisition of this capacity, then the thesis of the priority of interaction would be unproblematic; it would be a trivial and obvious truth.

But if it can be shown that the mastery of demonstratives, the correct use of one's own name, the developed use of negation, and thus one of the elementary conditions for the understanding of truth, can only be understood when a self-relation is presupposed, then the situation is quite different. We have to assume that linguistic behaviour emerges within a complex framework of intelligent performances which do not stand in a sequence of one-to-one relations with each other. It is clear that higher linguistic achievements, such as the mastery of identity and the relative pronoun, can only be acquired in jumps in which several functions are learned in one go, just as one might learn a difficult double grip required in a handicraft or a sport. They are indeed learned, not step by step, but through spontaneous strivings, oriented towards an example, which eventually result in the spontaneous and simultaneous emergence of a form of knowledge and a capacity. There is every reason to believe that even the first steps in the acquisition of language occur within such irreducibly complex networks of interdependencies.

But even if this is acknowledged, we are still a long way from being given *carte blanche* to imagine a metaphysics based on the self-relation of conscious life. In fact, instead of this, we have initially come closer to naturalism in one essential respect. For naturalism begins with the assumption that communicative activities – indeed, all those which involve the 'understanding' of 'meanings' – can ultimately be viewed as a series of functions in the cerebral cortex. Regardless of the fact that it is only in socialized living beings that these processes lead to a capacity for language, the cerebral cortex is the individual basis for the emergence and use of this capacity. We have reason to believe that the processes within it correspond to the ramified, complex performances which we observe in the development of intelligence.

In any case, no conception of a modern metaphysics would be at all plausible if it were unable to work out a relation to the data which provide the underpinning for naturalism. No one who regards self-relatedness as emerging alongside the capacity for language from the very beginning need fear that his arguments converge with those of naturalism at this point. The problem is to show in detail how the data of naturalism can be given their due, without endorsing naturalism itself at the same time.

XI Hope and Haste

To the problem of correctly determining the role of the relation to self in the use of language there directly corresponds, at a much higher level, another problem. This is the problem of how to reach a full understanding of the sociality of human beings, at the level of human intelligence which corresponds to the capacity for high culture. To this sociality belong both intimate relationships based on a shared humanity, which can be independent of the group, and self-realization in associations stabilized by the exchange of arguments (Buber's 'I–Thou relation' and Habermas's 'public sphere'). Even here, where the origins of the primary and personal (and thus authentic) motivation for Habermas's thought – along with that of many other interactionists – can be found, there are different notions in play, and questions to decide. These concern the best way of understanding how the self-relation of conscious life can be embedded in relations of shared humanity and communicative exchange.

The modern world brought into being not only experiences of withdrawal and the suffering of isolation. Under headings such as 'alienation' and 'diremption' it quickly transformed them into theoretical concerns, which were given their most powerful initial statement by Rousseau. Soon there emerged many theoretical efforts and political reform movements aimed at retrieving a protective community and a political life for those who had become depraved through isolation, a life in which the 'subject' could become a 'citizen' or a 'comrade'. The first intellectual efforts directed against a spirit turned solitary were Jacobi's doctrine that every 'I' finds its complement in a 'Thou', and Hölderlin's early philosophy of unification. These were followed by Fichte's social philosophy of recognition, as well as Feuerbach's and Marx's anthropologies of human beings as essentially social beings. After the First World War these sources flowed together into a broad stream. Husserl's theory of intersubjectivity, Lukács's concept of class consciousness and Martin Buber's treatise on the primordiality of the dimension which makes possible the opening towards each other which occurs between 'I' and 'Thou', were the most striking landmarks along its way. In Heidegger's thinking, this 'in-between' was more specifically defined as 'language'. It was therefore to be expected that the common features of philosophies stressing the linguisticality of human beings and the approach of American pragmatism, with its theory of social interaction, would be noted, and that Wittgenstein's doctrine of the primordiality of language-games, developed in England, would soon be combined with them.

Whenever the motives which can be traced back to Rousseau attained a hidden or open predominance within the syndrome which was formed in this way, the hopes which were bound up with the theory of intersubjectivity also flowed into it. These hopes nourished the conviction that a human life can only reach peace and completion when it finds its way back through praxis to the human community which precedes it, makes itself relative to this community, and – as Hegel puts it – gives itself up to this community and is absorbed into it. This conviction can become the single essential motive of an individual's thinking. Such an individual will then regard the goal of his thinking as attained when this conviction comes to play the key role in a theory which forms the basis for an entire intellectual edifice. In this case, even obvious theoretical deficiencies can come to appear unimportant. Although Habermas's thought is of course not as narrowly focused as this, this personal motivation for his theory can be seen everywhere. But in his work it does not have the orientation towards the intimate form of community, which is reflected in Hegel's Frankfurt theory of 'love', in Jacobi's and Buber's 'Thou', and in theories of dialogue and 'essential' communication. It is entirely oriented towards the political community, and is therefore not concerned with dialogue, but with discussion; not with the intimate understanding of the other, but with communicative action. For this reason its Rousseauistic origins remain concealed behind a theoretical orientation towards Peirce and Anglo-Saxon theory of language.

It is far from being my intention to argue that the problems and conceptions which emerged with Rousseauism and pragmatism can be dismissed as imaginary. There is no more reason to do this than to secure the primordial position of self-consciousness by claiming that logical and linguistic form can be derived from it. In any case, this is not the place to explore any further the various developments of dialogism and interactionism, or to investigate the possibilities for a defensible account of the social nature of human beings. But, in placing the motives for Habermas's thinking back in the history of modernity's motivations, two considerations can be added which directly concern the character of his objection to metaphysics, and in particular to a metaphysics which would emerge from the dynamics of self-understanding.

To believe that any prioritization of the speech community over the relation to self already provides support for those motives which orient thought towards the notion of a rational human community would be to draw far too hasty a conclusion. We have already seen that nothing is more likely to assist the triumph of naturalism than the discovery that the use of signs constitutes a self-contained system. The fact that linguistic interaction functions in a fluid way, that language-games are interwoven with everyday activities, even the fact that the 'discussions' of a political culture can develop in a stable way in accordance with established rules and facilitate decision making – all this can provide grounds for assigning all the pretensions of a universalistic reason to the realm of dreams from which we have long since awoken. But with this would also disappear any notion of a self-realization in which not only would the distress (*Not*) of the isolated subject be done away with, but his authentic hopes and true nature would be fulfilled. Quine made a great impression with the thesis that the fluidity of a form of speech tells us nothing about the reality of the intentions and 'inner' states of consciousness which are connected with it. And another experience which the reflective character of modern consciousness has made possible is a sense that the very stability of models of interaction gives us reason to suspect them of being fictions. Against a Rousseauism drunk on language, the poetry of our time long ago raised the objection that endless talk can be the manner in which a consciousness of the failure of all language articulates itself and works itself out. And the authentically poetic word lies on the borders of silence, where – as Wittgenstein also believed – everything which is essential in life finds its place.

However, anyone who recognizes metaphysics as part of modernity, and wishes to preserve a future for it, cannot accept this conclusion as the last word. He must entrust thought to a language, and allow subjectivity the chance of conversation and mutual understanding. To this extent he stands in comradeship with those who move in the stream of Rousseauism. But if it is true that subjectivity develops only where human beings are addressed, it is no less true that a conversation which is worthy of the name takes place only when those interacting are more than the dramaturges and 'speakers' of semantic theory, and of the theory of communicative action. Anyone must be true to himself and be capable of 'thoughtfulness' (*Besinnung*), who would say a word as a friend. And this capacity for reticence is not merely an intermediate stage, which understanding may require. It is based on that self-relation which is bound up with the capacity for language as such. It is truer to say that anyone who is able to turn a discussion towards measure and truth must have achieved a certain level of insight concerning himself. Two hundred years ago Herder objected to the philosophy of unification (*Vereinigungsphilosophie*) that 'love' – if it is to be more than mere exuberance – presupposes the 'selfhood' of the lovers. Hegel took this warning to heart, as did Hölderlin. Thereafter their thought was concerned with how to reconcile the freedom of the individual and the encompassing unity of life – including political life – without any one-sided reduction. Only in this way can indispensable experiences of modernity be made compatible with the human hope for a free, non-instrumental society. Both of them knew that a metaphysics was necessary for this task. Anyone who fails to acknowledge this falls back into the gravitational field of Aristotelian politics, which – as is well known – was also uncoupled from metaphysics.

XII The Refusal of Thought

Habermas is not entirely insensitive to this truth. But it has had no effect on the way in which he has constructed his theory. This is made clear by his structureless concept of the lifeworld; and by his readiness to derive self-relations from communication (with the support of Mead). It is also made clear by his empty concept of a 'subjective world', which is supposed to be communicated through dramaturgical actions and 'expressive' sentences. It is this last theorem above all (one taken over from Ernst Tugendhat) which should be dissolved into its elements and thus exposed in its weaknesses. Anyone who speaks of 'self-understanding', and of a conscious life which is organized in terms of self-relations, needs to take an explicit distance from this theorem. After all, we cannot advocate, rescue and comprehend the discourse of modernity by abandoning it to a life which our theoretical language has hollowed out. But here it will have to suffice to identify the place of this theorem in the system of basic concepts which Habermas thinks have enabled him to get beyond both subjectivity and metaphysics.

We can add the following observation. We have already recalled that Hegel was obliged to develop a conceptual form for modern metaphysics when he realized the need to bring subjectivity and sociality together without any one-sided foreshortening. This metaphysics is not yet one which is compatible with the self-understanding of conscious life, and thus not a metaphysics of resolving closure. It is a structural theory, which precedes this final stage. In the technical terminology of the old metaphysicians, it belongs to the domain which was referred to as 'ontology'. The structural weakness of Habermas's conceptual language has already been touched on, in connection with his concept of the 'lifeworld'. Under pressure of questions regarding the status of 'world' in relation to individuals, it turns out to be no clearer than Heidegger's early concept of the world. But questions of sociological method depend on such clarification. They are difficult to decide. Wittgenstein, to name but one, struggled throughout his life to find the right way to talk about the 'lifeworld'. In Habermas's theory the fundamental concepts remain indeterminate, and indeed in a state of oscillation, despite his declaration that the lifeworld is 'holistically' constituted. This oscillation is the result not of indecisiveness, but rather of a failure to see that a decision is required with respect to a basic problem of social theory. In the last instance, is it the individuals themselves whose interactive behaviour, along with the complex reasons which inform it, provides the basis for the the development of the concept of a 'lifeworld'? Or is it necessary to appeal to forms of association which precede individuals, which of course cannot exist without individuals, but – with respect to their 'ontological' status – are independent of individuals to the extent that they determine their social behaviour, just as Newtonian space determines the positions of the bodies within it? Are institutions also entities of this kind? Any social theory must evaluate these alternatives if its development is to be philosophically guided. Of course, it is always possible to undermine the alternative – for example, by a new return to arguments inspired by transcendental philosophy or pragmatism – but only after the pros and cons of the two opposing sides have been thought through. After such reflection, the renewal of a perspective based on the intrinsic limitations of knowledge would be apparent in the increased clarity and caution of theory construction in the social sciences.

In the case of Habermas, it is remarkable how uninhibited he feels about constructing his two-stage social theory by borrowing extensively from his most dangerous sociological opponent: namely, systems theory. How a system functions, and how its emergence and eventual 'uncoupling' from the lifeworld and from communicative action are to be made intelligible, remain just as unexplained as the constitution of the lifeworld, in view of the problems previously mentioned. 'Lifeworld' and 'system' are, in their fundamental implications, incommensurable concepts, which cannot therefore be related to each other as 'stages'. The lack of such considerations is all the more striking, given that Habermas's work is characterized by an extraordinary breadth of orientation and an extensive incorporation of specialist literatures which are significant or relevant for the construction of a social theory.

Given that such demands are evaded in the domain of problems which we could term 'ontological', it is scarcely surprising that, when we pose simple but fundamental philosophical questions, ones which are questions of modernity *par excellence*, it is difficult to identify Habermas's position at all. If we ask whether he would be willing to come out against naturalism, it is difficult to know how he would answer, or how he would feel obliged to answer. It is of course clear that the defence of naturalism is not one of the intentions of his theory. But, equally, it is hard to perceive any consistent attempt to oppose it. And the screening out of difficulties which encourage his belief that it is possible to stand pat with a defence of communicative rationality also makes him fall prey to the illusion that banishing metaphysics from the paradigm of modernity is a straightforward, cost-free enterprise.

With this observation we have closed a circle, returning to Kant's lucid diagnosis of the indifferentists, which served as a starting-point for our definition of the concept of metaphysics in modernity. Kant aimed to expose the posture of nonchalant superiority which the indifferentists favoured as their style of self-presentation. He objected that they all had their own secret metaphysics 'to the extent that they think anything at all'. The meaning of this qualification now appears in its continuing significance. Habermas's theory refuses thought with respect to precisely those questions which are decisive for the thinking which Kant has in mind – and which is called philosophy. This would be no objection against a theoretical proposal in sociology. But we have not been discussing the objections of a sociologist to the possible modernity of metaphysics. Conscious life must not have the paths indispensable to it narrowed down, overshadowed and eventually blocked off by discouragement – especially not by something which aims to be a philosophy of freedom (and should be esteemed as such), but which lingers in indeterminacy, and distorts the notion of such a life – and of freedom itself – in some of their essential aspects.

This discussion must now be brought to a close, if only for the time being. And here I would like to add some words in a different tone. No one has made more effort than Habermas to make debate possible again in German philosophy. He debates with an obvious interest in what the outcome will be, and with that undiminished energy which also drives the construction of a body of work which has rightly aroused universal interest. No one, not even Habermas, can have viable thoughts and insights about every topic, thoughts which are capable of restructuring the field of problems. We need competition between different approaches, in which everyone runs up against the limits of their competence, but in which what is at stake emerges for that very reason all the more clearly. And it is precisely Habermas's conduct in public debate which can teach us how our work must be subordinated to the genuine issues at stake. Without playing to the gallery, we must none the less seek to serve the causes to which we are committed with zeal. With regard to the cause which he is almost alone in defending publicly, and which – next to the emancipation of subjectivity from itself – is the most important for him, my theses put me side by side with him, despite the fact that they contradict him in every other respect. This cause is the defence of modernity against its learned despisers. Unanimity will not help this cause to prosper. A modernity which spoke with only one voice, or through only one voice, would already be moribund. This means that fundamental disagreements concerning modernity are in no sense a denial of modernity's continuing force.

Notes

*   Habermas's review first appeared as 'Rückkehr zur Metaphysik? – Eine Tendenz in der deutschen Philosophie', in *Merkur*, 439–40 (Oct. 1985), pp. 898ff. (Reprinted in ND 267–79). His reply to Henrich's critique, 'Metaphysik nach Kant', appears in ND 18–34 (English translation PT 10–27).

1   Habermas, 'Rückkehr zur Metaphysik'.

2   Kant, *Critique of Pure Reason*, A, X.

3   Kant, *Gesammelte Schriften, Akademie-Ausgabe*, vol. XXIX, I, 2, p. 765 (Kant's italics).

4   Cf. my 'Versuch über Fiktion und Wahrheit, in D. Henrich and W. Iser, eds, *Funktionen des Fiktiven* (Poetik und Hermeneutik X) (Munich: Fink, 1983), pp. 511ff.

5   The outlines of such a project can be found in my book, reviewed by Habermas, *Fluchtlinien* (Frankfurt am Main: Suhrkamp, 1982), pp. 125ff, and in D. Henrich, ed., *All-Einheit: Wege eines Gedanken in Ost und West* (Stuttgart: Klett-Cotta, 1985), pp. 33ff.

6   The following reflections are frequently a response to Jürgen Habermas, PDMo, and later also to TKH1 and 2.

7   Cf. my 'Wohin die deutsche Philosophie?', in *Konzepte* (Frankfurt am Main: Suhrkamp, 1987), pp. 66ff.

8   Cf. ibid.

9   Many years ago, in my *Laudatio* for Jürgen Habermas, I sensed the likelihood that this connection would emerge ('Kritik der Verständingungsverhältnisse', in J. Habermas and D. Henrich, *Zwei Reden* (Frankfurt am Main: Suhrkamp, 1974), p. 20.

10   Cf., for example, 'Erläuterungen zum Begriff des kommunkativen Handelns', in J. Habermas, *Vorstudien und Ergänzungen zur Theorie des kommunikativen Handelns* (Frankfurt am Main: Suhrkamp, 1982). This chapter also provides some very important clarifications of the basic concepts of Habermas's 1981 *Theorie des kommunikativen Handelns*.

11

The social dynamics of disrespect: situating Critical Theory today

Axel Honneth

In the essay which follows, Axel Honneth proposes a programme for the continuation of Critical Theory which differs significantly from that of Habermas. In Honneth's account, what is definitive of Critical Theory is its cognitive dependence on a 'pre-theoretical instance', an existing social interest in emancipation which it seeks to articulate. Honneth argues that the historical process of the communicative rationalization of the lifeworld, as Habermas understands it (the process whereby ever more validity claims come to require explicit, consensual resolution), is a process which takes place 'behind the backs' of social subjects. So although communicative rationalization preserves a link between reason and history, the unfolding potential of communicative reason is not necessarily reflected in the experience of social subjects as an enhanced moral sensibility. For according to Honneth, subjects experience 'the constriction of what we can call their moral expectations, that is their "moral point of view", not as a restriction of intuitively mastered rules of language, but as a violation of identity claims acquired through socialization.' Habermas's theoretical standpoint thus cannot be aimed, in the same way as Horkheimer's, 'at the idea of helping to give expression to an existing experience of social injustice.'

In order to establish a lifeline to the pre-theoretical, Honneth suggests, we need to develop a communication paradigm which is conceived not primarily in terms of a theory of language, but rather one of relations of recognition and their violation. Such a theory would be able to connect up with the experiences of shame, anger and indignation which are the typical response to such violations, and articulate the aspiration to social justice which is already implicit in them. In defence of Habermas, it might be said that his notion of communication is 'thicker' than Honneth supposes – that he is aware of the intertwining of communication and recognition, and sensitive to the ways in which distorted structures of communication have implications for our identies as subjects. Nevertheless, Honneth is right to point out that Habermas's social theory tends to focus on the general 'colonization' of the lifeworld by the rationality of economic and administrative systems. It thereby overlooks the consquences of the continuing conflicts between specific social groups, whose recognition, or lack of recognition, is often closely intertwined with their economic role and status. In short, the question of the precise the relation between a formal pragmatics of language and a theory of recognition is far from being merely an abstract philosophical issue. It bears directly on the relative weight which is given to two dimensions of critical social analysis. To borrow Marx's own terms, these would be the dimension of 'alienation' on the one hand, and that of 'class struggle' on the other.

Anyone who attempts to situate 'Critical Theory' today is readily suspected of nostalgically misjudging the current position of philosophical thought.[1] For in its original sense – that is, as the interdisciplinary endeavour to diagnose social reality critically – this tradition ceased to exist some time ago. If I nevertheless undertake such an attempt in what follows, this should not be seen as evidence of an intention to explore conditions for a revival of the old Frankfurt School tradition. I do not believe that the original research programme merits further development unchanged; nor am I convinced that a complex, quickly changing reality can be investigated within the framework of a single theory, even if it is interdisciplinary in character.

In what follows, therefore, the phrase 'critical theory of society' is not intended in the sense of the Frankfurt School's original programme. None the less, what is intended is more than just a reference to any theory of society, in so far as it submits its object to critical examination or diagnosis; for this applies in an almost self-evident manner to every kind of theory of society that really deserves its name – to Weber no less than to Marx, and to Durkheim no less than to Tönnies. Rather, by a 'critical theory of society' I mean in this context the type of social thought that shares with the Frankfurt School's original programme – indeed, perhaps, with the whole tradition of Left Hegelianism – a particular form of normative critique. Such thought is able to inform us about the pre-theoretical source of legitimacy (vorwissenschaftliche Instanz), the empirical interest or moral experience, in which its own critical viewpoint is anchored extra-theoretically.

Hence, as a first step, I wish briefly to recall Critical Theory's Left Hegelian legacy, since this can be considered the only theoretical element that functions as an identifying feature, as an unrenounceable premiss of the old tradition. The Frankfurt tradition of social theory differs from all other currents or directions of social theory in its form of critique. Only after recalling this methodological aspect can I begin to outline where the critical theory of society finds itself today. I shall endeavour to do this – in careful demarcation from Habermas's theory of communication – by sketching step by step the basic assumptions of an approach that can satisfy the methodological requirements of the old theory. The core of this approach consists in unfolding the social phenomenon mentioned in the title of my essay: the 'social dynamics of disrespect'.

I Critique and Pre-theoretical Praxis

The methodological starting-point of the theory which Horkheimer attempted to launch at the beginning of the Thirties is determined by a problem whose source lies in the acceptance of the Left Hegelian legacy. Among Hegel's left-wing disciples – that is, from Karl Marx to Georg Lukács – it was considered self-evident that a theory of society could engage in critique only in so far as it was able to rediscover an element of its own critical viewpoint within social reality; for this reason, these theorists continually called for a diagnosis of society that could bring to light a degree of immanent, intramundane transcendence.

Horkheimer has this task in mind when, in one of his famous earlier essays, he defines the uniqueness of Critical Theory by referring to it as 'the intellectual side of the historical process of emancipation';[2] to be able to accomplish this, the theory must always be able to reflect both on its emergence in pre-theoretical experience and on its application in a future praxis. In contrast to Lukács, however, Horkheimer realized that, by defining his point of departure in this way, he not only establishes a methodological requirement, but also calls for the regulated co-operation of the individual social science disciplines: for Critical Theory can assert its own link back to its pre-theoretical dimension of social emancipation only if it gives, in the form of a sociological analysis, an account of the state of consciousness or emancipatory readiness of the populace. The specific relation within which Horkheimer – continuing Left Hegelianism – brought together theory and praxis presupposes a determination of the social forces that, in their own right, push toward a critique and an overthrow of established forms of domination. For this reason, Critical Theory in its innermost core – whatever its congruence with other forms of social critique may be – is dependent upon the quasi-sociological specification of an emancipatory interest which is anchored in social reality itself.

However, a series of investigations in the history of theory have in the meantime shown (convincingly, I believe) that the explanatory tools provided by the Frankfurt Institute's social philosophy were not sufficient to realize this demanding goal in research practice. From the outset Horkheimer remains bound to a Marxist philosophy of history, which could tolerate a pre-theoretical interest in social emancipation only in one class, the proletariat. From an early stage Adorno had made Marx's critique of fetishism such a decisive point of departure for his critique of society that he could no longer find any trace of an intramundane transcendence in the social culture of everyday life. Perhaps the theoretical impetus to seek a different, more productive access to the emancipatory potentials of everyday social reality could only have come from the fringe members of the Institute, from Walter Benjamin or Otto Kirchheimer.[3] But Horkheimer and his circle as a whole remained bound to a Marxist functionalism that misled them into assuming a cycle of capitalist domination and cultural manipulation which was so self-enclosed that there could be no room for a zone of practical-moral critique within social reality. The problem this produced – namely, the embarrassment of being theoretically dependent upon a pre-theoretical emancipatory source whose very existence can no longer be proved empirically – could not help but become more acute for the theoretical tradition founded by Horkheimer, in so far as the practically nourished hopes for change inevitably lost their plausibility. The victory of fascism and the final triumph of Stalinism destroyed any possibility of giving the theory's critical perspective an objective foothold in a pre-theoretical source of legitimation, be it a social movement or an existing interest. Critical Theory's turn to Adorno's historico-philosophical negativism finally marked the historical point at which the endeavour to link critique back to social history failed completely. In the reflections contained in *Dialectic of Enlightenment*, the only remaining place where something like an intramundane transcendence could occur was in the experience of modern art.

After returning from exile to the Federal Republic of Germany, Horkheimer and Adorno did not make any significant changes to the empirical premises of their critical undertaking. True, it is open to argument whether both thinkers actually adhered to the approach of *Dialectic of Enlightenment* without correction until the end of their lives, but it is less debatable that neither remained willing to believe in an intramundane possibility for emancipation. In Adorno's case, this is shown in his *Negative Dialectics*; in Horkheimer's, in his turn to Schopenhauer's metaphysical pessimism late in life. Whatever the details may be, the fundamentally negativist orientation of their later writings bequeathed a problem that, ever since, has posed the first obstacle to every renewed attempt to link up with Critical Theory: if the Left Hegelian model of critique is to be retained in any sense at all, theoretical access to the social sphere in which an interest in emancipation can find a pre-theoretical anchoring must be re-established at the outset. Without proof – however this may be provided – that the critical perspective is supported by a need or a movement within social reality, Critical Theory cannot be continued in any way today. For it no longer distinguishes itself from other models of social critique by virtue of a superior sociological explanatory substance, or of its philosophical procedures of justification, but solely because of its attempt (which still has not been abandoned) to give the standards of critique an objective foothold in pre-theoretical praxis.

But because this sphere has been buried in the course of the history of Critical Theory, it must be brought to light again today by means of arduous conceptual work. For this reason, I see the key to updating critical social theory in the task of disclosing social reality categorially in such a way that an element of intramundane transcendence will again become visible in it. To this extent, the question of how contemporary thinkers respond to this problem can serve as a theoretical guide-line, one which can give provisional direction to an attempt to situate Critical Theory today.

II Alternative Ways of Renewing Critical Theory

With reference to the problem outlined thus far, two diametrically opposed responses can easily be distinguished. In the first of these, the negativist social critique practised by Adorno in his later writings is radicalized one further degree, such that a self-dissolution of the social core of society as a whole is anticipated; here the focus is on phenomena such as the wholly uncontrolled growth of major technological systems, the total uncoupling of system steering from the social lifeworld, and, finally, the accelerated hollowing out of the human personality. However much this list of developmental tendencies recalls the kind of diagnosis once drafted by conservative authors like Arnold Gehlen, today it is found primarily in theoretical circles which look to Adorno's negativist legacy. In the German-speaking world, the writings of Stefan Breuer most obviously represent this trend, while, internationally, it is frequently the disciples of French post-structuralism who focus on these social phenomena in their diagnosis of society.[4]

The theoretical image of the social lifeworld generated in the diverse versions of negativist social critique is always characterized by a tendency toward dehumanization. What generally transforms human beings into mere objects of an autopoietically reproducing systemic power is, for Breuer, a quasi-religious belief in the omnipotence of technology and science; for the Foucault of the middle years, it is a passive reaction to the strategies of the apparatuses of power; for Baudrillard, finally, it is the dramatically widespread tendency toward semblance, toward mere simulation. But if social reality is conceived in this way, the theoretical consequences for our problem are obvious: every form of critique attempting to locate itself within social reality must be considered impossible, since this reality is no longer constituted in such a way that social anomalies, even emancipatory interests or attitudes, can be found in it. The radicalization of the later Adorno's critique of reification removes the basis in social theory for any effort to identify an intramundane element of transcendence, and thereby to secure a social foothold for critique. With this form of a critical theory of society, the attempt to enter into a reflexive relationship with pre-theoretical praxis would have reached its end.

However, that this is not the inevitable outcome is made clear by the second theoretical current through which the tradition of Critical Theory is continued today. Habermas's theory of communication, which I am of course referring to here, represents a countermove to negativist social theories precisely in the sense that it has re-established access to an emancipatory sphere of action. The construction of the theory of communicative action can be understood as recovering the categorial means to allow Horkheimer's idea of social critique to be revived today. In a first step, this aim is served by shifting from the Marxist paradigm of production to the paradigm of communicative action, a framework which is intended to make clear that the conditions of social progress are located not in social labour but in social interaction. The next step proceeds from here to the development of a pragmatics of language that aims to identify the specific normative presuppositions that constitute the rational potential of communicative action. Then on this basis, in a third and final step, there is the formulation of a theory of society that pursues the process of rationalization of communicative action to the historical point at which it gives rise to the formation of social steering media (see TCA1 and 2).

As is generally known, Habermas's theory of society leads to a diagnosis of the times which suggests that the power of self-steering systems has grown to such an extent that they threaten the communicative achievements of the lifeworld. Under the corrosive force with which the steering media of money and bureaucratic power currently invade everyday culture, the human potential for reaching understanding in language is beginning to dissolve. In this image of a colonization of the lifeworld, Habermas's theory of society seems, in the end, to agree with the pessimistic social critique we found in the negativist current of contemporary Critical Theory: in their diagnoses, both models agree that systemic powers have today acquired such independence that the social core of society threatens to dissolve. The whole, decisive difference between these two approaches consists in Habermas's ability to provide a systematic account of what is currently threatened by the domination of systems. In place of the predominance of the unclarified premises of a barely articulated anthropology in negativist theoretical models, in his model we find a theory of language which is able to demonstrate convincingly that the endangered potential of human beings is their capacity to reach understanding communicatively. In contrast to all the other versions of Critical Theory, Habermas's contains a conception which can account for the structure of the forms of practical activity which are threatened by the tendencies of social development which are being criticized.

From this perspective, it is easy to see that Habermas's theory of communication satisfies in its formal construction the requirements Horkheimer placed on a social critique in his original programme. What the latter locates in societal labour, Habermas finds in communicatively reaching understanding (*Verständigung*), namely, a pre-theoretical sphere of emancipation to which critique can refer in order to confirm its normative standpoint within social reality. However, the comparison with Horkheimer's model of critique also brings to light a problem in Habermas's theory that I would like to take as the point of departure for my further reflections. It concerns the question of how we are to determine more precisely the reflexive connection presumed to obtain between pre-theoretical praxis and Critical Theory. When Horkheimer formulated his programme, he had – in keeping with the Marxist tradition – a proletariat in mind that, supposedly, had already acquired a sense of the injustice of capitalism because of its role in the production process. His idea was that these moral experiences, this sense of injustice, merely had to be systematically articulated by theory at a more reflexive level in order to give its critique an objective foothold. But we know today – and Horkheimer might have realized this, had he thought it through dispassionately – that social classes do not experience the world in the way the individual subject does; nor do they have any common, objective interest. In any case, there are good reasons for our loss of the notion that emancipatory interests or experiences can be attributed to a group of people who have only socio-economic circumstances in common. But what, in the construction of the theory, can today take the place occupied in Horkheimer's model by those moral experiences which he – in this regard entirely a disciple of Georg Lukács – attributed to the working class as a whole? As we have seen in our retrospective, Critical Theory must be confident of identifying empirical experiences and attitudes which already indicate at a pretheoretical level that its normative standpoints are not without basis in social reality. What experiences of a systematic kind – indeed, what phenomena of any kind – I would further like to ask, assume the role in Habermas's theory of giving everyday proof of the cogency of critique, that is, prior to all theoretical reflection? I surmise that at this point a fissure appears in the theory of communicative action, one that is not accidental, but has a systematic character.

III Pre-theoretical Praxis and Moral Experiences

In shifting Critical Theory from the production paradigm to the paradigm of communication, Habermas unveiled a social sphere that fulfils all the presuppositions of the claim to an intramundane transcendence. For, in communicative action, subjects encounter each other within a horizon of normative expectations whose disappointment becomes, over and again, the source of moral demands which go beyond the established forms of domination. The role which capitalist relations of production played for Horkheimer, in setting unjustified limits on the development of the human capacity for labour, is played for Habermas by the societal relations of communication, which restrict the emancipatory potential of intersubjectively reaching understanding in a manner that cannot be justified. With the help of his conception of universal pragmatics, Habermas reveals the specific normative justifications contained in the process of social interaction. According to this conception of pragmatics, the linguistic rules on which communicative action is based possess a normative character, since they also determine the presuppositions of the process of reaching understanding, a process which must be free from domination (see especially MCCA 43–115).

If these conditions, which are present in language, are regarded as the normative core structurally built into human communication, then the critical perspective embedded in Habermas's theory of society becomes somewhat more evident. It should be concerned with an analysis of the social and cognitive restrictions that set limits on the unimpeded application of those linguistic rules. By turning to universal pragmatics, Habermas has taken a course that leads to equating the normative potential of social interaction with the linguistic conditions of reaching understanding free from domination. However great the advantages which such a linguistic version of the communication paradigm brings with it may be, the disadvantages internally associated with it are just as great. A first difficulty already becomes evident when, following Horkheimer's lead, we ask what moral experiences are supposed to correspond to this critical standpoint within social reality.

For Habermas, the pre-theoretical source of legitimacy which secures a foothold in reality for his normative perspective has to be the social process which develops the role of the linguistic rules for reaching understanding. In *The Theory of Communicative Action*, this process is referred to as the communicative rationalization of the lifeworld. However, such a process is typically something which could be said – with Marx – to unfold behind the backs of the subjects involved. Its course is neither directed by human intentions; nor can it be grasped within the consciousness of a single individual. The emancipatory process in which Habermas socially anchors the normative perspective of his Critical Theory is not at all reflected as such a process in the moral experiences of the subjects involved. For they experience an impairment of what we can call their moral expectations, that is, their 'moral point of view', not as a restriction of intuitively mastered rules of language, but as a violation of identity claims acquired in socialization. A process of communicatively rationalizing the lifeworld may unfold historically, but it is not reflected in the experiences of human subjects as a moral state of affairs. For this reason, a correlate cannot be found within social reality for the pre-theoretical resource to which the normative perspective of Habermas's theory refers reflexively; his conception is not aimed in the same way as Horkheimer's (which was of course also under the influence of a destructive illusion) at the idea of helping to give expression to an existing experience of social injustice.

A way out of this dilemma can only be provided by the idea of developing the communication paradigm constructed by Habermas more in the direction of its presuppositions regarding the theory of intersubjectivity – indeed, in the direction of its sociological presuppositions. What I mean by this, provisionally speaking, is merely the proposal not simply to equate the normative potential of social interaction with the linguistic conditions of reaching understanding free from domination. I have already pointed in this direction with the thesis that moral experiences are not triggered by the restriction of linguistic competences; rather, they are shaped by the violation of identity claims acquired in socialization. Current studies pointing in the same direction include those by Thomas McCarthy, who attempts to give the Habermasian communication paradigm a more experiential formulation by reconstructing the normative presuppositions of interaction with the help of ethnomethodology.[5]

In order to get a better understanding of the moral expectations which are embedded in the everyday process of social communication, an appropriate first step would be to draw on the resources of historical and sociological studies devoted to the forms of active resistance engaged in by the lower social classes. Because members of these classes have no special cultural expertise in articulating moral experiences, we perceive in their utterances – prior to all philosophical or academic influence, as it were – what normative expectations are oriented towards in everyday social life. When considering these studies, it becomes evident again and again that the social protests of the lower classes are not motivationally guided by positively formulated moral principles, but by the violation of intuitive notions of justice; and the normative core of such notions of justice repeatedly turns out to consist of expectations connected with respect for one's own dignity, honour or integrity.[6] Generalizing these results beyond their particular research contexts, we arrive at the conclusion that the normative presupposition of all communicative action is to be found in the acquisition of social recognition. Subjects encounter each other within the parameters of the reciprocal expectation that they receive recognition as moral persons, and for their social achievements. If this thesis is plausible, then, as a further consequence, we get an indication of which occurrences are perceived as morally unjust in everyday social life: such perceptions arise whenever those concerned are – contrary to their expectations – denied the recognition they feel they deserve. I would like to refer to such moral experiences as feelings of social disrespect (Mißachtung).

These reflections have already brought us to the point where the first outlines of an alternative to the version of the communication paradigm which is based in a theory of language are becoming visible. The point of departure is found in the notion that the normative presuppositions of social interaction cannot be fully grasped if they are defined solely in terms of the linguistic conditions of reaching an understanding free from domination. Rather, what must be considered first of all is the fact that there is an assumption of social recognition, which subjects connect with their normative expectations when entering communicative relationships. If the communicative paradigm is extended beyond the linguistic framework in this way, it can then indicate the degree to which any damage to the normative presuppositions of interaction must be directly reflected in the moral feelings of those involved. Because the experience of social recognition represents a condition on which the development of the identity of human beings depends, its denial – that is, disrespect – is necessarily accompanied by an awareness of the threat of a loss of personality. Unlike Habermas's model, this model entails a close connection between the ways in which normative assumptions of social interaction can be violated and the moral experiences of subjects in their everyday communication. If the conditions of interaction are damaged by denying people the recognition they deserve, they generally react with those moral feelings that accompany the experience of disrespect – that is, with shame, anger or indignation. In this way, a communicative paradigm conceived not in terms of a theory of language, but in terms of a theory of recognition can ultimately close the gap left open by Habermas in his further development of Horkheimer's programme. Those feelings of injustice which accompany structural forms of disrespect represent a pre-theoretical fact which a critique of the relations of recognition can use to demonstrate its own basis in social reality.

Now, the idea I have just summarized contains so many unclarified presuppositions that I cannot justify them all in this context. Elsewhere, with the help of George Herbert Mead, I have reconstructed the model of recognition developed by the young Hegel; I have attempted to justify the communicative presuppositions of a successful development of identity.[7] In that context I proposed a distinction between three patterns of reciprocal recognition, a distinction I consider essential, but have so far only touched upon here. Furthermore, at the moment I am unable to justify in all its consequences the claim that the expectation of social recognition belongs to the structure of communicative action. For this would require solving the difficult problem of replacing Habermas's universal pragmatics with an anthropological conception that can explain the whole range of normative presuppositions of social interaction.

With regard to the question of where Critical Theory finds itself today, other issues are in any case of greater importance. If the social relations of communication are to be analysed primarily in terms of what structural forms of disrespect they generate, then the critical perspective of the diagnosis of contemporary society must also shift away from the viewpoint of Habermas's model. The focus of interest should no longer be the tension between system and lifeworld, but rather the social causes responsible for the systematic violation of the conditions of recognition. Critical social theory has to shift its attention from the autonomization of systems to the damage and distortion of the social relations of recognition. As we shall see, this will lead, in contrast to Habermas, to a re-evalution of the role that the experience of labour should play in the categorial framework of Critical Theory.

IV Pathologies of Capitalist Society

In the tradition of the Frankfurt School, there has been a tendency to regard the fact that instrumental reason has attained predominance over other forms of action and knowledge as the decisive 'disorder' of modern societies. All occurrences and phenomena that appear to be 'pathological' in social reality are interpreted as consequences of an autonomization of the attitudes connected with the objective of dominating nature. The same tendency is also continued in Habermas's work, in so far as his outline of a theory of communicative action leads to a diagnosis of contemporary society that finds its point of departure in the danger of a 'colonization' of the lifeworld by systems organized in terms of purposive rationality. Once more, the 'disruption' said to threaten the life of our society is the tendency of instrumental orientations to attain supremacy, even though this time their growth is not explained simply by the objective of dominating nature, but by the increase in organizational rationality. It is scarcely necessary to mention that the negativist social theories which follow in the wake of Adorno are, of course, also tied to a critical diagnosis in which a particular type of instrumental reason is perceived as assuming the dimensions of a life-threatening power in technology, science and systems of control.

What should be recognized as characteristic of all these models of social critique is the consistent measurement of social pathologies or anomalies only in terms of the stage attained by the development of human rationality. That is why only distortions which occur in the cognitive orientation of human beings can be regarded as deviations from an ideal that must be presupposed categorially as the standard for a 'healthy' or intact form of society. Accordingly, such a perspective is also accompanied by a narrowing of social critique to a theory of rationality – something which is another legacy of Left Hegelianism. As a result, all those social pathologies which do not refer to the developmental level of human rationality cannot come to light at all. For instance, those disorders of social life which Durkheim had in mind when he analysed the process of individualization cannot be perceived by social critique conducted in the tradition of Critical Theory; for these disorders arise in the form of the dissolution of a socially binding force, a dissolution that is only indirectly related to changes in human rationality.

Given the basic assumptions I have made so far in my attempt to situate Critical Theory today, there would be no point in resting content with such a narrow view of the disorders and pathologies of our society. How can the pathological developments of social life which are connected to the structural conditions of reciprocal recognition become visible, if the only criteria available for the measurement of anomalies refer to the stage of human rationality? As soon as the communicative paradigm is reoriented from a conception of rationally reaching understanding to a conception of the conditions of recognition, the critical diagnosis of the times can longer be pressed into the narrow scheme of a theory of rationality. The rational conditions for reaching understanding free from domination can no longer be employed as the criterion for what is to be regarded as a 'disorder' or pathological development of social life. Rather, the criterion is now provided by the intersubjective presuppositions of human identity development. These presuppositions can be found in the social forms of communication in which the individual grows up, acquires a social identity, and ultimately has to learn to conceive of him- or herself as an equal and, at the same time, unique member of society. If these forms of communication are constituted in such a way that they do not provide the level of recognition necessary to accomplish the various tasks involved in acquiring an identity, then this must be taken as an indication of the pathological development of a society. Thus it is pathologies of recognition that move to the centre of the critical diagnosis as soon as the communication paradigm is grasped not in terms of a theory of language, but in terms of a theory of recognition. Accordingly, the basic concepts of an analysis of society have to be constructed in such a way that they can grasp the distortions or deficiencies of the social framework of recognition, while the process of societal rationalization loses its central position.

However, my reflections so far have given no indication of the relationship between such pathologies of recognition and the social structure of a given society. If the model of Critical Theory outlined so far is to be more than a merely normative analysis of the present, then its primary task will be to reveal the socio-structural causes responsible for a distortion of the social framework of recognition in each particular case. Only then can it be decided whether there is a systematic connection between specific experiences of disrespect and the structural development of society.

Here I must restrict myself to a few remarks which will primarily serve the function of preparing for a further, final step away from Habermas's version of the communication paradigm. As I have mentioned, by returning to the young Hegel, I distinguished three forms of social recognition which can be regarded as the communicative presuppositions of a successful formation of identity: emotional concern in an intimate social relationship such as love or friendship; rights-based recognition as a morally accountable member of society; and, finally, social esteem for individual achievements and abilities. The question of how a particular society's framework of recognition is constituted can be answered only by research that concerns itself with the empirical state of the institutional embodiments of these three patterns of recognition. For our society, this would require studies, firstly, of socialization practices, familial forms, and relations of friendship; secondly, of the content and forms of application of positive law; and finally, of actual patterns of social esteem. With regard to this last dimension of recognition, and considering related research, we can claim with relative certainty (and not just surmise) that a person's social esteem is measured largely according to what contribution he or she makes to society in terms of formally organized labour. As regards social esteem, the relations of recognition are to a large extent interwoven with the distribution and organization of social labour. To understand this would require, however, that the category of labour be awarded greater significance in the programme for Critical Theory proposed here than it has in the theory of communicative action.

V Labour and Recognition

Even just a brief glance at studies of the psychological effects of unemployment makes it very clear that the experience of labour must be assigned a central position in the model emerging here. Even today, the acquisition of that form of recognition which I have called social esteem is bound up with the opportunity to pursue an economically rewarded and thus socially regulated occupation. Yet, on the other hand, this upgrading of the experience of labour should not mislead us into falling back below the level set by Habermas twenty years ago in his categorial purification of the concept of labour. For in the Marxist tradition, and even in Horkheimer, social labour, in combination with a certain philosophy of history, was elevated into a such a crucial factor in the cultural development of human beings that only a very dispassionate concept of labour, one whose normative implications had been purged, could guard against the danger of such an illusory construction. These contrary tendencies raise the following question: To what extent can the concept of labour be neutralized without at the same time surrendering the significance of a central source of moral experiences? On the one hand, the process of social labour must not be exaggerated, as in the tradition of Western Marxism, into the process of formation of an emancipatory consciousness. On the other hand, from a categorial standpoint, it must appear sufficiently embedded in the network of our moral experiences for its role in securing social recognition not to disappear from view.[8]

It is indeed the case that, in Habermas's recent theory of society, the concept of 'instrumental action', into which he had formerly transformed the

Marxist concept of labour, no longer plays a systematic role. The central distinctions he makes today in the praxis of human beings are no longer categorized according to differences in the specific object – that is, nature or co-subject – but according to differences in the co-ordination of actions conceived as being teleological in principle. However, this conceptual strategy has the result that the experience of labour no longer appears systematically in the categorial framework of the theory. The question of what experiences we have in dealing with external nature plays just as insignificant a role in Habermas's concept of personal identity formation as the question of how social labour is distributed, organized and evaluated plays in his theory of society. But if individual identity formation is also dependent upon the social esteem enjoyed by one's labour within society, then the concept of labour must not be constituted categorially in such a way that it suppresses this psycho-social connection. The dangerous consequence of this would be that any effort to re-evaluate or reshape particular forms of labour might remain incomprehensible – indeed, indiscernible to social theory. Certain zones of pre-theoretical critique become evident only to the extent that they are analysed in light of a concept of labour that also categorially encompasses the individual's dependence upon the social recognition of his or her own work.

What is currently most important for the further analysis of the connection between labour and recognition is the discussion, inspired by feminism, concerning the problem of unpaid housework.[9] In the course of this debate, it has become clear from two perspectives that the organization of social labour is very closely bound up with the ethical norms regulating the particular system of social esteem. From a historical viewpoint, the fact that child rearing and housework are not yet valued as equally worthy and necessary types of social labour can only be explained by pointing out the low social esteem granted them in the context of a culture determined by male values. From a psychological viewpoint, the same situation means that, given the traditional distribution of roles, women have had few chances within society to receive the level of social respect necessary to support a positive self-conception. It can be concluded from these two lines of argument that the organization and evaluation of social labour plays a central role in a society's framework of recognition. Because the culturally defined ranking of social tasks determines the amount of social esteem an individual can obtain from his or her occupation, and the attributes associated with it, the chances which an individual has of forming an identity through the experience of recognition are directly related to the societal institutionalization and distribution of labour. To gain insight into this pre-theoretical zone of recognition and disrespect, however, we require a concept of labour that has sufficient normative strength to be able to include the idea of our dependence upon the social acknowledgement of our own accomplishments and attributes.

VI Conclusion

All the reflections I have so far presented converge in the thesis that it is the multifarious efforts of a struggle for recognition that will enable Critical Theory to justify its normative claims. The moral experiences which subjects undergo when their identity claims are disrespected constitute a pre-theoretical source of legitimation, reference to which can show that a critique of the societal relations of communication is not entirely without a foundation in social reality. However, this thesis could easily give the impression that feelings of disrespect are something morally valuable in themselves, to which theory can refer directly and without qualification in its social self-justification. How wrong such an assumption is, how extremely ambivalent such experiences of injustice really are, can be seen clearly in a passage I would like to cite briefly:

> Most young people who spoke to us were frustrated. They had absolutely no future prospects. I supported them and praised them from time to time in order to increase their self-esteem. This kind of recognition made them completely dependent on what we called the 'group of comrades'. For many of them, this 'group of comrades' becomes a kind of drug they can't do without. Since they do not experience any recognition outside the 'group of comrades', they are mostly isolated and do not have any other social contacts.[10]

These sentences come from a book written by the East Berliner Ingo Hasselbach about the experiences he had while he was in neo-Nazi youth groups. Though the portrayal of his impressions may well be influenced by the language of the journalist who helped to prepare the manuscript, it nevertheless very clearly shows where the experience of social disrespect can lead politically. Social esteem can be sought in small militaristic groups, whose code of honour is dominated by the practice of violence, as well as in the public arenas of a democratic society. The sense of no longer being within the network of social recognition is in itself an extremely ambivalent source of motivation for social protest and resistance. It lacks any normative indication or direction that could stipulate in what ways one should struggle against the experience of disrespect and humiliation. For this reason, a critical theory of society that wishes to further develop Habermas's communicative paradigm in the direction of a theory of recognition is not in as strong a position as might have thus far appeared. It can indeed find in widespread feelings of social disrespect that element of intramundane transcendence which confirms pre-theoretically that its critical diagnosis is shared by those affected. Many people experience social reality as the theory critically describes it – namely, as incapable of adequately generating the experience of recognition. However, this pre-theoretical confirmation cannot be regarded by the theory as proof that the normative direction of its critique is shared by those affected. To this extent, we can no longer conceive of the theory as Horkheimer did: namely, as no more than the intellectual expression of a process of emancipation already under way. Rather, this theory of society will have to concentrate its efforts on answering a question that Horkheimer – under the spell of a grand illusion – could not even perceive as such: the question of how a moral culture could be so constituted as to give those harmed by disrespect and ostracization the individual strength to articulate their experiences in the democratic public sphere, rather than living them out in the counter-cultures of violence.

Notes

1 This is the text of my inaugural lecture at the Otto Suhr Institute of the Free University in Berlin in November 1993.

2 Max Horkheimer, 'Traditional and Critical Theory', in *Critical Theory* (New York: Seabury Press, 1972), pp. 188–243.

3 See, by way of summary, Axel Honneth, 'Critical Theory', in *Social Theory Today*, ed. Anthony Giddens and J. H. Turner (Cambridge: Polity Press, 1987), pp. 347–82.

4 Good examples are Stefan Breuer, *Die Gesellschaft des Verschwindens: Von der Selbstzerstörung der technischen Zivilisation* (Hamburg: Junius, 1992); Michel Foucault, *Discipline and Punish*, tr. Alan Sheridan (New York: Pantheon, 1977).

5 Thomas McCarthy, 'Philosophy and Critical Theory: a reprise', in *Critical Theory*, ed. David Hoy and Thomas McCarthy (Oxford: Basil Blackwell, 1994).

6 See, e.g., Barrington Moore, *Injustice: The Social Basis of Obedience and Revolt* (Armonk: Sharpe, 1978). I have also referred to this in Axel Honneth, 'Moral consciousness and class domination', in Charles W. Wright, ed., *The Fragmented World of the Social* (Albany, NY: SUNY Press, 1995), pp. 205–19.

7 Axel Honneth, *Struggle for Recognition: The Moral Grammar of Social Conficts*, tr. Joel Anderson (Cambridge, Mass.: Polity Press, 1995).

8 See my reflections in Axel Honneth, 'Work and instrumental action', *New German Critique*, 9/2 (1982), pp. 31–54.

9   See, e.g., the contributions to the topic 'Social Philosophy of Labour' by
     Friedrich Kambartel, Angelika Krebs and Ingrid Kurz-Scherf in *Deutsche
     Zeitschrift für Philosophie*, 41/2 (1993), pp. 237–75.

10   Ingo Hasselbach and Winfried Bonengel, *Die Abrechnung: Ein Neonazi sagt aus*
     (Berlin: Aufbau, 1993), pp. 121–2.

Select bibliography

Principal publications by Habermas in German

'Das Absolute und die Geschichte: Von der Zwiespältigkeit in Schellings Denken', Doctoral dissertation, University of Bonn, 1954.

Student und Politik: Eine soziologische Untersuchung zum politischen Bewußtein Frankfurter Studenten, with Ludwig von Friedeburg and C. Oehler (Neuwied and Berlin: Luchterhand, 1961).

Strukturwandel der Öffentlichkeit: Untersuchungen zu einer Kategorie der bügerlichen Gesellschaft (Neuwied and Berlin: Luchterhand, 1962).

Theorie und Praxis (Neuwied and Berlin: Luchterhand, 1963). Expanded edn, 1971, from Suhrkamp.

'Zur Logik der Sozialwissenschaften', *Philosophische Rundschau*, 14, supplement 5, 1967. Expanded edns, 1970 and 1982, from Suhrkamp.

Erkenntnis und Interesse (Frankfurt: Suhrkamp, 1968).

Technik und Wissenschaft als 'Ideologie' (Frankfurt: Suhrkamp, 1968).

(ed.) *Antworte auf Herbert Marcuse* (Frankfurt: Suhrkamp, 1968).

Protestbewegung und Hochschulreform (Frankfurt: Suhrkamp, 1969).

Arbeit Erkenntnis Fortschritt: Aufsätze 1954–1970 (Amsterdam: Verlag de Munster, N. V. Schwarze Reihe 10, 1970).

Philosophisch-politische Profile (Frankfurt: Suhrkamp, 1971). Expanded edn, 1981.

Theorie der Gesellschaft oder Sozialtechnologie: Was leistet die Systemforschung?, with Niklas Luhmann (Frankfurt: Suhrkamp, 1971).

Kultur und Kritik: Verstreute Aufsätze (Frankfurt: Suhrkamp, 1973).

Legitimationsprobleme im Spätkapitalismus (Frankfurt: Suhrkamp, 1973).

Zwei Reden: Aus Anlass der Verleihung des Hegel – Preises 1973 der Stadt Stuttgart an Jürgen Habermas am 19 Januar 1974, with Dieter Henrich (Frankfurt: Suhrkamp, 1974).

Zur Rekonstruktion des Historischen Materialismus (Frankfurt: Suhrkamp, 1976).

Politik, Kunst, Religion: Essays über zeitgenössische Philosophen (Stuttgart: Reclam, 1978).

Das Erbe Hegels: Zwei Reden aus Anlass der Verleihung des Hegel – Preises 1979 der Stadt Stuttgart an Hans-Georg Gadamer am 13 Juni 1979, with Hans-Georg Gadamer (Frankfurt: Suhrkamp, 1979).

(ed.) *Stichworte zur Geistigen Situation der Zeit* (Frankfurt: Suhrkamp, 1980).

Kleine Politische Schriften (I–IV) (Frankfurt: Suhrkamp, 1981).

Theorie des Kommunikativen Handelns, 1: Handlungsrationalität und gesellschaftliche Rationalisierung; 2: Zur Kritik der funktionalistische. Vernunft (Frankfurt: Suhrkamp, 1981).

Moralbewußtein und kommunikatives Handeln (Frankfurt: Suhrkamp, 1983).

Vorstudien und Ergänzungen zur Theorie des kommunikativen Handelns (Frankfurt: Suhrkamp, 1984).

Die Neue Unübersichtlichkeit: Kleine Politische Schriften, V (Frankfurt: Suhrkamp, 1985).

Der Philosophische Diskurs der Moderne (Frankfurt: Suhrkamp, 1985).

Eine Art Schadensabwicklung: Kleine Politische Schriften, VI (Frankfurt: Suhrkamp, 1987).

Nachmetaphysisches Denken: Philosophische Aufsätze (Frankfurt: Suhrkamp, 1988).

Vergangenheit als Zukunft (Zurich: pendo-verlag, 1990).

Die Nachholende Revolution: Kleine Politische Schriften, VII (Frankfurt: Suhrkamp, 1990).

Texte und Kontexte (Frankfurt: Suhrkamp, 1991).

Erläuterungen zur Diskursethik (Frankfurt: Suhrkamp, 1992).

Faktitizität und Geltung: Beiträge zur Diskurstheorie des Rechts und des Demokratischen Rechtsstaats (Frankfurt: Suhrkamp, 1992).

Die Normalität einer Berliner Republik: Kleine Politische Schriften, VIII (Frankfurt: Suhrkamp, 1995).

Die Einbeziehung des Anderen: Studien zur politischen Theorie (Frankfurt: Suhrkamp, 1996).

Vom sinnlichen Eindruck zum symbolischen Ausdruck: Philosophische Essays (Frankfurt: Suhrkamp, 1997).

Die Postnationale Konstellation: Politische Essays (Frankfurt: Suhrkamp, 1998).

Principal publications by Habermas in English

Knowledge and Human Interests, tr. Jeremy Shapiro (Boston: Beacon Press, 1971).

Toward a Rational Society: Student Protest, Science and Politics, tr. Jeremy Shapiro (Boston: Beacon Press, 1971).

Theory and Practice, tr. John Viertel (Boston: Beacon Press, 1973).

Legitimation Crisis, tr. Thomas McCarthy (Boston: Beacon Press, 1975).

Communication and the Evolution of Society, tr. Thomas McCarthy (Boston: Beacon Press, 1979).

Philosophical-Political Profiles, tr. Frederick Lawrence (Cambridge, Mass.: MIT Press, 1983).

Autonomy and Solidarity: Interviews with Jürgen Habermas, ed. and introduced by Peter Dews (London: Verso, 1986). 2nd, enlarged edn, with a postscript to the introduction, 1992.

The Theory of Communicative Action, vol. I: *Reason and the Rationalization of Society*, tr. Thomas McCarthy (Boston: Beacon Press, 1984).

(ed.) *Observations on the Spiritual Situation of the Age* (Cambridge, Mass.: MIT Press, 1987).

'Modernity – an incomplete project', repr. in *Postmodern Culture*, ed. Hal Foster (London: Pluto, 1987).

The Philosophical Discourse of Modernity: Twelve Lectures, tr. Frederick Lawrence (Cambridge, Mass.: MIT Press, 1987).

Theory of Communicative Action, vol. 2: *Lifeworld and System: A Critique of Functionalist Reason*, tr. Thomas McCarthy (Boston: Beacon Press, 1987).

On the Logic of the Social Sciences, tr. Shierry Weber Nicholsen and Jerry Stark (Cambridge, Mass.: MIT Press, 1988); first published 1967.

Law and Morality: The Tanner Lectures on Human Values, VIII (Salt Lake City: University of Utah Press, 1988), pp. 217–79.

The Structural Transformation of the Public Sphere: An Inquiry into a Category of Bourgeois Society, tr. Thomas Burger (Cambridge, Mass.: MIT Press, 1989).

The New Conservatism: Cultural Criticism and the Historians' Debate, ed. and tr. Shierry Weber Nicholsen (Cambridge, Mass.: MIT Press, 1989).

Moral Consciousness and Communicative Action, tr. Christian Lenhardt and Shierry Weber Nicholsen (Cambridge, Mass.: MIT Press, 1990).

'Martin Heidegger: Work and *Weltanschauung*', in *Heidegger: A Critical Reader*, ed. Hubert Dreyfus and Harison Hall (Oxford: Blackwell Publishers, 1992).

Postmetaphysical Thinking, tr. William Mark Hohengarten (Cambridge, Mass.: MIT Press, 1992).

Justification and Application: Remarks on Discourse Ethics, tr. Ciaran P. Cronin (Cambridge, Mass.: MIT Press, 1993).

The Past as Future, tr. Max Pensky (Lincoln, Nebr.: University of Nebraska Press, 1994).

Between Facts and Norms: Contributions to a Discourse Theory of Law and Democracy, tr. William Rehg (Cambridge: Polity Press, 1996).

The Inclusion of the Other: Studies in Political Theory, ed. Ciaran Cronin and Pablo de Greiff (Cambridge: Polity Press, 1998).

Selected books and special issues of journals on Habermas in English

Baynes, Kenneth, *The Normative Grounds of Social Criticism: Kant, Rawls and Habermas* (Albany, NY: State University of New York Press, 1992).

Benhabib, Seyla, *Critique, Norm and Utopia: A Study of the Foundations of Critical Theory* (New York: Columbia University Press, 1986).

Bernstein, J. M., *Recovering Ethical Life: Jürgen Habermas and the Future of Critical Theory* (London: Routledge, 1995).

Bernstein, R. J., ed., *Habermas and Modernity* (Oxford: Blackwell, 1985).

Calhoun, Craig, ed., *Habermas and the Public Sphere* (Cambridge, Mass.: MIT Press, 1992).

Cardozo Law Review, 17/4–5 (March 1996), Parts I and II (special issue on Habermas's *Between Facts and Norms*).

Cooke, Maeve, *Language and Reason: A Study of Habermas's Pragmatics* (Cambridge, Mass.: MIT Press, 1994).

D'Entrèves, Maurizio Passerin, and Benhabib, Seyla, eds, *Habermas and the Unfinished Project of Modernity: Critical Essays on 'The Philosophical Discourse of Modernity'* (Cambridge: Polity Press, 1996).

Deflem, Mathieu, ed., 'Habermas, modernity and law', special issue of *Philosophy and Social Criticism*, 4 (1994).

Geuss, Raymond, *The Idea of a Critical Theory: Habermas and the Frankfurt School* (Cambridge: Cambridge University Press, 1981).

Held, David, *Introduction to Critical Theory: Horkheimer to Habermas* (London: Hutchinson, 1980).

Holub, Robert, *Jürgen Habermas: Critic in the Public Sphere* (London and New York: Routledge, 1991).

Honneth, Axel and Hans, Joas, eds, *Communicative Action* (Cambridge: Polity Press, 1991).

Honneth, Axel et al., eds, *Philosophical Interventions in the Unfinished Project of the Enlightenment* (Cambridge, Mass.: MIT Press, 1992).

Honneth, Axel et al., eds, *Cultural-Political Interventions in the Unfinished Project of the Enlightenment* (Cambridge, Mass.: MIT Press, 1992).

Ingram, David, *Habermas and the Dialectic of Reason* (New Haven, Conn.: Yale University Press, 1987).

Keat, Russell, *The Politics of Social Theory: Habermas, Freud and the Critique of Positivism* (Oxford: Blackwell, 1981).

Kortian, Garbis, *Metacritique* (Cambridge: Cambridge University Press, 1980).

McCarthy, Thomas, *The Critical Theory of Jürgen Habermas* (Cambridge: Polity Press, 1978).

Matuštík, Martin J., *Postnational Identity: Critical Theory and Existential Philosophy in Habermas, Kierkegaard, and Havel* (New York and London: Guilford Press, 1993).

Meehan, Johanna, ed., *Feminists read Habermas* (New York: Routledge, 1995).

New German Critique, Special issue on Jürgen Habermas, 35 (1985).

Praxis International, 8/2 (January 1989) (special issue on Habermas).

Pusey, Michael, *Jürgen Habermas* (Chichester: Ellis Horwood, 1987).

Rasmussen, David M., *Reading Habermas* (Cambridge, Mass.: Blackwell, 1990).

Revue Internationale de Philosophie, 194/4 (1995) (special issue on Habermas).

Roderick, Richard, *Habermas and the Foundations of Critical Theory* (London: Macmillan, 1986).

Thompson, J. B. and Held, D., eds, *Habermas: Critical Debates* (London: Macmillan, 1982).

Wellmer, Albrecht, *The Persistence of Modernity*, tr. D. Midgley (Cambridge, Mass.: MIT Press, 1991).

White, Stephen K., *The Recent Works of Jürgen Habermas: Reason, Justice and Modernity* (Cambridge: Cambridge University Press, 1988).

White, Stephen K., *Political Theory and Postmodernism* (Cambridge: Cambridge University Press, 1991).

Wiggerhaus, Rolf, *The Frankfurt School: Its History, Theories and Political Significance*, tr. M. Robertson (Cambridge, Mass.: MIT Press, 1994).

Selected articles on Habermas in English

Apel, Karl-Otto, 'Types of social science in the light of human interests of knowledge', *Social Research*, 44 (1977), pp. 425–70.

Bohman, James, 'Formal pragmatics and social criticism: the philosophy of language and the critique of ideology in Habermas's Theory of Communicative Action', *Philosophy and Social Criticism*, 11 (1986), pp. 331–53.

—— 'System and "Lifeworld": Habermas and the problem of holism', *Philosophy and Social Criticism*, 15 (1989), pp. 381–401.

—— 'Complexity, pluralism and the constitutional state: on Habermas's *Faktizität und Geltung*', *Law and Society Review*, 28 (1994), pp. 801–34.

—— 'Modernization and impediments to democracy', *Theoria*, 86 (1995), pp. 1–20.

Cooke, Maeve, 'Habermas and consensus', *European Journal of Philosophy*, 1/3 (1993), pp. 247–67.

—— 'Realizing the post-conventional self', *Philosophy and Social Criticism*, 20/1, 2 (1994), pp. 87–101.

—— 'A space of one's own: autonomy, privacy, liberty', *Philosophy and Social Criticism*, 25/1 (1999), pp. 23–53.

Dews, Peter, 'Life-world, metaphysics and the ethics of nature in Habermas', in *The Limits of Disenchantment: Essays on Contemporary European Philosophy* (London: Verso, 1995), pp. 151–68.

—— 'Modernity, self-consciousness and the scope of philosophy: Jürgen Habermas and Dieter Henrich in debate', in *The Limits of Disenchantment: Essays on Contemporary European Philosophy* (London: Verso, 1995), pp. 169–201.

—— 'Morality, ethics, and "postmetaphysical thinking"', in *The Limits of Disenchantment: Essays on Contemporary European Philosophy* (London: Verso, 1995), pp. 202–11.

Ferrara, Alessandro, 'A critique of Habermas's Consensus Theory of Truth', *Philosophy and Social Criticism*, 13 (1987), pp. 39–67.

Gadamer, Hans-Georg, 'Hermeneutics and social science', *Cultural Hermeneutics*, 2 (1975), pp. 307–30.

—— 'On the scope and function of hermeneutical reflection', *Continium*, 8 (1970), pp. 77–95.

Giddens, Anthony, 'Reason without revolution? Habermas's *Theorie des Kommunikativen Handelns*', *Praxis International*, 2 (1982), pp. 318–28.

Gosepath, Stefan, 'The place of equality in Habermas's and Dworkin's theories of justice', *European Journal of Philosophy*, 3/1 (1995), pp. 21–35.

Hesse, Mary, 'In defence of objectivity', *Proceedings of the British Academy*, 58 (1972), pp. 275–92.

—— 'Habermas's Consensus Theory of Truth', in Hesse, *Revolutions and Reconstructions in the Philosophy of Science* (Brighton, Sussex: Harvester Press, 1980), pp. 206–31.

Honneth, Axel, 'Communication and reconciliation in Habermas's critique of Adorno', *Telos*, 39 (1979), pp. 45–61.

—— 'Work and instrumental action', *New German Critique*, 26 (1982), pp. 31–54.

Keane, John, 'On tools and language: Habermas on work and interaction', *New German Critique*, 6 (1975), pp. 82–100.

Larmore, Charles, 'The foundations of modern democracy: reflections on Jürgen Habermas', *European Journal of Philosophy*, 3/1 (1995), pp. 55–68.

McCarthy, Thomas, 'A theory of communicative competence', *Philosophy of the Social Sciences*, 5 (1975), pp. 163–72.

Mendelson, Jack, 'The Habermas–Gadamer Debate', *New German Critique*, 18 (1979), pp. 44–73.

Pensky, Max, 'On the use and abuse of memory: Habermas, anamnestic solidarity and the Historikerstreit', *Philosophy and Social Criticism*, 15 (1998), pp. 351–80.

Rawls, John, 'Reply to Habermas', *Journal of Philosophy*, 92 (1995), pp. 132–80.

Rehg, William, 'Discourse and the moral point of view', *Inquiry*, 34 (1991), pp. 27–48.

—— 'Discourse ethics and the communitarian critique of neo-Kantism', *Philosophical Forum*, 22 (1990–1), pp. 120–38.

Ricoeur, Paul, 'Ethics and culture: Habermas and Gadamer in dialogue', *Philosophy Today*, 2 (1973), pp. 153–65.

Rorty, Richard, 'Habermas, Derrida and the functions of philosophy', *Revue Internationale de Philosophie*, 194/4 (1995), pp. 437–59.

Scheuerman, Bill, 'Neumann versus Habermas: the Frankfurt School and the case of the rule of law', *Praxis International*, 13 (1993), pp. 50–67.

Tugendhat, Ernst, 'Habermas on communicative action', in *Social Action*, ed. G. Seebass and R. Tuomela (Dordrecht: Reidel, 1985), pp. 179–86.

Visker, Rudi, 'Habermas on Heidegger and Foucault: meaning and validity in the philosophical discourse of modernity', *Radical Philosophy*, 61 (1992), pp. 15–22.

Whitebook, Joel, 'The problem of nature in Habermas', *Telos*, 40 (1979), pp. 41–69.

—— 'Intersubjectivity and the monadic core of the psyche: Habermas and Castoriadis on the unconscious', *Praxis International*, 9 (1990), pp. 347–64.

Woodiwiss, Tony, 'Critical theory and the capitalist state', *Economy and Society*, 7 (1978), pp. 175–92.

Index

Adorno 77, 220, 233, 323, 324
  on philosophy 13
Alcoff, Linda 182
alienation 5, 260, 313
Apel, Karl-Otto 272–3
  on reason and interest 10
Arendt, Hannah
  on power 157–8
Aristotle 246–8, 252
Athenians 285–6
Auschwitz 211–12, 223, 233–4
Austin, J. L. 276–7
authenticity 128–9
autonomy 188–97
  ethical 201–3
  feminist critique of 179–84
  value of 191–3
  and validity 193–5

Baudrillard, Jean 325
Being and Time 126, 128
Between Facts and Norms 155–72
Bordo, Susan 182–3
Breuer, Stefan 324
Butler, Judith 180–2

Capital 64, 70–1
Castoriadis, Cornelius 22
Categorical Imperative 36–41, 46–7
civil society 156–8, 161, 165–8
community 313–14
Critical Theory 53–5, 120, 242–63,
    321–4
  conception of history 257
  Horkheimer on 6–7, 53, 243–5
  and praxis 246–8
critique 4–5
  aesthetic 19–20
  contrasted with reconstruction 11
cognitive interests 7–10, 57
cognitivism 31
communication 320–1
  and metacommunication 107
  paradigm of 325–7, 330–2
communicative action 67, 186, 324
communicative rationality 284
communicative reason 18, 99

decisionism 129–31
democracy 80–2
  capitalist 155

democracy cont.
  deliberative 156, 161
  liberal 166
Derrida, Jacques 88–90
  and intersubjectivity 89–90
Dewey, John 80–1
Dialectic of Enlightenment 4, 251, 323–4
discourse theory 32
Durkheim 331

Elster, Jon 64, 65
emancipatory interest 8, 24, 57–8, 322
Enlightenment 263
  and autonomy 183–4
ethical-political discourse 215
ethnomethodology 76, 329

feminism 333
  and post-modernism 181–4
Feuerbach, Ludwig 22
Flax, Jane 181–2
formalism 41
Foucault, Michel 88–9
  on dialogue 89
  on empirical and transcendental
    dimensions 108
Fraser, Nancy 159
freedom 87, 259–60
Freud 184

Gadamer, Hans-Georg 63, 255
Geertz, Clifford 68–9
Gehlen, Arnold 222–3, 254
Germany 12
  cultural heritage of 117–19
  Federal Republic of 222–3
  and globalization 227–8
  role of intellectuals in 215–16, 218
  university system 220, 225
the good life 247, 262
  conceptions of 197–9

Hegel 1, 12, 259, 261, 301

on Categorical Imperative 35–40
and comprehensive theories
on Kant's moral theory 29–30
on reason 91
Heidegger 12, 123–36, 222–3, 224–5, 233, 306–7
  on *das Man* 132–4
  on *Dasein* 123, 129
  and National Socialism 124–5, 130, 132
  on resoluteness 128–9
Henrich, Dieter 291–2
Herder 315
hermeneutics 66
Hillgrüber, Andreas 226
historical materialism 55–6, 63, 78
Historikerstreit (Historians' Debate) 213, 226
Hobbes 300
Holocaust 219, 224
Honneth, Axel 320–1
Horkheimer, Max 1, 56, 220, 243–5, 260, 322–4, 326–7, 336
Huntington, Patricia 182

identity 186
ideology 64
illocution 276–7
imperatives 278, 280
individualization 106
instrumental reason 250
interests
  cognitive 7–10
  and morality 42–44
intersubjectivity 88–90, 126–7, 241–2, 255, 328

Jünger, Ernst 222–3

Kant 300–1, 317
  and Hegel on pluralism 59–60
  moral theory 29–41
  on the will 39–40
Kierkegaard 12

Klemperer, Victor 211–14, 234
knowledge
    social distribution of 81
Knowledge and Human Interests 7–10, 18,
    57
Kuhn, Thomas 112–13

labour 252, 262, 333–5
Lacan, Jacques
    compared with Habermas 92–98
    and Hegel 98
    on speech 109
    on the unconscious 93
language
    and code 94
    and interaction 307–8
    and intersubjectivity 95
language-games 314
Left Hegelians 99, 249, 321–2
Leibniz 299–300
lifeworld 15–17, 21, 73–4, 229, 298,
    316–17
    colonization of 75, 331

macro-sociology 72, 73, 76
Mannheim, Karl 64–5, 67
Marcuse, Herbert 254
Marx 12, 54–5, 258–9
    on ideology 65–7
Marxism 22
    cognitive status of 4
    as critique 4–6
    role of philosophy in 11–12
maxims 38
McCarthy, Thomas 46, 328–9
Mead, George Herbert 100–8, 330
    compared with Lacan 103–4
    on 'I' and 'Me' 102–8
Melians 285–7
metaphysics 292–318
    Kant on 293–6
modernity 119, 317–18
    time-consciousness of 121
moral discourse 194–5

moral experience 328–30
moral norms 44–6
morality
    meaning of 20
    and reasons 44–5
    and *Sittlichkeit* 47–8
multi-culturalism 229–30

Nagel, Thomas 309
naturalism 301–2, 303–4, 312
nature
    in Critical Theory 248–9
    in Greek philosophy 244
    in Marx 253
    liberation of 251
    resurrection of 252
Negative Dialectics 101, 324
neo-conservatism 231–2
Nietzsche 8–9, 12, 120
Nolte, Ernst 226

O'Neill, Onora 38

paradigm-shifts 98–9, 122
    Kuhn on 112–13
parliament 160, 162, 165, 168
perlocution 277
Peters, Bernhard 163–6
The Philosophical Discourse of Modernity
    87, 136–7
philosophy
    of consciousness 90–1, 101
    as *Forschung* 12, 16
    of history 6, 243–5, 251
    as interpreter 13–14, 17
    and religion 112
    as stand-in 13–14, 17
    of the subject (*Subjektphilosophie*) 108,
        310–12
    and world-disclosure 21–2
pluralism
    methodological 54, 78
    in social science 58
    theoretical 54, 78

post–modernism 77, 304
post–structuralism 90–1, 180–2
power
  administrative 157–9, 169
  communicative 157–9, 163, 169
pragmatism 78–80, 82
principle D 194, 200–2
principle U 33–5, 41–8
  and Categorical Imperative 25–6
psychoanalysis 9, 184
  Habermas and Lacan on 92–4
Putnam, Hilary 2

Quine, W. v. O. 302, 314–15

rationality 284, 288
rationalization 2
Rawls, John 2
Raz, Joseph 189–90
reason 294
  desublimation of 3, 19, 22
  diremption model of 91
  Hegel's view of 1–2
  and history 1–2
recognition 320–1, 329–30, 331–2
reconstruction 13
reflection 298–9
Rorty, Richard 1, 19, 21
Rousseau 134, 301, 313

Schelling 4
Schmitt, Carl 222–3
science 246
Searle, John 303
Seel, Martin 15
Seinsgeschichte (Heidegger) 141
the self
  as disembodied 179–80
  post-structuralist views of 184–5
self–authorship 189–90
self–consciousness 306
  and language 308–10
self–description 298
self–determination 186–7

self–identity
  ethical 186–7
self–realization 187
self–reflection 9, 256
self–relation 311
semantics 309–10
separation of powers 170–1
Smith, Adam 43
social integration 61–2, 73, 74
Spaemann, Robert 14
speech acts 274–84, 302
Spinoza 300
strategic rationality 283, 287–8
The Structural Transformation of the Public
    Sphere 154–5
system 317, 326
  and lifeworld 68–77
system integration 61–2, 74

Taylor, Charles 129, 197–9
theoria 243–5, 247
The Theory of Communicative Action 58–9,
    273–80
Theunissen, Michael 241–2
transcendental pragmatics 275
truth
  Lacan on 95–6
  Nietzsche on 7
  and normative rightness 45
  Wellmer on 97
Tugendhat, Ernst 105

the unconscious 110
universal pragmatics 327–8
universalism 36, 216–17, 229

validity
  ethical 188, 191–203
  moral 194–5, 199–200
validity claims 31, 111, 276
  and meaning 145
Verständigung (understanding) 276, 326
Voltaire 1, 295–6

Walser, Martin 211–14, 221,
  234
Waugh, Patricia 183
Weber, Max 2, 56, 58–9
Weir, Allison 183
Wellmer, Albrecht 97

Wittgenstein 306
world-disclosure
  in Heidegger 122–4
  and philosophical argument 139

Young Hegelians 3